- Morris — Conundrum
- MORRIS — OXFORD
- Jan Morris — SPAIN
- Morris — The Road to Huddersfield: The Story of the World Bank
- CITIES — James Morris (Faber)
- Venice — Jan Morris
- Jan Morris — CORONATION EVEREST
- MORRIS — CORONATION E[VEREST]
- Jan Morris — South African Winter (Faber Finds)
- ELAND — Jan Morris — Sultan in Oman

307.
76
MOR

JAN MORRIS: A LIFE

by the same author

GLOWING STILL: A WOMAN'S LIFE ON THE ROAD
MUD AND STARS: TRAVELS IN RUSSIA WITH PUSHKIN AND OTHER GENIUSES OF THE GOLDEN AGE
O MY AMERICA! SECOND ACTS IN A NEW WORLD
ACCESS ALL AREAS: SELECTED WRITINGS 1990–2010
THE MAGNETIC NORTH: NOTES FROM THE ARCTIC CIRCLE
TOO CLOSE TO THE SUN: THE LIFE AND TIMES OF DENYS FINCH HATTON
CHERRY: A LIFE OF APSLEY CHERRY-GARRARD
TERRA INCOGNITA: TRAVELS IN ANTARCTICA
TRAVELS IN A THIN COUNTRY: A JOURNEY THROUGH CHILE
AN ISLAND APART: TRAVELS IN EVIA
(as co-editor) AMAZONIAN: THE PENGUIN BOOK OF WOMEN'S NEW TRAVEL WRITING
(for children) DEAR DANIEL: LETTERS FROM ANTARCTICA

JAN MORRIS
A Life

SARA WHEELER

faber

First published in 2026
by Faber & Faber Limited
The Bindery, 51 Hatton Garden
London EC1N 8HN

Typeset by Faber & Faber Limited
Printed and bound by CPI Group (UK) Ltd, Croydon, CR0 4YY

All rights reserved
© Sara Wheeler, 2026

Extracts from 'In Memory of W. B. Yeats' and 'September 1, 1939' and
Epistle to a Godson and unpublished letter to Jan Morris by W. H. Auden
Copyright © 1940 and 1972 by The Estate of W. H. Auden
Reprinted by permission of Curtis Brown, Ltd
All rights reserved

Extract from *Autumn Sequel* by Louis MacNeice
© Louis MacNeice 1954, published by Faber & Faber, reproduced by
kind permission of David Higham Associates

The right of Sara Wheeler to be identified as author of this work
has been asserted in accordance with Section 77 of the Copyright,
Designs and Patents Act 1988

A CIP record for this book
is available from the British Library

ISBN 978–0–571–37945–3

Printed and bound in the UK on FSC® certified paper in line with our continuing
commitment to ethical business practices, sustainability and the environment.
For further information see faber.co.uk/environmental-policy

Our authorised representative in the EU for product safety is
Easy Access System Europe, Mustamäe tee 50, 10621 Tallinn, Estonia
gpsr.requests@easproject.com

2 4 6 8 10 9 7 5 3 1

In Memoriam
Elizabeth Morris
1924–2024

What a nightmare hiatus we all pass through,
on the way from birth to death.

JAN MORRIS

AUTHOR'S NOTE

When Jan Morris wrote about her childhood – the choirboy years – and of soldiering with the 9th Queen's Royal Lancers in the aftermath of the Second World War, she referred to herself as 'he'. Out of respect for her decision, in these pages I have done the same. 'He' until 1970, when transition was approaching completion, 'she' thereafter.

SARA WHEELER, 2026

CONTENTS

Introduction		1
1	Twenty-Eight Knots for Sandy Hook (1926–1945)	9
2	Soldiering (1946–1947)	37
3	Bronzed Hero (1948–1952)	53
4	Knocking the Bastard Off (1953)	80
5	Perpetual Theatre (1954–1956)	98
6	Not What I Am (1956–1958)	119
7	Veil over Lipstick (1959–1962)	139
8	Trefan (1963–1965)	160
9	Half a Freak Show, Half a Miracle (1966–1970)	180
10	Being a Star (1971–1974)	209
11	Mon Dieu (1975–1979)	243
12	The Matter of Wales (1980–1984)	262
13	What's Become of Waring (1985–1989)	274
14	On the Brink (1990–1995)	288
15	Jester in Camelot (1996–2001)	300
16	Ancient Mariner (2002–2012)	313
17	Both (2013–2020)	337
Afterword		351
Source Notes		357
Acknowledgements		389
Picture Credits		393
Index		395

INTRODUCTION

I first met Jan Morris twenty-five years ago, at her home in Wales. We talked about the 1953 Everest expedition, among other topics. She had been the *Times*'s correspondent on the mountain and got the message back for Coronation Day. Morris spoke of her admiration for the leader, John Hunt, calling him 'a grizzled Hannibal'. There was a long pause, and I thought she was remembering her late pal, so I remained silent and looked out of the window. Finally she said, 'It must have been hard on the old boy. The sex change, I mean.'

I was with her for the day to gather material for a magazine profile, and earlier she had suggested a spin through the Welsh lanes. It was a fresh April morning, the sky cloudless. Once we had swung out of the gravel yard, Morris pressed a foot to the floor, gripped the steering wheel and set her face forward, eyes gleaming. She had rolled the window down, and a spring breeze ruffled a cumulus of hair. 'I'm *passionate* about sporty cars,' she said as the dun-coloured countryside raced by. 'This one has six gears. They advertise it by saying, "Add a little danger to your life." I like that.' After a few minutes she screeched to a stop to indicate, with a theatrical flourish, the embowered grave of former prime minister David Lloyd George, nestling in the live green shadows on a bank of the Dwyfor.

Later, after lunch in the kitchen, she showed me around the modest house: in her bedroom she flung open a louvred wardrobe door to reveal a poster of First Sea Lord Jacky Fisher, of whom she had written a slim biography. 'I'm going to have an affair with him in the afterlife!' she announced. Approaching eighty, she was purposefully skittish: as we were chatting in the doorway, she reached up to hang languidly from a crossbeam. It was raining by the time I left, and she escorted me to my taxi wielding a huge umbrella given to her on that fearsomely wet day in 1997 when Hong Kong was handed back to the Chinese. (She had been there, of course.) As the car lurched off towards Bangor amid homecoming cows, Morris shouted reproachfully, 'Shall I say goodbye to Ibsen for you?' Ibsen was the cat.

Some months later, I reviewed one of her books in a newspaper – a positive review, with one short paragraph expressing caveats. She asked, via her publisher's publicist, if I would chair a lecture she was giving at the Royal Society of Literature in London. We met at the theatre where the presentation was taking place and after the sound check retired to a private room to talk over a drink while the audience took their seats – the event was a sell-out, as Morris's usually were. The chat was relaxed and cordial; Morris laughed a lot, gulped her Sauvignon Blanc and made fun of me in a slightly flirtatious way. When the formal part of the evening began, I introduced her on stage with the customary encomium. 'Nothing is said, I notice,' she announced into the microphone after taking the podium, 'about the bad review.' She had not mentioned the review over our tête-à-tête. She had been saving it up.

I met her occasionally after that, but I only saw the mask slip that one day in Wales when she thought about Hunt. As the years went by, the enigma of Jan Morris puzzled me more and more. Is it possible to reconcile the larky persona with its flinty doppelgänger? How can a writer be superficial and profound at the same time? Why did she dress like a Walmart version of the Queen? How were both sides able to co-opt her as the battle over the rights and wrongs of Empire took on fresh urgency? Why did she carry on writing books when she had little left to say? What had she wanted to get out of transition, and did she get it? She had told me in 2001 that she did not give the gender issue a single thought 'from one year to the next'. She said she found Welsh nationalism far more interesting and asked if I did too, defying me to disagree.

What else lay behind the mask?

In 2021, a year after Morris's death, her literary executor and eldest son, Mark, asked if I would write her authorised life. I had published two

INTRODUCTION

previous biographies and a book of biographical essays, and my many travel books were full of capsule lives. I had always thought there would be one more full-length biography, but subjects had failed to seduce me – three or four years is a long time to spend with one person, even if they are dead. As a younger woman, I had needed heroes. In my seventh decade, Morris's contradictions and fallibilities stood in for life itself. Even at the outset I could see she was 'silly like us', to cite W. H. Auden, once a colleague of hers. Or I thought I could see that.

I began conducting interviews with Morris's family, friends and associates. A ninety-six-year-old former soldier turned watery blue eyes onto a South London street and went back in his mind to the Palestinian coast, where he and Morris had looked out for ships carrying Jewish refugees in 1947. Welsh independence hero Dafydd Iwan remembered taking shelter in the Morrises' house in 1970 after serving a prison term for defacing English-language road signs. Jann Wenner, co-founder of *Rolling Stone* magazine, recalled an eventful lunch with his star writer in San Francisco as the Me Decade unravelled. I interviewed Mark Morris seventeen times.

Jan's partner, formerly wife, Elizabeth was with us on the day I spent at the Morris home. I enjoyed her company immensely. By the time I came to write this book, dementia had taken hold. I have tried to let her speak in these pages through the letters and fragments I have uncovered. Jan once said that her 'union' with Elizabeth 'has given nobility to my mostly frivolous life', but Elizabeth had a life of her own. It was hard to reconcile the strong, fearless, independent woman I had met with the codependent victim so often present in versions of Morris's story, holding the fort in silence while Jan held the stage.

Unpublished material in the Morris Collection at the National Library of Wales in Aberystwyth included scores of notebooks and book drafts; the *Times* archive on an Essex industrial estate yielded febrile memos from the imperial and foreign newsroom as Israeli forces invaded Egypt the first time round, as well as everything else that unfurled in the Middle East in the cauldron of the 1950s. In addition to these and other archival resources, numerous individuals provided information in the course of the three years it took to write this book. A former newspaper editor, clearing out his shed, spotted a long and forgotten piece of Morrisania on its way to the recycling bin. Was there anyone who had not met Morris, I wondered, as anecdotes poured in (often the same anecdotes)? One man came forward to tell me he knew nothing.

I knew what Morris was trying to do on the road as I have spent my life trying to do it myself. She was a travel writer above all else, although she hated the term. I followed her through the backstreets of Nizwa, the ancient capital of Oman, to find the garden where bondsmen had set her typewriter on a carpet at nightfall. My notebook lay on the marble tabletops of the same cafés on Sharia Sherif Pasha as hers had lain in that 'strange little world' of semi-spies in post-war Cairo, and I stood on the deck of a *dahabiyeh*, houseboat, moored on the slow Nile in Zamalek. (Not her *dahabiyeh* – that sank.) Some months later in the foothills of the Himalaya I heard the slap-slap of laundry in a stream in which Morris had bathed and seen spires of blue smoke rising from the villages while white men with frozen beards sharpened ice axes. Those were good days.

I also spent many weeks back at Jan and Elizabeth's now unoccupied home. This time, I was sifting through letters tucked into thousands of foxed volumes or stored in Fairy Liquid boxes jammed under the stairs alongside broken fax machines, certificates from cat breeders and glass sculptures awarded for services to journalism. I slept in Morris's bed. It was often perishing cold, and a short row of pipistrelle bats sat it out on a ceiling beam, waiting for me to switch off the torch. (The bedside light wasn't working.) Late one night, I was forcing myself through a final bundle of quietly disintegrating letters recording dental appointments. Beyond a starburst of frost on the inside of the window, a cloudy moon lit the silhouette of Yr Wyddfa, Snowdon. I looked down at the dateline on the second piece of paper, handwritten on a friable airmail sheet. *Kathmandu, 2 April 1953*. The clock stopped but the pages went on, through April, up from the Nepalese capital to Dudh Kosi and Namche Bazar, through Thyangboche and the monastery and into the next tense

INTRODUCTION

month and Base Camp and deep snow and even up the Khumbu icefall, and here were Hillary and Tenzing, ice axes aloft. These letters, the ones Morris had written home to Elizabeth from Everest, had been missing for half a century. A current of electricity went through the freezing room, and even the bats turned their eyeless heads.

I went on to read mail Morris had sent home from the Casablanca clinic, and from many other places, unread since Elizabeth had slipped the sheets from their envelopes. Sometimes in those lonely Welsh days I glimpsed Jan Morris, as if she were in the same room; then she would wheel away into the mist in the lane, laughing.

She was present at many of the most significant moments of the modern era; she was among the finest *descriptive* writers who ever lived; she transitioned in 1972, when 'sex change' was unexplored territory. 'I think it could be claimed', Morris wrote in a late unpublished fragment,

> that during the second half of the twentieth century I wrote about more places than anyone else, and I was in a position to witness, and to reflect in my writing, many of the great historical events of the time. As I experienced all this first as a man, then as a woman, it might also be said (although I wouldn't want to make much of this) that my viewpoint was unique.

The contradictions and anomalies that kept on coming only made her life more alluring. She preached the virtues of kindness but after she died her daughter revealed unspeakable parental cruelty; she was a famous chronicler of the British Empire (some say an apologist for it) and a card-carrying Welsh nationalist. She was singular and contrary, yet I began to discern – and this surprised me – that her life reveals much that is universal. About addiction, for example: Morris was addicted to writing – to the creative process as a means of filling the void, or at least of trying to block it out. Was it through universality that she achieved the twin grail of sales and critical acclaim? This needed to be explored – so many have tried for that grail and failed. Few would put Morris in the very top rank as a writer (including me), but that is a high bar, and as a person she seemed to me more interesting than any man or woman who has ever made it into that minuscule band.

The politics of transition have risen high on the public agenda since that meeting in Wales a quarter of a century ago, and so, more predictably, have arguments over Empire. Morris's 1,600-page *Pax Britannica* trilogy charts the rise and decline of what she called an 'ambiguous epic'. She wrote it in the transition years and called it 'the centrepiece of my life', conceived as 'the recollections of a centurion in the dying days of the Roman Empire, telling us how the Empire worked in his province'. The role of the observant centurion was one she played for many decades all around the mutable world.

Taken together, the material revealed everything and nothing. What of the place where the documents stop? How to extract the essence of a person from the clutter of days and years? Sometimes I lost Morris in the dark. The depth of her ambition was hard to reach, as was her self-absorption. As I ploughed on, I wondered if the life was going to overshadow the work. She found irony in everything (she said), and there was irony in the gap between her words and her actions. It is hard for anyone wishing to honour Jan Morris's reputation to acknowledge family revelations.

The biographer's task is to breathe life into an inert mass of material, then discard most of it. She must at all costs (I believe) avoid the impulse to impose coherence. In other words, the life-writer cannot take a doggedly factual approach that ignores a whole layer of emotional and imaginative experience. All of us who do this so-called job seek to uncover an inner life. But whom do we really know? Motives are like deep-sea fish – even our own. Morris curated her image through more than fifty books, as well as many hundreds of essays and quite a few *Panorama* films. The image was the mask. She acknowledged it sometimes. In her eighties she made a film reviewing her life for her US publisher. When the interview finished, she said, off-camera, 'I've never heard such a lot of balls propounded.' I heard her saying it on the tape.

INTRODUCTION

At least we had some things in common. I took my first steps on Clevedon Pier, like her, and like her my earliest memories are of ships gliding up the Bristol Channel, headed, who knew, to Xanadu. I too have earned my living on the road for many decades. I know the loneliness of the empty hotel room and its bleak single bed, as well as the bleaker letter from HMRC. I too could remember, sitting on a warm rock on some foreign shore, twiddling the dial for what Morris called 'the grave sound of Big Ben on the BBC World Service, and the resonant, almost ecclesiastical way in which the announcer declaimed, "This is London."'

She drove me mad at times. Often when I read her tricksily asking me, the reader, 'Come with me now . . .', as she loved to do on the page, I had only one answer: no thanks. But when the chips were down, I found I agreed with her on most things. The right issues made her despair. She once began a review of a Ryszard Kapuściński volume: 'This is a book of essays and reminiscences about the Third World and it is enough to make a dead dog cry.'

When I slept in her bed, before switching off the torch I sometimes read the passages from her last book, *Allegorizings*, in which she wrote about her dreams. I thought I could actually enter into her unconscious life as well as her physical one by dreaming versions of her dreams. But at her house I dreamed of the Antarctic, where she had never been and I had. It was the only place she couldn't take away from me.

In 1946, then a nineteen-year-old cavalry officer, Morris sat on a bollard on a wharf in Trieste to write an essay about nostalgia. A steamboat eructating smoke left for Istria, ferrying indigent refugees home to bombed-out villages. Morris felt a sense of belonging in the city that did not belong, and on the wharf that morning laid the foundations of a whole career exploring nostalgia and its yearnings. Along the way, she would become a public figure as authors seldom do: she had star quality, someone said after she appeared on television tossing her white hair. Besides being read everywhere, she was famous everywhere. When she returned to Darjeeling in middle age she found a framed poem on the drawing room wall in the Windamere Hotel. She had written it in the visitors' book four decades earlier.

This is a story about longing, travelling, and never reaching home.

1
1926–1945
TWENTY-EIGHT KNOTS FOR SANDY HOOK

On 20 May 1910, in the indeterminate frontierlands of the Marches, the people gathered at St Mary's in the county town of Monmouth to mark the funeral of King Edward VII. Organist Enid Payne pulled out all the stops for Guilmant's *Funeral March*, her father, bank manager Charles Payne, conducted the choir, and head chorister Walter Morris sang 'Requiem Aeternam'. When Enid started 'O Rest in the Lord', clergy and choir filed into a sandstone porch where they met the civil procession, 'one of the longest ever seen in Monmouth'. Blue-robed mace-bearer James Morris, the head chorister's father, followed the entourage into weak spring sunshine.

The choirboy was fourteen, the organist twenty-four. Her people were burghers of the professional classes. His were house painters and grocery-store porters. Nine years after the king went to his final rest, the choirboy and the organist married in a Somerset church where they did not know the graven names. They never returned to the Marches. They were Jan Morris's parents.

Her maternal ancestors had built the turnpikes and smelters that had made Britain the richest country in the world – they were civil engineers, prototype hydrogeologists, manufacturing chemists. One of Morris's great-greats was secretary of the company which raised the first iron bridge over the Thames; a triple-great had employed Marc Brunel to bore the first tunnel *under* the same river. Another relative was provost of Eton, one sat as an MP, a few were even writers. Eliza Marten, Morris's great-grandmother, was a stylish storyteller who published books for older children exploring the coal country around Wolverhampton – travel books, effectively. A great-uncle emigrated to the US in 1871 and married the Nantucket-born author Annie Mitchell, an early graduate of Vassar. Annie's own aunt, astronomer Maria Mitchell, was the first woman elected to the American Academy of Arts and Sciences.

Charles Payne, the baton-wielding bank manager, married Edith, née McKenna, in Shifnal, Shropshire, in 1884. Enid, Jan Morris's mother, was born two years later. Charles had begun as a clerk in the Shifnal branch of Lloyds and worked his way up to the top job in nearby Ludlow. When his children were small (a boy and another girl had followed Enid), Lloyds posted him to its Monmouth branch. The market town, on the confluence of three rivers in the porous, ambiguous territory between England and Wales, was prospering. Assizes drew solicitors as well as bank managers, and when the Paynes arrived Monmouth had two railway stations and a gentlemen's club. The family and their two servants initially moved into Priory Farm, six miles outside town, then shifted across the Hereford Road to Trafalgar, a villa owned by the Rolls family, whose name was about to be linked for all time with the glamour of the motor car. John, Henry and Charles Rolls, sons of the 1st Baron Llangattock, were frequent visitors at Trafalgar. Like the Paynes, they were musical. It was the era of amateur choral societies, the world of Elgar and Bach. When Charles Payne made his debut as director of the Monmouth Musical Society, playing the organ in the Rolls Hall in Queen Victoria's Diamond Jubilee year, eleven-year-old Enid accompanied him on the violin, and when he conducted Gilbert and Sullivan's *HMS Pinafore*, Enid's little brother Geraint took the part of the Midshipmite.

Enid won a scholarship to Monmouth Girls' High School and went on to study piano for three years at the Leipzig Konservatorium under Robert Teichmüller, whose own teacher had been a pupil of Liszt, Mendelssohn and Schumann. When Konservatorium chaperones forbade female students from attending a performance of Strauss's opera *Salome*, Enid jumped out of a window at her lodgings to get there.

'Oh, she had heard the chimes at midnight,' Jan Morris wrote of her mother. When Enid's parents visited Leipzig, Charles packed a brace of Monmouthshire pheasant for Teichmüller. Enid continued her studies in London at the Royal Academy of Music, and after graduating moved back to Monmouth to become the organist at St Mary's, the church where people were to mourn the king, and teach music and German at her alma mater. She also played a water-powered organ in the Great Hall at The Hendre, the neo-Gothic Rolls pile where a cart brought in wood from the park. The swashbuckling Charles Rolls, who lived mainly in London, had already co-founded Rolls-Royce with Henry Royce; the first car he owned personally was one of only three in the whole of Wales. In 1906 he went up in a hot-air balloon from the Monmouth Gasworks, a thrilling event for everyone. Gareth, Jan Morris's brother, always maintained that Rolls had proposed to Enid and his family had disapproved, but that she had in any case refused him. Charles Rolls died in an air crash in Bournemouth in 1910, Britain's first fatality in a powered aircraft.

Of the three Payne children, Enid was the only one still living at home in 1912, when Lloyds transferred her father to Hereford, twenty miles away. The Monmouth branch gave him a silver tea service when he left. Charles and Edith took the unmarried Aunt Fanny (Edith's sister-in-law) to Hereford with them. Iris, the second Payne daughter, was a live-in teacher at a Monmouth school under headmistress Ethelreda Carless, a Dahl character *avant la lettre*. Geraint, the Midshipmite – the name was pronounced the English way, with a soft 'g' (as in Jerry), as opposed to the Welsh hard 'g' (as in Gareth) – was, like his sister, a scholarship student as well as a gifted artist and musician (a cellist, in his case). He trained as an architect in a paternal uncle's firm and after qualifying set up his own practice in Hampstead, North London. He was engaged to the artist Katharine 'Kitty' Clausen, daughter of the painter Sir George Clausen. When war broke out, Geraint enlisted in the Artists Rifles, initially in the London Regiment's transport section, and his sister Enid sent enormous care parcels to him in France ('It is ripping of you to do the thing so handsomely'). After officers' school behind the lines, in January 1915

Geraint Payne got his commission and the War Office posted him to the Highland Light Infantry in Neuve Chapelle. In February he returned to Monmouth on leave. The civic dignitaries had only recently installed a stained-glass window in St Mary's memorialising the Boer War – it depicted Henry V and the Monnow Bridge – and now a fresh cohort of young men from Lloyds and the assizes were in uniform. Back in Neuve Chapelle in March, Geraint wrote to his father, revealing that his platoon had persuaded him to play football for the first time in his life: his team had gone down 3–1.

> We are having a very pleasant time here for the present and the men are all getting surprisingly fit again after their trench work. We are weeding out a lot of the old crocks and replacing them with young drafts . . . I haven't got the Trenchscope yet [a periscope for looking over a trench parapet]. I went to the shop but they couldn't let me have one at once, but promised to send one when I sent them the address to send it to. I have since sent them the address, so I suppose it will come soon.

It didn't. A week later Geraint looked over the parapet to observe the lines and a German sniper blew his head off. He was twenty-six. George Clausen painted *Youth Mourning*, a naked female figure curled at the foot of a wooden cross in a wintry expanse of flooded craters. It is Katharine, his daughter. (The picture hangs in London's Imperial War Museum.) Charles Payne never listened to Bach's cello suites again. The next year he had appendicitis and died on the operating table in Hereford at the age of fifty-five. Katharine Clausen married a Sinn Fein gunrunner.

Walter Morris, Jan's father, was born in 1896 in Monmouth's Weirhead Street, close to the west bank of the Wye. He was the eighth of thirteen children, all with English names. When he was small the family moved to a house made of ships' beams next to a pub in Dixton Road. Walter's own father, James Charles, a house painter, worked on Saturday mornings and came home at dinnertime – dinner was taken at midday –

complaining that the town was 'full of the Welsh'. *His* father had been a porter who carted boxes for shops. In April 1915, six years after enrolling at Monmouth School for Boys, the teenage Walter signed up to fight along with his brother Tom. Two older brothers were already in uniform. 'The record of the Morris family is magnificent,' reported the *Monmouth and Over Monnow Parish Magazine*. Walter had broad shoulders and a high forehead, his chin slightly receding, nose large and spreading, and lips thin. He served as a private in motor transport on the Western Front, where he was gassed and hospitalised for thirty-eight days in 1916, and again for forty-eight days in 1918. His wounds, physical and psychological, never healed. When he got back to Monmouth, Walter proposed to Enid, the organist ten years his senior. The widowed Edith had moved back from Hereford when Charles died, bringing Aunt Fanny and the tea service. Enid's sister Iris, the teacher, was engaged to a farmer's son from Long Ashton in Somerset, thirty miles from Monmouth. It was there, in All Saints Church on the road from Bristol to Weston-super-Mare, that Walter Morris and Enid Payne married in 1919. It was a sort of elopement, with mother and aunt in tow.

Walter turned his back on an enormous loving family who would have taken him in and found him work whatever his gas-induced limitations. Did he think that in abandoning all he knew he would also leave his nightmares on the banks of the Monnow? Did Enid leave on account of the stigma, powerful then, of marrying into a class some way beneath her own? Whatever motivated either of them, there was no question of returning to Monmouth.

They rented accommodation ten miles west of Long Ashton in Clevedon on the Bristol Channel and stayed in that small town all their married life. In the mid-nineteenth century, merchants from the adjacent port of Bristol had built grey-stone villas in what was then a rural seaside village, and in 1869 the Clevedon Pier opened. By the time the newly married Enid and Walter arrived, the municipality had put a bandstand on the seafront and planted garden beds with China roses. The channel itself was gunmetal grey, and although it was almost always calm the water usually rippled a little, and the sky, with no hemming mountains or even hills, was so big it filled the frame of the eye. A branch line connected Clevedon to the Great Western Railway, which ended in London, and another went to Weston-super-Mare, where day-trippers breathed in the health-giving vapours that rose spectrally from the mud – Jan Morris remembered this when she was writing about the nineteenth-century mania for health cures. The entourage – Walter, Enid, her mother Edith and Aunt Fanny – rented an apartment in The Lookout, a villa on Marine Hill. Walter found employment as a mechanic and taxi driver at Pages Central Garage. He also worked as an undertaker's driver. So Enid had a hearse instead of a Roller. Undaunted – one wonders what could have daunted her – she advertised private piano and organ tuition in the newspapers, and in the summer secured a job as a pianist on pleasure steamers plying up and down the grey Bristol Channel. Later she played the organ at the two-hundred-seat Picture House, which had opened in 1912 for silent movies projected by means of gas power. (The first film shown raised money for survivors of the *Titanic*.) Enid was resourceful, energetic and generally tremendous; the family did not conform to what Morris called 'conventions of the day', in which 'man was for hard things . . . woman was for gentler, softer pursuits . . . In our family . . . such distinctions were not recognized.' Who wouldn't want to be like Enid Payne?

Gareth was born on 13 May 1920, Christopher on the same day two years later. (Three months after Chris made his appearance, Walter drove Clevedon's first charabanc on a day trip to Wells, an event reported with pride in the *Mercury*.) Edith, Enid's mother, had gone into a nursing home in Bristol; she died there in 1924. By then the Clevedon Morrises had moved to 37 Victoria Road. Before hazel-eyed James arrived in October 1926, they had shifted again to 1 Herbert Road, and he was born in that rented house. It was a three-storey semi-detached dwelling of pennant sandstone, heavily ornamented with a decorative parapet and carved window heads. More importantly for young boys, it faced a park with a small wood.

It was a happy time for all of them, even for Walter, when he wasn't having nightmares in which he was back in the trenches. Aunt Fanny, seventy-three when James was born, taught the children to read and took them for penny buns on the pier. Money was tight; when Enid sent them on errands, the boys had to ask for credit at Parker's grocery. But the family employed a maid. Walter was a loving husband, and when Enid was out teaching in the afternoon he boiled two eggs to await her return. (He liked tripe and onions himself, but only Chris would cook the dish for him. The fair-haired Chris, whom Enid called Kit, was closest to his father and most like him in looks.) Walter had unnamed health problems. He spent a lot of time in the bathroom. Mustard gas had affected his sight in one eye, as it had affected much else. Enid ran the house – even its finances. At home, she was always reading while she worked. When she washed up, she propped a book behind the sink. Half-open volumes lay around Herbert Road like partially eaten sandwiches. 'My mother,' Morris recalled, 'who preferred to read seven or eight books simultaneously, in two or three languages, left them all over the place open at her current page ... Perhaps it was the profligate intimacy of this habit ... that has made the book one of my own more ubiquitous delights.' The intimacy achieved through reading was more than a delight for Jan; it was a journey that ran in parallel with the travels, a source of happiness, a support, an escape – everything. As for Enid, she was lively and opinionated as well as a dedicated reader. The boys remembered her impressions – she was an excellent mimic. She liked to declaim a line made famous by Walter's boss, the undertaker. Once a coffin had gone into the ground, he would intone, 'Another one done, Wally.' And of course there was always music in the house. James, known in the family as Jim, sat under the piano while his mother played, close to the percussive creak of the pedals. Enid had taught them all to play and to read music, and often Gareth accompanied her: Chris remembered arriving home from school to find the pair tackling Stravinsky.

The family wireless set came of age in the twenties. That, and the gramophone, meant Enid could listen to music at all hours, and in the summer, when the windows were open, neighbours complained. In the same decade, the British Broadcasting Company and its successor the Corporation enabled the rise of classical music in Britain, and, as Enid noted with satisfaction, works for the piano ascended in the hierarchy of the overall repertoire. On Sundays she played a hydraulic church organ, like the instrument at The Hendre back in Monmouth. Gareth served as boat boy (a junior acolyte at the altar) and remembered that at climactic moments Enid would pull out every stop at once, disabling the central mechanism, and a churchwarden would have to descend through a trapdoor under the organ seat to coax the instrument back to life.

Enid was engaged with the world as she experienced it. She composed a musical ode to Queen Mary and sent it to Buckingham Palace. One of her grandfathers (he was among the manufacturing chemists) had been a keen contributor to the Letters pages; in 1876 he wrote to the *Journal of the Society of Arts* (actually more of a science journal, but to the explosively creative Victorians there were not yet two cultures), complaining about the deleterious environmental effects of a new sewage system. It was an enthusiasm – a compulsion to reach out – that was to run in the family. Enid complained to the *Musical Times* about 'the horrible fashion' in piano playing for 'attacking each note of a melodic group as a separate objective'. In April 1929 she weighed in to a debate about organ pedalling techniques. Jan Morris was to appear regularly on the Letters page of *The Times* (though not the *Musical Times*) for many decades; she inherited her mother's quick mind and her instinct to make contact with the unknown world pedalling around her.

The aldermanic Stanley Baldwin was the most constant figure on the political landscape beyond Clevedon. Pipe-smoking and phlegmatic, he projected, or tried to, a Disraelian notion of the Conservative Party: that of One Nation, an idea embodied in Morris's bank-managing grandfather. In 1924, the Liberal Party having shrunk to invisibility, Ramsay MacDonald had briefly presided over the first-ever Labour government in Britain, but by 1929, when he again took the helm, an economic storm was beginning to blow. Unemployment reached three million, or 22 per cent of the working population. Walter was among the fortunate – garages and petrol stations flourished, catering for the rise in motor ownership: in the thirties, the number of cars in Britain doubled to reach two million. Funerals also held up. The Depression did not bite as deeply in the prosperous South-West as it did in the Midlands and the North, the regions which suffered most after the National Government introduced the controversial Means Test for unemployment benefits in 1931. The residents of 1 Herbert Road just about maintained the respectabilities of their middle-class status, even if the boys had to ask for credit. They never let go of the maid. When one left of her own accord and a new girl appeared, Gareth overheard the outgoing one telling her successor that all the family were nice except him. His repetition of the story later in life was characteristic of his ability to laugh at himself. His youngest sibling could never mock herself with conviction: her self-deprecation was superficial. In life as in prose, comedy rebuffed serious analysis and fended off tricky questions, but, *au fond*, Jan Morris was not there to be laughed at.

The family sometimes visited Bath, twenty-five miles away, 'an exemplar of dingy respectability', and Morris recalled spotting Haile Selassie, the fallen emperor of Ethiopia, at that time in flight from the Italian occupation of his homeland. He was at Bath station, 'sitting alone, pale, dark-eyed and meditative, in a first-class compartment of a Paddington train'. The world beyond Clevedon impinged memorably on Jim again when he heard about Gandhi's visit to Buckingham Palace over the wireless. 'Gandhi was sixty-two, I was five [they shared a birthday], and I can dimly remember the commotion.' Thrillingly, the family visited the capital themselves once: Morris always remembered Londoners respectfully removing their hats as they passed the Cenotaph, Lutyens's memorial to the fallen from both Britain and across the colonies. Empire was in the air educated children breathed in the twenties and thirties.

The boys went to a nursery school two streets away, but Jim was expelled for tying a girl to a tree. At weekends and in the holidays, Gareth and Chris formed a unit, cycling off to Walton Castle or Ladye Bay or taking the bus to Bristol. Jim was often alone. He had thick, springy dark-brown hair and his father's high forehead, a good-looking, athletic boy, though not yet a tall one. He liked climbing to the iron-age fort on Wain's Hill. Ten miles of water lay between him and Wales, and when the visibility was good he could see the uninhabited islands Steep Holm and Flat Holm. Morris's primary memory of childhood was watching ships sailing up the Severn Estuary into the Bristol Channel.

> Only a grassy hill separated my home from the sea, and few anticipations have been more urgent for me than the climb up its flank, carrying my telescope, to see what vessels would reveal themselves for me on the other side – a plume of smoke, first showing itself above the ridge, and then a mast or two, or a funnel, until finally, panting with exertion and expectancy I would throw myself on the grass, opening the slides of my telescope as I did so . . . I can see those ships now. They were handsome white banana boats making for Bristol, and freighters from West Africa, and French wine ships and ships piled high with timber flying the flags of Latvia and Lithuania, and fleets of blackened colliers coming and going perpetually from the coal ports of Glamorgan . . . Occasionally I would recognise, from the silhouettes in my *Dumpy Book of Ships*, some famous liner diverted from its usual route, a Canadian Pacific *Empress* or one of the new three-funnelled P & Os. This would give me the utmost excitement, besides adding to the interest of the otherwise somewhat monotonous journal in which I kept a register of those observations; and so ineradicable are the pleasures of childhood that to this day, when I see a ship at sea that I recognise by name, I feel an irrational surge of pride.

It was Morris's eternal moment. She mentioned the colliers and the telescope in a publicity film when she was ninety-two. Ships enabled the boy Jim to see humanity in a seascape, and similarly, landscape moved the adult Jan for its role in the human story. During a relatively solitary childhood, with two brothers soon to be away at school, his telescope was his 'most prized possession except for my cat', and besides patrolling

Wain's Hill he also sat near the Sugar Lookout, where men had sat before him straining for the sails of their ship coming in. Jim was looking out too, 'identifying passing ships for my roster'. Before he turned ten he had completed the first pages of a book he called *Travels with a Telescope*. Spyglasses, as people sometimes called them, exerted a lifelong attraction: they 'gave private insight into different worlds'. Morris chose a telescope as the luxury item on her first *Desert Island Discs* outing, in 1983. You can see things clearly with a spyglass, without getting close.

The geography of childhood came to represent personal duality – Wales on one side, England on the other. Even Steep Holm, which is part of England, and Flat Holm – Ynys Echni, and part of Wales – conspired to formalise the divide. The English hills south-east of Clevedon, Morris recalled, 'seemed to me more disturbing by far than the stately old mountains of Wales that sheltered my father's people'. In autobiographical fragments, Morris cast off most family history in favour of choice nuggets which she polished until they gleamed: 'I could always see the mountains [of Wales], so close across the water and yet apparently so unattainable . . . A lumbering old de Havilland biplane used to fly heavily over each morning on its way from Bristol to Cardiff, and its slow passing gave me my very first intimations of *hiraeth*.' This was the ineffable Welsh homesickness, the fugitive longing for which there is no direct translation.

Dualities of class did not fit the narrative, so Morris made Walter an engineer in his accounts, rather than a private in a transport regiment. As Jan, she only told stories that signposted personal legends, highlighting for example 'the restrained mysticism' of the 'Quaker strain' in the family, or the biplane that came to represent transcendent longing. Authentic detail and romantic invention blended to powerful effect, and for many decades memory lovingly cultivated the image of a tiny machine buzzing up the Bristol Channel.

The view out to sea thrilled Jim for another reason: 'no land stood between us and New York'. America was the future – the boy sensed it. At sunset especially, Morris wrote, the shimmering red water offered 'tantalising visions of Manhattan's towers and palaces'. Jim had 'grown up' with 'great ships'.

> I pored over their pictures in shipping magazines, thrilled to their graceful lines, and marvelled to imagine their elegant shapes, streaming smoke from their two funnels, swelling foam from their prows, as they made at 28 knots for Sandy Hook – ships, names, places that spelt romance for me then, and excite me still.

Toponyms had already taken on significance in Jim's imaginative world; places on a map or in a book were symbols of potential, not merely geographic cyphers.

Enid faced the challenge of the boys' education as she had confronted the problem of *Salome*. As there was no possibility of jumping out of a window, she put the three of them up for scholarships at the cathedral schools. Gareth got his, at Bristol. The odds were better, Enid reckoned, if she spread her bets. Chris was eight when she took him up to Hereford on the train for an interview. Two boys were in contention for the single music scholarship, and Chris got it on the spot. Enid sent a telegram to Clevedon: *CHRIS SUCCESSFUL PLEASE MEET US TEMPLE MEADS*. There, at Bristol station, they arrived among the shopworn, hollow-eyed men of the thirties hawking themselves around as porters, and Walter was grateful for the taxi and the hearse.

Then it was Jim's turn. Enid had Oxford's Christ Church Cathedral Choir School in her sights. Part of the university (the cathedral is a college chapel), the school took between sixteen and nineteen choristers a year – enough for a cricket team, as Morris noted, but not enough to raise a side to play against. Jim got in, with a full scholarship. Enid had her hat-trick. She showed her sons they could do anything with their lives. Like Chris at Hereford, they got the news there and then, at interview, and another successful boy's father took them all out for a cream tea.

Clevedon celebrated Empire Day every 24 May with a costumed parade along the front, thumping activity in the bandstand and general flag-waving. Jim and his brothers had absorbed the novels of G. A. Henty featuring Britons swaggering round the pink-tinged globe. And they knew what they were celebrating, or thought they did. Embedded certainties and a sense of national exceptionalism were legacies of Empire. Morris wrote in the introduction to one of the *Pax Britannica* books, 'I was born just in time to see the schoolroom maps emblazoned pole to pole in the imperial red.' (Pink was the more usual colour.) But in a little-known 1963 volume about the World Bank, Morris described how swiftly the confidence drained away.

> I can myself remember, as a small boy, contemplating with what must have been a most displeasing complacency the huge red slabs that marked the British Empire on the map . . . only a couple of decades ago one of the commonplaces of political morality was the notion that men of one race had not only the right but often the actual duty to government of another. Today the idea of the White Man's Burden seems as outmoded as the Ptolemaic view of the universe, or the divine right of kings. Yesterday it was among the facts of life.

Morris said, 'A lost England made me.' But it was not lost yet. In 1935 the bunting came out early for George V's Silver Jubilee on 6 May. It was Jim's last spring at home, and an exceptionally cold one. Bristol had a Jubilee Carnival on Durdham Down, with a helter-skelter and roundabouts as well as a military review and a twenty-one-gun salute. It was the last imperial jubilee, though nobody knew that. Prime Minister Baldwin, keen to unite the nation at the start of his second period in office after recent public brawls between communists and fascists, used the occasion to tout the Crown as the 'great symbol of our race and of our unity'. The BBC broadcast an ambitious musical programme and the shopkeepers of Clevedon's Hill Road wore red, white and blue rosettes. Eight months later, the king was dead.

They had moved to Verwood, a smaller house in Madeira Road. It was plainer too, with bay windows on the ground and first floors. Walter had taken a job at the Seavale Road and East Clevedon Garages, and he kept up the hearse work. His health had not improved. 'In his dreams the war was raging still,' according to Jim, 'and when I crept awestruck into his bedroom he cried out warnings, tossed and turned, moaned and coughed uncontrollably, and sometimes bitterly laughed, so alive in his nightmare that I heard the guns myself, ducked to the screaming whistle of the shells, smelt the cordite and the treacherous, murderous gas.'

While Walter could not escape the past, the rest of the world looked forwards. 'Everything Victorian was generally derided' in the thirties, according to Morris. The new was what counted. So what was new? The wireless. The talkies at Enid's cinema. Women's ankles. (Women between twenty-one and twenty-nine had even got the vote in 1929 in the so-called Flapper Election.) Sliced bread and Kit Kats made their debuts. The boys were allowed into the Picture House for free, and in 1938 they squashed onto their bench at the back to watch the first Disney full-length animated film: *Snow White*. But according to W. H. Auden, the thirties were a 'low dishonest decade'. Abroad, the family heard over the wireless, Spaniards were fighting for freedom. Spain crystallised a struggle against fascism across Europe that came to dominate the airwaves. In 1932 Baldwin's cousin, a poet who was to become, in Morris's lifetime, a shibboleth for all that was wrong with Empire, wrote in his poem 'The Storm Cone': *This is the midnight – let no star/ Delude us – dawn is very far*. Hitler was not yet in power, but Kipling sensed what lay ahead.

In September 1936 Jim joined Christ Church Cathedral Choir School. (The word 'choir' was shortly dropped from the name, though it was a choir school by its nature.) He was almost ten. 'Exile was mine when, rising in Cathedral Choir House that first morning from prickly institutional blankets in a loveless dormitory, I crept to the window and saw outside a totally unknown landscape.' But he liked the great fortress front of Christ Church in twilight before evensong, punctured by a single lit window; the robed canons flapping like starlings through Tom Quad; the vaporous river chill that crept into the cathedral itself early in the morning when the boys, barely awake, dropped their music sheets on the flagstones and even paper seemed to clang. 'Everyone was happier there I think than boys were at other prep schools,' Morris wrote. 'I loved the daily cycle.' From 1938, the bespectacled classicist Reverend Wilfrid Oldaker was headmaster of the school and precentor of the cathedral; among themselves the boys called him Pip, after the *Daily Mail* cartoon *Pip, Squeak and Wilfred*. Choristers boarded under the watchful eye of Matron in a house down a lane on the other side of St Aldate's – 'We lived medievally, a nest of singing birds in an Oxford attic' – and filed across to the cathedral twice a day, albs, cassocks and surplices of their own fluttering, 'sometimes passed rather comically in the opposite direction by a parallel line of policemen, clumping in single file, helmeted and heavy-booted, towards their headquarters down the road'. One of the cops told Jim off sotto voce for picking his nose, a shame that lingered for eight decades.

Outside choir practice and lessons at inky double desks, the boys played sport on the Christ Church Meadow playing fields, which ran down to the River Cherwell. Jim hated all sport except cross-country.

> Three big chestnuts grew in the corner [of the playing field], and in the long damp grass beneath them I used to lie unobserved and ecstatic, in the heavy, sweet-smelling hush of an Oxford summer afternoon. Frogs leapt up there, and kept me amused; grasshoppers quivered on grasses beside my eye; the bells of Oxford languidly chimed the hours; if I heard somebody looking for me – *Morris! Morris! You're in!* – I knew they would not bother to look for long.

The life of the school was intimately connected with that of the cathedral and the wider community. It was far from the insular, shut-in prep school experience typical of the thirties. For Jim, Oxford offered 'my first intimations of a world . . . beyond my telescope's range'.

Canon Claude Jenkins gave the evensong benediction.

> The style of it, as he slowly recited it in the gathering dust before the distant high altar, fascinated me then, as it moves me in

memory now. So very old he looked up there, so mystical seemed his vestmented figure in the half-light and so lovely did his blessing sound in the words of the King James Bible that he seemed to me a very emblem of simple goodness, beyond all dogma, thesis, or even his own theology.

Morris wrote those lines at ninety, adding (in the journal *The American Scholar*) that it was Jenkins – canon by virtue of being Regius Professor of Ecclesiastical History – who instilled the precept 'Be Kind'. No single teacher had 'left a mark on my identity', Morris continued, but Jenkins was 'the one true spiritual influence on my life'. (Recollections may vary. According to a recent history of the college, Jenkins was 'grubby and malodorous in person, miserly and filching in his habits, archaic and untidy in his erudition'.) The spirituality did stick, even if the religion didn't: the adult Morris, like the Jenkins of memory, was 'beyond all dogma', but the candlelit early years left a deep sense of the mystical.

The rest of the college emptied at Christmas, but the cathedral was at its most hectic. Choristers returned to their homes only after the festivities were over. The canons arranged parties for their charges in their houses facing Tom Quad.

> How tall the candles were! How rich but wholesome the cakes! How twinkling the Regius Professors turned out to be, stripped of the awful dignities of office! What thrilling presents we were given – envelopes with penny blacks upon them, magnificent wax seals of bishops or chancellors! How happy the old clergymen's faces looked as, breathlessly piping our gratitude – 'Thank you very much *indeed*, sir!' 'It was jolly nice of you, sir!' – we last saw them nodding their goodbyes, a little exhausted around the eyes, through the narrowing gaps of their front doors.

'I spent a string of my childhood Christmases hard at it in the choirstalls and practice rooms,' Morris wrote. But he never minded. 'On the contrary, those Christmases far from home amid the dreaming spires have remained the high points of my life's long memory.' Boarding at prep school was not the endlessly repeated lesson in loss that it was for so many. Loss was part of being human for Morris, not something connected to life events.

Jim read and read. The first volume he bought with his own money was *The Welsh Fairy Book* by W. Jenkyn Thomas. When he moved on to his mother's shelves, he read the Russian classics. 'I was raised on Constance Garnett's Russia,' Morris recalled, referring to the translator of the Golden Age writers, and as a young man he scrawled 'This is the best novel ever written' in Enid's copy of *Anna Karenina*. The family had moved again two years after the last shift, this time to Langleigh in St Andrews Drive on Clevedon's coastal edge. It was an even smaller, modern house; at the end of the street, meadows led directly to Wain's Hill, where Jim took up his old position with his spyglass. Back at the dining room table, he made a Somerset gazetteer, pasting in illustrations – Bath's page showed a photograph of the Royal Crescent.

Gareth was at home full-time again: he had not cared for his cathedral school and had switched to a private tutor, and he also went to London once a week to study the flute under Robert Murchie. The Scottish flautist, another Bach disciple, had played the Fourth Army over the Rhine in the Great War. Gareth decided to continue under him full-time at the Royal College of Music. The task of posting the application form had been assigned to Walter. He forgot, they missed the deadline, and Gareth's appeal was rejected. But everyone always forgave the lovable Walter. (When he got home from a convivial skittles session at the Wessex Royal Engineers Social Club, he used to put his head round the door of one of the upstairs bedrooms and ask the boys to come down for fried onions.) Gareth went instead to the Royal Academy of Music, Enid's alma mater. When he returned to Clevedon in the holidays, he brought Dennis Brain, a young horn player, soon to be a famous one. Enid wrote cadenzas for Brain's concert performances.

One day, when Jim was twelve, Oldaker called him into his study. Walter had died. He had been ill – beyond the normal – for only a few days. He was forty-six. Morris wrote later, 'I hardly knew my father.' Representatives of the skittles team attended the funeral at Clifton Parish Church. Aunt Fanny had already died, and Walter was buried in the same churchyard. Another one done.

Mark Morris, Jan's eldest son, says, 'My father never once mentioned his own father to me – never. I wonder if ingrained shame about Walter's occupation led to his silence on the subject, and to a need to have visible status.' Mark thinks Jan resented Enid for marrying down. 'The Paynes were virtually lesser aristocracy, yet she married a working-class man ten years her junior.'

The previous May, Jim had filed into the stalls with the others to mark the coronation of George VI. 'All hearts seem open at the moment,' Baldwin wrote, egging the nation on after the horrors of Edward VIII's abdication. But the light now dimmed. In the last days of September 1938, the choirboys had gas masks fitted. The devices smelled of the disinfectant Izal and powerfully affected young imaginations, as did the trenches being dug in the Oxford parks. Although pottery models of beaming prime minister Neville Chamberlain waving a piece of paper briefly appeared in the windows of Carfax souvenir shops, it was not long until the lights went out altogether for the second time in the lives of the old canons. In 'September 1, 1939', Auden – a Christ Church man – dismissed the dishonest thirties, but the poem continued: *Waves of anger and fear/ Circulate over the bright/ And darkened lands of the earth.* By the time Jim went home for the next holiday, a Jewish refugee from Vienna had arrived at Langleigh, a boy of his age. 'He was the most brilliant person I had met,' Morris remembered. Having arrived without a word of English, the boy, also called Walter, 'seemed to pick up the entire language in a month or two. He excelled at cricket, he played the violin exquisitely, Latin and mathematics seemed equally easy to him and to cap it all he was almost excessively good-looking. Though I was hampered by no small modesty myself, he made me feel gauche.' Meanwhile Enid, the Germanophile, queued for her own gas mask in Clevedon's Old Church Road. Few civilians knew the cost of war like she did. Her husband had lost his health, her brother his life and her father his peace of mind. Now she had three sons to give.

The first winter of the war was the coldest of the century so far in Britain. In Oxford, a powdery film of lichen froze on the branches of the silver birches in Christ Church Meadow, and in their house the choristers clung to the asthmatic fire while Matron grappled with the new system of coupons and filled ceramic brown-and-cream screw-topped hot-water bottles. Jim and his cohort took the Common Entrance examinations for their public schools when daffodils were out in the meadow and countries in Northern Europe were falling one by one. Oldaker had discussed Jim's prospects with Enid: she had told him she could not afford more than £10 per term in fees, but they had put Jim in for Lancing College, where the full cost for boarders was £55 per term (about £2,650 today; Walter had earned about £5 a week). Just before France signed its armistice with Germany, Oldaker heard that Jim had won the top music scholarship and the sixth general scholarship. It was a remarkable double, recorded in the pages of the *Oxford Mail*. Oldaker wrote to Enid informing her that he would secure a benefactor for the rest of the Lancing fees. It was not to be the end of Christ Church for Morris.

After the Dunkirk summer, they heard, on the wireless in coastal Clevedon, about the start of the Blitz, and on cinema newsreels watched images of Spitfires coming out of the sun as the Few saved the nation. On 11 September 1940 Churchill told the British people that if invasion came, it would be in the next two weeks. Life somehow went on. Enid was still playing the organ at the Picture House, even when the talkies had taken over. Cinemas were attracting over twenty million people a week and films like *Victoria the Great* and *Sixty Glorious Years* expressed a national myth. For Jim, other kinds of films augmented dreams of America inspired by the vessels he spotted through his telescope. 'Even in the 1930s,' she wrote as Jan, remembering those days, 'when I imagine not one in ten thousand inhabitants of the British Isles had ever crossed the Atlantic, we were all strangely familiar with American scenes and idioms.'

Jim started at Lancing when he was fourteen. Founded on the Sussex Downs by a churchman in 1848, the school was a monument to the Gothic Revival. Evelyn Waugh, a pupil in 1917, referred to it as a 'flint-girt fortress'. But for the duration of hostilities Lancing had relocated to the Herefordshire–Shropshire border, and Jim never even saw the fortress. Moor Park, the school's main wartime location, was in the village of Richard's Castle, near Ludlow, where Enid's father had managed Lloyds Bank. Jim was put in Sanderson's House, which occupied Ashford Court in Ashford Carbonell. (The owners had moved into the chauffeur's cottage when the house was requisitioned and the chauffeur and his wife had shifted to the big house as butler and housekeeper.) Sanderson's boys bicycled to their lessons in Moor Park across Wheat Common, which deteriorated to a quagmire in winter, and cycled back for lunch. The River Teme ran along the bottom of the Ashford garden, and in summer the Spam-coloured pupils swam. Jim continued to abjure team sport wherever possible, but he still enjoyed cross-country running, pounding over the Downs in all weathers to the ominously named Further Steepdown.

Numbers had fallen away. More significantly for the boys, the labyrinthine public-school system of codes and regulations had not made the journey to Shropshire, nor had daily prayers ('dibs'): the only whole-school service was on a Sunday, the Lancing reputation for High Anglicanism among the mounting casualties of war. 'The old hierarchical structure broke down to some extent,' wrote a Sanderson's contemporary, 'and the rather rigid discipline was replaced by a more liberal approach.' Jim was allowed to cycle over to Hereford to see Chris, who had left school and become the organ loft apprentice at Hereford Cathedral, and on Sunday mornings he sat in the loft as Chris played. Back at Sanderson's, the boys helped housemaster Basil 'John' Handford plant potatoes and set up chicken runs, and in the evenings Handford played them gramophone records in his drawing room.

'Dear mum,' Jim wrote to Enid during his first Lancing winter, 'Thanks for the clothes parcel.' He had cycled to Richard's Castle but had had to abandon his bike halfway; the snow was two feet deep, so he turned back, even on foot. The letter continued:

> It's absolutely impossible to get into Moor Park till the snow clears and so we are having to work here. There are twenty-seven boys in this house . . . the standard of work is much lower than at Oxford, so I find it fairly easy . . . we have four meals a day, breakfast, lunch, a stand-up tea (tea and buns) and a hot supper, and the food is very good . . . Could you possibly send me some tuck? Everyone here has supplies of toffee etc and a bottle of tomato sauce would be very useful indeed!! . . . This afternoon I am going with a boy named Staddon to Richard's Castle again . . . I am having a fine time, love Jim.

Nothing was said about the beatings by the house captain over a packing case in the basement, with all the prefects watching. 'I was beaten more often than any other boys in my house,' Morris wrote later, acknowledging that, while 'not really unhappy' at Lancing, 'I was habitually frightened.' Besides the jungular anxieties of the playground, he had to navigate hierarchies of class. Lancing was a minor public school, but other pupils were not the sons of taxi drivers.

Jim liked the sex, however, or some of it.

> When I thrilled to the touch of a prefect's strong hand surreptitiously under the teashop table, I was able to forget that he had flogged me the week before. It seemed perfectly natural to me to play the girl's role in these transient and generally light-hearted romances . . . It was fun to be pursued. I enjoyed being kissed on the back stairs, and was distinctly flattered when the best-looking senior boy in the house made elaborate arrangements to meet me in the holidays.

Boys cavorted in haylofts and field-ricks. When it came to the mechanical business, Jim found 'nothing fitted'. He didn't enjoy that part, remembering most vividly 'not the clumsy embraces of Bolsover

Major, not the heavy breathing of his passion or his sinuous techniques of trouser-removal, but the warm, slightly rotted sensation of the hay beneath my body, and the smell of fermenting apples from the barn below'. In later life Jan treated the whole experience as a normal part of a boy's public school career. Perhaps it was. But Morris concluded, 'If any institution could have persuaded me that maleness was preferable to femaleness, it was not Lancing College.'

On a terribly hot day Handford told them about the fall of the Libyan port of Tobruk, a disaster dominating the news. The reality of war and its vicissitudes, relayed daily over the wireless, brought the boys' own military apprenticeships into focus. It would be them next. Every Thursday afternoon, at compulsory Junior Training Corps parade, they donned First World War uniforms and marched with guns captured from Italian troops in North Africa. On 8 December 1942 Morris passed War Certificate A for Individual and Section Leading. Old Boys on leave returned to address pupils. Their stories of tanks and battleships stoked enthusiasm, though not as had been intended in the case of Tom Sharpe, a year behind Jim at Lancing and a future satirical novelist. His father was a fascist, and Tom wore a German belt with his school uniform engraved with the words *Gott mit uns*.

The following term, Sanderson's pupils toured village halls with a show called *Bubble and Squeak*. It included a one-act play Jim had written called *This Is London* and his adaptation of an M. R. James ghost story. The Shropshire Lads, as they called themselves, travelled to venues on foot, on bikes and in a lorry carrying scenery. They went to bed at two in the morning, ate picnic food and raised nearly £30 for the Red Cross Prisoners of War fund. Morris wrote the event up in the *Lancing College Magazine*, beginning with a line of dialogue from a woman setting up with the boys in one of the village halls: '"You won't need those." She pointed to the extra benches. "We 'aven't 'ad a show here for five years. And then there was only 25 people come."' But six hundred came. Stoves disgorged cinders, moth-eaten curtains wouldn't stay up and all the lamps ran short of oil. Morris ended the report with the precociously good line, 'Though everything went wrong, everything else was a great success.' One can see the outlines of the whole Morris style in this school magazine piece: direct speech to reel the reader in, knockabout comedy, immediacy and above all a clear, resonant voice. He was writing to entertain an audience, and doing it with vigour, intimacy and a winning flippant touch.

The winter of 1941–2 was another perishing one, and more Old Lancings perished. Masters too old to fight knew every name on the lists. In the late spring of 1942, when the Axis looked like winning the war, Jim took his School Certificate. He was fifteen, and keen to leave. As one of his Sanderson's contemporaries wrote, 'The works of Aeschylus, Euripides, Tacitus and the rest seemed very unimportant just then.' Lancing did not give Jim gloss. He wasn't there long enough: any culture that might affect a boy had been diffused by the move to Shropshire, and Jim was anyway already set on an independent course. Five weeks into Lent term, he did leave. The college magazine reported in its valedictory, 'He was renowned for his wit and bright and often crushing remarks ... he left to undergo a course of journalism before being called up.' In the School Certificate, Jim received a Very Good in English Language and History; a Credit in English Literature, Latin and Elementary Maths; and a Pass in French with Oral. It reflected a school career which came in at a strong B grade. School gave him a grounding, but Morris was essentially self-educated via his prodigious reading.

He was not embarking on anything as formal as 'a course'. Jim had arranged to work on a voluntary basis as a cub reporter at Bristol's *Western Daily Press*. Already bristling with ambition, he had approached the paper while still at Lancing to ask if he could review a play at the Bristol Old Vic in the holidays, and they had said yes. Jim had decided, come what may, to become a writer. His brothers were to follow careers in music – distinguished ones in both cases – but music did not touch him. 'Miss Morris, is music important to you?' a BBC interviewer asked in 1983. 'No, I really don't think it is. I feel it ought to be.' It was words that explained the world, not crotchets on a stave.

Chris and Gareth were already away in uniform when Jim got back to Clevedon. Chris had been determined to serve in the ranks but changed his mind when he looked through the window of the officers' mess and saw an ironed white tablecloth and gleaming wine glasses. He fought in North Africa and Italy and ended the war as a cavalry captain. Gareth had completed a year at the Royal Academy when hostilities began. He joined the sixty-piece Royal Air Force Symphony Orchestra along with Brain, the horn player. The orchestra went around giving concerts to the troops which the troops weren't always keen to attend; one night the bassoonist said, 'There's such a sound of jangling manacles I hope they don't drown the music.' The orchestra played for Churchill at Downing Street twice. According to Gareth, the prime minister, with a glass of brandy in one hand and a 'huge' cigar in the other, said, 'Thanks so much for coming, pity you didn't play any Gilbert and Sullivan.' They toured the United States late in 1944, performing four concerts a day. 'Because we were in uniform,' Gareth said, 'all the Americans thought we were heroes, Battle of Britain people – after all we had propellers on our arms, and wings.'

Enid had soldiered on alone in Clevedon until Jim got back from Lancing. Between 1 September 1940 and 18 May 1943, German bombers heading for Bristol, Bath and Cardiff dropped explosives on the town sixteen times. On the night of 4 January 1941, more than a hundred Luftwaffe aircraft aiming for Bristol's Avonmouth Docks got lost when cloud cover obscured the route, and released most of their loads along the estuary shores. Nine bombs and six hundred incendiary devices fell on Clevedon. One bomb came down opposite Enid's cinema, killing a man.

Jim desperately wanted to serve. In April 1943 he turned up at the recruiting station of the 8th (Weston-super-Mare) Battalion of the Somerset Home Guard. At sixteen, he was underage, but he lied to the recruiting officer. Most of his colleagues were veterans of the First World War, including the commander, a baronet decorated in India. They wore the badge of the Somerset Light Infantry, exercised once a week and had their own cricket team. 'I was a young romantic,' Morris wrote much later, 'and I can half remember to this day my adolescent emotions when I was posted with my ancient Lee–Enfield rifle to a hillside above the sea, looking across the Bristol Channel to the Welsh shore.'

He began as a rookie reporter at the *Press* the same month, commuting by train from Clevedon to Bristol. His first published story concerned the conviction of a husband and wife who had neglected their baby. The court cases he attended with a notebook in his pocket started a habit which lasted a lifetime: if you don't have anything to write about, head to the nearest courtroom. But in fact there *was* something else to write about. American convoys were making landfall in Bristol, and with so many journalists away at the front the editor sent Morris to report on the first night of Irving Berlin's troop show *This Is the Army* at the Victoria Assembly Rooms. The fledgling theatre critic sat in the front row of the stalls not far from the enchained Lord Mayor, and his review, when it appeared the next day, began with a mature flourish. 'The English stage', it announced, 'is perhaps weakest in its presentations of musical reviews . . .' Later, Morris recalled,

> The soldier musicians of the band, only a few feet away from me in the orchestra pit, were amused by my callow presence there, and threw cheerful surmises at each other, loud enough for me to hear. 'Won a raffle ticket.' 'Bribed the usher.' 'Murdered the guard' . . . and in that very moment, as they looked laughing across at me, I was captured by the particular American mixture of quick wits, frankness, arrogance and good nature that has beguiled me ever since.

Berlin appeared in the show himself, 'singing in a very frail tenor, which I can still hear, a song he had written in the *first* World War entitled, "Oh! How I Hate to Get Up in the Morning".' Morris even interviewed the Russian-born composer. In lunchbreaks at the *Press* he prowled the second-hand bookshops of Bristol's Old Market – another lifetime's habit, and another precocious start: that first year he bought *Introducing James Joyce*, a selection of prose edited by T. S. Eliot. Jim had watched Gareth start a book collection (and invent a device with which he could read under the covers), and the pair colluded in high-mindedness: that Christmas Gareth gave Jim *Devotional Poets of the 17th Century*.

Morris passed his army medical in February 1944 as eight hundred Allied aircraft raided the German capital, and on 13 April he enlisted. (His recruitment form records that he was five foot nine; he stopped growing the following year at five foot ten.) Six weeks later he was called up and posted to Number 30 Primary Training Wing of the General Service Corps in Ranby, Nottinghamshire. Training in gunnery, driving and maintenance lasted four months, then Morris transferred to the Royal Armoured Corps and its 58th (Young Soldiers) Training Regiment at Bovington in Dorset, where he spent nine months in the Pre-OCTU (Officer Cadet Training Unit). The army refined his understanding of vocabulary. 'I learned that when a sergeant major barked "Get a fucking move on", he was being more or less convivial: it was only when he omitted the obscenity that he really meant what he said.' For a year Morris bounced between Bovington, Catterick (Yorkshire) and Aldershot (Hampshire); travelling from one to the other, he stopped over in London, eating artificial cream cakes at Gunter's in Curzon Street and paying eight shillings at the Berkeley Hotel for soup of indeterminate origin followed by minced chicken hash. When the weather was fine, Czech, Polish and French soldiers gathered in Hyde Park, and London was more cosmopolitan than ever before. In the evenings only the gleam of a torch or the dim blue lights of a car pierced the blackout, and even then just occasionally, for little traffic prowled the streets. Morris was in the capital in a yellow fog on Christmas night 1944, and he heard Noël Coward sing at the servicemen's Stage Door Canteen in Piccadilly. Coward wrote of that occasion:

> Canteen packed with troops who had nowhere else to go and greeted all of us who appeared with boisterous enthusiasm. There was a lightness in the air, a tacit awareness that this might conceivably be the last Christmas of the war. The show started at 8 and continued until 1.30, by which time a great deal of beer had been drunk and so many

cigarettes smoked that the atmosphere inside was almost as thick as the pea-soup fog outside.

Rocket bombs and doodlebugs ushered in the New Year. You could hear a doodlebug coming, at least, and take cover when it cut out overhead. The V2 rockets that had begun to fall in September dropped without warning.

Then it was over. On 8 May 1945 Private Morris stood in unseasonably hot spring sunshine and watched Churchill address euphoric and worn-out crowds from the Ministry of Health balcony in Whitehall 'at the very moment of his ultimate triumph'. It was the only time Morris ever set eyes on the leader who stalks the final chapters of *Pax Britannica*. 'All around us were grand old monuments of English history,' he wrote of that momentous day, 'Parliament and Abbey, Nelson on his column up the road, Admiralty and Banqueting Hall and Horse Guards Parade, and it seemed to me then that he [Churchill] was already one of them.' The royal family made eight appearances on the balcony. Back in Clevedon, the bunting came out again in Old Church Street. Chris had returned from the war with a twitch and Gareth with a pair of trouser braces ('suspenders', they had called them in America, where he bought them) with clips as opposed to buttons, an innovation not previously seen in the whole of Somerset.

Peace had broken out in Europe but Morris had no plans to abandon the military. He liked it, writing after the passage of many decades, 'The only authority I've ever really admired is the British army,' and once telling an interviewer, 'In the army of all places, I thought I was free.' He developed ideas in those years, had time to read, and liked being part of something, though there never was a less tribal individual. Morris even enjoyed parading. Besides, in the autumn of 1945, when he turned nineteen, he was longing to see what lay beyond the Bristol Channel, and the Occupation Forces needed men to keep Europe moving. In May 1945 he started Officer Cadet Training at the Royal Military Academy Sandhurst. A modest, blue-eyed Etonian called Bill Norman was among his peers. The pair remained friends for seventy-five years.

While Morris was eating Gunter's cakes, the newsreels at Enid's cinema had shown the first images of a death camp. It was Majdanek, near Lublin. The ovens at Auschwitz were still blazing at full capacity. The month Morris began his Sandhurst training, the US army liberated Buchenwald. Within weeks Soviet troops were at the camp, incarcerating political prisoners of their own. Morris used Buchenwald later as a symbol of the generalised inability to learn from history. There was only ever one victor, and that was war itself.

On 4 November he was granted an emergency commission as second lieutenant and joined the 7th Hussars. A week later, Morris was walking down the steps of the subway at Reading station ('resplendent in Sam Browne [military belt that passes over the right shoulder] and brand-new pips') when he recognised a soldier coming up the other way. It was Walter, the Jewish refugee who had dazzled Clevedon. He was a sergeant, not an officer. The pair celebrated their chance reunion with a cup of tea at the steamy station buffet counter, talking over the clanging in the rail yards, 'and as I remember it our conversation was not constrained: but I knew, and he knew, that if either one of us should really be the officer, he should. It was because of his Jewishness, we both understood, that in theory (though mercifully not in practice) he ought to have saluted me when we parted.'

2
1946–1947
SOLDIERING

Through the dirty window of a troop train he watched columns of the destitute moving in every direction through a battered France. Rails and bridges had been destroyed – by retreating Germans, by advancing Allies, by the Resistance. Post-war Europe was a literal Waste Land.

The train crossing the Alps into Austria ferried contingents of the Central Mediterranean Force on occupation duty. The fog of war might have lifted in Vienna, where the soldiers alighted, but the Viennese had been on starvation rations for a year. In the three weeks following the arrival of the Red Army, doctors had reported 87,000 rapes – and those were just women who had presented for medical attention. Yet Viennese matrons waited at the station with warm bread and real coffee for the good soldiers.

Two days later Morris's section set off again from the Südbahnhof, headed this time for Northern Italy, where yet more exhausted people were on the move. Between them, Stalin and Hitler had uprooted, transplanted, expelled, deported and dispersed thirty million Europeans. Italy had capitulated to the Allies in September 1943 and civil war in all but name had convulsed the north. The predominantly rural population of the north-eastern Veneto region, the majority of whom had existed in conditions of indebted penury before the conflict, had lived through the daily degradation of war and now battled on in disillusion rather than relief. No robust institutions existed at national, regional or district level in Italy. In this most centrifugal of European nations, it is hard to imagine what order of any kind there could have been when the train disgorged Morris and his colleagues at Venezia Santa Lucia at the beginning of 1946. Troops before them had installed gun emplacements and searchlights on the *altane*, the canopied wooden roof terraces that *i veneziani* had for centuries used as gardens: Carpaccio painted women playing with their dogs on an *altana*. Bombs had not fallen on the centre of the city, however, not even when the Allies had liberated Venice by air in Operation Bowler in March 1945, and the churches had never been stripped.

Morris had been happy in uniform since he first put one on. 'I was entering a man's world. I felt like one of those unconvincing heroines of fiction who . . . penetrate the battlefields to find glory or romance.' None of the others cast him in a womanly mould, as he was not remotely effeminate. Quite the reverse – he was virile and something of an action man, as well as popular and handsome: a fellow officer noted, 'Morris was rather better looking than any young man is entitled to be.' The hazel eyes were well spaced, the nose noble, if on the large side (he always said he didn't like his nose), the cheekbones high. His teeth were straight and his chin square. His dark-brown hair – almost raven, in some lights – was abundant, and springier than ever at the front.

Venice did, though, present the perfect setting for a heroine fantasy, 'half-empty, lonely, defeated – just my style'. He was billeted on the lagoon side of Giudecca Island and procured a gramophone to blast Mendelssohn's Italian Symphony (No. 4 in A major) over the water beyond. The composer had written it after his own visit to Venice.

> In the evenings especially, when the island was silent except for the lapping of water in our boathouse, or a sudden peal of laughter, perhaps from somewhere over our garden wall, I found the wistful loveliness of the place almost orgasmic – my first intimation that love for a beautiful place could be more than simply sensual, but actually sexual too.

But decades later Morris remembered the city as 'desolately impotent in the aftermath of conflict', even 'stricken', and the lagoon 'metallically motionless', like 'a dead lake in a fable'. Places changed like amoebae according to Morris's aims as a writer at the moment of composition. The true meaning of place was to be, through all the books and many scores of essays, subordinate to the meaning Morris wished to impose. And while Morris cast himself retrospectively as 'an unconvincing heroine', at the time he was very convincing indeed as its mirror image – a hero.

From March to July the Hussars seconded Morris to 513 Company of the Royal Army Service Corps. He drove the length and breadth of the Veneto from the Dolomites to the Po Valley, west towards Padua, and through villages he drew on later for a story he never published. He saw his first motorway on the way to Milan, and heard his first opera at La Scala: *La traviata*. One evening he dropped off a fellow officer at a brothel to find a real-life Violetta. It was the man's first visit, 'and I remember still how pale he stood there in the streetlight, looking back at me almost desperately as I drove my jeep away into the night'. Italy introduced him to paintings as well as opera. 'Giorgione's "La Tempesta"', he wrote, 'began a love affair of a lifetime,' and that artist's 'intenser masterpieces' made him feel 'I am in touch with God'. In Giorgione's few, elusive images, Morris glimpsed the transcendent unity he sought, and was to go on seeking – all his and everyone's hopes and fears and desires rendered for one moment absolute on stretched canvas.

His surroundings formed their own pictures. Morris and his fellow officers sometimes stayed at a duck hunter's house, where they sat by the fire in the kitchen 'drinking grappa, practising our Italian, the game birds hung upside down from their hooks, giving the room a still-life look'. The marsh glimmered outside. 'There were only oil lamps in the house . . . we would take the light with us to the table in the sitting room and squeeze ourselves in at the white-clothed table against the wall.' In April he went to Florence, freewheeling 'all but uncontrollably down from Fiesole in an armoured scout car whose engine had failed . . . as Firenze revealed itself to me, serene and towered beside its river, brown, green, golden, lightly misted, it seemed to me hardly a real city at all, but a kind of ideal urbanism.'

In June Italians voted by a narrow margin to amalgamate their country into a republic, but there was to be nothing ideal about it. Republican status did not put food on the table. At that time, Italy recorded the lowest average food consumption of all Western European populations. The soldiers, though, were not hungry. The immaculately dressed future television presenter Alan Whicker was editing the Forces' newspaper *Union Jack* from 'a grand office in the Venetian daily *Il Gazzettino*', to which he sauntered in uniform every morning along the Riva degli Schiavoni. Living in Venice in the spring of 1946, Whicker wrote, was like 'belonging to an exclusive club'.

Shortly after his twentieth birthday, Morris was posted to the 9th Queen's Royal Lancers – not the Guards, but higher up the class ladder than Lancing College. At that time the 9th had thirty officers and seven hundred men. Christian names were used among the former (James, not Jim) and so was courtesy. 'I loved it from the start,' Morris said of his new regiment. 'I loved its easy style, its grace, its humour, its sense of friendship and community among all ranks . . . I liked the lean, humped silhouettes of infantrymen and the swagger of paratroops and all the martial consequences of embarkation or parade.' Style, swagger, martial consequences: these were features that drew him in. The 9th, nicknamed 'the Delhi Spearmen', were famous for 'glitter and club-like exclusivity', and although members were proud of their history, nobody mentioned it, 'for if there was one attribute the 9th Lancers were not anxious to display, it was *keenness*'. Morris liked to cite the fact that in 1840 a 9th man had taken his cello on campaign in China. 'Among the officers,' Morris wrote, 'there was a powerful sense of family. It was hardly like being in an army at all . . . Nobody called anybody sir . . . It was generally understood that if you did not read Surtees [R. S., the Victorian sporting novelist] . . . then at least you would have the sense and taste to keep quiet about it.' Bill Norman, the friend from Sandhurst, had also been commissioned into the 9th – his father's regiment (Norman Senior was a general). The two soldiers met again in Venice. 'James had made great friends with a Count who had a place on the Grand Canal where we used to spend evenings. The horrors of the war were far off,' Norman recalls, talking a lot about 'swanning', which meant skipping occupation duties to have a high time. Morris said later he felt an 'impostor' in the military, but he seemed to fit in all right.

One morning, his commanding officer summoned him to his tent on the banks of the Tagliamento,

> and told me commiseratingly that I was to be detached for a time to help run the motorboats of Venice, all then requisitioned by the British Army ... He was extremely sorry to do this to me, for organising motorboats seemed a plebeian sort of task to such a professional cavalry colonel ... It was the best present anyone had in life.

Few visiting British generals had ever been to Venice before. Under Morris's command motorboats set out from the dock near the Piazzale Roma and, as they chugged up the Grand Canal, 'I watched the shifting expressions of astonishment and delight that passed over their grizzled warlike features.' The grizzlies put up at the requisitioned Hotel Danieli. At night Morris's pals pushed him into Harry's Bar ahead of them. (Harry's had swing doors then.) At the tables sat 'smoky looking, hooded-eyed, tweedy, sometimes hatted, heavily made-up, but rather weatherbeaten persons I took to be members of the Italian aristocracy'. Another world beckoned. 'Getting to know Venice', Morris wrote, 'changed everything for me.'

Three days after the war in Europe had ended, Churchill had sent a telegram to his foreign secretary, Anthony Eden, who was in America founding the United Nations. 'In a very short time our armies will have melted,' said the prime minister, 'but the Russians may remain with hundreds of divisions in possession of Europe from Lübeck to Trieste.' In the five separate treaties signed in Paris in 1946, Italy lost all its colonies and ceded the Istrian peninsula to Yugoslavia. But the Powers had not solved the problem of Trieste. Not only was it stateless, its identity unresolved; it was also a frontier of what was to become the Cold War. In autumn 1946, the War Office ordered the 9th 161 kilometres (100 miles) east. Their job, according to Norman, was to prevent Trieste falling into the hands of the 'Jugs'.

Having changed horses during the course of the conflict, Italy itself was an object of suspicion to West and East alike and it was widely believed in Western military circles that if a third world war broke out, it would be in the Trieste region. A few months after the panicky cable citing Trieste, the Bulldog made his 'Iron Curtain' speech. As late as December 1947, even Ernie Bevin, the British foreign secretary who had succeeded Eden, considered Russia less of a threat than a resurgent Germany. So who was the enemy as Morris and the others rattled down to the coldest waters of the Adriatic? Uncertainty was breeding a lack of confidence among the men, or at least a faint suspicion that Britain no longer sat at the top table. Morris remembered 'the subalterns of my regiment . . . fantasizing about a ceremonial end to the island kingdom, becoming the forty-ninth state of the American Union perhaps, or marching four abreast, all 40 million of us, off the peninsula of Land's End into the oblivion of the Atlantic'.

They settled in to Trieste all right. 'James was good at getting hold of motorised army transport for recreational purposes,' says Norman. 'We swanned endlessly in the bars. I learned how *not* to get drunk in Trieste after vomiting too many White Ladies. James would never have lost control like that.' Spearmen took launches to Muggia, where mangy cats haunted the trattorias, the white stones of the city glittering in the glare of the sun across the bay, and at other times, such as May Day 1947, they paraded in Comet tanks. The First World War had done Trieste in, as James Joyce had attested. The port was already a scene of desuetude. Cornices fell from windows, collared doves nested in the warehouses, ceilings caved. Mitteleuropa, not yet Central Europe, lingered in threadbare decorum and coffee. It was not Italy there, literally or in any meaningful sense. At Grignano, where Morris and the others swarmed over Miramare Castle searching for abandoned German materiel, they glimpsed the flash of a Habsburg epaulette through the gabled windows. Morris had always felt fluid in that way himself. As he sat on the bollard on the Audace wharf, notebook in hand, to write his essay on nostalgia as the black steamboat left for Istria, he pined for 'Europe distilled – the civilised continuity of culture that I imagined for my lost continent as a whole'. But that had never existed. In years to come he would realise he had been longing for unity for himself.

In December he went home on leave. It was an even colder winter than the one of 1939–40, in which he and the other choristers had huddled round the fire in their medieval nest. London was bombed out and exhausted. Since Morris had left on his troop train, Britain had brought in bread rationing, something Whitehall planners had avoided throughout the war itself. (Rationed loaves were grey, like everything else.) Papers carried pictures of housewives queuing for coal. They would wait all day for their weekly allowance and push it home in a pram. London still smelled of coal, even though families were burning less of it, and all the buildings were sooty. James saw Gareth, already a successful flautist (playing a wooden instrument that gave him a distinctive sound), and when he complained that the 9th was turning out to be an expensive regiment, Gareth paid his mess bills.

Before Morris returned to active service, the lorry drivers of London's Smithfield Market came out on strike along with many others, and newly elected prime minister Clem Attlee got the army to deliver horse carcasses to butchers. Britons were apparently unable to feed themselves, let alone govern, even as they and their continental colleagues still ruled much of the non-European world.

He got back to unexpected news in Trieste. The regiment was shifting to Palestine. The War Office had tasked 9th commander Lieutenant-Colonel David Laurie with the administration of the territory during a critical period of the Mandate. Morris revered Laurie, a war hero who, dragged from his flaming tank at the Battle of Wadi Akarit in 1943, had protested that he wanted to carry on fighting. Now he led the 9th as they embarked to serve in the Middle East Land Forces (MELF). Where even was Palestine? To Morris, the name conjured the stony desert wastes depicted in his *Children's Bible*, where beastly Philistines captured the long-haired Samson.

Britain was preparing to relinquish the mandate to govern Palestine received from the League of Nations after the earlier world war. But what would happen to the territory after Britain's departure? Committees and commissions had failed in their search for a compromise. Newsreels in Enid's cinema showed traumatised Jewish refugees who had survived the Nazis living in squalid camps in both Palestine and Europe. Yet the government in London, unwilling to alienate the Arab nations, refused to increase the slow pace of legal Jewish migration to Palestine. This was the situation facing the 9th. The previous July, Jewish paramilitaries, led by future prime minister Menachem Begin, had arranged for six men disguised as Arabs to carry milk churns containing five hundred pounds of explosive into La Régence, the basement restaurant of the King David Hotel in Jerusalem. The Secretariat of the British Mandatory Authority in Palestine, as well as the MI5 and Secret Intelligence Service (SIS, or MI6) stations, were housed immediately above La Régence. The bomb killed ninety-one. A photograph showed a typewriter in the rubble with two severed fingers still resting on the keys.

In the very week the 9th were sailing towards Port Said, Foreign Secretary Bevin told the House of Commons that the government was referring the problem of Palestine to a UN committee which would report its findings in the autumn. Bevin did not intend this to be the end of the Mandate. But it was.

The journey took five days. After disembarking at Port Said, Morris dined in a restaurant with a superior, who exclaimed, 'Rhine wine after all these years!' Morris said it was the first time he realised non-Italian wines even existed. That night, he boarded a train with an English colonel 'of particular gentleness of manner and sweetness of disposition'.

> As we walked along the corridor to find a seat we found our way blocked by an Egyptian offering refreshments . . . Without a pause,

apparently without a second thought, the colonel kicked him, quite hard and effectively, out of the way. I was new to the imperial scenes, and I have never forgotten this astonishing change in my companion's character, nor the absolute blank indifference with which the Egyptian accepted the kick, and moved.

From Port Said they travelled to Qassassin, a village in Lower Egypt (counterintuitively in the north, above Upper Egypt), where a prisoner-of-war camp had once held captured Italians. It was 230 kilometres (143 miles) south-east of Alexandria, in the desert near the Sweet Water Canal linking the Nile to the Suez Canal. Qassassin was grim, and everyone was pleased when the regiment moved to Al Bureij, near the port of Gaza. The village (the name means 'Little Tower') lay among citrus and banana groves tended by a population of seven hundred Arab subsistence farmers. In camp, the officers' quarters had a separate hardstanding for each four-man tent; port, wine and beer were served in the mess; and a garrison tailor made Morris a navy-blue blazer. They went swimming in the Mediterranean, pellucid aquamarine there on its easternmost shore. Norman had left the regiment in Trieste to go on leave and now rejoined his colleagues in Palestine. 'I remember going swanning with James to Subeita [now Shivta] in the Negev. We looked at Byzantine ruins.' They ran up to Alexandria, where, Morris said, 'we sampled the society of cosmopolitans – that shifting, glittering companionship of the Levant which still set the tone of Alexandria, with its pashas and its panderers, its cotton knights and its Maltese entrepreneurs'. Within a month of their arrival, the Irgun, a paramilitary offshoot of the Haganah insurgency, bombed the British Officers' Club in Jerusalem, killing thirteen.

Morris had been appointed regimental intelligence officer. The work required scouting, checking, reassessing and thinking on one's feet. He was good at all that. The operative traits of boarding school had prepared him. The role came with its own jeep, giving him 'licence to wander far and wide through the countries of the Fertile Crescent, Cairo to Kurdistan'. The intelligence officer was also the assistant adjutant, with a desk in the adjutant's office-tent. Morris sat clacking at his portable typewriter in the dry Gaza heat, ribbons gritty with sand. Besides reports, he wrote squibs for the regimental paper, *The Lighter Lancer*. 'James was very competent, unlike me,' Norman recalls. 'But "intelligence officer" was just the name given to the person doing intelligence within the regiment. The role was nothing to do with the "Intelligence Corps" – they were all pansies.'

As in Trieste, Norman had no doubt why they were there. 'Our job was to stop Jewish immigration.' Ships carrying hopeful refugees who vastly exceeded the meagre quotas put in at every port. Neighbouring Arab sovereign states had been busy for many months disagreeing among themselves over what to do with the latest round of displaced persons arriving in the Holy Land. Both sides, Arabs and Jews, needed arms. 'It was awkward,' Norman says,

> as we spent our whole time guarding our own camp! We had barbed wire. One night when I was orderly officer, a soldier on the top bunk of the guard tent had forgotten to attach his rifle to him with string. An Arab got through the barbed wire onto the top bunk and stole the rifle. We regarded the Arabs as thieves and the Jews as murderers. If we went to Jerusalem we had to go in a 15 cwt truck, with armed men besides the driver and two more armed men in the back. There were passwords all the time. I remember saying Arabs probably stole arms to sell to Jews but was laughed down.

Norman says, 'We made promises we couldn't keep to both Jews and Arabs.' Which side were the British on? Neither, according to one historian: 'They were on the British side.' Few could disagree with the sentiment Morris expressed in a letter to *The Times* in 1971 about the future of Jerusalem: 'The most fervent apologists for the Raj would scarcely claim the Palestine Mandate as one of its successes.'

Morris's duties included liaison. On one particularly clear afternoon he escorted a British district commissioner to a desert site where the regiment proposed to build a tank firing range. As they set off, the DC, in khaki drill, picked up a trilby from a hook beside his office door and put it on at a rake. This struck Morris as 'magnificently civilian, even Bohemian . . . [He was] the first official of the British Empire I had ever met, and he implanted in me a taste for the imperial aesthetic that has never left me.' At this time, the 9th B Squadron was cooperating with the Palestine Police to counter both the Stern Gang and the Irgun. Jewish militias were far better organised than their Arab counterparts, and they perceived British troops as their chief enemy – representatives of a colonial power that had illegally seized land sanctioned by holy scripture as the ancient Jewish homeland. Morris scoured villages for saboteurs, as had many men before him. 'Every blue-eyed Arab was said to have had an Australian father.'

Henry Otto Daniel Thwaites, who went by Otto, stood out in the regiment as 'one of the grand originals'. A slight, stooped figure with a lopsided gait and a stutter, his actual origins were mysterious, not least because he was fluent in German. He said one of his uncles was a panzer general. Thwaites had certainly won a Military Cross in France in 1943. He was, according to Morris, 'full of saturnine charm', and had elderly relatives (he said they were Habsburg princesses) with an apartment in Vienna, which they lent him from time to time when the 9th were in Venice and Trieste. Morris accompanied him on these jaunts and said Thwaites's behaviour was 'deliberately outrageous'. Now he joined Morris on saboteur-scouting missions, 'teaching me tricks of the desert trade'. Once, late at night in the Suez Canal Zone, then a British military enclave,

> we were being driven cross-country back to camp at Qassassin. It was one of those stunning starlit nights of an Egyptian winter . . . the sky looks so crisp you could cut it. Otto and I stood in the back of the open truck, leaning on the roof of the cab, and as we bumped across the open desert we stood close together for warmth, and he threw a great coat over both our shoulders. We travelled for a time in silence, as the truck shuddered and jolted on, and then Otto spoke. 'G-G-God,' he said, 'I w-w-wish you were a woman.'

'I loved him,' Morris wrote years later, after one of Thwaites's own men stabbed him to death on the Arabian Peninsula.

In March 1947 Washington announced the Truman Doctrine, a policy that pledged support for democracies against authoritarian threats. Its primary goal was to contain Soviet expansion. Three months later, Secretary of State George C. Marshall made his Harvard address announcing the plan to put American dollars in European hands so they might buy the tools of recovery. While US money had shored up disintegrating post-war Europe already, it was the Marshall Plan, a programme conceived and executed as an economic barrier to Soviet expansion, that exemplified the battle between East and West that was to shape the first half of Morris's working life. But, again, who was the enemy? The Labour MP Richard Crossman had visited Palestine and said Americans themselves 'represented the greatest danger to British rule in the Middle East today'. Oil had risen to the top of the British agenda just as the 9th arrived. The region had been crucial before, as a route to India, but India was now about to go. Like their American counterparts, Whitehall mandarins feared that British withdrawals from the colonies would leave a power vacuum the Soviets would fill.

The Cold War began in that Palestine year. All over the world, anti-British nationalist movements were already colliding with its frigid concerns. As regimental intelligence officer, Morris was in contact with the half-dozen defence security officers (DSOs) serving in Palestine in Security Intelligence Middle East (SIME). Initially set up as a multi-service regional agency, in 1946 SIME had become the sole responsibility of MI5. (MI5 covered internal security throughout the Empire as well as the homeland.) The Foreign Office had initially ordered SIME to focus on the fight against communists rather than on the defence of British interests against nationalist movements. But almost all wartime SIME personnel had gone home. The agency was operating with untrained new men, and with callow regimental intelligence officers such as Morris. Prime responsibility for internal security lay with the Criminal

Investigation Department of the Palestine Police, but both SIME and the Occupation Forces had to support it. In addition, MI6 officers were working alongside MI5. Everyone was spying on everyone else in Palestine in 1947.

The United Nations Special Committee on Palestine (UNSCOP) had duly arrived. Palestinian and other Arabs alike feared it was going to recommend partition. Morris drove alongside UN motorcades which had 'new Studebakers that looked the same front and back . . . and which seemed to me then, as they moved in convoy around the narrow, dusty lanes of the Holy Land, more or less like vehicles from Mars'. On 18 July a converted American river steamer renamed *Exodus 1947* appeared from Marseilles carrying 4,500 Jewish refugees. When it tried to dodge the blockade, Royal Navy destroyers rammed it and after a struggle towed it into Haifa, where British soldiers made the passengers – including many women and children – disembark and board three other ships which would convey them back to France. UN committee members were on the quay to watch this grotesque saga. The world's press led with the story.

Meanwhile, in Steimatzky's bookshop on Jerusalem's Jaffa Road, Morris found a copy of Charles Doughty's *Travels in Arabia Deserta*, the book that was to influence his writing style more than any other bar one (as we shall see). Doughty wrote 'in an idiosyncratic and sometimes all but unintelligible pastiche of Chaucerian and Spenserian prose', according to Morris; Doughty himself had said it was 'only nominally prose'. The tall, red-bearded author, who died in the year of Morris's birth, was the foremost European traveller in Arabia of that or any other age; he crossed the sands as the Ottoman Empire tottered. His was a life of heroic tragedy. The Royal Navy turned him down and he inadvertently lost his inheritance. In Arabia, nomads sold him toothless and arthritic camels. He was an outsider everywhere, as Morris felt himself to be. Doughty's 1,200-page book, a rich slab of velvety antique, proceeds with semi-obsolete vocabulary and with biblical cadences, hymning 'the soil of Arabia smelling of *samn* and camels', 'gaunt untrodden mountain rocks' and 'the glassiness of this sun-stricken nature'. Like Morris,

Doughty had grown up listening to the Authorised Version, not as a chorister in the stalls but as a son in the pew – Doughty senior was a parson. Also like Morris, he had grown up in poverty, not of means but of respectability. A sense of history informed his work, seeding a yearning for the faith he always feared he might lose. Morris had no faith to cherish, but the experience of reading Doughty in Palestine expanded his historical awareness, opening an emotional dimension. Doughty was not a romantic orientalist like so many English travellers. Instead he was in thrall to the links between past and present which he saw all around him. (His sense of time was geological – he'd started out as a geologist.) Morris chose *Arabia Deserta* as a favourite travel book for six decades.

Meanwhile, UNSCOP duly recommended the feared partition. The British government told the UN it would withdraw unilaterally from Palestine. Who was going to control the Middle East as post-war alliances shifted?

Morris always said that he learned his trade in the army. This 'trade' was the intelligence principle of 'watch and learn'. 'I developed in [the 9th] an almost anthropological interest in the forms and attitudes of its society: and sitting there undetected, so to speak, I evolved the techniques of analysis and observation that I would later adapt to the writer's craft.' Subject matter too was laid at his feet. In Palestine he was in on the start of British withdrawal from Empire – there on the untrodden rocks, he wrote, Britain 'first admitted impotence'. Two weeks before the UN committee recommended the partition of the Holy Land, at midnight between 14 and 15 August, three-quarters of Britain's imperial subjects had departed with the Raj. The Spearmen had heard news of the carnage following Nehru's 'tryst with destiny' over the camp wireless. As Jan, Morris was to spend her most creative years writing about the rise and fall of the Pax Britannica – the work she called 'the centrepiece of my life'. In those books Morris is a miniaturist of Empire; she avoids the overarching generalisation (in the main), sticking to the trade she learned in the army. Palestine had revealed that events as they unfold, before they become history, are coloured in shades of grey, and therefore history should rarely be painted in black and white. The present, after all – always muddled enough – is the ongoing past. This knowledge meant Morris could never be a determinist commentator; as Jan she did not read certainty into any story. She remembered how *un*-certain everything had seemed as Bill and the others swanned about in Al Bureij. She never wrote that Britain's decision to get out of India was *intended* to mark the end of Empire; she said it was in Palestine that British imperialists, 'for the first time, frankly abandoned the imperial responsibilities'. Morris was not a historian, as he and later she insisted, but he was already reading Edward Gibbon, and the six-volume *Decline and Fall of the Roman Empire* began working away in his imagination.

Between Palestine and the *Pax* trilogy, Morris would hear the death rattle of Empire as he travelled across the Sinai with the Israeli army during the catastrophe of Suez. But publication of the *Pax* books was a long way off. Morris had a few things to get out of the way first – including his own tryst with destiny.

He spent his twenty-first birthday on a troop train. Morris had decided to leave the army and make a serious start as a journalist. If he stayed, he feared he would become institutionalised, like some of his older colleagues. He was too much of an outsider to rise to the top of the military, and too ambitious to settle for the middle ranks. As the Middle East was in the news, and he liked Arabs, he thought he might return to the region as a newspaperman. First he had to get home, demob and find a job. As Norman, who had already left to take up a place at Cambridge University, put it, 'We got fed up with getting shot at and eventually we left them to it.' Just over a month after Morris sailed away from Port Said, the UN General Assembly endorsed UNSCOP's majority recommendation and voted for the partition of Palestine.

Morris had absorbed more, in the army, than the importance of watching and learning. 'I felt myself to be', he said, '. . . totally separate and distinct; for I realised by now how deeply a male sexuality lay beneath [my colleagues'] conduct, and how profoundly I liked it.' He liked it in that he was attracted to it, but he had no such male sexuality to govern his own conduct. At least in retrospect he considered that being a soldier cemented his belief in his own true gender. 'Far from making a man of me, it [the 9th] made me feel more profoundly feminine at heart.' The army, he said, 'confirmed my intuition that I was fundamentally different from my male contemporaries. Though I very much enjoyed the company of girls, I certainly had no desire to sleep with them . . . My own libidinous fancies were far vaguer, and were concerned more with caress than copulation.' At twenty-two, Morris knew his sexual preferences lay with men; he had not outgrown the lure of the Lancing 'romances'. At school it had seemed 'perfectly natural to play the girl's role'; it still seemed natural. 'I suppose', he wrote later of this period, 'I was really pining for a man's love.' Why did he not take some man's love, if he pined so? In the future, kindly friends were to arrange meetings with queers in their circle in the hope that they might help Morris unblock internal resistance to his sexuality. He met the men and baulked. It was not what he wanted. There was something else. He did not know exactly what it was; but he already had a vague idea.

3
1948–1952
BRONZED HERO

It had been a terrible year at home, with a coal crisis and a sterling crisis, the latter to become a post-war staple. In Clevedon, Enid was more worried about electricity than the New Look. But she had embraced the BBC's Third Programme with Payne vigour when it went on air on 29 September 1946. Old Lancing Evelyn Waugh said he too had listened attentively and it made him want to emigrate. A culture war was about to take over from the real one. Meanwhile, Morris, dependent on his own resources in London and now an ex-Lancer as well as an Old Lancing, found a room in a boarding house belonging to a retired brigadier whose wife had a poodle. It was in Nottingham Place in Marylebone, a part of the capital still gaping with bombed-out holes in its jaws. The other buildings in the street were medical establishments, nursing homes or, like his, providers of respectable transient accommodation, all minutes from Regent's Park, Baker Street Tube station and the multitudinous buses that ran east–west along the major artery of Marylebone Road.

He was there to start a career, and on the day he secured his room he enrolled on an Arabic course at the School of Oriental and African Studies in nearby Bloomsbury. There, in the frosty early weeks of 1948, he began daily lessons, and when they were over he rode along the Embankment on the top decks of buses to youthful male assignations. But on the way out of the house each morning he used to pass another boarder on the stairs, hurrying to catch her own bus. She had blue eyes and wore a red coat, one made in America that stood out among the grey plumage of post-war London. He found out she was working as a secretary for an architect in Hampstead, and that she took the 24 every day. She was also very beautiful, and her name was Elizabeth Tuckniss.

Elizabeth had grown up in Ceylon, on the Matugama rubber estate where her father, Austin Cecil Tuckniss, known by his second name, was manager. He came from a line of Quakers in Lewes, Sussex, and like Morris counted abolitionists among his forefathers. His wife, Margaret, née Bourne, known as Margo, was from Shropshire, where her father managed the Lilleshall steelworks. She was a gifted violinist. The couple had married in Colombo on 5 December 1922, honeymooned on Kandy Lake and moved into a bungalow with antlered heads on the wall. There was plenty of tennis and Margo wrote home to 'Darling sis Betty', telling her of crocodile shoots with Thermoses of cold tea and lime.

Elizabeth was born in the bungalow and christened Margaret Elizabeth; her brother, Trevor Richard St George, known as Dick or Richard, was exactly a year old when she appeared. Elizabeth's memories of Ceylon were 'a blur of shade and sunshine, heat and lemonade, horses, tea things on the veranda, a pet baby elephant, a bird in a wooden cage'. The bungalows were 'lofty and cool and lapped in lawns', Morris wrote when describing the Ceylonese planting community in *Pax*, and you could always hear the swish of a gardener's brush. The Tucknisses kept puppies and a Persian cat as well as the elephant and bird. The children learned to play the piano and went bathing with their Ceylonese nannies. Cecil was a tall man with glasses, a toothbrush moustache and a middle parting, and he liked to hunt. In 1926 they all went back to England on leave and Elizabeth celebrated her second birthday at Hatherleigh, the villa on Southfield Road that belonged to her maternal grandparents, the Bournes, in Paignton, Devon, and she and Dick took donkey rides on Paignton Sands.

Margo fell ill and wrote home about pains and X-rays. 'Oh if only I could talk to you darling mummie,' the last letter said. 'Don't worry.' Margo died among the planters aged twenty-nine. Elizabeth was four. For ninety-six years she kept a flower from her mother's grave wrapped in a tiny piece of paper. The telegram to Hatherleigh read: *DARLING*

MARGARET DIED FRIDAY NIGHT MUCH LOVE IN OUR MUTUAL SORROW CECIL. A photograph in Elizabeth's album shows him on the veranda at Matugama, hands on hips, wearing shorts and socks and white shoes, lonely.

The bereaved trio returned to Paignton almost every summer. The children bathed at Goodrington, where the water was rather colder than the Indian Ocean, fed the pigeons at Buckfast Abbey and rode Dartmoor ponies. Cecil usually went back to Ceylon before the other two. He wrote to the eight-year-old Elizabeth: 'My darling baba, Granny and auntie Betty [the dead Margo's sister] told me you had eight big teeth pulled and that you were very brave.' She was to need all her bravery. In 1937 Cecil died. Dick and Elizabeth, then fourteen and thirteen, were orphans. Aunt Betty was on her way to South Africa to have an adventure; a cable reached her on board ship, and she diverted to Ceylon to pick up the children and bring them back from Colombo to a cold country they knew only from summer holidays. 'My life has been ruined by you,' Aunt Betty told Elizabeth later.

At least Hatherleigh was already familiar, and so were grandparents George and Bessie Bourne. George had retired after forty-five years at the steelworks, and they had moved then to the Devonshire seaside. The Hatherleigh drawing room was a riot of wall-mounted china, shardy-leaved pot plants and tapestries on floor and chairs, still Victorian in the 1930s. The children went to school in Tiverton, and Elizabeth passed her School Certificate a few months before war was declared. In 1942 she joined the Women's Royal Naval Service (the Wrens), for four years existing on a diet of baked beans and 'vile sweet tea'. Aunt Betty had a second shot at life as an air raid warden. Dick went to the US with the convoys; by 1944 he was a sub-lieutenant in the Royal Navy Volunteer Reserve. Elizabeth became a leading Wren in the signals division and in 1943 was posted to Inverness in Scotland. She loved the Wrens: it gave her a purpose, and she found another family. In addition, she and her friends had invitations to dances at the Highland Hotel almost every night. Prior to the invasion of France they were transferred from

Inverness to Portsmouth to pack the Tommies' D-Day kit bags. Then the war ended. For Remembrance Day in November, Elizabeth took the train to London to stand below the balcony of the Home Office to see the princesses and Queen Mary come out. She left the Wrens in 1946 and enrolled on a secretarial course in London, taking a room in the boarding house in Nottingham Place. Once the course ended, she got the job with the architect. On 25 March 1947 *The Times* had announced the engagement of Elizabeth Tuckniss and Lt P. Anson, RN, elder son of Sir Edward Reynell Anson, 6th Baronet, of Templemore, Hatch Beauchamp in Somerset, sixty miles north of Paignton. Anson had spent three and a half years as a prisoner of war in the Dutch East Indies. Once Elizabeth had put on the red coat and collided with James on the stairs, Peter Anson left the stage. Morris had found his emotional home, and would never leave it.

He called her Tuppence, a nickname she had picked up in the Wrens, and took her to Clevedon to meet Enid. Some days he joined her on the 24 through the morning traffic up to Hampstead and came back down when she disappeared into architect Maxwell Ayrton's house in Church Row. (Then in his seventies, Ayrton had once been Lutyens's assistant.) On 24 March 1948, Morris spent the evening at the Public Schools Club in Piccadilly, his base in London's West End. He sat in the smoky clubroom to write her a letter. She turned twenty-four that year.

> Dear Tuppence, I've got to confess something to you. I've been trying to tell you for days, but I couldn't pluck up the nerve & I was determined to tell you this morning but I was enjoying your company too much. I'm not 23. I'm not even 22 yet. Please don't think I made it up just for you. I've been living the lie for years, I put myself up a year to join the paper in Bristol, & I joined the Army when I was 17 . . . I am most terribly sorry to have deceived you . . . if you're too furious, I'll give Mrs J. my month's notice.

A month later Elizabeth went home to Paignton for three weeks. He didn't like it on his own now. He already needed her. When he fell in love with Elizabeth, Morris knew she would understand whatever there was to understand; that was more important than erotic love. He had told her everything from the start, insofar as he himself understood what 'everything' might be. He loved her very much and never stopped loving her.

> I'm spending a miserable evening without you & tomorrow I shall spend a miserable day thinking of how miserable the evening's going to be. Can't you possibly get back sooner? Three weeks of this is just too fantastic to contemplate. It's the first time I've ever been lonely . . . If I can, I'm going to try & get down to Torquay the weekend after this coming one – I'll put on battledress and hitchhike . . . I had yet another menacing letter from the School of Oriental Studies but my mother very foolishly & very wrongly insisted on paying the bill for me. She doesn't know how grateful I am! I spent today at the Arab office, Pakistan House, the Islamic Cultural Centre, India House, Pan American Airways and the Society of Motor Manufacturers . . .

Journalism, in Morris's career plan, was to be a route into creative writing. To get on fast he decided he needed a degree, so he would have a shot at that, even though nobody else in the family had ever been to university. It would have to be Christ Church: that was his spiritual home. He filled in the forms for what would be the last of the two-year undergraduate courses for ex-soldiers, telling Elizabeth, 'There are really very few chances indeed of my passing the examination.' In the meantime, he bought and read T. S. Eliot's new *Notes Towards the Definition of Culture*. Then he went to Venice on holiday without her. 'Don't expect a bronzed hero,' he wrote on a postcard, 'because I don't go brown.' A few days later he sent her another en route from Venice to Zurich: 'I've got a boil on my nose that needs your loving care.'

He had spent the first three months of the year sweating over his Arabic and finding he had no facility for it, worrying how he was going to pay the school's fees and looking for a reporting job in the Middle East. He said later that he had looked up the Arab News Agency

(ANA) in the telephone directory, but the outfit that hired him was the government-owned Britanova, part of the new Information Research Department, the Cold War propaganda arm of the Foreign Office. A Special Operations Executive (SOE) cover to penetrate Turkey and other neutral countries, Britanova had offices in Yugoslavia and elsewhere, largely to pump material into the Soviet Union. It had established ANA as a branch office in Cairo to do the same in the Middle East: both were Secret Intelligence Service (MI6) front companies. Morris put in sub-editing shifts at the Britanova headquarters in London (later expanding the job to a full-time year on his application form to join *The Times*; he also elongated his tenure at the *Western Daily Press*). In the autumn of 1948, ANA duly hired him for Cairo. The Communist coup in Czechoslovakia in February was still on people's minds. Which country would fall next?

What a year to be in Cairo. In May the Palestine Mandate had ended and Israel had declared independence. The next day the Arab states had invaded, Egypt among them. Bombs, assassinations and martial law dominated headlines. The First Arab–Israeli War, known in Israel as the War of Independence and in the Arab lands as Al-Nakba – the catastrophe – was to grind on until 10 March 1949. The subsistence farmers at Al Bureij, where Morris had camped with the 9th, had fled. Egypt's defeat by Israel reinforced a sense of national crisis, and hostility to King Farouk expressed itself in hostility to the British. Every dissident group, of whatever hue, believed that the fight against imperialism – as represented by the continuing presence of tens of thousands of deeply resented (and bored) British troops in the wilderness of barracks and warehouses strung out across 120 miles of the Canal Zone – was linked with the fight against their country's corrupt regime. The previous year, 1947, the half-million-strong Muslim Brotherhood had declared jihad against the British. The truth, and Morris unlike many was beginning to see it, was that the end of the Mandate was the beginning of the end for British power and influence in the Middle East. The events of 1948 had detonated a crisis that was to remain desperate and unresolved down the generations.

Britain's strategic interest in the Suez Canal and the Nile Delta meant the country had to maintain friendly relations with Farouk and his cronies in peace as it had in war. Military commanders understood it was their duty not to knock the Egyptian king off his perch. But everyone knew he was an ass. The best-known Anglo-Egyptian song, Morris recorded, 'performed with disrespect on every route march, started with the words, *King Farouk, King Farouk, Ang 'is bollocks on a 'ook*'. In addition, the British intelligence community was certain that the Soviet Union was bent on global domination – that the civilised world as agents knew it might shortly disappear under a tide of commie horribleness. Cairo was at the heart of the battle, strategically, geographically and militarily, and Morris was there. On 1 January 1947 Foreign Secretary Bevin had written privately to his friend Prime Minister Attlee to express fear that the whole region was slipping away. 'You cannot read the telegrams from Egypt and the Middle East nowadays without realising that not only is India going, but Malaya, Ceylon and the Middle East is going with it, with a terrible repercussion on the African territories.' When Morris arrived in Cairo, the Communist coup in Prague had already fomented unrest in Italy and France, and the Berlin Blockade was still causing dismay in Whitehall and Washington. A sense of doom prevailed at home. Since mid-July there had been a permanent American nuclear presence on British soil, inaugurating an age of nuclear malaise. Historians agree that US loans under the Marshall Plan 'opened the way to silent infiltration of American influence into almost every walk of British public life'. 'Coca-Colonization' became a sustained theme for Morris, even though he was to fall in love with the United States.

The disreputable inscrutability of Cairo drew him in. It was the most densely populated city in Africa. Hundreds of thousands of impoverished fellahin lived less than a mile downstream from the sugar and cotton pashas who hobnobbed at the Turf Club and Shepheard's Hotel. The economy was tottering even before the war: Auden had visited with

Christopher Isherwood in 1938 and found the city an 'immense and sinister Woolworth's where everything is for sale'. But Morris wrote, 'I was happy working for the Arab News Agency.'

> My friends were mostly in the office [in the Immobilia Building on Sharia Sherif Pasha], and we were none of us rich. We were boulevardiers, but of a modest rank, frequenting the shabbier of the downtown pavement cafés, murky places with marble-top tables where the coffee was as thick as porridge and the water glasses were a perpetual dingy grey. There we would sit and talk in the early evening when the long siesta was nearly over, until we heard the rattling of the heavy steel shutters being raised one by one from the shopfronts, and it was time for us to saunter to the office and start work on the evening bulletin.
>
> The news that greeted us there was always full of drama and piquant intelligence – wars and corruptions, desert crime, court conspiracies, religious polemics, family feuds – and we worked in a spirit of Bohemian release. Once we were inside our dim-lit, crowded and untidy rooms we would forget the truth about ourselves, forget the impending misery of the midnight tram, forget the shabby villa off the airport road, forget the swarming children and the skinny black-veiled wife, forget our lost hopes for a career in the law or the Ministry of the Interior, forget that we were indigent Egyptian effendis or struggling Levantines [he was neither], forget even our sexual ambiguities [he had them], and lose ourselves in that strange little world of ours upstairs.

He bought a Canadian-manufactured Ford in one of the oily mechanics' caves in the backstreets, a convertible four-seater painted desert khaki. When he had a puncture on the road to Suez, a truck driver lifted the car up with one arm. Alexandria was three hours away; once, he took his first-ever flight there instead, hitching a ride in a de Havilland Dragon Rapide biplane on a brilliant Egyptian summer's day. Both engines cut out over the Delta. After a few minutes, in which Morris prepared for death, the pilot turned and shouted over his shoulder, 'Just saving a bit of fuel!'

Pursuit of sources involved vigorous socialising. The expatriate community gathered at Shepheard's (not yet on its Nile site), where Morris sat in a wicker chair on the terrace, scouring the faces of the drinkers. As well as the popular Turf Club there was Gezira Sporting Club at the south end of an island cut with long, straight boulevards lined with plane trees, and, for loucher evenings, the nightclub Auberge des Pyramides. Dilapidated Thornycroft buses and trams wheezed through the fumy streets, with blue beads, protection against the evil eye, dangling from the rear-view mirror, if there was one. Pack animals and carts loaded with oranges and dates and cucumbers lolloped alongside the buses, led by men in tarbooshes or turbans. Hacks gathered at Groppi in Talaat Harb Square to eat the chocolate ice cream Farouk had sent to King George during the war.

The British embassy did look onto the Nile. Morris knew everyone there and met contacts at the bar of the Semiramis. That autumn, Donald Maclean arrived as counsellor and head of chancery. After American government official Alger Hiss had been unmasked as a spy that summer, Maclean, himself under deep cover as a double agent codenamed HOMER, had started drinking even more heavily than he had before. Morris witnessed him going off the rails in Cairo: Maclean woke up shoeless on a bench in Ezbekiah Gardens, told a dinner party at the Dutch ambassador's residence that Hiss had been right, and pissed over the side of Farouk's palace staircase in full view of *le tout Caire*. (Melinda Maclean said much later that her marriage ended in Cairo in 1948.) Being half a generation younger, Morris walked in the vapour trail of Maclean and the other traitors who came to be known as the Cambridge Five. (The Morris children remember Jan telling them she had 'done something' for the spooks.) Cairo was an intelligence hub: the Foreign Office had installed a regional security officer there at the end of the war, and SIME had first been headquartered in the MI5 Cairo offices; in 1946 it had moved to Fayid in the Canal Zone.

Nine days after Israeli ground fire shot down four British reconnaissance Spitfires, mistaking them for Egyptian bombers, Morris walked to the cablehead in the Carlton Hotel and dictated to the man in a jellabiya sitting behind the counter: *PLEASE MARRY ME STOP WRITING LOVE JAMES MORRIS*. He had set aside the 'sexual ambiguities' he referred to so obliquely. In fact, he had already proposed over the phone the day before. *ANSWER AS OVER TELEPHONE YESTERDAY*, Elizabeth replied. *IF YOU ARE SURE ALL LOVE*. They gabbled plans: Elizabeth would travel out on her own, and they would marry in Cairo Cathedral. Once they calmed down, they soon realised an Egyptian ceremony would suit nobody. James would instead return home for a Paignton wedding and take Elizabeth back to Cairo for their first year of married life. She thrilled to the idea of Egypt – she might surely recapture the heat and light of Ceylon. On 29 January she asked: *SHALL I MAKE ENGAGEMENT OFFICIAL IN PAPER?* In fact, he had arranged to sit his Oxford entrance examinations and had already booked leave; he would fit the wedding into those three weeks. This stunt marked the start of a long and successful career maximising every opportunity a trip offered. Time management coupled with driving ambition made everything Morris achieved possible.

While Elizabeth was making all the wedding arrangements, he went to see *Carmen* with Clare Hollingworth, the *Observer* stringer. She bought Morris a whisky and soda during the interval. He did not care for that kind of reversal of gender roles: 'She's really rather awful.'

On 18 March, twenty-two-year-old Morris married Elizabeth in St Andrew's, a red-brick Victorian church in Paignton. He wrote later that he had known, as an infant of three or four, that he was really a girl. He had always felt an outsider, and he did in 1949, standing there in a morning suit with a carnation in the buttonhole, waiting nervously for his bride to come down the aisle. Marriage saved him. He was no longer an outsider when he came out of St Andrew's into the last rays of winter sun. Elizabeth – who was getting over mumps – wore a long satin gown buttoned at the front to a Peter Pan collar, with a short train and a long veil which the wind ballooned in the church porch. She accepted everything he had told her, and would continue to accept everything. Her understanding, Morris said, was 'fathomless'. The word was apt.

It was spring when they reached Cairo, and the *khamseen*, the hot desert wind, left a film on the skin. After a one-night honeymoon in the royal suite of the Semiramis they found a houseboat, called a *dahabiyeh*, to rent among a flotilla on the Nile, north of the Gezira Sporting Club. Its name was *Saphir*, and Morris always said it belonged to one of Viscount Montgomery of Alamein's sisters, and that on one of the Field Marshal's visits he had discovered two German spies on the next boat. The other vessels at the mooring, Morris wrote in an unpublished piece, ranged 'from a magnificent steamship with gleaming brass rails to the muckiest of derelict water shacks, the ultimate in dampness and dankness and decrepitude'. They hired a cook and an aged crewman who both slept below deck, and a stately Sudanese steward called Abdu. The *dahabiyeh* community was 'a place of incessant terrible barking but precious few bites. There were also threats and accusations in abundance, but a scratched finger was quite an event.'

> Scarcely an hour went by without some appalling tragedy being averted by the narrowest of hair's breadths before our very eyes. Savage fires broke out, threatening us all with utter extermination. Poor old men fell overboard and were sucked under by the paddles of passing steamers. Enormous trees toppled over into the river, throwing up great clods of earth with their mighty roots. Cows leapt the rails of the swing bridge and plunged down into the swirling waters. Maddened husbands attacked their wives with choppers. Babies dangled perilously from lifelines . . . Horrible crocodiles emerged from the slimy mud. Imams fell from the minarets of neighbouring mosques. But amidst all this whirlpool of catastrophe, experience taught us, no one was to be in the slightest degree inconvenienced for more than a fleeting instant.

As for work: talks over the ownership of the Anglo-Iranian Oil Company reached a critical phase and clients of the Arab News Agency all had a stake in the outcome. Then, on 4 April, NATO was signed into being. Its purpose – the remark is usually attributed to Hastings 'Pug' Ismay, the first secretary general – 'is to keep the Russians out, the Americans in, and the Germans down'. Still, despite the shabby drama of the office and the murk of the cafés, and despite the pleasures of conjugal life, Morris was restless, and unhappy. The 'ambiguities' had not gone away. They flickered like *Saphir*'s lights on the surface of the Nile.

He passed the exams. When he told his boulevardier colleagues he was leaving to enrol at university, they greeted the news with

> profound consternation . . . it was considered highly undignified and in doubtful taste to exchange the high calling of a journalist for the menial status of a student. I noticed a definite cooling off of the atmosphere. Our translators no longer introduced me quite so fulsomely to their friends. No longer, I fancied, did the messenger boys spring quite so smartly to their feet to open the door for me.

Married undergraduates were not permitted to live in college, so when they reached England, and eventually Oxford, the Morrises rented the thatched Tudor Cottage in Appleton, a village then in Berkshire and ten miles from the university. The house, down a green lane off the main thoroughfare and dating from very early in the seventeenth century, had a bountiful cooking-apple tree at the back and an ancient yew at the front; the deep thatch attracted sparrows, which the new residents heard nesting from their own nest in the bedroom under the eaves. In the first week they made friends with neighbours Reg and Audrey Mutter; Reg was a poet and was to begin his own university degree that year. Elizabeth wrote chatty letters to Enid, who had moved to London and was living in Clapham with Gareth. She concluded one missive, 'Must go and make his tea.'

Morris's tutor at Christ Church was the Scot J. I. M. Stewart, a new 'Student' (the equivalent of a fellow) who wrote crime novels under a pseudonym. After the first term, Stewart reported that Morris was 'a mature and able man, bent on doing well'. His overall tutor was C. H. Stuart, a historian who had operated as a spy under non-official cover in the war. The college was embedded in the intelligence services. Among many alumni in the game, the politician Tom Driberg, a generation above Morris, served the spooks with distinction, having joined the Communist Party at Lancing. Hugh Trevor-Roper, a junior censor when Morris went up, was among the wartime recruits to intelligence in the Senior Common Room, and it was he who had got Stuart in. The pair played the roles of mischievous bachelor lieutenants at Christ Church until Stuart married, though all the colleges, like everywhere else, were straitened after the war – 'You can't believe how frightful Oxford is,' Trevor-Roper wrote to Stuart in 1946, meaning there was less food, less drink and less fun. Halfway through Morris's undergraduate career, Trevor-Roper, recently promoted to senior censor, was obliged to reprimand him for a minor infraction. They were to meet again.

At home in Tudor Cottage, Morris continued to read and read. He had discovered *Eothen* by Alexander Kinglake. In telling the story of a journey to Cairo and beyond (the tricky title means 'from the east'), Kinglake's refusal to leave the fun out of travel – an almost unique decision when the book appeared in 1844 – set the young Morris's mind alight. *Eothen* became a model for prose to come, the one book that influenced him more than Doughty's. 'There is no pretending that Kinglake was a profound thinker,' Morris wrote. '*Eothen* is a terribly self-centred book.' He and then she were often to say the same about themselves and their own work. Kinglake's achievement overall 'was to make something altogether new out of a relatively commonplace experience'. And that is what Morris did. It was not a small thing.

Then there was Lawrence of Arabia. For their first Oxford Christmas, Elizabeth gave her husband a 1935 edition of *Seven Pillars of Wisdom*. Morris admired T. E. Lawrence, 'poseur that he was', and *Seven Pillars* paid homage to Doughty, Lawrence's 'master and perhaps his conscience'. Doughty, as we have seen, was not a romantic orientalist, but the long history of British Arabism culminated in figures like him, and like Lawrence. Morris was drawn to places where the desert met the sown literally and figuratively, and though he did not succumb to the mythologisation, he was prepared to indulge a taste for literary musings on the lone and level sands. Too astute a reader to rate the *Seven Pillars* author for his prose ('"I am no writer," he [Lawrence] used to say, and by God he was right'), Morris was interested in something more personal in Lawrence, though he didn't yet know quite what. Much later, when Jan Morris had some idea what it was, she wrote, 'I believe T. E. Lawrence to have been one of those tormented but privileged persons who, finding themselves in the wrong shell, change it for another, but presently aspire to a condition of universality, beyond sex, race, class, or age – beyond body, in fact.' The second 'but' is revealing: you could 'change' the body 'for another', but that wouldn't solve the problem.

Morris also used this student period to write, setting up a desk in the bedroom under the thatch and ransacking everything he had done to come up with short stories and even a radio drama set in the Veneto marshes. His imagination needed direct experience – whose doesn't? – so as he tried to achieve lift-off he turned to places he knew. He was honing his style, fumbling towards a personal process of storytelling; finding a voice. As the engines of Morris's fiction repeatedly stalled (most of the work completed in this period remains unpublished), he was learning to use the same techniques in non-fiction, as Kinglake did. At Appleton he was already experimenting with autobiographical accounts within the genre, and some, like the houseboat stories, were very good. He began to recognise, and develop, his descriptive gifts.

He kept up with university work. At the end of his second term, his report read: 'Confident, vigorous, and has a dangerous facility with pen and typewriter. His command of a pointed and vivacious style is all to the good, but he must dig deeper if he is to do justice to his abilities.' Stewart, his main tutor, recognised the resonant voice of the *Lancing College Magazine*, but wondered if it expressed anything of significance. Morris wasn't sure he wanted to dig deeper. He wanted to be like Kinglake and 'make something new out of a commonplace experience'. In that first Oxford year he did have stories about a hack's life in Cairo accepted on the undergraduate page of the *Spectator*, and he started writing squibs for *Cherwell*, the then-fortnightly student newspaper. Elizabeth was left on her own a good deal as the spring days grew longer in 1950. They made a few friends as a couple, but there was little time for joint socialising, especially after Morris became editor of *Cherwell* in Hilary term of his first year, a period in which Elizabeth was more alone than ever in the thatched cottage.

The *Cherwell* editorship indirectly launched Morris's career. When he wrote to *The Times* to ask permission to use a drawing they had printed, his letter landed on the desk of the typographer Stanley Morison, a kind of genius as well as a ferocious Catholic and part-time Marxist. Many years later Morris described the encounter in a letter to Morison's biographer:

> Morison . . . invited me up to look at it [the drawing], and gave me a cup of tea in his room in the old Private House [the eighteenth-century dining room at the back of Printing House Square]: and when we had talked about it a bit, and he had arranged for a print to be made, he asked me if I was interested in working for *The Times* . . . I said yes of course, and he said he would see what he could do. What he did do was arrange for me to spend the following long vacation working as a sub . . . the kind assumption of equality he showed a very insignificant stranger reminded me far less of Oxford than of attitudes in the old-school cavalry mess I'd served in.

On 17 July he started a summer job at *The Times* on nine guineas a week, staying in Clapham with Enid and Gareth. He worked in the Home sub-editor's room. The paper was under the editorship of William Casey, a Cape Colony-born playwright of Irish stock who had started as a sub-editor himself. Talk of Europe edged onto the Home pages in Morris's first weeks, even though Europe was not home. He pored over copy as continental politicians unveiled plans for a European Coal and Steel Community (ECSC), a prototype Common Market. But the British did not want to be part of any community – they 'had not had their pride broken and their factories destroyed'. Neither Morris nor his masters at *The Times* knew it then, but in missing out on the beginning of the institution Whitehall lost control of any future bloc that was going to emerge from the ECSC; the French and Germans were forging ahead, shaping the federalism in which, Morris came to believe, Europe's future lay. In the midst of it all, on 25 June, the newsroom had to cover the Korean invasion. Everyone agreed that this unwelcome development made war with Russia more likely.

At the end of Michaelmas, Morris returned to the paper for a month, this time in the Foreign subs room. He even had the opportunity to write himself, though nobody outside the paper knew, as everything in *The Times* was anonymous then – the cult of public personality was unknown and news did not even appear on the front page until 1966. Back at Tudor Cottage he was restless, and critical of Elizabeth and of domesticity in general; he felt hemmed in and confused – about himself, and about everything. She was endlessly forbearing. It was in Elizabeth's nature to compromise. It was in James's (and Jan's) to do what he and then she wanted. In this second year of his shortened degree, Stewart wrote in Morris's report, 'Graduated from the *Cherwell* to the *Spectator*, and to *Times* Fourth leaders. And this is his real line of country.' The Fourth leaders were light, loosely topical pieces that followed the more serious leaders, and one of Morris's first concerned a small boy watching a cricket match through a telescope. In Hilary term, Stewart's report repeated, 'Could go deeper.' But there was no need: in May, as Morris was taking his final examinations, *The Times* offered him a permanent job as a graduate trainee at £650 a year (about £18,000 today), at first 'covering the chief aspects of our work on the foreign side'. The paper had put a brake on the graduate programme lest it end up with too many trainees and not enough post-training jobs. But manager Donald Tyerman wrote a memo to the directors suggesting they make an exception for Morris, as he was 'quite out of the run of normal candidates'. His success during his two stints as a sub, Tyerman informed his colleagues, had been 'quite remarkable'; his academic superiors thought he was going to take a first-class degree; and, Tyerman was keen to note, Morris had served as an intelligence officer. Like Christ Church, *The Times* was heavily involved with the clandestine world. Networks of journalists and commercial travellers had reported back to news outlets for decades; sometimes a paper or agency was a cover, more often bone fide foreign correspondents saw it as their patriotic duty to relay tips. Graham Greene called the set-up 'the old firm'.

To celebrate the end of exams, James and Elizabeth went to Llanthony in the Black Mountains in south-east Wales. The *Daily Telegraph* had also offered him a job, at a higher salary. One afternoon Morris walked to a telephone box and rang *The Times* to accept their proposal, coins crashing one after the other as he looked out at the hills that extended over the border with England, the bifurcated, ambiguous land of his fathers. He valued prestige above money. *The Times*, he wrote much later, 'affected my attitudes forever'.

On 20 June he began as a full-time employee, working in Room 3, below the writers' floor. A commissioner stood guard in the front hall wearing his Great War medals, coal fires burned in the leader-writers' rooms, scholarly specialists stalked the corridors and Morris dined in the eighteenth-century Private House, which opened onto the square. A butler offered snuff from a box enamelled with an image of St Petersburg.

He sub-edited long articles, still called turnovers even though they had long ago stopped extending onto a second page. Perry Worsthorne, also a sub at *The Times* then, recalled that they had to take corrected proofs to the 'god-like specialist writers' for approval, 'a high-risk activity, requiring great gifts of diplomacy, charm and sensitivity, with all of which James was preternaturally endowed'.* Morris took over from Worsthorne as assistant to the imperial and foreign news editor, Ralph Deakin. A grammar-school boy from the Midlands, Deakin had

---

* Sir Peregrine, as he became, rose to the editor's chair at the *Sunday Telegraph*.

worked in the Berlin office before being appointed to his current position where, in the late thirties, he had hired Kim Philby. He sat upright at his desk wearing a grey alpaca jacket, his bowler on a shelf behind him, and lunched at the Reform Club, usually with a correspondent home on leave. 'The lunches never varied,' wrote Louis Heren, who had started at *The Times* as a messenger – his father was a printer there: it was feudal – and whom Deakin had subsequently employed on the Foreign desk. 'Dry sherry in the rotunda, a carafe of the club claret with the meal and coffee, port and a cigar upstairs.' Deakin worked long hours and usually came in at weekends. Worsthorne, like everyone, was fond of him. Mrs Deakin used to join them sometimes for lunch if the correspondent brought his own wife and if Deakin had not invited his secretary, which he sometimes did. Deakin's wife embarrassed him (Worsthorne said) by ordering 'bangers and mash' and saying Ralph would order it too if he weren't worried it was common. Deakin had not gone to university and was, according to Worsthorne, 'chippy'. At that time he was coordinating dispatches from the Korean War. He heard the cadences of prose all right but had a tin ear for communication of the verbal variety. He told the widow of a foreign correspondent killed in that war, when she came into the office to complain about her pension, that at least *The Times*'s two-column obituary had done her husband proud.

Morris continued to write Fourth leaders; one concerned the proposed flooding of the Honddu Valley in the Black Mountains, where he and Elizabeth had celebrated the end of exams. He quickly absorbed and marshalled an argument, he was efficient, and his prose was a model of clarity. He instinctively knew where to add a dab of colour – journalistic pieties required light, subtle dabs in the 1950s, but they made a difference. He stood out as one of the most promising young reporters on the paper. In the autumn of 1951, they unleashed him on foreign assignments of his own, and he learned the ropes in Norway and Denmark, rushing round briefings and interviews, dictating the story over a telephone line, typing it on a cable form or punching it into a telex tape. When he came back, he went for long lunches with Worsthorne at Boodle's or the Naval and

Military on Piccadilly. 'In those days,' Worsthorne recalled, 'James had a marked military aura . . . What one imagines the First World War poets looked like when on leave in mufti – well-polished brown brogues, soft and finely woven tweeds, in such striking contrast . . . to scruffy bohemians busily engaged in drinking themselves into an early grave.' When Worsthorne introduced Morris to his mother, she said he had something of Lawrence of Arabia about him. He never saw his other best chums on the paper sober, and he never saw James drunk. 'At no point', Worsthorne said, 'was James ever one of the boys.' Morris fitted in at *The Times*, though, as he had in the cathedral and the army. Much later he referred to the paper as 'that daily tapestry of orthodoxy'. In all three institutions, orthodoxy kept him on the rails. He knew it.

Elizabeth was pregnant. They were renting a flat in a terrace in Hammersmith in West London, and she had thrown herself with zest into her new life in the capital, making friends with other expectant mothers at the antenatal clinic round the corner while James worked long hours at *The Times*. He had got his degree: a good second. Stewart included a caveat in his letter of congratulations: 'You will have had – as I had – some hopes of you doing yet better.'

One story gripped the panelled newsroom in Printing House Square that year. On 25 May 1951 HICKS and HOMER – diplomat Guy Burgess and Morris's Cairo acquaintance Donald Maclean – had vanished, aware they were about to be unmasked as Soviet agents. (The year after Maclean had pissed over the side of Farouk's staircase, he had been appointed head of the American department of the Foreign Office.) Poetic types who knew their Robert Browning now asked, *What's become of Waring/ Since he gave us all the slip*; Morris was also to use the fictional Waring, fixing on the Browning character who vanished and was found in Trieste, as a representation of concealed identity. As for the double defection: reverberations were still being heard in Wapping, where *The Times* had decamped, decades after the two spies had tired of their Soviet masters.

The Home pages, meanwhile, also had to struggle on with coverage of the Festival of Britain, which had opened in May on the South Bank, the Skylon tower its already famous luminous exclamation mark. The month after the festival finally closed, to widespread relief among reporters who had long ago exhausted all there was to say about it, Labour called a snap election. They had won narrowly twenty months earlier and thought they could do better, but the gambit failed, as it so often does, and in October 1951 Churchill returned to Downing Street and Eden to the Foreign Office. Two months later, Deakin told Morris he was sending him to the Canal Zone near Cairo at short notice to replace the ailing special correspondent there. The baby was due in January.

The Cairo air was warm after a damp London winter and Morris spent his first day back with an old friend, Cyril Quilliam. Brigadier, *Times* Middle East correspondent, Arabic speaker and long-term spy, he lived in an elegant villa in Zamalek; he was a regional expert, really, not a journalist. 'Quilliam was most friendly,' Morris wrote to Elizabeth,

> he's a thoroughly nice chap and I enjoyed his company very much . . . I walked to the houseboat [*Saphir*] in the middle of the Sunday afternoon 'at home' . . . I had some remarkable conversations with Quilliam which I will report to you when I see you . . . The colleagues [in the press corps] are a pretty ghastly lot.

From the capital he headed to RAF Ismailia, an air base with sprawling barracks 125 kilometres (78 miles) north-east of Cairo. As Quilliam had explained, nationalists wanted foreign forces out. British corpses floated in the Sweet Water Canal, where Morris had camped with the 9th, and in October a mob had attacked targets including the Turf Club and Shepheard's. A long historical story was approaching its Wagnerian conclusion. Quilliam had sent *The Times* an analysis of the latest failed negotiations over the Anglo-Egyptian Treaty. 'The Foreign Office', he declared, 'has contributed substantially to the present mess by its lack of understanding of Egypt and its people and its apparent disregard of Egyptian history.'

The ongoing dispute over ownership of the Anglo-Iranian Oil Company had fuelled this latest Suez crisis. Before becoming prime minister of Iran in April, the patrician Mohammad Mosaddegh had called for nationalisation of the British-owned firm. (The echo of that call too was to reverberate through many decades.) Everything in the Middle East now came down to hot oil and Cold War. *The Times* had tried to be conciliatory. 'No true incompatibility divides the British from the Persian interests in Persian oil,' a leader declared valiantly on 30 April 1951, going on to note, crucially, that over Anglo-American the British and American governments had not supported one another. Listening to the debate at the UN as politicians from London fought for a toehold in 'Persia', the American ambassador to that institution noted, 'The British gave me the impression of singing the last act of the *Twilight of the Gods* in a burning theater.' Morris's first turnover ran with the headline 'British Task in the Suez Canal Zone'. He filed every afternoon, often long pieces informed by Quilliam's intelligence, returning late to the Officers' Club by the marshy Lake Timsah. It turned out that there were two 'particularly nice' correspondents after all: 'David Walker of the *Mirror* (who spotted me in a House [Christ Church] tie and turns out to have been there himself!)' and Noyes 'Tommy' Thomas, a 'surprisingly civilised' man with the *News of the World*. On Boxing Day he wrote to Elizabeth, who had her old neighbour Audrey Mutter from Appleton staying, to say:

> Christmas Day was ghastly – I got a little tight but not enough to make the RAF anything short of awful. Fortunately Sunday night I spent with the squadron of the Royal Dragoons who run the patrol in Ismailia and they gave me an absolutely first-class time . . . The 9th Lancers was a magic password – I had the squadron leader's luxury tent for the night.

Fighting and looting broke out sporadically across the Zone, and in Cairo. In those tense December days he was on the telephone to the

Royal Dragoons every hour for updates. Besides Thomas and House-man Walker, colleagues included 'Alan Whicker of *Exchange Telegraph* (he has a beard) and a completely sexless and rather shy American lady from AFP [Agence France-Presse]'. Whicker, five years Morris's senior, had volunteered as a teenage subaltern and served in the Army Film and Photographic Unit for the entire Italian campaign; he'd been at the Anzio Bridgehead, where, he wrote, 'we all ceased to be young'. It was he who, editing the Forces' paper in Venice, had described the city in 1946 as 'an exclusive club' for British officers. He and Morris had not met in the heady days of the Riva degli Schiavoni, but from now on they maintained a loyal friendship which lasted until Whicker's death. Meanwhile, 'I'm afraid I got rather tight again last night,' Morris confessed to Elizabeth. He had received what Louis Heren called 'herograms' from Printing House Square praising his dispatches. Editor William Casey cabled on 25 January 1952: MANY THANKS FOR EXCELLENT STEADY AND SHREWD MESSAGES FROM THE CANAL ZONE THEY DO YOU GREAT CREDIT AND I HOPE YOU CAN KEEP THEM UP. Donald Tyerman had appealed for a Christmas bonus on his behalf. Morris, he wrote in a memo, 'is doing much more than we have the right to expect any trainee in his first year to do'. In February they raised his pay to £850 retrospectively and told him formally that he was no longer a trainee but a regular member of staff. He was not yet twenty-six.

On 16 January he wrote home, 'The chief of staff began his press conference by saying "I hear we have to congratulate *The Times* on an addition to strength".' On 12 January Elizabeth had given birth to Mark at Hammersmith Hospital. In fizzy, chatty letters she told him, 'I'm sent flowers and letters by the dozen,' reporting visits from Chris and his wife Ruth (who had married the same year as James and Elizabeth, after Chris had had a first marriage annulled), and Gareth and Enid, whom Elizabeth called Mummy. When she and baby Mark left hospital they went to stay with the Mutters in Appleton. Elizabeth made the best of it, without him. She was good at that.

Fresh lava of discontent erupted on 26 January, a day that came to be known as Black Saturday. The morning before, British troops had launched an operation to disarm auxiliary policemen fighting as fedayeen (guerillas, effectively). On the Saturday, mobs of all stripes set fire to British property and ignited chaos: hijacks on the tarmac and slaughter at the Turf Club. In total, seven hundred buildings went up in smoke, including the British Council. The head of MI6 Middle East ops, who was there, wrote later, 'When the British Council premises go up in flames the odour of roasting pansy is incense in the nostrils of Allah.' It was one of the greatest upheavals in Cairene history. 'Poor time here,' Morris wrote to Elizabeth a fortnight later, 'and anyway the king's death has filled the papers' (he was referring to George VI). He'd flown to Aqaba with Walker, but after one day an explosion had gone off in a train so they'd had to rush back. He concluded the letter with reflections on their time together in Egypt. 'What ages ago it seems, and how very, very much happier I am now than I was then.' Work gave him focus, and the camaraderie of the mess filled a void, at least for now, especially when the glittering figure of Ralph Izzard appeared. The *Mail*'s six-foot-four Egypt correspondent was, according to Morris, the '*beau idéal* of the old-school foreign correspondent'. (Izzard was going to represent something quite different to Morris, once they were both at higher altitude a long way from Cairo.) Meanwhile, to fill her own void, Elizabeth had taken Mark to Yorkshire to stay with their friends the Busks near Doncaster; Martin Busk, another giant of a man, had received his emergency commission the same day as Morris, and they had served together in the 9th.

Things got worse for him in Cairo. 'Living here is really rather bloody now,' he wrote home. The paper had given him a camera, which added to the vexing practicalities, as he had to get the rolls of film to London. The others in his billet snored and he had to have an infected tooth extracted. He told Elizabeth that a letter from her 'transformed' his day, and that he had bought two pairs of French nylon socks. 'They are absolutely splendid – I wash them myself, as easy as pie.'

On 27 February Deakin wrote, 'It is difficult to form any opinion of how long this is to last, and I am quite sure that you would like to be at home and see your new baby. You can assume that we shall not want to keep you in the Canal longer than is absolutely necessary.' But how long was that? Elizabeth was struggling with the uncertainty. Might James be sent off to another hotspot before even meeting Mark? Karachi was mentioned. In March she sent him what he called 'a rocket'. He promised to press Deakin, and wrote to her, 'I tell everyone about you and how much I love you. It astonishes me how much closer I feel to you now than I did a couple of years ago in my criticising phase. I've met a great number of people since then but none I could ever love like you.'

When Churchill and Harry S. Truman had met in DC in early January to discuss the unravelling situation in the Middle East, both sets of advisers had read Morris's dispatches. The British prime minister asked the president to send troops to the Suez Canal to boost Western influence. But Truman wouldn't do it. Morris was in on one of the biggest stories in the world. Back in London, everyone in the newsroom was fidgeting about the forthcoming coronation of the young Elizabeth II, the first queen since Victoria. He was to be in on that, too.

Elizabeth wrote to Deakin herself from the Busks': 'Thanks for the kindness since J went to the Canal Zone . . . As you can imagine, I keep my eyes glued to the Egyptian news. I nurse the fond hope that you may even recall James in time for Easter.' She returned from Yorkshire on the Pullman, with Mark in his basket on the table in the dining car. To celebrate their third wedding anniversary she had sent James a message via the paper; not wanting to be 'personal', she wrote 'Many Happy Returns'. *The Times* thought it was his birthday so added their good wishes. A fortnight later she wrote to him from Appleton: 'I just can't wait to know what your "new post" will be . . . I'm really getting rather desperate . . . What a year to remember already – your son born – a new queen – Oxford winning the boat race – a new appointment for you and last but not least a wife who loves you more than ever before.'

Deakin cabled on 23 April: *PLEASE COME HOME SOON AS CONVENIENT*. It was over.

He met his son at Heathrow, and family life began in Hammersmith Terrace as the Thames at the end of the garden ran high with spring tides. Morris was seeking freelance commissions to bolster both his bank balance and his portfolio, and his byline soon appeared on both sides of the Atlantic in outlets including *Harper's*, *The Economist*, *Vogue*, the *Times Literary Supplement* (*TLS*), *London Calling* and *The Nation*. He had succeeded in honing a personal style under the Appleton thatch, and editors everywhere wanted to publish it. His mind worked in metaphors; he rarely perceived a fact in isolation, and in these early essays Morris learned how to tease a story from a fact or a single image, taking what he needed and no more. He then solidified the fact or the image so that it might take on a life of its own, imaginatively developing a process – one that became automatic – of writing about a place to a short length.

Encounter was among his clients after it launched in 1953. Clutching his typed pages, Morris would make his way in a creaking cage lift to the office off London's Haymarket, where editor Stephen Spender sat in a collage of books, paintings and ashtrays. The CIA was funding the magazine in an attempt to convince the world at large that the US was no evil empire – indeed, that it had a soft cultural centre. America had tested its first hydrogen bomb the year before *Encounter*'s inaugural issue came out, and the Soviets were about to test theirs, so the Cold War opened a cultural front. *Encounter* was aimed at writers and readers who thought art should be free of political control, unlike its rival the *New Statesman*, a sort of anti-*Encounter* publication urging political engagement. Morris, not being engaged, wrote for both. John Berger, born just a month after Morris, was the Marxist art critic for the *Statesman* (and one of the so-called 'kitchen sink' painters, as well as a writer). Their politics were radically different, but Berger and Morris breathed the same air. Berger acknowledged the generational influence of the First World War on himself and his peers, transmitted in both his case and Morris's through the father. *I was born of the look of the dead*, he wrote in a poem, *swaddled in mustard gas*. Both of them tried out many forms over six decades and – this was fairly unusual at the time – blurred the lines between fiction and non-fiction; both were to be Booker contenders. (When Berger actually won in 1972 for *G.*, partly set in Trieste, he gave half the money to the Black Panthers.) In the sixties a vibrant new sense of European identity was to inspire them after the ration-book fifties. But all Berger's work sprang from the historical realities of his time, and creatively he was indigenous to the moment. Whereas beyond his reportage, the shadow of Cold War polemics fell hardly at all on Morris, a writer who had other wars to win.

In the autumn, Morris produced a long essay about 'gypsies' for *The Times*, travelling round southern England to carry out interviews: the piece was an appeal against prejudice and for the accommodation of cultural integrity. Sir William Haley, who had taken over the editorship from Casey, sent a personal memo to praise the feature. Six weeks later, a polluted fog fell on London, so dense that people could not see their feet. On 19 December Ralph Deakin died. The paper had told him he had to leave, even though his retirement date had not yet arrived, and Morris sensed that he had grown increasingly bitter and confused,

> until finally, one winter evening, he gave me a letter. If anything should happen to him, he said, buttoning his thick black overcoat . . . I was to hand it to the higher authorities of *The Times* . . . he nodded at me in his usual way, said goodnight with his habitual icy trace of a smile, and went home to kill himself with sleeping pills.

Heart disease was cited as the actual cause of death, but the coroner found that worry and emotion had exacerbated the condition. Deakin had left a note, which was read out at the inquest, confessing his love for the secretary he had sometimes taken to lunch. Worsthorne later said that, after her husband's death, Mrs Deakin appeared regularly at the office at dusk underneath the window where the secretary sat, looking up and shaking her fist.

Morris was appointed acting foreign news editor, grappling with the new teleprinter at the same time. Britain was beginning to decolonise, and the USSR was looking hungrily at vacant territory as well as clamping down on its satellite states in Eastern Europe. But something else was afoot in Printing House Square.

4
1953
KNOCKING THE BASTARD OFF

Before he died, Deakin had been liaising with the Royal Geographical Society over the paper's sponsorship of a forthcoming Everest expedition. This fresh attempt on the summit, led by Colonel John Hunt, was to be from the south, through Nepal. British mountaineers had been tackling Chomolungma – 'Mother Goddess of the World' in Tibetan – for more than thirty years, and *The Times* had sponsored most of the expeditions in return for exclusive copyright in dispatches. The news value of big climbs had risen and, as Morris wrote, 'Sport was now a chief medium of nationalist fervour.' In 1953 it was Britain's 'turn' on Everest, and prestige – a lot of it – was at stake. French climbers had posed on the top of Annapurna 'with a flourish of national pride'; people who called Nanga Parbat 'the German mountain' now openly referred to Everest as the 'British' equivalent. In addition, it was the country's last chance: French climbers had Everest booked for 1954; the Swiss, who had nearly made it to the top in 1952, had claimed 1955. A race was on for what people called the Third Pole – one of the greatest sporting contests of all time.

Hunt was supposed to be writing the dispatches. But on 11 October 1952, RGS director Laurence 'Larry' Kirwan had written to Deakin to say the colonel would not after all be able to report due to his other responsibilities on the mountain, and that the Joint Himalayan Committee had 'discussed Shipton being invited as your special correspondent'. Eric Shipton had led several Everest expeditions himself; he had been slated to lead this one, but when the committee unceremoniously parachuted Hunt in as co-leader, Shipton resigned. The RGS had wisely decided against appointing him as 'reporter', and Kirwan had then put to the committee 'whether some of the burden of writing despatches to *The Times* might perhaps be lightened for the Leader by one of [the paper's] Correspondents'. The captious committee had not wanted this either. 'They would prefer greatly', Kirwan had informed Deakin with confounding abstruseness, 'that despatches should be written by the Leader or by a member of the actual climbing team deputed by him.' As deputy foreign news editor (as he signed himself, rather than 'acting'), Morris took over the liaison role with this crucial issue unresolved.

Another baby was due in May. At the end of October, the family had moved to rented accommodation in Lower Lodge in Taplow, Buckinghamshire, but it was a short-term let, and Elizabeth was understandably anxious. On 19 January Morris wrote to Iverach McDonald, the Highlander recently appointed foreign editor. 'I know so little about my future. We plan to move into a new house in London in May but the landlord is a little chary of letting it to someone who may only live in it for a few months.' Morris had brought more uncertainty upon himself by applying for a Commonwealth Fund Fellowship, which would allow him to travel in the US for a year. It was not an obvious career move – he was a young star at *The Times*, with options to shoot even higher in the sky, or at least pick his postings. But America was the future, as he had glimpsed when he'd lifted his telescope at the Sugar Lookout to watch ships at full sail. In addition, he wanted acknowledgement of his status through external means, and he wanted to pack in as much as he could as quickly as possible, as if something lay in his path ahead which would prevent him taking up opportunities. A year in America represented a remarkably egocentric project for a man with a growing family. He didn't even know if *The Times* would pay his salary if he took up the fellowship. Morris was obsessed with himself, and seemingly incapable of taking Elizabeth into account.

At the end of March, he heard he had got the fellowship: Morris was heading for Sandy Hook, at twenty-eight knots. Elizabeth was going to have to put up with his absence and with the lack of clarity; she had no idea even where they would live, as they could not now take the London house. But there was no time – for him – to dwell on domestic arrangements. *The Times* was moving at full speed itself. In February they agreed syndication rights on the Everest story – whatever the news from the mountain turned out to be, and whoever carried it down – with outlets from *Le Figaro* to the *Melbourne Age* and *Time*. But how to get the reports home without the interference of rival newspapermen? It was decided that the paper's Delhi correspondent, Arthur Hutchinson, who had covered the Swiss expedition the previous year, would fly to Kathmandu, 'if only to keep an eye on the opposition'. This last contingent presented such perils that the men at *The Times* set about compiling codes: 'icefall' was to be SAUSAGE or CABINET, and 'failed because of' DENTIST or CONTINENT, while the news that someone had been killed was to be indicated by SIGNALBOX or KNIGHTHOOD. Hutchinson was to shepherd the dispatches through the cablehead once he received them from runners, interpreting them where necessary. Meanwhile, the committee, notwithstanding their reverence for the Soviet-styled Leader, had realised they needed a professional journalist on the mountain after all. On 4 February the new foreign news editor, Gerald Norman (he had been brought back from Paris to relieve Morris of his temporary position), wrote to Hutchinson in Delhi to say they 'have twenty-six-year-old James Morris in mind, at present my assistant'. Norman continued, 'He is tough and wiry and has on previous assignments survived v well extremes of heat and cold.'

One wonders what these extremes were. Nobody cared. Morris seized the moment. He didn't particularly fancy Everest or indeed any mountain, but 'I was horribly ambitious, and I went like a shot.' ('I wish Morris didn't look quite so pleased,' said Iverach McDonald after he told him to pack for Nepal.) He was so lacking in empathy that he was prepared to race off to America and leave an impoverished Elizabeth holding two babies, but there was no shortage of Boy's Own courage. Hunt requested his presence at his club for lunch. Over brown Windsor soup in the coffee room at the Garrick, oils hung salon-style all around, Morris revealed that he had never set foot on a mountain. Hunt 'summoned up a wan smile' and hurried off to tell *The Times* that Morris was 'utterly inexperienced and physically substandard . . . we should find someone else'. There was nobody else. His code name was CARPET or ARMCHAIR.

CARPET left London with his bags on the last day of winter, Everest-bound on a Comet jetliner. He had joined some of the climbers for one brief training session in Snowdonia, Elizabeth manfully propelling Mark in his pram up the footpaths around the Pen-y-Gwryd Hotel. 'Eggs and bacon in Rome at 3:00 am,' he wrote to Appleton after setting off. Now seven months pregnant, Elizabeth had again decamped to the village with Mark. 'Everything is less strange than it might be,' Morris wrote home when he finally reached Delhi, 'because it is all so much like Cairo. Especially the general sense of developing seediness.' Hutchinson was already in Nepal, but his young wife, June, helped with arrangements in India despite being 'rather a common girl'. Morris was quick to find people 'common', evidently acutely aware of his own position in the unyielding British class system. Common or not, June was among the few in possession of a complete copy of the sacerdotal codes that would enable Morris to get the story home without being intercepted.

In a Delhi bazaar Morris shopped for a tent, pots and pans, as Hunt had stipulated that he had to bring in his own supplies and do his own cooking (which in practice meant that his personal Sherpas would do it). On 25 March he flew up to Kathmandu and checked in at the Nepal Hotel, a converted palace 'of incomparable discomfort' where staff abluted in the ornamental fountain and two stuffed leopards grappled in a death lock in the hall. Hutchinson was there, but Hunt and his team had left a week earlier to acclimatise; Sherpas and porters – 362 in all – were carrying in fifteen tons of equipment. As there were no roads into Nepal, every pound had arrived by 'cable railway'.

Morris's attention turned to 'the opposition', omnipresent actors in the Everest drama. Ralph Izzard, the six-foot-four *beau idéal* from the *Mail* first seen in the Canal Zone, was to stalk the Everest story like a villain in a snowy pantomime. 'The embassy people in Kathmandu are virulently anti-Izzard,' Morris wrote to Elizabeth, 'but the more I see of him, the more I like him; he's quite first class.' The Essex-born Izzard, who had already left Kathmandu for the foothills, was sixteen years Morris's senior, and 'not only brave and resourceful, but also gentlemanly [which meant not common], widely read, kind, a bit raffish, excellent to drink with, fun to travel with, handsome but louche, honourable but thoroughly disrespectful'. Already an old Cold War soldier, he was glamorous (he had a daughter with a film star) as well as quirky: he was an expert on lichens and wore gym shoes on the mountain. In 1947 Izzard had married Molly Crutchleigh-Fitzpatrick, whom he'd met at Bletchley Park, the hub of wartime codebreaking, and given her a chestnut mare as a wedding gift. 'In his cups' earlier that week, Izzard had told Hutchinson that the *Mail* 'had some final surprise up its sleeve'. Hunt had written to Gerald Norman before Morris even arrived in Nepal to fulminate, 'I have been having a great deal of trouble with the press. The *Daily Mail* man got hold of Tenzing and has concocted a story which is seriously inaccurate, in particular regarding a decision about Tenzing going to the top alone.' Sherpa Tenzing Norgay was the expedition sirdar and also, unusually for a British expedition, an official member of the climbing team.

Assembling his gear on the veranda of the British embassy, Morris met Major J. O. M. 'Jimmy' Roberts, leader of the rearguard supply party with whom he was to walk up to Base Camp. The bald but otherwise ursine Roberts, on leave from his regiment in Malaya, had once commanded a Gurkha battalion. 'He has a rather good dry soldier-like sense of humour,' Morris reported; 'you couldn't ask for a better chap to trek with, especially as he knows the language.' In that heady week, Morris sent off his first dispatch, a filler about Sherpas, and bicycled about town with Hutchinson. 'The squalor in Kathmandu is worse than Egypt,' he decided as he threaded below tiered wooden pagodas with golden finials and fantastic carved stone animals. The politically tense capital was under a curfew, 'passwords passed from hand to hand on grubby pieces of paper', and villages like Bhatgaon ten miles to the east, where the expedition had assembled supplies on an army parade ground, were 'instinct with the spirit of the Middle Ages'. 'Give my love most of all to MARKETUS,' Morris ended one letter, 'who really is a thoroughly bad goblin. I love you always, darling.'

Kathmandu was at 4,000 feet, the foot of Everest at 18,000. One hundred and seventy-five miles separated the two – a west-to-east trek of about two weeks. Primroses were out and Morris started for the Dudh Kosi valley with seven Sherpas of his own, including Sonam, a personal servant Tenzing had selected for him; Roberts; and seventy-seven more porters loaded with goods, including sixty crates of oxygen tanks. The berberis were out too, along with primulas and orchids, and so were five-inch flying beetles. One night Morris found an immense frog in his sleeping bag and for days the Sherpas shouted, 'Sahib! Sahib! One frog in your bed!' On 4 April he camped 'outside a Buddhist temple on a very high ridge, about 6000 feet, with deep valleys on either side'. Roberts doled out medicine to villagers while Morris typed, canvas bellying as he sat on his inflatable mattress. 'There's an audience around me of about twenty very ragged people who've never seen a typewriter before,' he wrote to Elizabeth. Nepal did not allow long-range transmitters to be brought in, and wags at the paper had suggested dispatches might go telepathically via Buddhist holy men. Following previous expeditions, Morris was to rely on Sherpa runners to carry his copy back to Kathmandu. But, on his way up, Hunt had discovered an Indian military radio transmitter at Namche Bazar, the Sherpa capital in Solukhumbu district and the jumping-off point for Everest thirty miles away; its role was to monitor the unstable Tibetan border. The operator powered the transmitter by pedalling a stationary bicycle. But was the station and its transmission route secure? Morris resolved to use it only for the crucial final dispatch announcing success or failure. He was tense – everyone was. 'The further one goes on the journey,' he wrote home, '... the more one gets keyed up for Everest.' His face splintered and his lips swelled painfully. But he was able to pick up the BBC sporadically on his own radio, which had a tall tripod aerial, and on one occasion heard Dennis Brain, Gareth's pal, playing a Mozart concerto on his horn, and all the Sherpas pushed into the tent to listen. 'How is Markytarkytus?' he asked Elizabeth. At the villages he showed the women a photograph of her and Mark, and he bombarded her with questions about the imminence of the baby, whom they called Beppo.

On 6 April he wrote:

> My dearest darling just a note scribbled on my knee to tell you how much I love you... Easter day's [march] was a brute – right down into a deep river valley and then up the other side to 8000 feet. Yesterday we had a petrifying bridge to cross: it consisted of single planks laid end to end and not joining properly with chains to hold onto across a deepish gorge... you can easily avoid it by wading through a river below and most of the porters did but I felt I owed it to myself to cross it... While I remember could you possibly send me some packets of lemonade powder... Though I'm looking forward to seeing Mt Everest I am counting the days till we're together again. <u>What a state to be in!</u>

Every day he watched runners melt into the mist with misgivings. Almost every returning Sherpa brought 'a sombre bulletin from Hutchinson, warning me of the intricate nets laid across the way to catch our news'. Rumours filtered down concerning Izzard, four days ahead of Morris. Then the man himself appeared, on his way back to Kathmandu. Without acclimatisation he had walked to over 18,000 feet in the gym shoes and reached the lower reaches of the icefall. A *beau idéal* indeed. The pair greeted one another cordially: Izzard had apparently shaken off his villainous mantle, as Morris gave him a letter to send on to Elizabeth. 'We get to Namche in about 3 hrs time,' he wrote to her on 16 April, 'and then to Thyangboche in the morning... This is wonderful country...

But I can't say I'm keen on the much-boosted Sherpas – they're such a lot of drunks!' Hunt's rear base at Thyangboche Monastery, ten miles up the valley from Namche and twelve miles south of Everest, nestled in a 12,000-foot saddle which cut across the valley of the Imja Khola.

Despite the 'wonderful country', both Morris's public and private writings reveal a man engaged with his work but not with the landscape. He experienced no sense of the sublime, even as oceans of rhododendrons shifted in the wind and peaks shimmered in the haze beyond. One scene was 'too dead and aloof for beauty', another 'odious'. He felt excitement only in relation to his professional goals. On 20 April he wrote in exhilaration, 'I can see the end of the icefall from just outside my tent, and the shoulder of Everest itself and the peak of Nuptse are above us!' He and his Sherpas were heading to Base Camp the next morning, then back to Thyangboche to rest, and at the end of the month he was going to walk up to Base Camp again 'in time for the fun to begin'.

On 22 April he wrote to the wireless officer at the embassy, the man who was to send the final message to the Foreign Office on the secure diplomatic link. 'One new major problem has arisen,' he revealed. The bicycling Namche radio operator would not send messages he could not understand, so a coded message announcing the final news would not be transmitted. 'I think it would be suicidal to send messages in clear [not in code],' Morris explained, '. . . as they would be public property in Kathmandu.' Therefore a new code had to be devised for that final message – one that did not look like code. 'Hunt agrees that the best way to do this is to send a message which appears to be in clear but which is really in a sense a code. This message need only say: a) that Everest has been climbed and b) which members of the expedition climbed it . . . I shall begin it with the phrase SNOW CONDITIONS BAD. This will mean to you that Everest has been climbed.' Morris also told the embassy man that, according to Tenzing, Indian journalists had bribed the Namche radio officers.

Base Camp south-west of the summit lay at the foot of the precipitous Khumbu icefall, which tumbles 2,000 feet from the broad glacier basin known as the Western Cwm. Men were fixing this route when Morris arrived, tiny figures beetling up and down in relay. Hunt had decided that he should eat with them after all, and when supper was over they took it in turns to read W. H. Murray's *Story of Everest*, which Morris had carried up with him, signing the flyleaf when they finished. At seven, Hunt dimmed the camp lights, and the tents fell silent. Morris crawled out of his to wander round then, windproofs wrapped tight, and said he felt like Henry V. He wondered if he should start thinking about obituaries, should the worst happen. One afternoon, forty-four-year-old Hunt asked him if he had the information he needed for the day's dispatch. '"Everything, thank you John," I replied, wondering if half a column would be enough for him.' He had his tent moved a little further from the rest and went back to eating his own food as he preferred it to theirs, especially Sonam's tea, though he visited for shards of their chocolate. He told Elizabeth,

> My tent is far and away the most comfortable and best organised – I have had a wall of stones built around the entrance and roofed with my waterproof cape . . . the climbers are in some ways the worst organised people I've ever met, and it seems to me they live in far worse squalor and discomfort than they need.

Hunt, constantly adjusting plans, invited Morris to Camp IV once it was established on the Western Cwm, despite his lack of climbing experience. He went up roped to Mike Ward, a doctor and pioneering high-altitude physiologist, ice cracking all around them in ribbed blue crevasses. Morris had never before worn crampons or handled an ice axe, yet he made it up the fearsome icefall, 'so I'm feeling rather pleased with myself; it's probably as high as I'll get on the mountain and certainly I don't much want to do the icefall journey again . . . It makes you realise what a simply monstrous mountain this is.'

He would climb the icefall again. It was among Morris's most astonishing achievements – few amateurs at that time could have made it to 22,000 feet, more than six times the height of Snowdon, the nearest proper mountain to Clevedon. Meanwhile, he sat at his typewriter alongside Hunt, 'ghastly with glacier cream', and imagined the triumph of rivals as the wind whipped up showers of ice and his paper tore while still in the carriage.

By 8 May, having gone back down to Base Camp to wait it out, he had sent twelve news pieces, another turnover about the Sherpas and a shorter article on the Abominable Snowman. Time was running out, weatherwise, as the advance climbers tried to struggle through to the South Col, the bleak, windswept saddle at 25,800 feet between the upper slopes of Everest and Lhotse. Morris told Elizabeth, 'I know who the climbers are going to be, though I mustn't tell you in case there are changes.' Breaking trail took much longer than planned and Hunt made the difficult decision to send two more men up with precious oxygen. In the rising tension of this last week, Morris filed a dispatch almost every day, paying his runners on a sliding scale according to how fast they were. It had always been supposed that the journey to Kathmandu from Base Camp took ten days, but some did it in six, and on one occasion two runners made it in five.

Every evening when Hunt was higher than him, Morris climbed to a vantage point on the moraine at 7 p.m. to talk with the leader over the walkie-talkie. He describes stowing the transmitter batteries inside his sleeping bag to keep them warm ('uncomfortable bedmates').* Already he had come to admire Hunt deeply; the colonel was, Morris felt, 'authority and responsibility incarnate'. The leader was an army man, and Morris felt comfortable in the framework of military discipline. If someone was coming down, Hunt sent a note to augment the walkie-talkie bulletin. On 23 May Morris received an account of that day's events at Camp IV. 'PS,' Hunt added, 'Congratulations on your son!' The BBC had broadcast the news over the wireless after the weather, and the others had assumed Morris had heard it. (Or perhaps they were blasé about sons. Major

---

* I can confirm the discomfort of this manoeuvre. I have done the same many times with bulky batteries, at the first two Poles.

Charles Wylie's wife had had one two weeks earlier.) 'You've no idea how the news has cheered me up,' he wrote to Elizabeth. 'I'm having a hell of a time here, a rival firm has turned up with a radio transmitter, so we're beaten from the start. But WHO CARES?' This fresh cast of scoundrels, who had 'turned up' in Kathmandu, not at 18,000 feet, were Indian, and they were monitoring all outgoing telegraphy between the capital and home.

Tom Bourdillon and Charles Evans, the first assault party, had gone up to the awful South Col using experimental closed oxygen circuits, and from there made it to the South Summit, just 430 feet short of the top and only 330 feet below it, higher than any man had ever climbed – but not to the peak of peaks. ('I could have done it,' Bourdillon wrote in his diary that night.) If the weather held, Ed Hillary, 'big and bold and piston-like', and Sherpa Tenzing were to make the final push with traditional open oxygen systems. But the weather closed in, and 27 May was a wasted day ('movement between tents is itself an ordeal'). Hunt wrote a long note to Morris from the South Col detailing 'momentous events' involving support parties, faulty oxygen cylinders, 'foul, breakable crust', dumped stores, sick Sherpas and Evans and Bourdillon's 'first ascent of the South Peak of Everest'.

At Base Camp in those final days, the official expedition physiologist, Griff Pugh, asked Morris on the spur of the moment if he'd like to go back up to Camp IV with him. 'Terribly rushed now,' Morris wrote to Elizabeth, back at Taplow, before leaving. 'The weather is the very devil.' The enormous Jimmy Roberts, with whom he had trekked in from Kathmandu, had him sent him a tiny pair of Tibetan boots for Henry, Marketus's new brother.

At Camp IV, Hunt paced outside 'his high shanty tent, still hideous with ointment; a heroic figure, I thought . . . awaiting the arrival of the elephants'. Hillary and Tenzing had slept in a lonely tent at nearly 28,000 feet the night before their attempt on the Mother Goddess. They had been seen at nine the previous morning crossing the South Summit, 'going strongly up the final ridge'. The hours dragged by. The waiting men went round and round discussing the chances of success. Then they saw dots descending the Lhotse Face. A feverish hush fell over the camp. The sun was shining, the sky a dazzling blue. Hunt sat outside on a packing case, his sun hat jammed on his head, 'as tense as a violin string'. The dots disappeared – the climbers had come off the Lhotse Face and were hidden behind a hummock at the top end of the Cwm. Tom Stobart stumped up with his cine camera. A radio sputtered to life with a bulletin from All India Radio: 'Agency messages confirm that the British assault on Everest has failed and that the expedition is withdrawing from the mountain.' Someone twiddled the knob, half amused, half irritated. And then:

'There they are!'

The elephants themselves.

Everyone rushed out, sinking and slithering in soft snow, Hunt in his dark goggles, Alf Gregory with the bobble on his hat jiggling as he ran, Bourdillon with his braces hanging down and bouncing on his windproof trousers.

George Lowe led the incoming party. He put his thumb up.

For Morris, it was just the start. At about 2.30 on the afternoon of 30 May he sat in the communal tent taking down Hillary's story as the climber forked down an omelette. Morris never asked which of the two had stood on the summit first. He did record Hillary's comment to his fellow Kiwi, Lowe, modestly summarising the achievement: 'Well George, we knocked the bastard off.'

The coronation was three full days away. Morris had to set off for Base Camp immediately in order to get a message to Namche the next morning. Would the Indians break the code? Mike Westmacott offered to go with him. (It was Westmacott, chiefly, who had pioneered the route through the glacier and kept it open with ropes and markers.) The way crossed an 'oozing icebog' in which Morris floundered up to his thighs. Long and deep were the crevasses that evening. They stopped at Camp III at twilight for lemonade and sweets but pushed on through a 'loathsome, decaying wilderness'. Dizzy and feverish in the growing darkness, Morris hit a block of ice and half his toenail came off. (He had the other half removed in Calcutta. It grew back and fell off again every five years for the rest of his and then her life.) At an almost deserted Base Camp, legs 'stiff as ramrods', his face burned from the sun, 'I extracted my typewriter from a pile of clothing and propped it on my knees to write a message. This was that brief dispatch of victory I had dreamed about . . . SNOW CONDITIONS BAD STOP ADVANCE BASE ABANDONED YESTERDAY STOP AWAITING IMPROVEMENT ALL WELL. This meant *Summit reached May 29 by Hillary and Tenzing*.'

Two mornings later, the message dispatched, Morris met Tenzing by chance near a yak herder's hut.

> He was going to a neighbouring village to see his aged mother and tell her the news of the ascent. We had breakfast together beside one of the clear streams that came rushing out of the Khumbu Glacier. He really was like some legendary mountain creature then – brown as a nut, supple as a willow, and when he stripped to the waist to wash himself in the icy water of the stream, how slim and sinewy he looked as he grinned at me through his shivers, rather like a deer that had come splashing out of the shallows and was shaking the water from its antlers.

Tenzing handed him a photograph of himself. Morris asked him to sign it, 'so he did – just the one word, TENZING. It was a kingly sort of signature, I thought. It was the only word he could write.' (Morris observed much later the effects when 'the jackals of fame' descended on the regal Tenzing.) That night, Sonam put Morris's tent up among the pines on the west bank of the Dudh Kosi, about six miles south of Namche. Dusk had settled, and the air, cool and scented, filled with the rushing sound of the swollen river.

The morning of 2 June broke fair, and as the sun's rays crept up his sleeping bag Morris reached a hand out of his mummified wrappings towards the wireless knob. 'A moment of fumbling; a few crackles and hisses; and then the voice of an Englishman. Everest had been climbed, he said. Queen Elizabeth had been given the news, he said, on the eve of her coronation. *The Times*, he said, had broken the story.' Morris continued:

> I jumped out of my bed, spilling the bedclothes about me, tearing open the tent flap, leaping into the open in my filthy shirt, my broken boots, my torn trousers; my face was thickly bearded, my skin cracked with sun and cold, my voice hoarse. But I shouted to my Sherpas, whose blurry eyes were appearing from the neighbouring windows:
> 'Chomolungma finished! Everest done with! Okay!'
> 'OK, sahib!' the Sherpas shouted back. 'Breakfast now?'

Foreign editor Iveragh McDonald had picked up the telephone in his panelled room at *The Times* one minute before the 4.15 p.m. editorial conference on the day before the coronation. It was William Ridsdale from the Foreign Office. McDonald took his fountain pen and a piece of blank paper and began to write as Ridsdale dictated.

Climbed
29 May
Hillary – Tenzing – All well
<u>Climbed.</u>

A few minutes later Ridsdale rang back to ask if they could give the Queen the news. *The Times* felt it was theirs to give, so the editor himself rang Sir Alan 'Tommy' Lascelles, Her Majesty's private secretary. John Astor, the paper's owner, was dining at his London residence that evening. Before pudding, the butler called him to the telephone. When Astor returned to the table, he told his guests that Everest had been climbed, instructing them not to tell anyone until the next morning. The news was not 'held back' as was tirelessly repeated in years to come. It could not have appeared in print any sooner than it did.

Morris began to feel ill once this dam had been breached, and Sonam took him to his village to recuperate. Chaurikharka consisted of a cluster of huts surrounded by potato fields, and Morris lay in his sleeping bag in a dark room on the upstairs floor of Sonam's house. Butter candles flickered over a dozen images of the Buddha in an alcove. There was no other furniture. Everything was woody, smoky, creaky, and he woke in the morning to the chatter of voices and the sweetly rotten vegetable smell of the monsoon. Meanwhile, *The Times* had secured vantage points for thirty-three correspondents at the coronation and its leading editorial on the day praised the young Queen with the words: 'the splendid trophy brought to her from the summit of the world's highest peak is the earnest hope of a new heroic age'. The press took up Morris's story the world over; on 2 June the *New York Times* splashed it over the front page. The reporter emerged as a romantic image of lean young manhood, and Hunt acknowledged that his initial judgement over the Garrick soup had been wrong. In his own comments, Morris did not say then what, as Jan, she wrote much later. For that suddenly world-famous journalist, the triumph was to become an allegory, as 'The British nation was approaching the end of its career as a great world power – signing off, though its people did not always recognise it, after so many victories, such grand tragedies and accomplishments.'

Morris recovered from his sickness and badly wanted to get home. On 14 June he wrote to Elizabeth in despair from the embassy in Kathmandu, having 'marched' for nine days 'in the hope of getting on a plane to India'. Instead, he found

> the firmest cable from PHS [Printing House Square] instructing both Hutchinson and me to stay here until the expedition left, and adding that I was to fly home with the climbers. It's madness having us both here . . . the story is now really dead . . . life here is perfectly bloody.

The story was not dead.

The sultry monsoon period brought out both insects and journalists, the latter from across the globe. They had been pouring into Kathmandu for weeks, 'like converging scavengers, to pick up what they could, using their claws if need be'. Morris was once more at the centre of the world's biggest news story. *HAVE BEEN OFFERED VARIOUS ATTRACTIVE TEMPTATIONS IN RETURN USE OF MY NAME IN ADVERTISEMENTS WOULD THIS BE DISASTROUS TO MY CONNECTION WITH THE TIMES?* he cabled Norman on 15 June. *YES DISASTROUS* came the immediate reply. At the Nepal Hotel, staff had spread all the laundry including their own over the front lawn.

Morris had been away for three months and all he could think about was home. He revelled in Elizabeth's news. When she reported that the Breitmeyers, friends they had met at Oxford, had asked him to be godfather to baby Peter, he replied eagerly, instructing her to tell them that he would be honoured to accept the role. Hillary, in the meantime, had agreed to stand as Henry's godfather.

'Morris has returned,' Norman told Hutchinson, who was back in Delhi, 'and has now shaved.' He had lost fourteen pounds and recuperated with his two sons and Elizabeth in Taplow, where they had extended their rental, while the world went mad: invitations poured in, in July alone from India House, Lancaster House, the Mansion House and St James's Palace. When he went to Buckingham Palace with the others to receive the Queen Elizabeth II Coronation Medal with *Mount Everest Expedition* engraved on its rim, the Queen told him how the news had been brought to her in her bedroom in a red dispatch box. After hours, the climbers went to the Coconut Grove on Regent Street to listen to rumba. Hillary had never tasted champagne before. He liked it. Tenzing liked it more. After a fuss in Nepal about Tenzing's invitation to fly to the UK with the rest of the team, he had said he wouldn't go anyway unless his wife and two daughters went too. (This was true heroism.) Meanwhile, Morris noted that at every formal dinner, after the ladies had withdrawn and the port was passed, the men asked how they had managed about the lavatory.

Everyone rejoiced. Or almost everyone. 'Furious about this,' the author, gardener and chatelaine Vita Sackville-West wrote in her diary the day she heard the news. She resented the violation of the unknown.

*

It turned out that Morris was not quite the Tin Man his actions suggested: he had approached the Commonwealth Fund to see if Elizabeth, Mark and the baby could join him in the US. While waiting for an answer, he had asked her from Kathmandu, 'Do you want me to back out of America?' One might have expected him to ask in advance if she minded him going at all. But the fund turned out to be amenable, and before he returned from the Himalaya he told her to book passage for the three of them across the Atlantic; he would sail ahead. *The Times* had agreed to bail him out of the first of many financial jams by continuing to pay his salary in return for dispatches; he was after all the most famous journalist in the world. So he had pulled it all off.

He left Liverpool on the RMS *Mauretania* in early October, missing the premiere of Tom Stobart's film *The Conquest of Everest* in Leicester Square in front of the Queen and the Duke of Edinburgh. Gerald Norman from *The Times* accompanied Elizabeth. Stobart (EAGLET) had filmed until the final push. His footage began with crowds in the Mall cheering the golden coach, switching to a garlanded Tenzing in a coach of his own, a palanquin weaving through the streets of Kathmandu. The production company had commissioned poet Louis MacNeice to write the script ('The Sherpas set off, carrying a dream . . . all of them bound for a cold white world'). At the low altitude of the early camps, the pale, shirtless bodies of the climbers appear in front of teetering towers of chapatis, Sherpanis behind plaiting one another's hair and the handsome Bourdillon (THUNDERSTORM or CANTEEN), in a string vest, supine on the grass reading a letter. Further up the mountain, Morris in orange trousers fiddles with gear while Ward (FIREPLACE) laughs at him. (Morris narrates a few minutes of the film, reporting his climb up the icefall.) Stobart, an accomplished man of action, also turned out to be a fine cinematographer. (He progressed to a third career writing cookery books.) The film was named one of the ten best of the year in the *New York Times* and won a British Academy Film Award. 'Why did they climb it?' the script ends. 'They climbed it because it is there.'

KNOCKING THE BASTARD OFF

MacNeice wrote about the experience of viewing the rushes in his long poem *Autumn Sequel* – itself a little-known sequel to the Everest saga. The poet had taken the train to the Beaconsfield studio through suburban Buckinghamshire. *A weir of whirling celluloid spewed images of ice Twenty-nine-thousand and two feet high, a clean/ Rebuttal of the verities of Bucks/ Where a projector clamps it on a screen/ And I write words about it.*

Hunt got his book out on 12 November. It had the whiff of the military commander about it, and is framed in moral earnestness, but it told the story with clarity. Morris emerges with distinction. Of his second ascent of the icefall, Hunt remarks, 'We all admired his enterprise: he had well earned his place as a full member of the expedition.' *The Ascent of Everest* was translated into thirty languages. Morris, desperate to write his own book, had discussed the project with publishers Hodder & Stoughton. But *The Times* wouldn't let him. 'Can you help me win over whatever Powers that be that object?' he pleaded with McDonald.

> Both the RGS and H & S 'cleared' the project, and H & S indeed gave me a contract for the book: and I am willing for it to be signed either Special Correspondent of *The Times* without my name; or my name alone, or both, and I am also willing to let anyone in the office vet the text . . . I shall never have so wonderful an opportunity to write a book that would sell again: I really don't think I can afford to let the chance slip without putting up a little more of a fight.

They still said no.

5
1954–1956
PERPETUAL THEATRE

'The dining car coach doors', Morris reported to Elizabeth from the New York–Chicago train, 'work by an invisible electronic ray, and they simply open when your body crosses it!' This, then, was America. The thirty-seven-storey Palmolive Building dominated the Chicago lakeside, and the city Morris found was 'still the stormy, husky, brawling place that Carl Sandburg had celebrated, "laughing the laughter of youth, half naked, sweating".' (The slightly adjusted quotation is from Illinois-born Sandburg's poem 'Chicago'.) The previous year the Republican Party had taken the White House and both houses of Congress, and Senator Joe McCarthy's anti-communist campaign led the news cycle.

Commonwealth Fund Fellowships (not yet called Harkness, but already funded by the Harkness family foundation) ran in academic years and each cohort included twenty UK graduates; fellows were required to submit a travel report at the end. Morris bought a 1949 Chevrolet saloon – '650 dollars, it has a radio and heater' – and toured for a month before Elizabeth and the boys arrived. In Milwaukee, Madison and Minneapolis, 'The combination of Commonwealth Fund, *The Times* and Mount Everest gives me a wonderful means of entry into all kinds of society! The last of the three got me an introduction the other day to Adlai Stevenson [one-time presidential candidate and until recently governor of Illinois].' Not everyone impressed him: the British vice consul in Sandburg's Chicago had been 'common'. Morris was effectively still a foreign correspondent in Eisenhower's America, but he was not covering the day's hard news. He was creating a panorama through observational minutiae.

After Wisconsin, St Louis, Kansas and DC, he was on the wharf in New York to meet the family off the Cunarder *Franconia*. They had had an appalling journey. Mark had a throat infection, Henry had whooping cough and Elizabeth was seasick. After they had disembarked, she wrote in her diary, 'The doctor in New York said that in another twelve hours Henry would have been dead.' But she rose above it, as she always did, and immersed herself in the spangled excitements of America. 'It was marvellous to be in New York after such a terrible journey,' she recorded in her diary after watching ice-skaters at Rockefeller Center. Overall the city was 'more magnificent and exciting than I could have hoped'. After a screening of the Everest film on New Year's Eve at the Fine Arts Theater on 58th Street, to inaugurate 1954 they drove to New Jersey, where they had rented a wooden row house in Cranbury as a base for the first three months. Morris's portrait of Cranbury, with children skating on the pond and weatherboard houses shining in the moonlight, could have been painted in 1854, or 1754, except for evidence of startling technological advancement like 'devices that change the TV channel by a radio impulse from your armchair'. A delighted Elizabeth wrote, 'I can't get rid of the feeling that it is not quite real.' She disliked the village doctor after he prescribed Mark Coca-Cola, but took to pizza, 'a wonderful dish' which she hoped to eat again. 'I still can't get over the fact that Americans seem to live on tins and frozen foods,' she recorded. 'They even buy orange juice canned.' When they left the boys with a babysitter, aspects of their journeys were novelties for them both. 'Some motels', Morris reported, 'provide coffee for the early traveller. It comes in powdered form in a little cardboard cup, together with sugar, milk powder and a cardboard spoon . . . you have only to add hot water (from the tap).' Touring in Connecticut, the Morrises observed Mamie Eisenhower launching the first nuclear submarine, and drove over to Princeton to see their friend Al Alvarez, who had a Procter Fellowship; he was still in his twenties, like them (Elizabeth turned thirty that year).* Alvarez had gone up to Oxford the same year as James. He went on to become a poet, critic and mountaineer, and in his autobiography revealed that while a student he had lost his virginity to the wife of another undergraduate who lived in a thatched cottage in a village outside Oxford. The relationship had tailed off after they left university (Alvarez recorded), as his unnamed lover began writing too much about her husband's achievements.

Hillary and some of the other climbers began a lecture tour across North America in February, and Morris joined them. His contract with 'the Thunderer' did not allow him to earn income from public speaking on *Times*-sponsored activities, but he was permitted to perform as a warm-up act and receive expenses. 'We have been staying at the Waldorf Astoria for the past five days on the first lap of their lecture tour,' Elizabeth wrote to Aunt Betty in Paignton. 'What an exciting time we have had.' The mountaineers went on to the White House, where Eisenhower mistook Hunt for Hillary, but Hollywood at least doted on them. Walt Disney, Morris wrote, 'went to great trouble explaining to me how his cartoon chipmunks conversed' (sound men played the tape backwards, very fast, at least according to Morris). Lyle R. Wheeler, the Oscar-winning art director of *Gone with the Wind*, then the most profitable movie ever made, took him to play bingo. Wheeler won a dollar and was thrilled. Beverly Hills, 'a caricature of a stockbrokers' suburb', yielded, in Morris's *Times* turnover, the first published instance of his dislike of financial men – he forgot that his maternal grandfather was a bank manager.

Ike was not Morris's last president that year. In the Midwest he chatted with Eisenhower's predecessor, Harry Truman, as 'the Haberdasher' sat at his desk in the town of Independence sorting material for deposition

---

* For the previous six months Alvarez had lived across the corridor at Princeton from V. S. Pritchett, the visiting Gauss lecturer. Born in 1900, Pritchett, known as VSP, had emerged during the Second World War as Britain's leading man of letters; over the course of the hostilities he had broadcast more than eighty morale-boosting talks for the BBC. He and Morris were to cross paths at one remove several times more.

in his Presidential Library ('"It's a lot of work," says Mr Truman in his flat Missouri voice'), spinning a globe as he reflected on the foreign affairs over which he had presided. (It was only two years since he had met Churchill to discuss the unravelling situation in the Middle East and his advisers had read Morris's dispatches.) In June it was 103°F in the shade in Vicksburg and black beetles infested the Morrises' rented apartment. Sometimes James had to find his own copy: travel writers, like reporters, cannot sit around waiting for things to happen, in case they never do. He visited local newspaper offices to interview the editor (who was usually also the typesetter and general factotum) and even wrote a piece himself about the Kentucky Derby for the *Louisville Courier-Journal*, regrettably misnaming the winning horse. Curious about Elizabeth's unusual maiden name, Tuckniss, he leafed through telephone directories to find relatives; he never discovered any, but while engaged in the task Morris realised that, in a land of immigrants, names yield clues. Thus, in American hotel rooms kippered with the smoke of the 1950s, Morris forged a habit of trawling phone books. He admired the immigrant's ability to blend in. 'The melting pot has done its work, and is cooling . . . there emerges the familiar figure of *homo Americanus*.' He had found Walt Whitman's 'teeming nation of nations', and he liked it. Their friend Alvarez said, 'America changed my life.' By the time Morris had motored through all forty-eight states, it had changed his too.

Norman had written to say a piece he had filed on New York was 'absolutely brilliant'. Morris's Everest fame, to the world at large, lay in the feat of getting the story home, but his colleagues at *The Times* recognised other abilities. He wrote with clarity and authority, and applied a sheen of humour. His masters did not want to lose him to an American paper, and on his twenty-eighth birthday Morris opened a letter from McDonald offering him the position of Cairo correspondent, his salary to include the colonial bonus. The foreign editor proposed he return to the London office for four months before Cairo 'so we can get to know one another again'. The whole family would then move to Egypt. In the meantime, Morris was still trying to persuade *The Times* to let him write his Everest book. To outfox them he concocted a plan whereby Eric Shipton would appear as the main author of a lavishly illustrated *Times Book of Everest* – Shipton had agreed in principle and again Morris sent a proposal to publishers. But *The Times* was not to be outfoxed.

Everyone wanted this unwritten Everest book, however. Charles Monteith was one. On the strength of the mountain dispatches, before Christmas he had approached Morris from the prestigious publishing firm Faber & Faber. An Ulsterman and – the supreme intellectual accolade – a fellow of Oxford's All Souls graduate-only college, Monteith, who had been with the firm just three months, had been hired in part to reduce the workload of director T. S. Eliot (who really was a bank manager, albeit one who had won the Nobel Prize in Literature). He had immediately embarked on the pursuit of authors. When Morris, already in America, replied to the Faber office in Russell Square revealing the *Times*'s no-book rule, Monteith himself tried to persuade the paper to relent. Having found out there was 'no hope', he wrote to Morris again: 'All I can add is that if you plan to write any other book – possibly about your present trip to the US – we should be very grateful indeed if you would give us the opportunity to consider it.' After Cranbury, the Morrises had settled in Lake Forest, a North Shore suburb on Lake Michigan, and Morris read Monteith's letter standing in the kitchen with a cup of Maxwell House in his hand. The moment set the pattern for his whole professional life. He could recycle all his American material by turning his Commonwealth Fund report into a book, and he could also incorporate the features he had sent back to *The Times*. He hurried to the dining room table to reply once more to Monteith: 'I don't know if you were really serious about the thing, but I am in fact planning to write a travel book about my American journey.' *The Times* agreed to the plan, on condition that Morris finish the book before starting in Cairo. So it was Everest that brought Morris his first publishing contract. If Hillary and Tenzing hadn't taken the last few steps, if the bicycling radio operator had cracked the code, if Izzard had triumphed – there might never have been any Morris books at all.

Monteith had recently engaged with another aspiring writer – a teacher in Salisbury – and succeeded in bringing him too into the fold after initial difficulties. Nobody had wanted to publish *Strangers from Within*, at Faber or anywhere else. ('Rubbish & dull. Pointless,' the Faber reader scrawled on the author's handwritten submission letter.) The rookie Monteith had seen something in William Golding's typescript, and had written to suggest a title change: why not call it *Lord of the Flies*?

On 12 November the family boarded the SS *United States* for Liverpool. Morris, who still loved big ships, recalled, 'I wanted to be lean, fast and raffish, like her.' What had he made of the country, as opposed to the eponymous ship? First, he had found Southern attitudes 'profoundly disconcerting'. He was in Atlanta the day after the Supreme Court decreed racial segregation illegal in schools in *Brown* v. *Board of Education*, and heard 'abuse so theatrical and so repetitive that I could scarcely believe it had not been plucked wholesale from some common phrasebook of prejudice'. Besides the monsters, 'other, gentler Atlantans . . . drugged by the sentimentality of the Old South, would say, like sanctimonious jailers . . . "Leave it all to us. *The South takes care of its own.*"' Second, he who knew Cairo was shocked at the endemic corruption in public office in Chicago. It had brought grit to the prose of Morris's turnovers and would do the same for the book that became *Coast to Coast*. Both of these characteristics – racism and corruption – saved Morris from idealisation, along with 'the whole performance' of the McCarthy hearings: from April until June every bar, diner and hotel lounge had televised 'that unlovely politician . . . [as he] stalked the land ruining reputations and demeaning the Constitution . . . New as I was to the scene, I was dismayed by this spectacle . . . the same ugly faces, the same baffled victims and alas, so far as I could see, the same public apathy.' A confounding fourth issue had presented itself in the business of what he called cultural Americanisation. While Morris had seen much to praise in the emerging *homo Americanus*, he noticed that everywhere was starting to look like everywhere else. 'The

American Way is winning,' he observed, referring to the homogeneity of which he was soon to become suspicious as it crept across the planet. In continental Europe, resentment over America's role in the war had already transferred to fear over its encroaching cultural hegemony. On 29 March 1950 *Le Monde* had announced, 'Coca-Cola is the Danzig of European culture.' (A few years earlier, war had virtually broken out over control of the Free City of Danzig on the Baltic.) Arguments had stormed to and fro in France over whether the country should allow the Coca-Cola Company to invest; the drink was, according to the president of the firm, bottled 'essence of capitalism' (which was supposed to be a good thing). As a reporter, Morris would have to engage in issues of post-war economic politics and market liberalisation, many towing in their wake similar concerns over national pride and national identity.

There was much to dislike, but Morris, just twenty-seven when he arrived in the US, was armed with the hope of youth. He applauded the nation's economic prosperity and efficiency. America was more productive than Europe in those post-war years — it was notably better at growing food and at making things. Morris saw much that could be learned, and went on to express frustration at the reluctance of Britons to learn it.

They celebrated the New Year in London, a city still permeated by what another army intelligence man, Dennis Potter (born in 1935 in the Welsh Marches), remembered as 'the great greyness'. A modest tide of affluence had at least eliminated grey bread, and with 'Rock Around the Clock' in the charts, it seemed popular culture might begin to infiltrate the other kinds of culture. (Potter's television dramas were to embody the phenomenon.) Both Morrises noticed that young British men were starting to look different from their fathers for the first time. America had followed them back too: they shopped in supermarkets now. The first had opened in 1948, in East London, but within a decade Britain had more than five hundred.

They found the wider family thriving. Gareth had already established himself as principal flautist of the Philharmonia Orchestra (a post he was to hold for twenty-four years), and he had started even earlier as professor of flute at his alma mater the Royal Academy of Music (a role he held for forty years). The distinctive sound of his wooden flute was often heard on the BBC airways. It turned out that James had not been the only Morris to contribute to the coronation: Gareth had been fluting in the orchestra positioned above the screen in the Abbey. Years afterwards he remembered craning his neck over the edge of the organ loft to witness the exact moment when Archbishop Geoffrey Fisher placed the crown on the royal barnet.

James had little time, however, for family. He began the book about America on New Year's Day – he had Morris graft as well as Payne panache. Like Kinglake, he wanted to paint a picture of light and shade, as he had seen the good and the bad of the US, or some of it. In February he sent Monteith a specimen chapter, and back came an offer: £100 on delivery of an acceptable typescript (about £2,000 today). Morris was to have his hard covers before he turned thirty, and with the most distinguished publisher in London. Meanwhile, there was the office. What had changed at *The Times*? Square-jawed Haley had reorganised the foreign department since appointing McDonald to the post of foreign editor. Stalin's death while Morris was preparing to struggle with his typewriter carriage in Himalayan winds had quickly led to what Churchill called 'the supreme event' – a release of Cold War tensions. When the Thunderer, which was supposed to be supporting East–West detente, gave Morris the role of diplomatic correspondent for two months, he rushed around interviewing ambassadors and writing confidential reports on topics from Formosa to disarmament.

In March 1955 the whole family decamped to Cairo, where, to Elizabeth's delight, they were able to reoccupy *dahabiyeh Saphir* on Gezira. Morris set up his workroom in the former wheelhouse. It had wraparound windows and the sun had blistered the paint, but Morris always remembered it as 'the most glamorous room, the most suggestive and the most unforgettable that I've ever occupied'. It was soon crowded with maps, telephones, official handouts and stacks of newspapers, cables from head office pinned to the wall 'if laudatory, crumpled under the table if not'. He had a couple of hundred books shipped out, a library 'which represented, so to speak, the state of my mind so far'. Reflections of the Nile rippled on the ceiling and a radiogram beside the door played Mozart, accompanying the chanting of a blind Koran singer who sat in a chair on the bank all day. When a felucca passed, Morris, bent over his new Olivetti, could hear 'the grunts and phlegmatic coughing of the crews. And sometimes I looked up to see a prickly face grinning back at me through my window only a few feet away.' Abdu, the Sudanese steward, would appear at the door with a silver coffee pot on a silver tray, a jug of buffalo milk and a plate of Playbox biscuits; the new cook smoked his hashish hubble-bubble in the privacy of the rope locker; Idris, the aged deckhand, who wore a long brown jellabiya topped in cold weather with a navy maritime sweater, shifted the moorings according to the seasonal rise and fall of the Nile, 'which sometimes raised my room high above the street and its trees, and sometimes left us cowering in the lee of the bank'. Two cats became central to family life – the animals were to be fixtures in all of Morris's homes, as well as in his and then her imagination – and when one fell into the Nile, Abdu dived in to rescue it.

What had changed in Cairo? King Farouk, still an ass, was out of the picture, and of Egypt. Three months after Morris had left to meet baby Mark at Heathrow, the Naguib–Nasser coup, also known as the Free Officers' coup, had brought the government down at last. Gamal Abdel Nasser had got the upper hand and was delivering anti-British speeches, but Her Majesty's ambassador still drove through the capital with an escort of whistle-peeping motorcyclists. A building boom was in progress, and the thrum of pile-driving machinery added to the symphonic Cairene mix. Much, however, remained the same – the teetering donkey carts, the morning visit to the embassy, lunch at the Mohamed Aly Club. Morris loved Cairo even more than before, embracing the contradictions Kinglake had expressed in the first sentence of *Eothen*: 'The din of a busy world still vexed and cheered me.' Friends they made together included

Ian Skeet, an Arabist and the PR man for Shell. Morris was not fond of horse riding but Elizabeth was, so she began to ride in Giza with Skeet. Guests came to visit, and myths started to accrete around the *dahabiyeh* like its barnacles. Not only was Monty involved: Morris told everyone *Saphir* had borne Kitchener to Khartoum.

He rented an office within the Arab News Agency building and began his first regional tour by air, starting in Amman at the wedding of King Hussein. After the First World War, Britain had sponsored the creation of the Hashemite monarchy, of which the young Hussein, just out of Sandhurst, was a representative. The matrimonials, Morris reported, were 'almost the last demonstration of the hybrid sense of ceremony which had been born out of Turko-Arab tradition by British imperialism'. In the receiving line, King Faisal II of Iraq stood next to the groom, his cousin and childhood playmate, both of them in ill-fitting dark suits. Morris wrote of 'Circassians in long black cloaks, astrakhan hats, high boots . . . lancers in scarlet tunics and white breeches . . . When the Queen Mother of Jordan arrived a sibilant Arabic whisper rippled through the hall: for the first time, she was appearing in public with no veil above her sumptuous silk gown.'

He went on to Habbaniyah in Faisal's Iraq to file on the farewell parade of the Assyrian Levies, the first military force the British had established when they had taken control of the country. The Royal Air Force was handing its bases over to the Iraqis 'and the Assyrians were left to look after themselves . . . they marched away to oblivion to a martial arrangement of "Old Folks at Home".' Besides 'multiple rivalries which were themselves innumerably subdivided', he had to engage with negotiations over the Suez Canal Treaty, which was up for renewal the following year. Half of Europe's oil flowed through the Canal. Espionage played a vital role in these unfolding dramas in the Middle East. The headquarters of SIME had moved to Cyprus, but 'diplomats and countless intelligence agents swarmed around the region', Morris wrote, and he kept up with them: John Slade-Baker, *Sunday Times* correspondent and MI6 spook, recorded in his diary that he enjoyed dining on *Saphir*.

In August Morris had to investigate a mutiny in Sudan, leaving a stringer to hold the Cairo fort and joining forces with Izzard, still wearing out his tennis shoes for the *Mail*. Their accommodation on the Khartoum waterfront was 'still very much a tea-and-biscuits hotel', English cars patrolled the streets and a two-shilling coin stamped with George VI's head was legal tender. Back in Cairo, and later than agreed, Morris finished the American book on 2 July. It had taken six months, and during that period he had held down a full-time job and changed countries. But he had also found a method, setting a target of twelve pages a day (double-spaced).* He had given the typescript the appalling title *America, Thou Half-Brother* (taken from a nineteenth-century poem). Monteith retaliated with *Over There*. They compromised on *Coast to Coast*. Pantheon, who had bought the American rights, called their edition *As I Saw the USA*.

Two months after finishing *Coast to Coast*, Morris began an Everest book in his sweltering cabin. *The Times* had not yet relented, but the other climbers were getting books out and Morris was so furious to be left lagging that he started anyway – he was the writer of the group, after all. Schoolmaster Wilf Noyce (RADIATOR) had sent his volume with a personal note: 'I hope you will like it, a memory of a good time.' Morris appears in Noyce's book in Chaucerian garb as 'a very parfit gentle journalist'. In the autumn he broke off for a visit to Israel, taking Elizabeth with him. 'We had a simply wonderful week's holiday in Jerusalem,' she told Norman. (She was on the warmest of terms with him, as she was with all her husband's employers.) 'We also went up to Baalbek – goodness what a place. Apart from the ruins, the setting is so superb.' Stewart Perowne showed them round; he was *The Times*'s Jerusalem stringer. A friend of both Morrises, Perowne was an archaeologist, historian, unsuccessful colonial official, writer and Arabic

---

* Some years later, Morris's target was 2,000 words per day, more like eight double-spaced pages. Both were ambitious goals. Graham Greene aimed for two pages (500 words) a day, as did Hemingway; Balzac achieved ten times that rate. Stephen King's goal is 2,000 words, the same as Morris's, and Maya Angelou's was 2,500.

speaker, as well as a witty and waspish man of deep learning. Though a bachelor of the confirmed variety, he had married another explorer, the writer Freya Stark – Morris had bought her book *Baghdad Sketches* actually in Baghdad that very year. The union had been dissolved some years earlier.

If there is a dominant theme to the stories Morris filed during this period, it is the upswelling of American influence. The Great Powers had left 'a crippling backlog of grievances', and the US, 'that noble amateur of Middle Eastern diplomacy, had turned professional'. Truth was in plain sight: 'Coca-Colonization' had replaced the Pax Britannica. In 1938 the American share in Middle Eastern oil production had been 13 per cent compared with Britain's 30 per cent. By 1956 the split was 65:30 in US favour. The oil business was transforming the region itself. 'The air of get-rich-quick to every corner' of 'brash and noisy' Kuwait, according to Morris, exemplified 'a change of values as complete and as significant as any contemporary social transition, even including the metamorphosis of Communism'. The eleventh ruler of the Kuwaiti sheikhdom (not yet an emir, though the same man became one upon independence in 1961) had a yacht, a gift of the oilmen, with 'a throne-room of elaborate magnificence' and a sheep pen on the upper deck.

Towards the end of November, Morris set off on a journey so secret that he had to conceal it from Elizabeth – she pieced together his movements from dispatches in the paper. He was to travel a thousand miles across roadless Muscat and Oman in the company of Sultan Said bin Taimur on a mission partly funded by the Iraq Petroleum Company. The Foreign Office resident in the Gulf, married to a co-proprietor of *The Times*, had arranged exclusive access for the paper – it was to be an Arabian Everest. Two *Times* men were in the party: one departing from Fahud, the other, Morris, with the sultan himself from Salalah; they would meet in Nizwa, the ancient capital. The purpose of the double-headed assault was the subjugation of one of the sultan's rivals, an imam in the interior. (This inland region represented the 'Oman' part of the two-pronged name of the nation.) The imam cherished 'separatist ambitions', allegedly encouraged by Saudi arms. But, as Morris acknowledged, the whole caper was 'concerned essentially with oil'.

Morris insisted that he had no support from the Foreign Office for the operation codenamed GRAND DESIGN. But he had plentiful access, and the British government was heavily involved. Muscat and Oman was part of the informal Empire; as Morris put it, Whitehall 'protected the Sultan's domains for him and largely handled his foreign affairs'. Britain was 'still the basic power in south-east Arabia', controlling seven of the desert sheikhdoms, including the peaceful fishing village of Dubai. The British-backed paramilitary group Trucial Oman Levies had expelled Saudi forces from Buraimi only three months before Morris flew in. (Shifting loyalties, along with suspicions, were endemic. Morris's colleague from the 9th, Otto Thwaites, had commanded the Levies and was investigating a dispute in Buraimi in 1952 when one of his men murdered him.) Britain's reduced oil holdings meant it was vital to maintain puppet-master status over the coastal sheikdoms. Morris knew – everyone knew – that his own nation's grip on the strings was loosening ('a certain niggling timidity and mediocrity' was creeping over 'our British policies'). This journey to the interior, and the years in the Middle East overall, were an incubator for Morris's project to ponder 'the huge antique mosaic of imperialism'.

Morris's group, pioneering a route skirting south of the Rub' al-Khali, or Empty Quarter, travelled in a convoy of seven American Dodge trucks painted red, with Black indentured labourers wearing blue jerseys hanging on to the rear. 'The soft scent of frankincense' drifted around the sultan's tent at nightfall and in the small towns goldsmiths worked in dim-lit, open-fronted shops. 'The sultanate of Muscat and Oman', Morris wrote, 'was a truly medieval Islamic state.' Bondsmen set his typewriter on a carpet in his tent each evening, and in the morning, after a plate of goat kidneys, he shaved in the wing mirror of his truck, the tin basin filled from bulging goatskin waterbags. The forty-four-year-old, luxuriantly bearded bin Taimur, a foot shorter than his exotic foreign guest, was unfailingly polite, to Morris if not to his slaves. Morris wrote of his 'antique paternalism', a phrase straight out of Doughty, though paternalism was even more antique now that trucks were rolling into the desert.

As for the other *Times* man on the job, his name was Peter Fleming. Although allegedly neither was aware of the other's plans, they were, the actually fully briefed Fleming claimed, 'like two ends of a pantomime horse'. Nineteen years Morris's senior and another Christ Church man (he had got the first Stewart had thought Morris deserved), Fleming had shot into literary skies as a precocious star in 1933 with his book *Brazilian Adventure*, the first of several travel volumes. ('Well, we've been on a journey with Fleming in China,' Auden wrote after *To Peking* came out, 'and now we're real travellers for ever and ever.') He cemented his image with marriage to the actress Celia Johnson. In the war, Fleming had been in intelligence at such a high level that he had been cleared for access to the decrypts from Bletchley Park, information known as ULTRA. His star then fell as his brother Ian's rose (the first Bond novel, *Casino Royale*, had appeared two years before the Omani journey), but Peter was the better writer. After the hostilities, he maintained his undercover role behind a desk at *The Times*. According to a colleague, 'He went into the office in well-cut tweeds, pipe clamped in jaw, to sit at "Colonel Fleming's table" in a lobby outside the Intelligence Department to write his gently witty Fourth leaders. He would then motor back to Oxfordshire in the old Rolls-Royce he had converted to an estate car and which, he would say, had room for a stag in the back.' Fleming dwelled in the shadow world of the Secret Intelligence Service (MI6) and journalism – Greene's 'old firm'. In Oman he wore a red turban. Morris told Elizabeth, 'He is such fun; in fact I think the most consistently funny man I have ever met.' At Eton, Fleming had been '[o]ne of the great almighty tremendous ones', according to a contemporary. But when Duff Hart-Davis's biography came out, Morris was the only reviewer to suggest there was nothing behind Fleming's glittering surface: 'it was almost as if he had a secret, assiduously disguised in humour'. She – it was 1974 – noted in the review that Fleming recorded his first in *Who's Who*. Readers who had worked with the colonel wrote to Morris to agree. In short, whether he was fun or not, Morris didn't fall for the Fleming myth.

The sultan's minister of external affairs, Neil McLeod Innes, a balding stalwart of the Colonial Service, accompanied Morris on his leg of the journey. At the end, after a triumphant Field Force parade in Nizwa, McLeod Innes and Morris sat typing at fold-out tables outside their respective tents. The sky was striated like bacon, as it often is over Nizwa, and late-afternoon rays varnished the crown of the minister's head. Morris courteously asked him if he would like to read the report he was about to send. McLeod Innes revealed that Fleming and Morris were anyway obliged to show him their copy before filing: it was part of the exclusivity deal. When Morris irritably showed him the dispatch (it was one thing to do it out of politesse, entirely another to be compelled), the minister asked him to change the word 'slaves', as Morris had called the bondsmen in blue hanging from the trucks. It wouldn't do for the British Empire to be involved with a slave-owning nation. Morris reluctantly agreed to cast the men as 'retainers', while pointing out that they *were* slaves. Journalists always said that they knew they were onto something when Foreign Office figures warned them off it.

The imam was apparently pacified, temporarily at least. As the expedition came to a close, the sheikh of Abu Dhabi 'roared' up to the sultan's convoy in a yellow Cadillac and got out to profess fraternal allegiance. Sitting in his steamer cabin on the way to Bahrain, the Gulf sparkling outside, Morris wondered 'how cordial their smiles would be if all this testy frontier region became the centre of a vast oilfield'. Back at the office, Norman wrote to thank a Mr Parks at the Iraq Petroleum Company. (The sultan had granted the firm a seventy-five-year concession.) 'Colonel Fleming has told me how much he and Mr James Morris have owed to your constant and unstinting assistance . . . I'm writing to express on behalf of *The Times* my very sincere, very warm thanks.' Norman sniffed an opportunity. 'We should naturally be very interested to know when your borings strike oil, as we hope they will.' He went on to suggest 'a simple code'. (They were mad for codes at Printing

House Square now.) For example, Norman continued, '"We have struck oil on May the 27th at a depth of 273 feet" would be, "met Simpkins, May the 27th at Birmingham, Gloucester, Cheltenham."' Meanwhile, Morris's salary rose to £1,300 a year (approximately £30,000 in 2026) plus a generous £4-a-day cost-of-living allowance. For intelligence on what had become his beat, he continued to cultivate the political advisers keeping the Empire alive on the Arabian Peninsula. The current crop included Hugh Boustead, a distinguished former soldier and a member of the 1933 British Everest expedition; when Morris visited him in Mukhalla, Boustead used to blow a silver whistle at breakfast to summon in a servant with more haddock. As Morris was skirting the Empty Quarter with his sultan, Boustead, then resident adviser in the Hadhramaut down the coast, was overseeing territory which ran for many hundreds of miles alongside it. He went on to work as development secretary in Muscat and Oman, finding the sultan opposed to development of any kind. ('That is why you lost India,' bin Taimur told Boustead when he tried to introduce schooling. 'Because you educated the people.')

After the Omani adventure, Morris hurried back to Cairo and set about finishing *Coronation Everest*. *The Times* had finally allowed it, along with *Coast to Coast*, but only as special exceptions to the rule. Since his triumph on the mountain, publishers had regularly approached Morris with ideas, and Norman was embarrassed when he had to forward their imploring missives, as 'this of course his contract does not allow'. According to a colleague, in the spring of 1955 Morris was 'resolved to hold out for permission to publish a book a year', which was quite the target for a writer with a full-time job and two tiny children, and who had not yet published a single volume. But he was determined, and Monteith was patient. (He was also waiting for Samuel Beckett to deliver the Faber version of *Godot* that year.) Now, six days after receiving the *Everest* typescript, the editor sent Morris 'a thousand congratulations' and offered an advance of £150.

Tom Pocock of the *Daily Express* hunted with the Middle East pack. He had visited *Saphir* and met James's 'beautiful wife'. Pocock wrote,

'The family had made themselves at home with the nonchalance the educated British had often shown in exotic places, yet the charming, clever and amusing James whose idyllic domesticity I, a bachelor, envied so much, still seemed to be nursing some curious little secret.' Pocock may have been as perspicacious as he claimed. But Morris *was* actively exploring the possibilities of the procedure then called 'sex change'. In other words, while all this was going on – *all this* – he was looking to overturn his entire life. He spoke, later, of 'the mystic conviction that he was inhabiting the wrong body', and felt it getting stronger as his twenties progressed – taking hold. Everyone lives with secret desires, but it is hard to imagine what Morris went through in his private moments during those years. He is at his most human as he interrogates himself, knowing just how terrifying the consequences of self-fulfilment might be. He had drawn on reservoirs of courage in the Himalaya; courage of an entirely different nature was required now. But he went on; he found the courage. In 1956 he wrote to Roberta 'Betty' Cowell, the first known trans woman in Britain to have gender surgery. Morris enquired about her experience of transition, and where she had found doctors willing to operate. The press had fallen on Cowell's story, dwelling on her pre-transition exploits as a fighter pilot and prisoner of war, and journalists trundled it out whenever a man donned a frock. Morris had read *Roberta Cowell's Story by Herself* when it appeared in 1954; the book spoke to him, as it apparently spoke to many: one British GP claimed to have received 456 requests for vaginoplasty as a result of the publicity around Cowell. The memoir itself offers few insights into the author's inner life, and no information about practical routes to transition. It presents instead gender stereotypes that could have filled several episodes of a 1950s Monty Python. 'When my first soufflé was in the oven,' Cowell reports in a section on the reality of womanhood, 'I was tremendously thrilled to find out how it would emerge.' Morris, who discussed everything with Elizabeth, looked beyond kitchen excitements.

    Cowell's reply was as unhelpful as her book and Morris faced the first of many dead ends. But at least he knew others had felt what he felt, and that they had discovered a medical solution. Cowell was not the only proof. As he was heading to the Canal Zone four years earlier, Morris had read many pages of breaking news concerning Christine Jorgensen's gender reassignment. Four months older than Morris, Jorgensen had been born a boy in the Bronx. Following clerical duties as a GI, the twenty-five-year-old had travelled to the Gentofte Hospital in Copenhagen (the family was of Danish descent) to undergo two operations. The second procedure, thirteen months after the first, was a penectomy. (When she wrote to tell her parents, they cabled: *WE LOVE YOU MORE THAN EVER.*) Jorgensen was recovering in hospital when a nurse brought her a telegram reporting a headline in that day's *New York Daily News*: 'BRONX GI BECOMES A WOMAN'. Soon the papers wanted to know whose shirts she wore (actually they asked whether she favoured pyjamas or a nightgown) and the story edged Jonas Salk and his polio vaccine off the front pages. By the spring of 1954 the US trade publication *Editor and Publisher* was reporting that Jorgensen had generated more newsprint during the previous year than any other individual – over one and a half million words. Future trans memoirists must have known they were to face the same obsessive public prurience.

After *American Weekly* flew Jorgensen home from Denmark in February 1953, she had a third operation in New Jersey using skin grafts taken from her thigh to construct a vaginal canal and external female genitalia. America seemed to think this was all new. In fact, German sexologist Magnus Hirschfeld, a pioneer in sex pathology, had been performing surgical and hormonal reassignment for more than twenty years at his Institute for Sexual Science in Berlin – Jorgensen noted that her doctors were familiar with dozens of Hirschfeld cases. But she was the first transsexual glamour symbol, and Morris knew all about her. He recognised much in her pages, notably, as he put it, the 'riddle' of the conviction, the absolute certainty, 'that I was born with the wrong body, being feminine by gender but masculine by sex'. He read the few other memoirs that had been written by trans people, 'and as I groped towards their [the authors'] presence . . . if they did not quite share my riddle, at least they would have understood it'.

He stored it all in some hermetic part of him, miraculously, and carried on working with brilliance, winning applause from all quarters: he had pulled off a wildly impressive feat by anyone's standards. In March he returned to Jerusalem, and Perowne. 'His [Morris's] article in last Tuesday's *Times* about Arab radio propaganda was quite brilliant,' Perowne gushed to Norman. 'I'd just been talking to our Embassy information man, and he had not one tenth of James' information. He seems to captivate everyone he meets, and to find out all there is to know by instinct.' The following month the pair were in Amman together, making fun of the *Telegraph* man, who had been one of the Kathmandu lurkers; it was all part of what Morris later called 'the perpetual theatre of the foreign correspondent's life'. While in Jordan, Morris analysed, across several pieces, King Hussein's dismissal of Glubb Pasha from his post as head of the Arab Legion. Norman wrote to say his coverage was 'first-rate, and put us in the forefront of newspapers in dealing with that matter'. Meanwhile, Selwyn Lloyd had made an official visit to Egypt. Morris told Norman,

> I was extremely depressed by the deportment of the Foreign Secretary when he was in Cairo the other day. He neither pleased, amused, frightened, impressed, invigorated, mollified or reassured anybody, but merely left us all with a sense of baffled irritation. If we can't do better than that, we deserve all we're getting. I'd rather have Nasser!

When Lloyd had sloped home to be useless at the Foreign Office in King Charles Street, Morris unwrapped a copy of *Coast to Coast* on the burning foredeck of *Saphir*, 'its handsome dust jacket glinting in the sun'. No writer forgets that moment.

Morris now had proof that he could produce sustained prose a hundred times longer than a *Times* turnover. There was more of him in the paragraphs between hard covers, and the vocabulary was fruitier.

'Pungent' appears three times in the first sixty pages: the word appealed to the author's sense of secret meanings beneath surface appearances. *Coast to Coast* does usefully deploy the techniques of reportage – direct speech, for example, the yeast that makes the dough rise. Morris understood – again, instinctively – that a writer aiming to be popular loses ground if a dictionary comes into it. He never wanted readers to think he was cleverer than they were; he just wished (the prose suggests) to share the journey like a kind of Everyman. So he addresses his audience directly, creating the illusion that he is taking them into his confidence. 'And if, one summer night, you stroll alone through the city [DC] after a mellowing dinner . . . Jefferson in your head and Chesapeake prawns in your belly, then I defy you to resist the magic of the American experiment, or evade its ever noble pathos.' He looks forwards in these pages, whereas in almost every other book, across a stupendously vast output, he aims at 'projecting my view of today into an evocation of yesterday'. But one sees the signature style forming in *Coast to Coast*. He refers at one point to 'the American strain of historical romanticism', and it was something he made his own; the pages shimmer a bit, like Doughty. Above all, the volume brims with youthful liveliness, even if, like most first books, it is uneven. 'Hawaiians', it turns out, 'seem to me the very sweetest of people, even if they did eat Captain Cook.'

Reviews were favourable on both sides of the Atlantic. *Coast to Coast* won the Café Royal Prize and was runner-up for the John Llewellyn Rhys Prize – a huge achievement for a rookie author. Meanwhile, Morris had already started his third book, about the sultan journey, and had written to *The Times* asking for permission to use material he had gathered while in their employ. Then he had to rush off to the Sudan again. When he got back he opened a letter from the paper's manager, Francis Mathew: 'No. With best wishes to you and your wife.'

On 13 April 1956, he resigned. He told McDonald, 'I'd much rather stay with the paper, but absolutely and irrevocably not on terms which limit my description of a six-week journey across virgin territory with a sultan, five sheikhs and a *wali* [a sort of holy man] to 2000 words on the Foreign page.' Finding an audience had set the course of his life. He wrote to Norman, 'I don't know yet what I shall do instead . . . I might try spending a year doing some miscellaneous travelling and writing. Don't think me sentimental if I thank you for your very many kindnesses to me since we first met.' They appointed, to replace him, their Washington number two, Sunderland-born David Holden, who was a keen spy. Elizabeth enquired if Holden wanted either *Saphir* or her nanny ('I have the best nanny in Cairo and would like to pass her on'). Holden did not have children but he did want the boat. Later, when he did have children, Morris got to know him on their various foreign beats, and the pair turned into postcard friends.

On 23 June, Nasser became president. One of Morris's last pieces for *The Times* was an interview conducted in his family's 'modest Cairo house that was plain to the point of ugliness'. The interview was pleasant, the interviewee 'relaxed and friendly, in shirtsleeves, his vest showing between the buttons . . . he liked to call himself the first indigenous ruler of Egyptians since the Pharaohs'. The pair sipped thick camomile coffee from little cups edged with gilt-and-blue roses. 'The hours slipped smoothly by as he expanded his theories, the coffee cups came and went, until at last the President rose from the table, his sandals flip-flopping across the linoleum to see me to the door . . . and wave me goodbye into the night.'

Morris filed his final dispatch from Beirut. Nasser nationalised the Suez Canal two weeks later. There was talk of bombing Cairo. Elizabeth took the last flight out with the children and Mark got lost at the airport. It had been so hot on *Saphir* that one of the cats had burned its paws walking on deck.

6
1956–1958
NOT WHAT I AM

At the end of the wet summer of 1956, Morris met Charles Monteith in person for the first time. The Clean Air Act had just been passed, and Bloomsbury, where Faber had their office, seemed fresher already. Monteith had replaced T. S. Eliot on the Book Committee and besides Beckett was working at that time with poets Philip Larkin and Thom Gunn and playwright John Osborne. A trim figure who wore round spectacles, Monteith had just seen Osborne's smash hit *Look Back in Anger*, but he was anything but an Angry Young Man himself – he seemed to have been born middle-aged, although in fact he was only five years older than Morris. Three months before their meeting, Monteith had accepted a dinner invitation from Kenneth Halliwell and John (later Joe) Orton, free-spirited writers working jointly at that time, with whom he was in discussion. 'I never thought', Monteith recorded privately after a meal in their flat of rice and tinned sardines followed by rice and tinned golden syrup, 'human beings could live this way.' Much lay ahead in the unconventional-author department. He never did publish Orton, but he appears in the latter's *Between Us Girls* as Liz Monteith, a brothel madame. He wore pinstriped suits into the office and vanished every Friday afternoon to Paddington station, where he boarded the Oxford train in order to dine at All Souls. Eliot said Monteith had 'flair rather than taste', and in this regard he was an ideal editor for Morris.

James and Elizabeth had decided to winter in the French Alps, where he would write another book before taking a permanent job and she would do everything else. They had rented Chalet Sibel in Samoëns, among the pines of the Giffre Valley near the Swiss frontier, and they motored across with the boys in a 1936 Rolls-Royce 20/25. It was the first but not the last of Morris's Rollers. He loved cars as he loved the raffish SS *United States*: for their power and style. They symbolised the opposite of the costive bank manager puttering about in a Ford Popular or Hillman Minx. This first model still had the chauffeur's screen between front and rear seats (ideal for not hearing children). Before leaving, they drove it to Kent to stay with Johnnie and Isabel Kerr (pronounced 'Carr') in Otham. The two couples had met at Oxford, where Johnnie and James, among the few married undergraduates at Christ Church, had the same tutor. The great-grandson of the 7th Marquess of Lothian and, through a maternal line, great-great-grandson of the 5th, Johnnie was a committed Catholic, a prodigious reader, more or less a Liberal and, according to him, 'middle-aged since I was twenty' (rather like Monteith). The graceful and fine-featured Isabel had worked at Blenheim for the Secret Intelligence Service (MI6) during the war. She had stood as a godparent to Mark in Christ Church Cathedral, along with Bill Norman and the giant Martin Busk. The Kerrs had three small boys, bringing the small-boy total to five when the families got together at The Limes, the Kerr house in Otham. In the evenings that year, the adults settled down in amazement to take in blaring advertisements on commercial television – another US import.

Samoëns was a success for everyone. They skied, and the Kerrs came to visit. A miniature electric train ran up the valley in the middle of the road, whistling as it went, and neighbours brought the cows down as winter closed in – in warm farm kitchens you could hear bovine breathing in the next room. Morris collected his mail from the village bar as the postman enjoyed his mid-morning cognac. The Roller was a hit with officials. 'On the French side, the gendarmes were jolly, careless and often had wine on their breaths', and

> they were delightfully amused by this vehicle, and sometimes asked permission to sit at its wheel. To the Swiss border police, on the other hand, a Rolls-Royce was an image of wealth, and a quaint, middle-

aged example like mine ... seemed to confuse their responses. They habitually greeted us with a mixture of respect and condescension, covering all contingencies.

As for permanent jobs: the *Observer* offered him Delhi, the *News Chronicle* wanted him for Washington and the *Mail* would have employed him anywhere. Thrillingly, he was in talks with Hillary about a place on the Commonwealth Trans-Antarctic Expedition – he would have to complete a course at an army baking school in New Zealand so that he could double up as official scribe and bread-maker. This came to nothing, and anyway Antarctica did not in fact thrill Morris: too much landscape and not enough people (besides the fact that one can't imagine him up to his elbows in flour). He had opened negotiations with the *Manchester Guardian* off his own bat soon after resigning. Unlike the flourishing *Telegraph*, the *MG* was not then a threat to the circulation of *The Times*. (It sold under 200,000 but was attracting proportionately more readers year on year than the antique Thunderer.) Alastair Hetherington, editor-in-waiting, was enthusiastic: while the paper didn't have an opening 'immediately', something would surely come up soon. Thirty-six-year-old Hetherington had been a tank commander, a major in the Intelligence Corps and a Commonwealth Fund fellow. By October he had hired Morris, who was to start in the spring.

Meanwhile, on his thirtieth birthday, Morris started writing a book-length survey of the Middle East – his fourth, in writing order, and another stitched together from dispatches and notebooks. Monteith had offered £150 for the Oman book, which was finished (Peter Fleming had provided an introduction), and *Coast to Coast* was already earning royalties. Morris had permission to use material he had filed for *The Times*, and as cowbells tinkled he started cutting and pasting, settling down for a peaceful autumn.

Nasser had nationalised the Suez Canal on 26 July. Three months later, on 30 October, Israel invaded the Sinai Peninsula. Former foreign secretary Anthony Eden, prime minister of the United Kingdom for just over eighteen months, issued a joint ultimatum with his counterpart in France, ordering Egypt and Israel to cease fire and withdraw to a distance of ten miles from the Canal. Hetherington, not officially editor of the *Manchester Guardian* for another three days, wrote an uncompromising leader for 31 October which began 'The Anglo-French ultimatum to Egypt is an act of folly . . . it pours petrol on a growing fire.' Many papers supported military action; the *MG* and the *Observer* were outliers.* On 3 November, pandemonium descended on the House of Commons and thirty thousand protestors on Trafalgar Square. On the fourth, British and French allegedly peacekeeping troops embarked in Cyprus, itself soon to go up in flames as guerillas brought an end to British colonial rule, and pilots launched secret air attacks on the Sinai. Russian divisions were killing Hungarian hopes that day (one thousand Soviet tanks attacked Budapest before dawn), and Hungarians. On the fifth, Morris drove the Rolls to Geneva and boarded a plane for Tel Aviv. The paper had been caught without a correspondent in the region and he had hurriedly joined the staff three months early. While he was in the air, soldiers of the Parachute Regiment dropped out of it onto El Gamil airfield, while French paratroopers landed south of the Raswa Bridge and at Port Fuad.

'What do you think about James dashing off at a moment's notice?' Elizabeth asked Monteith. 'On reading the *Manchester Guardian*, I'm really rather ashamed he is writing for them, for his slogan is always "Act first and quickly, with good judgement" – the consequences can come later!' Elizabeth disliked criticism of British policy. 'From this distance, England divided horrifies me. Why can't the Englishman be loyal to the government, right or wrong?' On the morning of the sixth, the desperate chancellor of the exchequer, Harold Macmillan, telephoned Washington and asked for help – Britain's gold and dollar reserves were in full flight. The Americans would only support an

---

* The two papers were not then under the same ownership. They later were; now they aren't again.

International Monetary Fund loan if the British government agreed to a ceasefire before midnight. Economics decided it. Morris's brief was to observe the Israeli army in the field at the moment of its ambiguous victory. He started his first piece 'A rainbow appeared this afternoon here. Nobody seemed to see it but me.' He

> was struck by the vast numbers of Egyptian lorries, tanks and half-tracks disintegrated by the impact of napalm bombs. More often than not the bomb seemed to have struck them smack in the middle, pulverising everything combustible. It is possible that the Israelis themselves have supplies of napalm bombs, but it is said that most of this ghastly accuracy was the work of French fliers.

Censors in Tel Aviv would not let him file, so he flew to Cyprus (where nemesis was four months off). There, 'killing time while awaiting my flight back to Tel Aviv', he observed a line of Mystère fighter jets with French markings in a distant corner of Lydda airfield. The French paras ('seasoned in the Algerian war') talked gaily of attacking Egyptians in the Sinai, of flying cover over Israeli territory and of dropping supplies to Israeli paratroopers at Mitla Pass. 'They told me quite frankly that they had been in action in support of the Israelis during the Negev fighting, and had used napalm.' The French airmen had covered up the markings on their planes when they went into action. Morris had his proof. It was he who broke the story. On 20 November his dispatch led the front page, headlined 'FRENCH COLLUSION WITH ISRAEL'.

> French aircraft flown by French pilots in French uniform played an important, possibly even a decisive part in the recent Israeli offensive in the Sinai desert. Israeli censorship has stifled the startling fact, and General Moshe Dayan, the Israeli chief of staff, flatly denied it when questioned at a recent press conference. There is, however, no doubt at all that French fighters took part in the battle, and it is suggested that the accuracy of their napalm bombing was one of the most important factors in the rout of the Egyptian army.

French and Israeli ministries also denied Morris's dispatches. Fifty years after Suez, another *Guardian* editor, Alan Rusbridger, asked Morris how he (then) could have been so sure in the face of such widespread and blank denials. 'Well, I suppose I was perfectly convinced by what the men had told me, and also, I fear, I was prepared to take a gamble.' The whole campaign had been based, in Morris's words, on a 'Big Lie: the pretence that the British and French were seizing the Suez Canal in order to separate the Israelis and the Egyptians, when they were really seizing it with Israeli collusion in preparation for the overthrow of Nasser'. Everything Morris wrote was corroborated later, though the full details of the conspiracy took years to seep out. Eden and Macmillan's ludicrous plan unravelled, and nothing would ever be the same again. It was, Morris wrote, 'a sorry tale about second-rate people'.

This, then, was the new heroic age *The Times* had promised on Coronation Day. It was a small irony that Morris had 'always thought the government's action was right, and welcomed anything that weakened Nasser's position' – this privately to Hetherington. In her assessment of her husband's response to the crisis, based on his character, Elizabeth had been correct. The *Manchester Guardian* was too socially liberal for a man of his essentially conservative temperament.

He flew on from Cyprus in a Royal Air Force aircraft to Port Said, which the British had taken by force ('there are Union Jacks everywhere'), and filed from the quayside. 'The decline of Empires,' he wrote, 'the rise of the new Asia . . . all these portentous movements are suddenly illustrated with peculiar clarity among these shabby urban streets.' Nasser kept full control of the Canal. Eisenhower, who had been re-elected the day after the ceasefire, now knew Britain, his ally, had been lying for months about its plans in the Canal Zone. Former Hungarian prime minister Imre Nagy said, before the Soviets hanged him, that had it not been for the invasion of Egypt his country's uprising would have succeeded. The UN threatened oil sanctions. Cyprus, a Crown colony since 1925 and a key strategic ally, continued to make headlines, and its guerillas continued to humiliate Whitehall. Eden resigned as prime minister on 9 January.

After Suez, British people no longer deferred automatically to politicians. Morris had written of 'shameful . . . swift decline into deception', and there was no way back up. The conflict even damaged British relations with France: when the US and Britain between them forced France to withdraw from the Sinai, the German chancellor comforted the French prime minister with the words, 'Europe will be your revenge.' (And it was.) On 11 February that same year, Guy Burgess and Donald Maclean had resurfaced in Moscow to give statements to four British journalists. Everyone read about the two spooks in every paper – they were perceived to be upper class (they weren't) and trust in what came to be known as the 'elite' and 'the establishment' went anticlockwise down the public plughole. For Morris, it was time to look back, not forwards.

By the end of 1956, distrust of the hitherto impregnable ruling classes in Britain meant you could laugh at anything. The UK-supported action in Oman in which Otto Thwaites had perished emerged as 'The Nasty Affair at the Buraimi Oasis' in the popular BBC radio comedy *The Goon Show*. Sheikh Rattelland Roll led the rebels.

Morris returned to Samoëns after Suez, spotting the opportunity to jemmy in another book or two before rejoining the *MG* in March 1957. Ian Skeet visited – the Egyptian authorities had expelled Shell following the conflict – and he and Morris skied, played ping-pong with the boys, ate dates and drank chartreuse in the village bar. Snow did not fall until Christmas Day, 'and we woke up in the morning to find sledge tracks miraculously on the hill, and the great face of Mont Buet glistening with sheen'. But what to do next? The diplomat Sir Harold Caccia had tried to tempt Morris into following him to Washington, where he was about to become ambassador, as what would now be called a special adviser. But the Foreign Office was not for Morris. He had appreciated the culture of departmental trust that had existed until Burgess and Maclean were unmasked – it was what he had liked about the army – but that had gone. Furthermore, he wanted to make a mark beyond that rigid diplomatic society, in part at least to show he could rise above his bifurcated background. His son Mark says, 'The world of British class was central to my father's personality. His mother, the daughter of a bank manager, from an upper-middle-class family of important engineers, even upper-class ones, married into a tribe of house painters and labourers. My father had something to prove.' Work was the arena to prove it, and Morris had a vision of a future without newspaper deadlines and silly press conferences. He said later, 'I got tired of the whole racket of impending wars that I thought were rather masculine.'

The year before Suez, Harold Macmillan, then foreign secretary, had publicly exonerated Kim Philby. The spy was among those who did not admire Morris's interpretation of events in the Middle East, and he said so, but ideological differences did not put Morris off: the pair had met in Beirut when both were foreign correspondents, and Jan confessed later she had fallen for Philby, as so many had. Indeed, the traitor was a man 'I thought I could have loved'.

In June 1957 Supermac, now prime minister, invited Hetherington to Downing Street, steering him after lunch

> to a window seat, where we talked about the Persian Gulf. The ruler of Oman, faced with tribal turbulence which he believed was being backed from outside his territory, asked for British help. Macmillan said that he had sat up late the previous night reading James Morris's book *Sultan in Oman* [which had come out in March] . . . it had given him a sense of the country and its character which did not come from any official brief. That morning, therefore, he had ordered a dozen copies and sent them round to the chiefs of staff and the relevant ministers, suggesting that they read the book quickly.

Sultan in Oman has a unity, like a Greek tragedy. (It covers a week, not twenty-four hours, but projects a temporal unity.) In addition to close observation, rueful acknowledgements of links between past and present, and set pieces like the stupendous scene in Nizwa when the sultan receives 'Sheikhs innumerable and indescribable', Morris introduces an undertow of humour which is not yet whimsical. He had found his voice. Like Kinglake, and like the best travel writers between the wars (Waugh in particular), Morris positioned himself as a comic character, walking shoeless with his toes curled under in front of dignitaries so as not to reveal the holes in his socks. Ceremonial occasions have a *Carry On* flavour – every time the Nizwa cannon sounds, a bit of masonry falls off. But beyond the jokes, the book sounds a klaxon. Chapter four opens with a lengthy disquisition on what oil might bring. ('I had seen it all before, most depressingly at the sheikhdom of Kuwait, at the top of the Gulf, a place much more closely tied to British apron strings than Muscat was.') Morris had reported from Doha in the protectorate of Qatar ('an appalling hole'). 'The transition between values was hideous to watch,' he wrote in *Sultan*. Oil was liquidating the romance of the old Arabia for Britons of Morris's temperament.

Between hard covers he had put the word 'slaves' back in. Still, decades later academics called it out. One referred to *Sultan* as 'one of the more unctuous effusions of the imperial imagination'. It is true that the country Morris called 'a little backward paradise on the seashore' actually bounced along the bottom of all social indices (or would have done had they existed), even within the Peninsula. Morris might have found his voice but, again, he was not in tune with most *Manchester Guardian* journalists. Even the newspaper's official history acknowledges that 'he had a fine talent for choosing the words best calculated to annoy the conventional stereotype of the Left-leaning *Guardian* reader ... [the sultan in] *Sultan* has since been regarded by all progressive Arabists as a grotesque and insufferable tyrant'. Morris had barely registered the culture shift from *The Times* to the *MG*: he was too preoccupied with himself to bother much with what colleagues were doing or thinking.

In February 1957 the Morrises had moved back to England, initially staying with the Kerrs at The Limes. They were house-hunting, this time to buy. It was a miserable experience, and for three years they decamped from one rented property to another while Morris shuttled from one foreign assignment to another, maniacally sequestering himself in between to get the latest book off to Monteith. In May of the first spring at home, the *MG* sent him to South Africa to cover the treason trial: the previous year, the Security Police had arrested Nelson Mandela and 155 others, ostensibly enforcing the Suppression of Communism Act, and the court case was set to begin. 'Things seemed to be approaching a climax,' Morris reported, not just in the trial but in general, as the Nationalist government 'manned the barricades against history'. (He wrote this at the time, not with hindsight.) He didn't want to go, Elizabeth told Monteith, 'shrinking from the ordeal of tensions ahead. Who can blame him? We had enough of that in the Southern States.' But the paper led on the trial. This, by him, appeared on the front page on 25 May:

> In a wire compound inside the red-brick drill hall at Johannesburg, 156 men and women sat this morning in attitudes of cynical or buoyant resignation. Some were black, some were brown, some were white. One wore a vivid green, yellow and black blazer. Some read newspapers, some wrote letters, some appeared to be asleep.

He travelled when the court wasn't sitting, filing from Black townships and visiting a witch doctor in the Transkei. She told him he was shortly 'to enjoy a metamorphosis into being a witch doctor myself. "But don't be alarmed," she added kindly. "You'll stay white."' Elsewhere, on the veldt, something of the romance of the lonely Boer guarding his cattle lingered in his mind – he had a receptive imagination which allowed him to appreciate folk stories and legend. But only up to a point. While most myths embody a truth, Morris thought tribal eulogies to Boer history rivalled 'the dottiest ambitions of Welsh nationalism'. This latter was about the 'dottiest' idea he could conceive in 1957.

He had dropped the Middle East survey to race off to Suez, and that trip now provided a set-piece opening in which the author stands in the Sinai alongside a triumphant Israeli colonel. The centripetal force of the book returns to this November day: Suez turned the volume into a portrait from that fixed perspective. There is no narrative arc.

Arranging material geographically over nine principal territories, Morris selected stories both to evoke cultural landscapes and to reveal political realities: in an inn hosting poor Shia pilgrims in Iraq's Karbala, Morris 'clumped' up a winding staircase to the roof to gain a view of the tomb of Muhammad's grandson. In each of the open-doored rooms off the stairwell, a man bent in prayer. 'I shall never forget', Morris wrote, 'the detestation that overcame the faces of those merciless old men when they observed a Christian on the stairs.' He had honed his gift for narrative as a foreign correspondent – who can forget the flashing white teeth of young Israeli tank crews as they ate sandwiches on the sand while Mystère jets swept overhead, the fish with 'eyes of porcelain', or 'the Ovaltiney talk' of myopic 'semi-nationalists' who call themselves 'the Queen's Arabs'? He had found his title – *The Market of Seleukia* – in a Constantine Cavafy poem about divinity in depravity. The book came out in the same year as *Sultan*. *The Sunday Times* serialised it, and in the US, where it was called *Islam Inflamed*, the *New York Times* reviewer said it was 'one of the best books of literary journalism I have ever read'.

'Shuttered' had joined the favoured-word list, deployed both literally and metaphorically to express the opaque fastnesses of desert lands. It expressed something more too – the sense of something closed, or closing, that infused almost everything Morris wrote in this period as he grappled with the weakening role of the British; with an overweening US presence; and with the Soviets, poised to pounce. He instinctively reached for negative words to describe Empire: 'impoverished', 'dwindling hegemony', 'ageing jets' and 'second-rate warships'. The concept was gathering mass, like cumulonimbus.

By the end of 1957 the Morrises had been able to rent a house in Ickham in Kent, and stayed for more than a year, the longest time in one place in this peripatetic period. Friends there included Nancy Harmsworth, widow of the great-nephew of Alfred, press baron and 1st Viscount Northcliffe. When her daughter Gillian, known as Puff, got married, Mark and Henry were pages. While he was living in the village, Morris made a documentary for BBC television about it, writing the script and conducting all the interviews. It was the first of his many creations for the small screen. 'We dedicate this little film to all the inhabitants of the village, young and old, nice and nasty,' he says in the introduction, standing with his sleeves rolled up in front of a telephone box. Half of those inhabitants had never been out of England, and Mrs Holliday had never been to London. None of the five hundred supermarkets had chosen Ickham: in the film, white-jacketed, tie-wearing servers fetch goods from high shelves in the single shop. 'Is there any point in keeping Britain as a first-class power in the world?' Morris asks passers-by through an open window. The vicar shudders up in a Ford Popular, past a sheep perambulating in the main street. Mrs Harmsworth herself sits on a sofa with a dog, the latter looking suspiciously at the camera. She (the biped) doesn't like some of her neighbours and finds it 'a cramping kind of life' in the village. Pub pundits express misgivings about the feudal system and Morris comments, 'The tenants are catching up with the squire.'

As James came and went, Elizabeth grew close to Monteith's assistant, Rosemary Goad. Known in the office as Rose, she kept Elizabeth informed about publishing schedules while offering commentary on the vagaries of her own life, reporting with despair when she gained seven pounds in weight on holiday. The two women made up half the Morris–Monteith team. 'My Dear Rosemary,' Elizabeth wrote on 5 March 1958. 'Well, James just popped off to France asking them if they want the H bomb . . . he will only get a few days at home before dashing off to the West Indies for three weeks.' The French did want the bomb, and on the Caribbean trip Morris visited Jamaica, Trinidad, Barbados, St Vincent, Martinique and Puerto Rico. 'A marvellous way to earn a living!' he wrote on a postcard to Enid at Millstones, her house in Walberswick on the Suffolk coast, where she had moved to annoy a fresh set of neighbours with loud music. His last stop was New York, where he bought Elizabeth a Dior Trapeze dress, narrow at the top and very wide at the hem. 'I wore it at a large wedding in London,' Elizabeth reported to Goad. 'I am not so sure that I like all the men's heads to turn and I hear a lot of whispering going on among the women.' The unmarried

Rose was in love with Monteith, according to Faber staff. Although his interests lay elsewhere, he – they said – once proposed to her, but she turned him down. Both women led double lives, and both men.

Money was tight, and Morris began to ask Faber for an advance on his typescripts before he had finished them: besides *Market*, he had squeezed in a book on South Africa, and while he was in the West Indies, *Coronation Everest* came out in both the UK and the US. It was another largely cut-and-paste book, but Morris's sixty-thousand-word memoir is funnier than the other volumes that melted off the slopes of 1953; its wry jokes and playful tone depart also from the sardonic reportage of his own *Coast to Coast*. Describing his system for paying the porters, Morris repeats advice he was given: the men would only accept coin. He duly spent hours at the bank in Kathmandu filling sacks with blackened metal discs ordered by cable from London. 'Two porters had to be paid just to carry the cash,' he wrote, 'a system that surely violates some fundamental economic law.' He subordinated literal truth to art. The news of Henry's birth, which had reached him in the congratulatory PS from Hunt, breaks in the book in a volley of static over the radio. '"Your *sugsugsugsug*! Your *switchabubblebubble*! Your s-o-n." My *son*! So I had another son! I must make a note of that.' Peter Fleming, writing under his nom de plume Strix in the *Spectator*, said *Coronation Everest* was 'a very funny, very exciting book', assessing correctly that its author was 'with but not of Sir John Hunt's expedition'.

As he darted around the world, flying direct from the fish war in Iceland to the actual war in Algeria, Morris often crossed paths with the ludicrous Randolph Churchill, another foreign correspondent and Winston's son. The pair shared a chartered aircraft to Algeria. 'Halfway there,' Morris revealed, 'Randolph suddenly ordered the pilot to make for Malta instead, for reasons entirely of his own convenience. It was my last Churchillian straw, up with which I would not put.' When Churchill *père* was allegedly dying in Monte Carlo in 1958, the paper sent Morris to maintain a vigil outside the Villa La Pausa at Roquebrune-Cap-Martin along with the press corps of the entire world – or so it seemed. They were all desperate for copy, and not a word emanated from the sickroom. Morris spotted a page torn from a pornographic magazine fluttering on the street, and when other hacks pored over it he turned the event into a column. Churchill lived for a further seven years. (Morris was in bed with flu at the newly rebuilt Shepheard's in Cairo when the old man extinguished his last cigar. Egyptian staff came in to offer condolences.) Randolph was an idiot but most colleagues in the corps were congenial enough; in Paris, Morris always called at the Ritz, where correspondents gathered for a restorative Martini. He never felt he was one of them, but he was afraid only of Darsie Gillie, the *MG* man in Paris. Gillie was a six-foot-four patrician. Once he secured Morris 'an otherwise totally unobtainable seat' on another aircraft going to the Algerian conflict, finding out later that the supplicant had missed the plane because he had been dining at Maxim's. Morris was ten times more frightened of Gillie after that.

When Iraqi revolutionaries mounted a coup against the Hashemite monarchy, the *MG* hastily dispatched Morris to Baghdad. The country had been a client state of the British for forty years, and Morris arrived a few days after the murder of young King Faisal and his prime minister, Nuri al-Said. At Said's house, which had a pretty garden running down to the Tigris, Morris found a packet of the dead man's denture fixative. He flew on to Jordan, where the lingering Hashemite King Hussein, whose wedding Morris had attended on his first tour out of Cairo, paid tribute at a press conference to his childhood playmate Faisal and the rest of the royal family. Raising his head from his notes, jaw twitching, he said, 'They are only the last in a caravan of martyrs.'

In September 1957 the Morrises had rented a house in north Devon for two weeks, and there James had begun yet another Middle East book after a day trip to Lundy Island by paddle steamer. It was the story of the Hashemite monarchy, the dynasty yoked to Britain and in the news on account of the Baghdad murders. Immediately after the 'holiday', Morris flew to Japan and Formosa on a joint *MG* and BBC mission; he was supposed to be on leave from the paper but had temporarily rejoined for the assignment. He filmed a *Panorama* with producer Jeremy Murray-Brown; they eventually made eight together. In 'Reflections on Tokyo', Morris in jacket and tie pontificates on 'that rambling and materially backward continent' – Asia – and on the city, which is 'not altogether the real thing – a next-best kind of capital'. Japan itself turned out to be 'a chain of ill-endowed islands', and what the viewers could see as the camera panned in and out was 'a copycat culture. Most of these cars were made in Japan [points at traffic], but it's odd how they naggingly remind you of last year's motor show at Earls Court.' Confident, patronising, prejudiced: this was the cultural and intellectual framework of the Pax Britannica. Morris was an adroit television journalist, going on to make documentaries for independent television as well as for the BBC; he also wrote and presented radio talks for the BBC's *At Home and Abroad* slot (one was on the first federal elections in the West Indies). Between 1958 and 1960 he returned often to what was still called the Far East, making his first-ever trip to Hong Kong and filing on the 'hollow men . . . [and] skull-like emptiness' of Hiroshima fourteen years after the bombs fell.

Morris had not forgotten Venice. As a maturing writer he felt sure he could harness the magic that had enchanted him at twenty, and he had been working up an ambitious plan in which the whole family would decamp to the City of Masks for six months. It was not hard to persuade his publishers. Morris had to get all the other wretched books out of the way and wait until he had a break from the *Guardian* (they had now dropped the 'Manchester'), but at the end of 1958 the four of them set off in a powder-blue Vauxhall Victor estate (the Rolls had gone), spending Christmas in Monte Carlo on the way. They had rented a flat with polished-wood floors in a palazzo on a curve of the Grand Canal; on the first vaporous winter nights, all they could hear was the slapping of water. From a corner balcony they watched *vaporetti* and squat fruit barges, and later in their stay enjoyed a grandstand view of sumptuous ceremonials when the body of the former Patriarch of Venice, Pope Pius X, by then canonised, returned on the Grand Gondola to lie in state for a month in St Mark's Basilica, a prolonged death in Venice. They engaged a housekeeper (she said she would like the Grand Canal filled in as it would make walking home easier) and a nanny: Mark remembers that the Venetian nanny wasn't as nice as her Egyptian predecessor and, regrettably, that he spat at her. Neighbours lowered baskets from the top floors of their own palazzos in preparation for the mail (the *postino* yelled each name), and when someone moved house a removal truck was floated to the front door on a barge. The Morrises had their own boat, which they moored round the corner. As the months passed, 'everything movable was filched piece by piece . . . First a bollard, then a seat, then the ropes, then the very floorboards, until at last she rode there, chained to the wall, stripped, ravaged and forlorn.' To make up for it, to the delight of both adult Morrises, Venice turned out to be 'one of the world's supreme cat cities'.

Seven-year-old Mark lasted two days at a beastly Italian school. The British consul suggested he join his own infants, who had a governess and enjoyed field trips in the consular boat. 'I just can't make out whether the children speak Italian or not,' Elizabeth told Goad. 'Henry goes to an Italian school, and I often see him in apparently animated conversation with his friends – but neither of them will admit to a word of Italian at home.'

Morris had taken on an immense amount of work. He was like Sisyphus in this regard. He finished *The Hashemite Kings* in Venice just over four and a half months after he had begun it in Devon, though bother in Iraq meant he had to rewrite the ending. He had recycled material from *Seleukia*, most of it had appeared in *The Times* before that, and those stories were not dead yet. 'Here you are, the sixth and worst of my collected works,' he told Monteith in a cover note. Jeremy Murray-Brown appeared from London with a crew to make another *Panorama*. And Morris soon started writing dispatches for the *Guardian*, which effectively serialised *Venice* before it came out. He had looked through the telephone directory to see which former doges were represented still, finding a single Dandolo. After visiting him, as the old man 'looked down from an open window to wave me goodbye, across the dark water of the side canal, a gleam of old battles seemed to enter his eye, his deep voice echoed down the centuries, and all the sad pride of Venice was in his smile'. A Titian in itself.

The Hashemite Kings duly came out, a precursor to *Pax Britannica* if there is one. 'Nationalism' is a huge word in this book. Morris was working out his own response. 'And when I criticise my own country in these pages,' he wrote in the first draft of the foreword, 'I do so only out of pride and admiration'; then in the second draft he crossed out 'admiration' and replaced it with 'affection'. Twice he cites T. E. Lawrence's assertion that Britain came out of the Arab Revolt 'with clean hands'. Few reading *The Hashemite Kings* (let alone current scholarship) would agree. 'In its early stages the Revolt was almost mystically Arab,' said Morris, and it is this 'mystical' quality that had appealed to many white men before oil flowed – the craggy figure in a turban standing noble in the desert. That, and the route Arabia offered to India. Standing on those shifting geopolitical plates, Morris had to decide which way to face. In the last chapter of *Kings* he produces a twenty-two-line paragraph to conjure *éminence grise* Glubb Pasha, whose demise he had so ably reported, 'lifting the telephone' to summon Bedouin soldiers to disperse the rabble streaming through the streets of Amman in the cold dark 'like a muddy flood'. The set piece reaches a natural conclusion, like an aria. As for the 'tasselled riding-camels' – it would be hard to find a descriptive phrase more emblematic of Morrisian style. This was narrative history at its best, and in the next book, *Venice*, he was to put a match to the kindling by inserting himself into the story. The *Sunday Times* reviewer said *The Hashemite Kings* was '[a] book as brilliant, as beautiful and as moving as any that has come my way for a long time past'. When Sir Reader Bullard, once ambassador to Iran, wrote to Monteith to say it was 'slapdash', he was right – it is a bit slapdash. But does that matter? Morris himself pointed out in *Kings* that he undertook 'only a modicum of original research' and that he had 'no pretensions to scholarship'. A fine line separated that from the slapdash. He once said, 'I am a very superficial kind of researcher,' and he was not ashamed; he knew what he wanted to do in his prose and he did it.

For every book Morris published, another failed to come off. A Nile volume almost reached fruition, as did a book on music in collaboration with Gareth, and a children's book about Venice with drawings by Osbert Lancaster. There had also been talk of something on the homeland – 'which, by the way,' Morris wrote to Monteith, 'I propose to be on England – none of your Welsh charlatans or Scottish hangers-on'. Rabid Welsh nationalism lay in the as yet unimagined future.

Chris came to stay in Venice, and so did the Skeets, the latter plural since Ian was about to marry another Elizabeth. When the Kerrs visited, the five small boys ran wild, inciting alarm among palazzo neighbours, one of whom, spying them on the loose close to the canal, yelled from the window, 'Be careful! The water in Venice is very wet!' William Kerr, rising ten then, remembers James's 'immense talent for doggerel – it was so very flattering when he made up lines specially for me'. Throughout his life Morris enjoyed composing doggerel, and reading other people's. It represented an instinctive reach for the demotic. 'Purple' was acceptable; pomposity was not.

Even as visitors came and went, Morris started *Venice*, settling almost straight away on a tripartite form (People, City, Lagoon), and just as quickly he found his beginning, in which an unnamed navigator, 'sailing up the Adriatic coast of Italy, discovers an opening in the long low line of the shore . . . gusts pungent with the heady past'. He explained later, 'I was a foreign correspondent then, and I planned this book as a dispatch about contemporary Venice.' But it came out as a 'highly subjective, romantic, impressionist picture less of a city than of an experience', a description a reader might apply to much that Morris wrote thereafter as both James and Jan. The early history of Venice is 'hazy and debatable', Morris fudged; 'legend though is always precise'. There was always a truth that was truer than the truth – a distillation more pungent than the realms of the scholar. Nowhere is this clearer than in the pages of *Venice*.

'It is not a history book,' Morris insisted. The volume marks a break. He had found the confidence to let go.

Morris's chief accomplishment in *Venice* is the ability to present the city as a stage on which things happen. Previous books had shown it as still life. The continuity of the past within the present (like the Titianesque descendant of the last doge) was still tolling like a bell – Morris barely got through each day's twelve pages without dragging it in. The manner in which the two are 'curiously interwoven' suits the travel writer. He has the old and new in the same frame. 'If you look through the window of the trattoria, shifting your eye beyond the red Coca-Cola sticker, you will see a small square house across the canal . . .' Morris was continuing the theme of crumbling empire. 'The Venetians have never quite recovered from their loss of glory,' he wrote, going on to note 'a wistful sense of wasted purpose and lost nobility, a suspicion of degradation, a whiff of hollow snobbery, the clang of the turnstile and the sing-song banalities of the guides, knit together with crumbling masonries, suffused in winter twilight'. This too was a prelude.

There was something more. 'In Venice the Orient began,' he wrote, positioning 'the frontiers of East and West' as two parts of a whole. In a subsequent revision of the book (one of three), Jan Morris overtly identifies this meeting of halves with herself. But when he, James, was writing in 1959, he had not yet resolved the two parts of his own whole. He was trying, but he had not got far. Frenetic work – manic, really, with six books in four years – dampened the inner noise. Without the work, and without the emotional stability Elizabeth provided, it would not have been possible to go on. The worlds – the almost insanely demanding and challenging writing life, and the fearsome, perhaps insoluble, yearnings of the internal life – left no room for other people. Morris cared less in 1959 about what was happening on the Grand Canal than he did about what was happening inside him. This tension between the inner and the outer, the two halves, made both fissile. In the meantime he wrote many thousands of words. They were like a curtain. In a newspaper piece on Prague, Morris compared the city under Communism to the Chevalier d'Éon de Beaumont, the French diplomat who lived as a woman 'sensibly adjusted to her new condition'. (The first support group in Britain for men and women then called transsexuals was named the Beaumont Society in honour of the pioneering chevalier.) Morris was nowhere near sensibly adjusted. He was moody. 'I don't think I was awfully nice to you that last day,' he wrote to Elizabeth from one foreign assignment. 'But if I wasn't you know I didn't mean it, don't you?' There were three people in the marriage, and two of them were Elizabeth's husband.

He returned to London from Venice alone to see a doctor who prescribed a suite of oestrogen-based feminisation hormones including diethylstilbestrol (DES), a non-steroid first synthesised two decades earlier. Side effects of the crude dosages included bloating and nausea; it is now known that counterindications are life-limiting – many countries have banned the drug. Morris got some of the effects he wanted, including female fat distribution and the development of breast tissue. But it wasn't enough; it made him too ill; where was it leading? Every time, in these increasingly punishing years, he flushed away another set of pills, despair rushed in to fill the void, 'and the older I grew, the more abjectly I realised, when I allowed myself the melancholy thought, that I would rather die young than live a long life of falsehood'.

7
1959–1962
VEIL OVER LIPSTICK

Morris finished the book many have called a masterpiece in a rented rectory on the eastern edge of Wiltshire. At the last moment he turned the city of Venice into a living thing: in the final draft, a shallow canal becomes a 'sluggish' one; a silent channel turns 'listless'; the water of the lagoon 'reclines' in a trance rather than 'lies'. He also refined the way he used history. Deploying information 'magpie-style', as he called it, Morris began 'embedding passages where they seem to glitter most effectively', a technique he was to hone in the *Pax* trilogy. In his handling of detail, Morris for the first time reveals the ability to show a world through the tilt of a hat, or the twitch of a cat. Carpaccio does the same on his canvases. Morris mentions him fourteen times in *Venice*.

Meanwhile, he was frantically juggling other professional commitments. In August 1959 it had been agreed that he would work six months a year for the *Guardian*; in his time off he could contribute as a freelance ('the more the better from our point of view', according to Hetherington). An LPA, leader page article, was worth fifteen guineas. As soon as it had been arranged, Morris asked if the six months could be split in two so he could work three months on and three months off. Hetherington, almost a saint in this regard, said yes. And while they were talking money, Morris asked if the *Guardian* would like a series on the Nile. By which he meant, would they pay the expenses for a Nile book? In addition, he contributed to an ever-expanding range of magazines, toting his typewriter and filing before the flight home. *Encounter* sent him on a press trip to Mariánské Lázně (Marienbad) in Czechoslovakia, one of many in which the 'leaden burden' of Communism got an airing. In Helsinki, Morris craved carrots after the bland diet – bland everything – of Leningrad; he bought a bunch, washed them in the hotel sink and ate them with a glass of schnapps.

He was human like us, irritably lugging his bags around and wilting as delays dragged out the days. In a piece on Rawalpindi, Morris bemoaned 'the whole blighted concept of modern travel'. Flying seemed to him especially invidious: swooping from one continent to the next in twenty-four hours with no meaningful sense of actually going anywhere. This was not Charles Doughty, lolloping across Arabia Deserta on a camel, or even Robert Byron, the travel-writing star of the thirties, shuddering to Isfahan in a charcoal-powered car. In addition to the indignities and inconveniences of queues, bad weather and terrible hotels, Morris was still coping with the debilitating side effects of medication. Few so ill have worked so hard. But by his mid-thirties his inner life devolved on the increasingly urgent conviction that he must transition or die. He thought of that when he dragged himself out of his hotel room to look at another lifeless landmark. On the Russia–Finland trip he had written an account of his anguish. Leaving Leningrad, the customs official searched his bag and found the typescript. 'Ah,' said the Soviet, 'a psychological novel,' and waved him through.

He spliced assignments to maximise income and expenses, for his medical bills were already fearsome. In the autumn of 1960 he went to New York and Canada for the *Guardian*, then on to Singapore and Bangkok, the costs of which were shared by the paper and *Life* magazine. Morris still teemed with book ideas, even as he was turning out elegant short-distance pieces, and as his thinking evolved so did the reach of his ambition. 'My mind is turning ever more inevitably towards India and Us!' he told Monteith. 'I would rather like to take a nibble at the theme by writing a book on the First Afghan War.' It was the seed of *Pax Britannica*. Monteith offered an advance of £400, and Morris took off for Kabul to file for the *Guardian* and follow the British army on its wretched march to Jalalabad in 1842. (The Afghan book never came off.) He was also reviewing, beginning one piece with the reprise of a theme.

> 'The writer of travel books today,' remarks Mr Carrington [the author of the volume under review], 'has a less enviable task than his predecessors.' Nothing could be more sadly true. Gone are the great days of the Curzons and the Kinglakes, or even the Starks. So little of the Earth's surface is left unfamiliar, so many people have done it all before, the sheen has gone, and you can book a passage to Kathmandu in Piccadilly or Cedar Rapids.

One hears again the eternal threnody for the travel book, a tune as old as Odysseus: we have been everywhere and seen everything. Yet Morris shows more convincingly than anyone that the journey never ends.

The rectory proved a congenial billet. Great Bedwyn had enjoyed a new lease of life in the nineteenth century with the arrival of the Kennet and Avon Canal; the railway had also puffed in, and Mark loved to watch the stand-by Great Western steam engine idling in the sidings. Family life remained calm, outwardly at least. Mark remembers, 'We [the family] had little sense of physical roots and only a small number of rarely seen close relatives. We were nomads, however much we tried to learn a place and quietly merge with it. We became a close-knit and self-reliant family.' The children hadn't yet noticed physical changes in their father. It seems nobody had besides Elizabeth, who knew what was happening. James covered up the emergent breasts with careful dressing.

By the end of October 1959, they had found a permanent house to buy. It was another former rectory, this time in Waterperry in the adjacent county of Oxfordshire. 'I shall now have it surveyed,' Morris told Monteith, 'and presently you can all come and eat crumpets beside the Agamatic.' When Faber requested a biographical note for a jacket that month, Morris ended it, 'He has just bought a Georgian rectory near Oxford.' He was staking a place in the world even as he struggled to find a way out of his own body. While the Waterperry purchase lurched off and then on again, they moved briefly to Gloucestershire, then for a longer period to East Woodhay on the Hampshire–Berkshire border, where they rented an upstairs flat in a large house called Burlyns Steps. Elizabeth was pregnant again. She had coped with different countries and languages as well as the uncertainty of where they were going to live next, not to mention a man unable to live in his own skin. Morris asked a lot of Elizabeth, and she gave it. What it cost her, no one can know.

Virginia Mary was born at the beginning of April, when daffodils were blooming in the flowerbeds around Burlyns. A month later she died of pneumococcal meningitis at the Royal Berkshire Hospital. They buried her in the Saxon churchyard of St Mary's at Waterperry.

Numb with grief, the baby's parents took a cottage for a fortnight in a place where nobody knew their names – Portmeirion on the Dwyryd Estuary. That part of the lonely Welsh coast was to loom large in the future, but neither Morris knew it at the time.

Then it all started up again; it had to. In July Morris flew to Cuba to interview Che Guevara, and the following month he was in Moscow for the downed US pilot Francis Gary Powers's espionage trial ('he was obviously frightened and so was I'). Morris suspected, as he sat in the courtroom, that Powers had not been shot down at all, but when he told Hetherington this on the telephone that night, the line went dead. While he was in the Russian capital, Guy Burgess called on him at the Hotel Metropol on Teatralny Proezd, where everything smelled of synthetic-cherry floor wax. The pair shared champagne and caviar, and Burgess 'confided in me, as he confided in everyone, about his lingering affection for England'. Morris had tickets for the Bolshoi later in the week and, as 'I could not help feeling sorry for him', they agreed to go together. 'We arranged to meet outside the theatre door, and when I got there he was waiting for me on the steps. I waved a greeting as I approached him through the crowd, and he waved a response, but by the time I reached the door he had vanished. I never saw him again.'

VEIL OVER LIPSTICK

It is hard not to conclude that Morris was present at all the really great events of those years. A month after the episode on the Bolshoi steps, the *Guardian* sent him to the UN General Assembly in Manhattan, where both Macmillan ('a gleam of smooth grey Etonian hair') and the Soviet leader Nikita Khrushchev ('sprawling and pouting in his seat') were in attendance. One day the first secretary banged his shoe on his desk in protest at Macmillan's boast of happy decolonisation, and the urbane Supermac asked for a translation. Late that night, Morris was nursing a whisky in the bar of the Waldorf Astoria Hotel when Macmillan shuffled through. 'Everyone there, barmen and all, burst into applause. But I found myself obscurely on Khrushchev's side. It seemed to me that there had been a peasant honesty and humour to his behaviour.' Perhaps he was a *Guardian* man after all. Not long afterwards, Morris was in Tokyo, witnessing 'live on television, as I sat idly in my hotel lounge, the assassination of the Japanese politician Inejiro Asanuma'. A man wielding a *wakizashi* (a short samurai sword) had rushed onto the set and murdered Asanuma in one of most shocking things yet seen in the age of the small screen.

Reporting from Addis Ababa, Morris had described what he called 'the long humiliation of colonialism', and it is this, not Macmillan's windy images of freedom, that emerges from the short-form work of the early 1960s. The topic often collided with the problem of Americanisation, and of modernisation in general. 'One of the sad results of the Western mission in Africa has been the vulgarisation of the continent,' he wrote from Kano. Even Madrid 'stood as a microcosm of a divided world', as did the UK's own Chester in Cheshire, where he covered the races (it was a place 'torn between the old and the new': by now the reader might wonder what place isn't, and to what degree the notion of a divided self governed Morris's subconscious). The gulf between East and West, so recently seen in Venice, also makes frequent appearances in the cuttings. 'Cairo is a half-way city,' he wrote in *Life* magazine, 'half way between age and modernity, between East and West... between the sublime and the ridiculous.' Anachronistic juxtaposition is a hazard of place-writing, as Morris himself noted: 'The best-flogged horse in the whole stable of travel imagery is the Sheikh-and-Cadillac piebald.' Yet he used it in *Life*: 'camel beside Cadillac, veil over lipstick'.

Morris often said that the success of *Venice* changed everything. The book, which came out in high summer, sold in the tens of thousands within the year. It resided on the *New York Times* bestseller list for weeks (the US edition was called *The World of Venice*) and in Britain won the Heinemann Award and topped the *Evening Standard* bestseller list. Freya Stark captured something of the tone of the book when she wrote to Morris from Cairo: 'It is very enjoyable and better than *The Hashemites* [in which she appeared] because you have lived yourself into it.' Nancy Mitford sent a letter from France in flamboyant writing on thick, creamy paper to say, 'Dear Sir, Your book is too lovely. I have lived in it.' Not everyone liked it. The *TLS* said, 'At worst, his comments on painting and sculpture are intolerably pert. (On architecture, he's almost as bad.)' Not everyone had to like it, because overall it had worked: the avoidance of scholarship in favour of a little light learning conveyed in a playful style had led to the grail: sales, reviews in the respectable press and status as *a popular writer*. Michael Palin, who was to make the last-ever documentary film with Morris, and a popular writer himself, read *Venice* as a young man. 'When you got there, it made perfect sense. It was like a flower opening.' The success of the volume gave Morris permission to consider himself, from now on, a book writer rather than a journalist. He did not yet want to retreat fully into the past – America, which he loved and visited every year, stood for the opposite of the past, with its shouty television ads and space-age supermarkets. It was the present Morris wanted to avoid – the tiresome news cycle of coups and strikes and arguments about cod. *Venice* crystallised a style antithetical to hard news that Morris went on to develop and consolidate, deploying it on literary smash-and-grab raids from Aix to Zululand. A touch of purple, a throwaway parenthetical remark, a little old-school grandstanding and an instinct for matching style with content – these were constituent features. But Morris's creative gift was bigger than the sum total of its parts.

Thirty years after that triumphant summer when Morris was the toast of literary London, Monteith wrote, 'Reading and then publishing *Venice* was one of the most exciting things that ever happened to me. Bless you for writing it. Much love, Charles.'

They moved to Waterperry at the end of 1960, the *Guardian* having guaranteed a building society loan. The Old Rectory dated from 1777; its garden sloped to the River Thame, a tributary of the Thames. Mr and Mrs Forward, a local couple engaged as housekeeper and handyman–gardener, moved into a specially built wooden cabin on the opposite side of the road. (Mrs Forward was allegedly of Romany stock. Morris felt instinctive empathy with 'gypsies' and had researched their history for the feature he had written. When he tackled Mrs F. on the subject, she took offence.) Besides the staff accommodation, Morris oversaw the conversion of a barn into a study, commissioning a carved ship to float above the lintel. He bought a punt, and a horse, going all out for the image of the squire. A Rover 2000 replaced the Vauxhall Victor in the drive. Despite his class snobbery, manifest in that tendency to label people he considered socially inferior 'common', and although Morris did not genuflect to grandees or revere titles in the English manner, the acquisition of trappings at this time in his life conferred an identity.

Johnnie and Isabel Kerr, last seen in Otham, had moved to the Victorian Gothic Holly Bank on a hill in the hamlet of Wootton, only fifteen miles away. Mark, Henry and the small Kerrs – a girl had joined the ranks – climbed trees in its broad acres and caught crayfish in the Dorn assisted by Rig, the irascible Kerr dachshund. Inside Holly Bank they gathered round an enormous kitchen table, where heat from the coke-fired stove caused flakes of paint to fall from the ceiling into the food. 'The Morrises were just always a part of life,' Andrew Kerr remembers. Johnnie had recently set himself up as an antiquarian bookseller; in 1964 he joined Sotheby's book department as an auctioneer, grew impressive sideburns, and eventually he founded his own auction house. Elizabeth was close to him at this time; he called her Biz and wrote beautiful letters. She confided in him. 'Is James really going to go the whole way, do you think?' he asked. Morris confided in him too. Johnnie's letter to Biz continues, 'James told me yesterday the doctor can't see him till March.' Kerr supported Elizabeth and she appreciated it.

Enid came to visit from Suffolk, where she still played the organ at a church in Reydon outside Southwold. Her eyesight was failing, and she once got through a whole service playing with her apron on, as she prepared lunch at home before morning service. When Chris and his wife Ruth visited Waterperry with their young children, Paul and Sallie, Paul remembers looking through an expensive telescope purchased out of fees from the Philadelphia-based weekly *Saturday Evening Post*, for a time the most widely circulated magazine in America. Besides being organist and director of music at St George's, Hanover Square, Chris was music editor at the London office of Oxford University Press, and he was composing work of his own.

Mark was already at prep school – a key identifier in the English class system – and Henry was about to start. As Morris's fan and *Encounter* stablemate Nancy Mitford was keen to point out, one had to spend one's money in the right way. Class was determined not by what one earned, but by what one paid for. Morris, however, cut an isolated figure. Despite being personally involved in many of the major events of the early sixties, he showed little interest when Harold Wilson became the first Labour prime minister since Attlee. He walked a longer road, along Harley Street to analysts, many of whom were quacks. These were years of tension and anxiety. It was clearer than ever that there were only two ways out, and one was suicide. Morris said so. It is hard, for those not engaged, to understand an internal dilemma so urgent that life literally depends on its resolution. Lack of understanding results in a failure of empathy. Some might say – have said – that Morris could not accept his homosexuality. But nobody could have taken the path he followed, with its years of sickness and endless half-secret tittering, for that sad reason.

VEIL OVER LIPSTICK

In the new year of 1961, Elizabeth was again pregnant. They both went to the US for a month and Morris covered one of Kennedy's first press conferences. 'I was never a very astute political observer,' he wrote later, 'and I really did not know what to make of Jack Kennedy. I was charmed by the look, sound and presence of him, as everyone was, but some vague instinct told me that although he was only in his mid-forties, he was already in his prime.' On solo assignments he reported on the lowering of the flag in – among other countries – Cyprus, Nigeria, Sierra Leone, Tanganyika, Jamaica, Trinidad and Tobago, Uganda and Kenya. The process was always muddled and, in Whitehall, grudging, for all Macmillan's efforts, and the general public in Britain was wholly indifferent.

Something had to give, and it was not to be the pursuit of medical help. At the beginning of spring 1961, Morris resigned from the *Guardian*. His departure was to come into effect at the end of the year. 'I have come to the conclusion', he wrote to Hetherington, 'that it is time for me to get out of daily journalism, if I am ever going to write something that will last.' He thanked the editor for 'an arrangement which is, I suspect, the kindest any newspaper has ever given an employee. You will think me a wretched flibbertigibbet ... but I am now thirty-four, and I think this is the moment to take another plunge! Into poverty and ignominy, I expect!' The plunge was to end somewhere else entirely. Long Island University had just awarded Morris the George Polk Award for Outstanding Foreign Reporting, though a reader had written to the *Guardian* the previous year to say the paper's dispatches from the Powers trial in Moscow were 'too emotional' for reportage, and in a postscript to his resignation letter Morris said he believed this to be true of much of what he'd produced for the paper. 'The elements I craved', he wrote elsewhere, 'were fire, salt and laughter. The *Guardian* specialties were fairness, modesty, and rational assessment. I liked a touch of swank. The *Guardian* shied from it like a horse from a phantom.' Meanwhile, Morris wrote to Monteith suggesting a book on the British Empire at its zenith – a reiteration of his 'India and Us' concept. But months of hard travel and almost constant filing lay ahead before he could focus on imperial matters. In spring he toured the Mediterranean and missed his wedding anniversary, sending a letter of apology from the Hotel Jolly in Cagliari in Sardinia, assuring Elizabeth, 'I love you more each year and the best thing that ever happened to me was meeting you! In your red American coat on the stairs! Indeed I really don't think I can go on much longer with these constant separations, even if it means living in poverty in a potting shed.' He ended the letter, 'Thank you for twelve such happy years.'

Adolf Eichmann was that year standing trial in Jerusalem for the crime of the century. Morris arrived from Greece (where he had gone from Sardinia) to cover the first week of court proceedings, bringing the Mediterranean tour to a close in Israel. Hundreds of journalists had descended to witness the stony-faced and stone-hearted Eichmann wearing headphones in a bulletproof-glass booth in the Beit Ha'Am tabernacle. Morris stayed at the President, and during the evenings, when he wasn't in his room pounding out features on the past weeks' travels, he went out with illustrator Ronald Searle, who was reporting on proceedings for *Life*, and with Indian poet Dom Moraes, in action for *The Times of India*. Morris found Moraes, whose wife was also present (they were on their honeymoon), 'fascinating though usually a bit tight'. More elevated scribes, such as Morris's old censor from Christ Church, Hugh Trevor-Roper, there for *The Sunday Times*, were at the King David, where the severed fingers had lain on the typewriter in 1946, though they all met up in search of food, as restaurants were closed for Passover. 'The hotel is full of appalling colleagues,' Morris wrote to Elizabeth, 'reinforcing my decision to get out of the trade.' He was attractive to women, a little feminisation notwithstanding, and news hotspots are febrile as well as far from home. A particularly annoying American correspondent, 'Susan somebody', whom he diagnosed a nymphomaniac, had pursued him from Athens. 'Never mind,' he ended the letter, 'I'll soon be in your arms.'

*

Still suffering a bad bout of pharmaceutical side effects, not long after the extended stint in Europe Morris set off on a South American tour for the *Guardian*. Presidents lavished him with attention and aviation ministers with private planes, and in Lima he made a rare excursion to the slums, where the miasma of garbage and excrement on San Cristóbal was 'even eddying around the cross on top of the hill'. Later he reflected that his piece on Peruvian poverty 'made me sound (just for once) like a proper *Guardian* reporter'. He found thirty-five Smiths in the Santiago telephone directory and overall loved South America. 'Cuzco and Machu Picchu was one of the best trips of my life,' he told Elizabeth. He finished on a bus which a tractor dragged over an Andean pass through deep snow. 'What a journey it has been!' he wrote from Bariloche. 'It will keep me in material for travel essays for a lifetime.' It did.

He knocked off as many as he could before departing for Africa, proceeding from there to Pakistan via Cairo, where he called in to see *Saphir* and Idris the aged deckhand, still wearing the same long brown jellabiya. At the Hotel Metropole in Karachi he sent three LPAs to the *Guardian* and a long feature to the *Saturday Evening Post*, then wrote to Elizabeth before he dashed for the Rawalpindi train. After much discussion with her, he had decided to stop the latest round of medication. It made him too ill.

> You'll be pleased to hear that I threw away my pills! I couldn't trust myself not to take them so I popped them down the lavatory. They make me happier, because more f. [feminine], but I'm not sure what effect they have on me otherwise, either on my writing or on my health – also only a fool would grumble, when I have so much happiness already possessing you (though of course my idiosyncrasy really goes beyond rational judgement – I know I am one of the luckiest people alive, but I still can't resist the feeling that I am not what I am! You know what I mean!).

Ten days later he wrote from Lahore, having mailed three more long essays. Although he had flushed the drugs away, their effects lingered. 'I've been having nosebleeds and pains the last couple of days, effect of pills I suspect.' The stop–start nature of medication that was at best experimental exacerbated the anxiety and distress of the long transition years.

In the middle of 1962, Morris toured Australia and New Zealand on a joint mission for the munificent *Saturday Evening Post* and the *Guardian*. He landed in Darwin, where the barmaids called him Jim ('I resent the laboured bandying of my Christian name as though I were participating in a television quiz show'). Furthermore, 'the beeriness of life itself sometimes borders upon the bestial'. *I LOVE YOU*, he telegraphed from Brisbane, as if clinging to a life raft, and six days later he wrote from Canberra, 'Australia strikes me as perfectly ghastly – perhaps the most unalluring of all the countries I've ever visited.' He couldn't get a purchase on anything in Australia; couldn't find a theme. After Melbourne, Adelaide, Alice Springs and Perth, he had discovered 'the women in particular are perfectly horrid, so cold and dull'. But out of thirteen LPAs from Australia it was the one on Sydney that people remembered thirty years later. The city – in the published stories, let alone the letters home – was 'pallid or frigid at the soul', the bronzed lifesavers on Manly Beach lacked 'lofty memories or aspirations' and nobody was kind. Sydney, Morris continued, 'was founded by the scum of England only six generations ago'. He found no great ideas, no visions of nobility, 'only starker impulses of self-advancement or survival . . . [the city] seems full of reproach, sneer, and grumble . . . The dinkum Aussie all too often seems to cherish racial prejudices of the nastiest kind . . .' Letters poured in on two continents, and Australian papers clamoured for reprint rights.

When London's privileged Travellers Club elected him a member in 1962, Morris told Monteith the subscription was a further blow to his finances, as if someone were forcing him to join. A club in the capital – in Pall Mall like the Travellers, of course, unless it was White's – was part of the package, along with the cars and the rectory and the prep schools.

Morris still aspired to social status, cleaved to its class implications, which was in part why he disliked Australia, as it didn't have them, or not in the same way. In his professional life, hardcover publication affirmed status. He had already achieved that enviable and elusive combination of critical approval and sales, and he was content with popularity, even if he usually felt he deserved more of it. Neither the literary elite nor the pretensions of the *nouveaux romanciers* interested him, nor did he identify with the resentment of Kingsley Amis and the modish Movement poets. They had battles to win, and he had none, beyond himself.

He consistently spent more than he earned. Subsidiary revenues made little inroads into outgoings, notably as Morris insisted on expensive changes to typeset proofs, the costs of which were deducted at source. He was racking up medical costs at gender-reassignment clinics. 'My position [financial] now approaches the desperate,' he wrote to Monteith. (Morris did better than many in the Faber stable – Monteith was about to offer the poet Philip Larkin £75 for *The Whitsun Weddings*.) To raise more cash he was constantly proposing new projects or reincarnations of old ones. He committed to books in the *Venice* style on San Francisco and Jerusalem, and was working up an anthology called *Comparisons*. None of those came off, mainly as he had no time to write them, though he did finish a wonderful children's book. *The Upstairs Donkey* retells sixteen folk stories, all 'stolen from unknown authors of indeterminate date . . . wherever my work as a newspaper correspondent has taken me'. Pauline Baynes produced line drawings – that same year, her work appeared on the cover of the paperback *Hobbit*, and she had already illustrated all the *Chronicles of Narnia*. In the pages of *Donkey* crocodiles talk, hobgoblins hop on one leg and soldiers trudge home in tattered uniform. When the team at Faber voted to drop three of the 'more horrid stories', among them 'How the Dotty Afghan Woodman Died', Morris rang Russell Square to say that was the whole point of the book. *Donkey* died a painless death itself in terms of sales, which was a tiny tragedy, really. And Morris still didn't have enough money to stay afloat.

Something, however, had come up to save his day. Writing to editorial assistant Rose Goad as far back as March 1958 during one of her husband's absences, Elizabeth revealed that immediately prior to departure James had sped up to Claridge's Hotel for a meeting with Eugene R. Black, longtime president of the World Bank (though she referred to him as president of the Bank of England, which would have been a promotion). This titan, at the helm since 1949, had admired *Islam Inflamed*, 'had great ideas for expansion in the Middle East' and wondered if James might 'do something for him'. Elizabeth finished the letter to Goad, 'Do pass this on to Charles [Monteith], but tell him it's strictly confidential. And don't let him have all the chocolate.'

Black wished, as retirement approached, to commission a book on the institution he had stewarded. (Conceived at the Bretton Woods Conference in 1944, the bank currently had eighty-one member states; its actual name was the International Bank for Reconstruction and Development.) Morris explained that he had no interest in finance, but in May 1960, when Black offered a £3,500 fee plus royalties (about £70,000 today), total access, additional travel expenses and editorial freedom with no right of veto, Morris could not afford to say no. In addition, as an independent author with no obligations to the bank, he could place the work with whichever publishing house he wanted.

The World Bank had been founded on a good idea. In an increasingly interconnected world (the originating theory went), less-developed countries were going to fall further behind without the support of more affluent counterparts. The bank was to present a model in which the business sector would partner the development sector, offering the same interest rates to all and loans that could function as guarantees of a nation's probity; private money, it was argued, would follow. (With hindsight, 'development' in this context looks a lot like imperialism.) To showcase this model, Morris was to visit World Bank-funded projects and write them up into discrete essays which would feature in magazines before they appeared as a book. Pantheon, his American publisher, duly bought the rights – *Venice* was on the US bestseller list, so they really had to. So did Faber.

VEIL OVER LIPSTICK

The birth and growth of manufacturing lay at the heart of the whole World Bank enterprise, and Morris picked, for his central image, the defenceless mill town of Huddersfield in the West Riding of Yorkshire, as it was the birthplace of 'the technical revolution . . . that has changed half the world already'. The town was not so much symbol as synecdoche: other writers landed on the same region to express the looming alienation of modernity. Stan Barstow had set his novel *A Kind of Loving* near Huddersfield just three years before *The World Bank* appeared; the film of the book (the action relocated to Manchester) was selling out the Ritz cinema in Oxford's George Street at the time Morris was writing. The preoccupations of the kitchen-sink boys, like those of Dennis Potter and the Movement poets, were not Morris's, but their work showed they all lived in the same dismal world.

Morris picked five regions, and in November 1961 flew to Ethiopia, the bank's first African client. At the Ghion Hotel in Addis Ababa, in between touring nascent business enterprises, he found forty-five entries in the telephone directory for members of the imperial bodyguard. As he slogged on through the project, his heart elsewhere, Morris recalled the 'huge red slabs' on his schoolroom wall, and contemplated the 'vacuums and anxieties' left by the collapse of the Raj and other colonial rules. 'Nowhere', he wrote in his fifth case study, 'did the end of empire have more fearful consequences than in the Punjab.' The British-built irrigation system that cross-hatched the Indus and its tributaries had enabled crops to flourish, but for reasons 'partly natural, partly political', after independence the watering system failed. Morris looked closely, for the first time, at the arbitrary line marking (literally) India's partition fifteen years earlier: half the Indus Basin lay in India, half in Pakistan. 'This', he wrote, 'is an imperial legacy of the most perilous kind.'

It was not at all clear that World Bank cash had done any good. The Ethiopia chapter ends with some of the most interesting pages in the book – why aid of any kind, repayable or not, is a tricky business, and why capital projects fail. In the end, *The World Bank* is not about the World Bank. It is a disquisition on the leap from the donkey to the Mercedes, or from the sick poverty of subsistence farming to the exploitation of the factory floor. Does the material succeed as a book? Not really. Morris provides no sense of context: there is nothing on the failure of the 1933 London Economic Conference, or the World Bank's position within the interconnected institutions created during or after the war to address global problems of finance and development (the International Monetary Fund, for example, or the aborted International Trade Organization). Nor does he mention the related movement in the forties towards what a political scientist called embedded liberalism, to which the World Bank, at least at first, gave expression. The anonymous *Economist* reviewer found that '[t]he final effect of the book is a little invertebrate. The flesh is brilliant, but one looks for more bones of hard administrative and economic fact.' It was not the last time an absence of economics would attract attention. That said, the range was astonishingly wide; one reviewer noted, 'What a many-sided man Mr Morris is!'

On the home front, the economy was tottering – it tottered on and off for most of the later fifties and early sixties, notwithstanding a rise in consumer spending much trumpeted by the government. Production was sluggish and Britain consistently lagged behind other major European nations, not least because the things Britons were buying came from abroad. In rolled a tide of books, pamphlets and essays diagnosing the national malaise. Dennis Potter's *The Glittering Coffin* came out in 1960, when the author was still an undergraduate; he said the title was a metaphor for the condition of England. When some of the volumes borne in on the tide, like Michael Shanks's *The Stagnant Society*, became bestsellers, Faber fidgeted about cashing in. Morris had in fact recently flirted with political engagement. He had been discussing the role of the renascent Liberal Party with Hetherington, who was close to its dynamic leader, Jo Grimond (even putting him up for the *Guardian* editorship when Grimond was thinking of stepping down from politics). Morris had become a Liberal by default, as both Conservatives and Labour appalled him. 'May a Liberal suggest . . .' he wrote to *The Times* in October 1964, continuing with an appeal for tactical voting. 'Our time hasn't come yet,' he concluded with a flourish. 'When it does, we shall make of this a country that will beguile and astonish the world.' The party had at least sprung back to life under Grimond, even if it had so far astonished only Torrington in Devon, which its candidate had taken in the first Liberal by-election victory for three decades. 'I believe in style as a political force,' Morris told Hetherington. (People can believe that when they are thirty-five.) 'Look at de Gaulle or Churchill or Kennedy. And I think Liberals will be wise to try and harness it for themselves.' Hetherington asked if he would consider standing for Parliament himself as a Liberal candidate. Sir Harold Caccia had already invited Morris into the political ring around the time of Suez, and he had declined. He was an outsider by nature, and over the long run a writer could say more. But he was still dithering over political involvement when Hetherington invited him for dinner with Grimond. The morning after the soirée, Morris wrote a proposal for 'a single brisk volume to express the whole Liberal point of view, the theme being the excitement and sense of proper purpose that we ought to still get from being British'. The World Bank project had represented a prescription for what would now be called levelling-up. This was something similar, but for domestic consumption. The two books were all of a piece and, as Morris admitted, he wasn't really interested in either of them. They, like fashionable literature, were about *ideas*.

Faber, eyeing the Shanks bestseller, were amenable, though Morris told Hetherington 'they won't tie themselves to a party (mainly I suspect because of the right-wing objections of T. S. Eliot)'. He called the book *The Outriders*, with the subtitle *A Liberal View of Britain*, explaining, 'We are the outriders of Europe, poised precariously between the American language and the continent of Europe.' It portrayed a rotten empire within a carapace that glittered dimly, like Potter's coffin. (There was something of Venice to the image as well.) The tone is avuncular rather than headmasterly. The nation should reform the House of Lords, abolish hereditary titles, shrink the army, modernise the monarchy, overhaul the unions and introduce proportional representation. The author called for fairness. 'It must be among our inalienable rights that if you prefer to . . . dye your beard blue . . . then you are honourably welcome to do so.' Abroad, Morris felt, 'Morally there is no alternative to Britain-in-Europe.' (On 31 July 1962, Macmillan had revealed Britain's application to join the European Economic Community, known as the Common Market, an institution signed into being five years earlier.) In October he finished a second draft and sent it to the Liberals for approval. Grimond wrote an introduction, *Encounter* and *Punch* ran extracts, and French president Charles de Gaulle vetoed Britain's application to join the Common Market.

Macmillan had actually said, in a famous Bedford speech to the Tory faithful, '*Most* of our people have never had it so good,' and *The Outriders* is a call to arms. Does it succeed as such? No, but it is an easy read, even entertaining in parts. Anthony Sampson had published the vastly more sophisticated *Anatomy of Britain* the previous year. (The author had been a near contemporary of Morris's at Christ Church. He respected and admired him, and had sent a copy of *Anatomy* to Waterperry, inscribed 'For James, with anxiety'. More of the redoubtable Sampson later.) Shanks, author of *The Stagnant Society*, as industrial editor of the *Financial Times* had experience to bring to bear on his analysis of the labour market and unions at a time when strife was paralysing Britain; Morris, whom one reviewer said displayed 'an over-insistent manliness' in his tone, got lost when he tried to extrapolate. Yet even if, as the author himself wrote privately, there was not an original thought in the book, the call to arms was predicated on a true analysis of the state of the nation. In Manchester in 1961 nearly a fifth of households did not have exclusive use of a hot-water tap, and in Birmingham 15 per cent did not have their own WC. The standardised mortality ratio (SMR) decreased between 1931 and 1961, meaning Britons were living longer, but the mortality-rate differential between social classes *widened*. Morris knew only the people who did have it good, which in the end is why *The Outriders* fails. He had never been to Huddersfield. He had little awareness that it was, up and down the land but not in Waterperry, the era of slum clearances

VEIL OVER LIPSTICK

and vertical development. In the piece on Chester mentioned earlier, the youth of Cheshire disgusted him.

> Stoop-shouldered and greasy-haired, loud-mouthed and loutish, physically pitiful and mentally apparently half daft, slouching through rallies, chalking rude inanities on walls, misbehaving in the shadows of the Rows [timbered galleries], retching outside pubs. One Saturday morning in race week I saw a young mother, heavily lipsticked and violently dressed, directing her small son to relieve himself against the wall of the Grosvenor Hotel.

The Outriders and *The World Bank* marked the beginning and end of an engagement with social betterment, and years later Morris dismissed both projects as tosh. 'He was treading water, bookwise, after the spellbinding Middle East ones,' Mark says. The truth was that he couldn't go deeper in his work even now, because it took up only the top few layers of him. The ones underneath – they burned with permanent heat as topsoil came and went with the winds of shifting professional commitments. As for the dear old Liberals: Morris's highly developed sense of self precluded submission to a programme imposed by others. He liked style and vigour, not theory. He soon let his party membership lapse. When he joined another one – Welsh nationalist Plaid Cymru – much later, it was for its emotional appeal. Mark also wonders if the uncertainties of Morris's predicament undermined him in these years. 'Jan always thought she was in control of her life. In the fifties she was, and in the seventies she was again, certainly after 1972. In the sixties she wasn't in control.' Morris was still ill from the effects of the drugs half the time, and anxiety over what lay ahead – its possibilities, even – bordered on the unbearable. Again, the tension besetting the country – between the Beatles and the new consumer spending on the one hand, and gloom about national decline on the other – mirrored interior tension. Morris was engaged in a surfeit of glamorous and demanding work, yet was battling despair and survival itself. He said of the period, 'I was cultivating impotence' – hence the compensatory 'over-insistent manliness'.

He kept up appearances. When he went to London he had his hair cut at Sissors, a gratifyingly unisex Chelsea salon where the sixties swung with more vigour than they did in Waterperry. He bought his suits at Jaeger (the firm had tried to keep up with the invention of youth by launching a range called Young Jaeger) – there was a turquoise one people remembered. He cut a dash, and when he next visited Chicago the elevator man at the Merchandise Mart asked him if he was a singer.

Tom was born in October 1961. (As an adult he changed his name to the Welsh Twm.) Monteith stood as a godparent at another ceremony in Christ Church Cathedral. Mark, now the proud eldest of three, had begun boarding at Marsh Court on the Test in Hampshire when he was seven. Elizabeth wrote long letters. From his father, Mark received postcards signed 'JAMES'. (Morris had an eye on his cards' potential as future material, so if one of them regaled a striking anecdote, he wrote 'PLEASE KEEP' at the top.) Through it all, Elizabeth was heroic. In December 1961 she wrote to Goad, 'I collect the boys from school on 21st and James from the airport [he was arriving from Delhi, having gone on to India from Pakistan] on 23rd!! Cutting it fine isn't he?' Still, the children heard the clacking of the typewriter in the barn on Christmas Day. Work had become a survival mechanism in itself; writing filled a metaphorical void, as well as the hole in his bank account. Between tours of South America, Africa and Asia he had prepared a second edition of *Coast to Coast*, adding so much fresh material that Faber had to reset the whole volume; new books were in the works; and on one occasion he mailed the finished typescript of one and a proposal for another in two separate posts on the same day. Unsurprisingly, the sales team at Faber expressed misgivings at *three* Morris titles on one autumn list. But after *Venice*, his value had risen. He had told Monteith that rival publisher Collins had offered £1,000 for a book on any subject, 'more than twice any advance dear old Faber have ever given me'. In addition to work, correspondence absorbed many hours, as he answered every letter. Morris enjoyed engaging with fans – he preferred it to engaging with real people with actual faces. In his prose he sets up a kind of love affair with readers, and they had always responded, feeling, as they told Morris in their mail, 'as though I know you'. The particular communion between writer and reader partially explained the success of the books: it was a dialogue. As were the letters. When a Swede wrote on the headed paper of a glass-blowing firm in Nybro to enquire about a reference in *Venice*, Morris replied with the information and went on to say he needed replacement stoppers for his decanters and could the Swede recommend a British firm?

He made a television programme on Oxford which went out in October 1962, and during the shoot he had an idea. Why not do a *book* on Oxford? The city was on his doorstep, Americans had heard of it and the whole thing could be over by Christmas. Meanwhile, Britain experienced the coldest winter for two hundred years. Fish froze in the river at the end of the garden and it snowed and snowed. Morris, to the children's delight, put on his boots and recreated Everest and the icefall in the garden.

8
1963–1965
TREFAN

Morris spent much of his thirties treading 'the long, well-beaten, expensive and fruitless path of Harley Street psychiatrists and sexologists'. Only one man in the whole teeming cast offered hope, and he was not in Harley Street, nor even England. Berlin-born Harry Benjamin had started his American career as a young endocrinologist in 1915, moving into the specialisation known as sexology and treating his first transgender patient in Manhattan in 1948. By the time he retired two decades later, still speaking with a heavy German accent, he had seen over 1,500 men and women who expressed a desire to 'change sex'. As a proper doctor, Benjamin believed in what we now call data (unlike many among the Harley Street pirates to whom Morris trekked). He gave currency to the term 'transsexualism', usually spelling it with one 's'.* Benjamin understood that gender dysphoria – a term not yet coined – is part of the human condition. In the 1960s the fashion in psychiatry was to prescribe what is now known as conversion therapy to sexual 'deviants' of all kinds; Benjamin rejected this as barbarism, guided his patients to examine their internalised transphobia, and exposed taboos against surgery within his profession. By the mid- to late sixties, several clinics in both the US and Europe were offering transition surgery. From the compassionate Benjamin, Morris wrote, 'I learnt what my

---

* Another pioneering American sexologist had first used the word in English in a 1949 clinical publication; Magnus Hirschfeld, whose work had inspired the doctors who treated Christine Jorgensen, had coined the term in German in the twenties.

future would be.' Transition was, in other words, possible. The relief was immense, even as the struggle that lay ahead was, to say the very least, daunting. Pre-operation for male-to-female patients Benjamin prescribed Premarin, a conjugated oestrogen extracted from pregnant mares' urine. He had treated Christine Jorgensen with it before she went to Denmark for her first two operations. The doctor who transformed Morris's future is often described as a maverick, but he had to be. He was a pioneer. Benjamin's 1966 book, *The Transsexual Phenomenon*, was the first even to set out an affirmative treatment path. (Benjamin credited Jorgensen in the book, and wrote privately to her: 'Without you, probably none of this would have happened: the grant, my publications, lectures, etc.') Unlike everyone else, even clinicians, Benjamin had been distinguishing between transvestism and transsexualism in published papers for two decades.

In 1963 he moved his practice to 1045 Park Avenue, between East 86th and East 87th. Morris came to know the address well. He was facing what trans writers have described as pre-transition 'existential terror' and an all-absorbing 'complex dance of knowledge and denial'. But there was to be no turning back. 'By my mid-thirties,' Morris wrote, 'my self-repugnance was more specific and more bitter, and I began to detest the physique that had served me so loyally.'

Loneliness emerges in every personal account. How could it not? The BBC broadcast the first programme about 'transsexualism' in 1966, a documentary called simply *Sex Change?* In the film, British dentist Georgina Somerset recalled her own long, solitary search for medical solutions. 'You just go from place to place,' she explained. Somerset – actually intersex, but nobody was clear what that was then – was the first woman to marry legally in church after officially changing the gender assigned to her at birth; her book *Over the Sex Border*, not a memoir but a study of transsexualism in all its known manifestations, published in 1963 under her maiden name, preceded even Benjamin.

Desperation over money ran in parallel with desperation over destiny, and work had to go on, with five mouths to feed, a mortgage and school fees. In New York, Harcourt, Brace & World had launched a series of large-format topographical books with a volume on London, illustrated with photographs by German-born Evelyn Hofer. VSP – Victor Pritchett – had written the text; when *London* reprinted twice, director Bill Jovanovich asked if he would take on Spain next, as he was an expert on the country and had reported throughout the Civil War. But Pritchett was committed for most of 1963, so Jovanovich asked Morris, a similarly impressionistic descriptive writer, though one who had never set foot in Spain – he barely perceived the country, he said, as part of Europe. Nobody seemed to mind about that. The advance was $5,000. *Oxford* (now signed up) could be postponed, Morris, Elizabeth and eighteen-month-old Twm could enjoy a five-month adventure, and the two older boys could fly out in school holidays. Everyone declared themselves delighted, worries receded, Hofer went ahead to Spain and in the autumn of 1962 Morris bought a set of Spanish Linguaphone cassettes, though he had no more facility with the language than he had had with Arabic. The boxes of new-fangled cassette tapes stared reproachfully from the drawing room table until it was time to depart, which, at the end of January, the Morrises did, in Elizabeth's Volkswagen Westfalia campervan.

It was still Franco's Spain, even if the regime was less intent on brutalising its own people than it had been, but Franco had begun to suffer from Parkinson's, and Luis Carrero Blanco held the reins. 'I vividly remember', says Mark,

> sitting with my parents at an outside café in a small one-street village near Malaga. Up the main road out of the village came the sound of sirens and a cloud of dust. A motorcade of police motorcycles sped through, scattering chickens . . . in the middle of the motorcycles was a single long black limousine. The motorcade flashed past, and the sirens were soon lost in the distance on the other side of town, leaving the dust swirling around the café. My father leaned over to me. 'That', he said, 'was General Franco.'

They were constantly warming up or cooling down. In May, Morris read in a newspaper that the previous day the temperature in Córdoba had reached 32°C, while in León it had fallen to 4. He carried a sketchbook, which became a habit; over the decades his own pen-and-ink drawings appeared often in his publications. The family called on the English writer Gerald Brenan, a Hispanophile (and confidant of VSP) who, having inherited an income, lived in the manner of a seventeenth-century *hidalgo* with his cat-loving wife in Churriana, an Andalusian village then in the middle of lush countryside, now *en plein* Torremolinos. During long, warm nights round the outside glass table, as fireflies whirled above the leaf litter of the holm oaks, Brenan, then sixty-nine, talked of feelings of detached romance concerning Spain. Once a part-time Bloomsberry, he had written widely on the country; his *South from Granada*, about the Alpujarra, the lovely Andalusian region on the southern slopes of the Sierra Nevada, remains a classic. Brenan and Morris wrote for the same magazines and were both obsessed with telescopes, in Brenan's case for voyeuristic purposes. They shared too a strangely intimate relationship with the past: a few years after the visit, Morris's old Christ Church censor Hugh Trevor-Roper told Brenan he was 'my ideal historian – you *see* the past in the present and the present in the past, imaginatively'. At Morris's best, the same applied. At any rate, Brenan influenced the book that became *The Presence of Spain*.

Because the country was so little affected by cultural contamination, on this trip Morris realised how much he hated the Americanisation of everywhere else. Spain, he wrote, 'stands apart because she has not yet felt reconciled to the twentieth century – has not quite succumbed to those pressures of materialism which we, like so many dim Frankensteins, half regret having devised'. Again and again 'the magnificent balefulness of things Spanish' drew him in, notably the grandiose, dark, overbearing Philip II style that he started to see everywhere. It suited his mental landscape. He was 'in a somewhat hallucinatory state' on account of the drugs, and of what he called 'my wondering alienation'. The Spanish people, one-dimensional, devout and rooted to the soil, became a symbol of what the itinerant, spiritually wretched writer was not. 'Nobody', Morris wrote later, 'could have been less Spanish than me.'

There were high points, hallucination or not. In March, sitting in a café in Bilbao, he opened a telegram from Monteith forwarded from the vice consul in Malaga: *TORRENTIAL CONGRATULATIONS*. The US Book of the Month Club had chosen *The World Bank* as its midsummer choice, paying the unthinkable advance of $60,000, of which half went to Faber, the originating publisher. *CARAMBA INDEED!* Morris cabled back. The club wanted to change the title to *The Road to Huddersfield: A Journey to Five Continents*. For that money, Morris would have called the book anything.

Still he strove to work harder. 'As you foresaw,' Morris had written to Hetherington at the beginning of the year, 'I miss not having the opportunity to comment on crises!' – going on to ask if he could contribute a monthly political essay. Engagement still glimmered, on his good days. As Morris had recognised, no newspaper could have been more supportive than the *Guardian*. Hetherington had run extracts from the Liberals book and commissioned nine LPAs on Spain at twenty guineas each. Morris offered a long piece on London he'd already written for a forthcoming anthology. 'Do send the ms along,' Hetherington replied by return, 'and we'll try to split it up into three units of about our normal length, and pay you three times twenty guineas for that.' When the tenth anniversary of Everest loomed, Hunt convened a reunion at Pen-y-Gwryd. Did Hetherington want anything on it? Of course he did. In which case, could he pay for Morris to get back from Spain?

Morris's primary professional relationship in the US had been, until this point, with his editor Helen Wolff. She and her husband Kurt, both German-born, had founded Pantheon Books (which had published *The World Bank*, the Middle East suite and *Venice*), leaving when Random House swallowed their imprint. Helen had been involved with Morris at Pantheon, batting for him in-house when the Middle East books didn't sell, and she had learned how to deal with his outbursts. In 1961 the couple started again with their own imprint within Harcourt, Brace & World, which itself became Harcourt Brace Jovanovich in 1970. Kurt died in a motor accident in 1963. Helen's relationship with Morris lasted decades and he became immensely fond of her. When he was glued up in the middle of *Pax* she wrote to him, 'What matter empires fall, so long as authors rise?' After the US rights to *Venice* reverted from Pantheon, where she herself had originally published the book, she bought them again for her new firm. She was a publishing grande dame and a redoubtable figure, the antithesis, in many ways, of the courtly Monteith. But as Morris started writing the Spanish book, he decided he needed American representation as well as the guidance Wolff supplied, and he engaged Julian Bach as his first literary agent. Bach, who had only recently entered the 15-per-cent world, was tweedily formal and spoke with a carefully crafted refined accent, 'though unlike Wolff he wasn't to the Manor born', according to an editor who worked with both. The attachment Bach formed with his client endured until he sold the agency almost three decades later. Astonishingly, during that whole time he and his assistants arranged all Morris's travel.

Morris wrote *The Presence of Spain* in less than three months, adding the accents by hand as his English typewriter considered them a foreign affectation. Brenan read the manuscript and made suggestions. The book traces an arc: from 'the beginning of history to the sixteenth century' Spaniards progressed upwards, 'steadily accumulating wealth, culture, prestige, and unity'. From then on they have been 'almost constantly slithering downhill'. Always looking for shapes, Morris seized on this arc as a central image. 'Spanish history does not form a happy pattern,' he wrote, 'but at least it looks symmetrical.' *Presence* came out in 1964, gorgeously illustrated in black and white with a dozen colour plates. Hofer used a four-by-five-inch-view camera and her photographs were both sumptuous and precise, and like Morris she switched from close-up to wide-angle to achieve specific effects. Brenan sent a publicity blurb – 'Perhaps the best general book ever written on Spain' – and the *New York Times* said it was 'one of those very rare books in which the writer and illustrator are in perfect accord'. Morris told Monteith he considered *The Presence of Spain* his best book so far.

In 2008, forty-four years after first publication, Faber republished the book as a slim paperback without photographs. Morris began the new introduction, 'Franco died in 1975 and in a sense this book died with him.' But that is not true, as *Spain*, the new title, magics up a timeless land.

He had spent most of Michaelmas term 1963 in Oxford, before *The Presence of Spain* came out, researching the postponed book. University College granted him temporary membership of the Senior Common Room, so he had a base on the High Street. ('Dinner jacket Sundays in term. Five shillings for lunch and nine shillings for dinner, rising to thirteen on a guest night when wine served.') He had breakfast at George's Café in the Covered Market and on Shakespeare's birthday joined the traditional malmsey-drinking lunch in the only surviving room of the old Crown Inn (probably the Crown Tavern). The most august dons at the most august colleges competed to host him at high table, flattering his already immodest vanity. When it was the turn of All Souls, Morris passed the port 'with three men who had reviewed my books'. On warm summer nights, he said,

> I sometimes used to park my Volkswagen bus in Radcliffe Square, unroll my sleeping bag and go to bed in the shadow of the Bodleian... very early in the morning I look through my open roof to see the top of Radcliffe's dome, and the comical pinnacles of All Souls, and the pink-grey sky above it all: and being of a romantic turn, and half-asleep too, I sometimes imagine I hear voices mingling with the first birds and bells of the morning.

(He probably did it once, if that.) In the evenings he and Elizabeth went to donnish drinks parties in north Oxford, where a regular remembered that James did not like talking to women, especially if they were glamorous and bright. 'I think they made him feel unfeminine, and when they flirted with other men, he could not compete.' On 23 November he sat in on a meeting at a Quaker House in St Giles', thinking of his ancestors who had practised that faith. The quiet worshippers offered only one prayer: for Kennedy's assassin. He had fired from the Texas School Book Depository the previous day.

The third Morris title Faber published in 1963 while he was still writing *Presence* was an anthology of seventy-three essays on cities that had appeared in 'the ten years of my prime, between my twenty-fifth and thirty-fifth birthdays'. Carrots in Helsinki were served up cold and Hiroshima's hollow men turned up again, as did the camel beside the Cadillac and the sensibly adjusted Chevalier d'Éon. Morris arranged the selection in alphabetical order, so serendipity took the upper hand – a good joke. Besides the organising principle of a single decade – 'unity of vision, unity of time' – familiar themes knitted the collection together: Americanisation, the Cold War, 'the long humiliation of colonialism', North America hardening into power, South America uncertainly maturing. Read together, the pieces reflect an agreeably idiosyncratic brand of boundless energy and minute curiosity; but they are not meant to be read together, and the remorseless anthropomorphising grates. 'Quite the most indigestible book I have read for ages,' reported a Faber in-house reader. The *Observer* reviewer, like Monteith a fellow of All Souls, panned the volume. 'I may be giving the whole thing up anyway and taking Holy Orders, owing to that shattering review,' Morris wrote to his editor. 'You must have been quite ashamed of having the book under your imprint. I am sorry.' *Cities* quickly fell out of print and was never reissued. But read individually, the best pieces have stood the test of time. Morris captures the effervescence of Bangkok and its essential lack of seriousness; it was a thrown-together city with little real beauty but a diaphanous personality contemporary visitors recognise in the essay. Morris pointed to a Thai readiness, or ability, to absorb rather than create. *Cities* was reviewed alongside *Thrilling Cities*, a book a newspaper had commissioned Ian Fleming to write, casting a thriller writer's eye as he jetted pointlessly round the world. Decades later Morris contributed the introduction to a new edition of Fleming's volume. 'The essays display the kind of patrician defiance . . . that gave the Bond novels their style,' he wrote, before applauding the depiction of 'Bond's world . . . as it seemed in the time of its invention'. There is little whiff of Bond's world in Morris's own essays – one can't quite picture 007 scrubbing carrots in the sink.

In an envoi to *Cities*, his own book, he wrote, 'When I caught myself packing fluffy slippers in 1963 I knew it was time to stop skimming and dig deeper!' He turned once more to the past. While he was preparing *Oxford* he sent Monteith a memo on the project first mooted three years earlier as 'India and Us', now with the working title *Climax of Empire*. He had never given up on it. His publishers on both sides of the Atlantic made offers straight away, Harcourt for a hefty $8,250. By March 1964 the title of the single volume had become *The Empire at Midday*. Morris began planning an ambitious programme of travel to India that was to extend over a decade. He needed to be alone; to dissolve into the teeming millions.

On 25 March 1964, Susan was born at the John Radcliffe Hospital in Oxford. (As an adult she changed her name to Suki.) Her eldest brother, twelve-year-old Mark, was in his final year of prep school. Morris had decided to send him on to Marlborough, the public school in Wiltshire, but changed his mind at the last minute, opting for Eton. Elizabeth went along with it. She had too much on her plate to argue, and anyway she didn't like arguing. For Morris, offspring at Eton, like the punt, were part of the life of a gentleman – even one with a funny haircut. At Marsh Court, his prep school, Mark had first had

> the vague intuition that there was more than mere nomadic existence that set our family apart from most others. Something about my father did not quite fit my notion of what a father was . . . I had been selected for the school cricket First XI, the highlight of which was the match against the fathers . . . but my father remained on the boundary line, and I felt that there was more than just a distaste for cricket, or for

sports... looking back, I recognise a reaction against the manliness of that particularly English game, the team spirit and the changing-room male banter.

The nomadism, like so much else, was drawing to a close. The month Suki was born, architect Clough Williams-Ellis had written to Morris to praise *Venice* and 'lure' him to Portmeirion, the fantasy village he had built on the estuary of the Dwyryd. The family had already been to Wales on holiday, and James and Elizabeth had rented the Watch House in Portmeirion after Virginia's death. When they returned there, James met Williams-Ellis and ended up writing a publicity brochure for what he called the 'folly-village'. (Privately he agreed with the first American he took round, who called it a cut-price Disneyland.) Now they began scouting for a permanent home in Wales. Removal from England was all part of the impotence-cultivation; it symbolised distance and seclusion, which suited more radical changes to come. He had found a partial way out of his agonies, or at least a country-sized bolt-hole. The shift west would also facilitate, in time, the embrace of his Welsh heritage, a gesture towards the unity he craved.

While they were house-hunting they rented Ogoronwy in Croesor, among the Snowdonia foothills above Llanfrothen. They had initially been looking to buy in Radnor, but in the first months of 1965 found Plas Trefan in what was then Caernarvonshire, close to the village of Llanystumdwy, a mile from the sea at Cricieth (Criccieth, in English) and, on the other side, in the shadow of Yr Wyddfa itself – Snowdon. These were the Welsh-speaking heartlands, once part of the independent kingdom of Gwynedd, a region Morris referred to as 'a last bastion of the Welsh against the conquering English'. (In 1974 Gwynedd reclaimed its ancient identity when a new eponymous county replaced Caernarvonshire.) Plas Trefan was at the easternmost edge of the Llŷn Peninsula, the finger of land that extends into the Irish Sea, specifically in the part called Eifionydd after the grandson of Cunedda ap Edern, founder of one of the earliest royal dynasties in Europe. An estate had existed there since the fifteenth century, and the current house was built in the 1770s. It was known grandly as Trefan Hall in English, and it was this name Morris chose for his letterhead. Everyone else called it 'the Big House'. In July they sold Waterperry at auction 'to a lady who flies aeroplanes' (Rowan Atkinson bought it later) and moved to Wales the same month, arriving round the circular carriage drive in the Rolls-Royce Silver Dawn that had replaced the Rover. 'For me,' Morris wrote of Trefan Hall,

> it will always be the most beautiful house in the world . . . It had an easy amateur air that I liked. Its east elevation was accomplished enough . . . with its climbing magnolia and bay window, but the north side, where the front door stood, was palpably unprofessional – a gaunt, very Welsh facade, one floor too high for elegance, with a funny pillared porch in a manner more neo- than Classical, and rows of windows, oblong and many-paned, such as children like to draw . . . It was a magic house.

Chaste architectural simplicity contrasted with the wild landscape. Beyond the Plas the wiry sessile oaks of the woods began, then fell away to the River Dwyfor. In winter, frost rimed the pools on the islet Ynys Llyn Allt y Widdan – the Island of the Pool of the Cliff (or Slope) of the Enchantress – and in spring, daffodils turned the leafmeal wood floor luminous with yellow radiance. The Dwyfor, which flows over seven miles from the mountains to Bae Ceredigion, is celebrated for its sea-trout; the locals were equally celebrated for poaching. Behind the walled kitchen garden lay a jungle, hidden within it ruined kennels which once accommodated the pack of the local hunt, and beyond that an old ice house and the remains of an early water-generated electricity system. Out of sight elsewhere, outbuildings included a two-storey stable block where owls nested and an equally dilapidated coach house with a wooden cupola.

Morris always described the Plas as a place between the mountains and the sea. He liked to use the phrase on book jackets. It was David Lloyd George who had coined it: Llanystumdwy was his boyhood home.

(Before going into politics he had set up a law firm with his brother William, now a vigorous centenarian who acted for the Morrises in their house purchase.)

Indoors at the Plas, a staircase swept up from the entrance hall (which they hung with red wallpaper) to a drawing room with tall windows that looked west over lightly landscaped parkland. The sea was just visible. They put the Bechstein piano in there. Mark, who is himself intensely musical – it was he who played the Bechstein – remembers a wooden cabinet with a lid containing the record player, though they never had many records, or listened much; the musical gene, present in Paynes, Morrises and Bournes and so manifest in James's gifted brothers, came out in his case in the melodic resonance of the prose. Next to the drawing room, Elizabeth had a sewing room which doubled as the snug where they watched *Coronation Street* and, from 1971, *The Two Ronnies*. Five bedrooms led off behind, and dingy back stairs rose directly from the kitchen to a self-contained flat on the third floor occupied by the Forwards, who had followed them from Waterperry, 'gypsy' enquiries having ceased. The principal rooms all had their own pulley-ropes to summon servants, still connected to bells in the pantry. Each one had a different pitch. 'Trefan is paradise,' Morris wrote to Monteith.

Soon after they moved in, the first Abyssinian cat arrived by train from the breeders (on its own, in a basket with the guard); generations were to chug in, all with Ethiopia-related names. Morris loved them and, being 'feline by nature', identified with them. 'I'm convinced that cats have contact with the profound,' she wrote later as Jan, 'and he [Prester John, an incumbent named after a patriarch who may have lived in Ethiopia] is my link with a wilder sort of nature.' After a cat died, Morris believed the next one to be its reincarnation. 'When I lost a child I thought the same thing would happen,' she told an interviewer years afterwards, 'and it did. Another child came along and I'm convinced it's the same one that we lost, the same spirit come back to us.' Didn't the new daughter mind? asked the startled interviewer. 'Oh no, she's perfectly alright about it.' But she wasn't.

To extend the menagerie they installed donkeys in the wood-storage area underneath the house. When Twm started at the local Welsh-language school, he sometimes went in the Rolls, sometimes on a donkey. Over the course of the first year at Trefan, Elizabeth cleared the jungle running down to the Dwyfor. Mark says, 'My mother was very happy at the Big House. She enjoyed the gardening – the garden was a place where she could express herself.'

The tall, gaunt Williams-Ellis was first to sign the visitors' book. He became a regular, often arriving to consult Morris's sixteen-volume *Dictionary of National Biography*, and when he was not there he sent tides of affectionate postcards written in a mandarin hand. Forty-three years Morris's senior, Williams-Ellis was a national figure – even an international one. A big and effective committee architect in the new science of national planning, he was an apologist for and populariser of environmentally judicious development. Both he and Morris were of Welsh heritage on the paternal side, both were atheists keen to display irreverent humour, and Williams-Ellis had even enrolled in the 9th, a family regiment, in the First World War, though in the end he had served in the Welsh Guards. Raspy and patrician-voiced, Williams-Ellis was also a committed writer and traveller like Morris, and had a similar weakness for splendour and display – he wore mustard stockings, but was nothing like Malvolio. He had bought the land which became Portmeirion in the twenties; it was at the time called Aber Iâ (Ice Mouth) and it lay between the twin estuaries of Traeth Mawr and Traeth Bach, draining the Vale of Maentwrog. Williams-Ellis invented the name Portmeirion and planned to make the place 'a holiday retreat for the discerning' as well as a 'living folly'. (His Welsh was ropey – he spelled toponyms wrong on his drawings.) Unlike Morris, he liked entertaining, and James then Jan and Elizabeth often visited Plas Brondanw, the house five miles from Portmeirion which Williams-Ellis shared with his wife Amabel, née Strachey, also a writer. Morris recognised that in some ways his older friend had created Portmeirion as a response to the sterile technology and automata of a brave new world – the world of Huddersfield. When he wrote his obituary for *The Times*, he concluded that 'Clough was his own best work, splendid in all proportions.'

Williams-Ellis was at the centre of a vaguely intellectual and artistic Anglo-Welsh set clustered round the Cardigan Bay side of Snowdonia. Richard Hughes, author of *A High Wind in Jamaica* and known to everyone as Diccon, was currently slaving over the second volume of his trilogy *The Human Predicament*. Bertrand Russell was a fixture at both Brondanw and Portmeirion from 1955 until his death in 1970; sometimes, out on an afternoon walk, Morris would spot him having philosophical thoughts in the gorse. Russell and Williams-Ellis were close, both habitués of the Bloomsbury crowd in the old days. Rupert Crawshay-Williams, a music critic, teacher and philosopher, had moved to the area in the forties with his wife, Elizabeth, and it was they who had lured their fellow humanists the Russells. When Elizabeth Crawshay-Williams became terminally ill, the couple wrote letters to their friends and overdosed on sleeping pills. The double suicide had a profound effect on the community, and on the Morris family.

At Christmas in 1965 they dragged the first huge tree into the hall and the children decorated it by hanging over the balustrade. A crib had followed them from Egypt and Elizabeth put a baby Jesus in it early on Christmas morning. 'I remember running down to see it,' Suki remembers. 'Mummy made it magical.' For stockings the children had the red-and-green-striped socks James had worn on Everest. (Luckily two pairs had survived.) They threw a Boxing Day party, inviting neighbours and local tradesmen for refreshment in the light first-floor drawing room. This sufficiently controllable form of entertaining became a tradition. 'It was feudal,' Mark remembers. 'Jan liked being a big fish, and maintaining the established order. The Anglo-Welsh were part of the community then, not the enemy they became.'

Enid came to visit, and so did the Skeets and the Kerrs, and Morris drove them all to Pen-y-Gwryd, the village at the head of the Nantygwryd and Nant Cynnyd rivers where the climbers had once trained for Everest. Many of Hunt's team still turned up there for reunions every

May, and the hotel displayed memorabilia from Everest 1953 along with photographs of other gnarly expeditions. The owners, Colonel Chris and Mrs Jo Briggs, became family friends. Twm, then a small boy, remembers the colonel taking out his glass eye.

The Welshness hadn't yet taken off, but it was a draw. Morris admired the priest–poet R. S. Thomas and had written to him even before the move asking if he might be kind enough to send a handwritten copy of his poem 'Song at the Year's Turning', which is about old rectories, so that it could hang framed in the Waterperry rectory. A preacher of sermons on the evils of fridges, R. S., as people called him on his home turf, was a very fine poet indeed. He really was Welsh, but had learned the language as an adult, and wrote his poetry in English. Much later he settled on the Llŷn Peninsula, chiefly because it was the heartland of Welsh speakers, and he and Morris got to know one another. Morris wrote:

> I think I understood him, for like many other Welsh persons, we both reached the conclusion . . . that we could glimpse the divine in the matter of Wales – not Wales as it is today, but a Wales with its language unthreatened, its landscapes unspoilt, its people serene in their own beliefs and loyalties. It was an old, old dream . . . an existential sort of Wales, a virtual Wales of our imagination and our longing.

R. S. was a genius, a narcissist and an eccentric. Someone else usually pays the price for those traits, and Thomas's only son, Gwydion, said it was him. The poet had grafted himself onto Welsh Wales, that true country of his imagination, and Morris was to do the same.

A dependence on American magazines to defray costs for Empire travels 'gets more and more of a bore', Morris complained, turning again to the loyal Hetherington, who had moved the *Guardian* editor's office from Manchester to London following the paper's name change. When Morris had told him, 'We are in the throes of buying (we hope) a half-derelict, wildly impracticable, cripplingly expensive and really rather beautiful house in North Wales,' Hetherington had immediately asked if he wanted to write something about that – buying a house. Was there anything the man would not commission? (Later, Morris banned the locution he himself used here, 'North Wales', on the grounds that it was a divisive weapon likely invented by the colonising English.) Morris was away for most of that first Trefan autumn. The itinerary started in Ceylon, where he found his parents-in-law's graves. 'I went to Matugama yesterday!' he wrote to Elizabeth from the Mount Lavinia Hotel.

> Met an elderly Tamil who told me, what I don't suppose he told your aunt or your grandmother, that in his latter years your father had a Ceylonese mistress, who had a child by him . . . I tried to trace him [the child], but couldn't . . . about three years before [your father's death] he and his mistress broke up . . . your father actually died in a hotel in Colombo where he had gone with his servant for a few days . . .

Small hardback notebooks purchased in Criccieth for sixpence include memos to himself ('1 lakh: 100,000') and to unknown persons ('The gears seem to be stuck on this car. It happened when we were just driving along, + the driver can't be blamed. I hope you won't make him pay! JM'). He started number 4 of the Ceylon notebooks with a hand-drawn map and a potential opener for a piece for *Venture*, an American colour monthly: 'On ~~my~~ your minibus, ghoulishly, a shiny-feathered crow.' He drew the reader in by personal address again, setting up the love affair. The technique adds to the antique faux-intimacy of the signature style.

He filed twelve articles for the *Guardian*, proceeding from Ceylon to Madras, Poona, Bombay, Delhi, Jaipur, Darjeeling, Lucknow and Calcutta, where Elizabeth joined him, and the books that became *Pax* began gestating in the notebooks. Back at home Morris made numbered lists denoting potential chapter and topic word counts, with other numbers alongside, evolving a sophisticated private cuneiform that laid down the subterranean patterns of what became a trilogy. He also listed 'things to look into'. He liked lists. Morris added shopping lists at the back of the notebooks. 'Eggs Bread lettuce fish writing paper Bras shoes?'

And what of his emotional response to India? Ancient history lives on in the daily present there more than anywhere. Yet Mark says, 'I never got the sense that the romance of India captured Jan's sensibilities like the Middle East or Trieste or Venice. It was Wales that was to replace the great romantic involvement with those places.' Morris never spoke about India at home. When he was there, he did not hear echoes of the Vedas. He was not emotionally involved with the country, like Paul Scott, the novelist six years his senior whose *Raj Quartet* was guilty of simultaneously glamorising Empire and being anti-British. (The first of the quartet, *The Jewel in the Crown*, came out in 1966, just two years before *Pax* made its debut.) Morris wasn't interested in contemporary India, in Indians or in the problems a hastily departing Britain had bequeathed. Scott, on the other hand, knew that Britain had ceded India to get the country off its hands as quickly as possible. Creeping Raj nostalgia irritated him: 'To hell with the peepul tree,' Scott fulminated in *The Times* in 1975, just as Morris was declaiming, 'It was in India that the martial heroism of Empire had found its most sacred apotheosis.' Morris's India was the veranda of the Windamere Hotel in 1897. He was seldom to return after he had finished the trilogy. India had served its purpose.

That same year, he fitted in France, Canada, the West Indies, the US and Australia. He paid for his travel – through the Bach Agency, which arranged it – and never accepted free trips. Morris hated having to think about money, and despised the very concept of a budget. When he won a prize in the US he came home in triumph bearing a Questar telescope in a leather case. He had bought it with his winnings. Elizabeth had wanted a new kitchen. An accountant came to the Big House every year to do the books on the dining room table. 'Take this tea to the most boring man in the world,' Morris told Twm once, handing him a cup Mrs Forward had brewed. Twm did so, not forgetting to address the man by his new moniker. Mark tried to persuade Morris to invest sensibly when the going was good, or at least to start a private pension. But he wouldn't, though he countenanced the purchase of premium bonds, as it didn't involve seeing a bank manager. He never missed an opportunity to smuggle a cutting reference to a stockbroker into a piece. Money was vulgar. He loathed the petit-bourgeois world of privet hedges that the pecuniary caste represented. Losses were to be written off on the page, not on the bank balance.

Oxford, which came out in 1965, celebrated the life of the mind – the antithesis of the bank manager's dreary existence. Like India, the city drew little emotional commitment at a time when Morris had heavier commitments to his future self. Besides the aftermath of the Anglo-Catholic Oxford Movement, the fantasies of Alice and the eighteenth-century university telescope, Morris briefly covered 'the new industrial towns' in the environs. 'Another England has emerged now,' he wrote. This was a theme of Morris's books from his first to her last – Spenglerian decline. 'The world shrinks and uniformity presses in.'

The strongest pages evoke the pity of war. Of the triumphant Trinity College rowing crew in 1939, six out of the eight perished in the Great Adventure to follow. 'All these sadnesses are hammered home to you', wrote Morris from the cloister walls, 'brass by brass.' The German Rhodes scholar and dazzler Adam von Trott zu Solz, after going down from Balliol, took part in the bomb plot against Hitler, 'one of the supreme tests of courage of our time'. After conjuring photographs of beaming youths raising oars to the camera, Morris writes of the very few years that separate those golden summers from 'the court that sentenced him [von Trott] to death, after torturing him almost to insanity, and compelling him to stand in degradation before the cameras with nothing to hold his trousers up but his own shaking hands'. Morris was to bring von Trott back again in *Pax Britannica*: the image of shaking hands stayed in his mind's eye, and it doesn't matter that a reader cannot actually see the picture, or that a photograph cannot depict a shake.

The book is a brilliant synthesis of days spent hurrying across quads and pretending to sleep in a campervan. But, as Mark says, 'It was duty rather than passion. *Oxford* should have been another *Venice*, but it wasn't.' When Dennis Potter, last seen celebrating the great greyness of the fifties and writing about glittering coffins, reviewed the book for *New Society*, a sub came up with the headline – Christmas was two months away – 'Ding Dong Dismally on the High'. 'If you slam the book shut,' said the playwright from the Marches, 'the purple ought to ooze out like the juice of squashed plums.'* But it was Christopher Ricks's review in *Encounter*, a publication in which Morris himself was appearing regularly in the mid-sixties, that cut deep. The formidable Ricks was not yet the sultan of lit crit he became, but he was already an Oxford don. 'James Morris's *Oxford*', the review began,

> is good at all those matters that have nothing to do with mind: gossipy anecdotes; portraits of Oxford 'characters' . . . watercolours. The only thing that is taxing about it is its sweet determination never to tax anybody. On every page there is some little pointless fact of the kind that children's comics trail along the top of their pages.

Ricks went on, at length, suggesting *Oxford* failed to 'transcend the limitations of this predictable genre, the whimsical, chattering travel book'. Morris knew he was a superficial writer – he said so – but that did not mean, in his opinion, that he was not sometimes a serious one. He immediately fired off a letter to Ricks. 'It's a terrible thing to see oneself depicted with such cruel and contemptuous dislike . . . Most wounding of all', he told the young don, 'was the suggestion that my style (i.e. my self) cannot rise to anything above flippancies and anecdotage.' Ricks stood firm. 'I have little room for manoeuvre,' he replied, 'since I thought the book demeaned its subject for the reasons that I gave.' Morris stormed off to Worcester College for a second round in person, and it was Ricks who brought matters to a close firmly but with dignity, signing off his final letter, 'After all, when all is said and done one still hankers to be liked.' The *Listener*, apparently not a subscriber to the publications cited, said the book 'has been rightly praised everywhere'. It was true that the historian A. J. P. Taylor was not actually nasty in the *New Statesman*

---

* When Potter adapted Christabel Bielenberg's autobiography *The Past Is Myself* for television in 1984, he focused on von Trott. So something lingered, beyond soft fruit.

('a mixture of rhapsody and anecdote recorded in an over-sweet style') and that Evelyn Waugh was reasonably nice in *The Sunday Times* ('agreeable'). The *Financial Times* noted shrewdly that Morris was 'more at ease in the past than in the present', though whether this was a fault the reviewer did not say. 'It is sure to be a bestseller,' Ricks had written in his review, and it was, appearing at number five in the *Evening News* list and reprinting twice in the month following publication.

Morris read the cuttings on the road, where his mail pursued him. Bedrooms seemed inhospitable as he sat on a single mattress and the cacophonies of the bazaar rattled the windows. He wrote to Monteith from Bombay to say he was sorry *Oxford* was being criticised for being too purple.

> I know how the leopard must feel, when nagged by reformers to change his spots! The awful thing is that as I wander round the Raj in pursuit of Pax Britannica, I feel my style getting florider every minute. I shall end life a living whirligig.

The postman, meanwhile, pulled round the circular drive with corrections by the sackful. A man from All Souls filled five pages, the chaplain of Lincoln College six. Later, Morris began a new introduction to a revised edition, 'Oxford is a dangerous place to write a book about.' The book had so many mistakes that he hired a student to prepare the second edition and later enlisted Mark to do the third, revealing with disarming candour that several people had written to say there is no such thing as a double first in Greats, several hundred had sent letters to tell him that Oriel College has a provost not a president, and 'a couple of thousand wrote in horror to find St Edmund Hall called St Edmund's'.

The new introduction brought an opportunity to be spiteful about Ricks, but Morris's heart was no longer in the fight, not really. 'I had a world at my feet,' he wrote of those years, but in grotesque counterpoint he was ill a lot of the time and increasingly desperate to resolve an inner conflict that verged on the unbearable. It was 'the worst period of my life'. The end game approached.

9
1966–1970
HALF A FREAK SHOW, HALF A MIRACLE

John Randell, physician for psychological medicine, headed up the new Gender Identity Clinic (GIC) in the forbidding nineteenth-century Charing Cross Hospital off the Strand in London. The medical establishment had reluctantly recognised transition surgery. The first International Symposium on Gender Identity took place in the capital in 1969, five days after Apollo 11 had touched down on the moon. Randell, a Welshman, had published a paper on 'transgenderism' in the *British Medical Journal* as early as 1959. Initially he had opposed surgery, like most of his colleagues. The reports of patients returning from successful operations abroad, and his physical assessment of those patients, had changed his view. In the late fifties he had begun a long association with a urologist who, at Randell's recommendation, performed castration and penectomy surgery at Charing Cross, later adding vaginoplasty. In 1969, when Morris saw him, Randell had just published a paper reporting on twenty-nine male-to-female and six female-to-male surgeries. Of the male-to-females, just over a third had undergone vaginoplasty, not always with satisfactory results. It was not an altogether encouraging picture, even though transition was in theory now possible.[*]

If nobody had a bad word to say about Harry Benjamin and his German accent, few said anything good about the despotic Randell. He believed he had the right to total control over those under his care (not

---

[*] Randell also kept up his regular psychiatric clinic at Charing Cross. In 1962 Dennis Potter was a patient.

an uncommon attitude in the National Health Service at that time) and exercised it without regard to their well-being. ('I don't like it one bit,' he squeaks – without a trace of a Welsh accent – in a rare few minutes of documentary footage when a patient reveals she has had top surgery independently while technically under his care. 'He was talking down to me as though I were an animal,' the woman remembers.) Randell insisted that any person attending his clinic should 'be able to be accepted socially without detection in the new gender role', and by this he meant his own view of the gender role. He banned 'his' trans women from wearing trousers. 'I think', he wrote in a conference paper, 'if they're going to be ladies they should be ladylike.' He had the monopoly, almost, of a despairing market. Where else could trans men and women turn? Randell embodied the conundrum of their dilemma, or one of them. He was grossly unempathetic, even unsympathetic, yet when he died in 1982 his obituary in a trans newsletter concluded, 'More than any other single psychiatrist in the UK, he helped us.'

At the clinic, Randell had devised a protocol he called the Real Life Test, obliging those under his care to present in their chosen new gender for a full year before he would consider recommending surgery. The RLT itself transitioned later into the RLE (Real Life Experience), to remove the suggestion of an endurance exam. Morris had in fact already made preparations to live a public life as a woman away from Trefan: in 1965 she had bought a terraced house in Oxford's Jericho for the purpose. For five years either side of turning forty she effectively led a double life. This was not quite like being a spy, though she had learned a good deal about concealment. It took a toll, psychologically: of course it did. (One can only try to imagine what it was like for Elizabeth.) There was little emotional support for the so-called 'transsexual experience'. The Beaumont Society had formed in the UK in 1966 as an offshoot of the American Full Personality Expression (also known as Phi Pi Epsilon), but Morris made no approach on either side of the Atlantic and did not seek out peer support, in 1966, in 1972, or at any time. She never in her life had a transgender friend. As an engaged writer recorded of those years, 'Trans people had nowhere of their own to go; nothing of theirs to belong to. If they wanted somewhere safe – transvestite or transsexual [the two were lumped together] – then the only places available were those where the gays and lesbians and drag queens hung out.' The verb 'to hang out', which suggests lack of purpose, would be hard to apply to Morris in any context. 'The division between transvestite and transsexual interests', another activist wrote, 'took shape [later] with the emergence of the first organisation specifically focused on the needs and interests of transsexual people – the Self-Help Association For Transsexuals.' This was SHAFT. (Yes.) Marooned in Jericho, Morris rang the Samaritans suicide-prevention charity. She had learned to depend on the anonymity of the telephone. The truth is that, however many support groups there might have been, she would not have joined one. She did not see herself as marginalised. She was above the margins, she felt, in some less constricted space which, when she could enter it fully, would set her free.

It was also Health Service policy, Randell had informed her, for a married candidate to obtain a divorce before he would consider recommending surgery. Morris said this was the issue that turned her away from Charing Cross. But if not the UK, where? French gynaecologist Georges Burou led the field in male-to-female operations in his Clinique du Parc in Casablanca on the Moroccan coast. He did not footle around with psychiatric assessment. 'I don't change men into women,' he told *Time* magazine. 'I transform male genitals into genitals that have a female aspect. All the rest is in the patient's mind.' Casablanca was nearer than anywhere else outside the UK, and April Ashley had been there.

Since 1961, when the *Sunday People* had exposed Ashley, she had been in the news. Born nine years after Morris, Ashley later said of her Liverpudlian childhood, 'I didn't know what a present was until my eleventh birthday.' And that was the least of it. 'I merely wanted to be whole,' she said – almost Morris's words. Following transition surgery, Ashley moved to London, became a model, lived the high life and married the Honourable Arthur Corbett, son of Lord Rowallan.

HALF A FREAK SHOW, HALF A MIRACLE

After the press exposed her, Morris's 'surprisingly civilised' *News of the World* colleague from the Canal Zone, Noyes 'Tommy' Thomas, wrote a six-part ghosted serialisation in his paper: he had befriended Ashley, and she had told him her story, or an edited version of it. 'As a result of the newspaper series I had a monstrous postbag,' Ashley wrote, echoing Cowell and Jorgensen. 'Hundreds of people wanting sex changes, wanting help . . . plus the usual quota of abuse.' But, as she said, 'You move one mountain only to find yourself at the foot of another.' In 1965 she was so broke she asked Corbett for a divorce (they had been separated for some time) in order to liquidate her share of their villa in Spain. Corbett fought the request in the High Court, asking Lord Justice Ormrod to rule that the marriage was illegal as the bride was male. When Ormrod eventually agreed, Ashley lost the villa and all trans individuals lost their marriage rights. Harry Benjamin commented publicly from New York, 'The judge's ruling is terribly illogical.' The law effectively created a third sex for whom marriage was not possible. 'Is it the function of the law to create non-people?' Ashley asked. The narrow framework of Ormrod's decision set back trans rights in the UK for more than thirty years. Papers led on the story for weeks, and Morris, away on an assignment, read about it day after day as she watched the black waters of the Jhelum swirl around a Kashmiri houseboat. The annulment verdict made her very nervous indeed. Perhaps she really would end her life as a living whirligig, spinning endlessly in the vortex between fulfilment and public opinion.

Ashley had been Burou's ninth patient. He had refused to testify at the trial. Randell, on the other hand, had appeared as an eager expert witness for Corbett. He had always made it clear that in his opinion nobody could ever *really* change gender, no matter what their new genitals were. The outcome of the Ashley case revealed that psychiatry still governed transgender clinical practice in the UK. Nobody was listening to Benjamin, or to Dr Robert Laidlaw, chief psychiatrist at Roosevelt Hospital in New York, who stated, 'Psychiatry has nothing to offer in these [transsexual] cases as far as any cure is concerned.' Whereas the medical and judicial establishment had abandoned the psychiatric approach to homosexuality (one that considered homosexuality an aberration to be cured, for example by the conversion therapy mentioned earlier), at the Ashley trial experts still cast the trans condition as a psychiatric one. As a doctor at the Gender Identity Clinic put it in 2018, in the sixties and seventies his profession 'tended to pathologize that which made mainstream straight society uncomfortable'. Doctors couldn't seem to stop themselves. Morris herself discovered that, however sympathetic an individual clinician might be, most still held the view that transsexual people suffered from a psychiatric disorder. Health services had all sorts of suggestions. Electroconvulsive therapy often came up. In 1968 Norfolk's mental health authorities suggested putting a trans patient to sleep for three months, the proposed victim reported, 'to rebalance my mind and see whether I would wake up right'. Casablanca beckoned.

The house at 26 Nelson Street in Oxford nestled near the canal among Jericho's red-brick terraces, 'last witnesses to the days when the Thames was the chief thoroughfare of the city – when wool came by barge for the Oxford weavers, and manuscripts for the Bodleian Library, and wines for the Oxford colleges, and arms for the garrison in the Civil War'. For Morris, the waters brought the first intimations of contentment. Once she had begun wearing a skirt in public and all the rest of it, she no longer needed the Samaritans. 'I felt myself', she wrote, 'to be passing through an ante-room of fulfilment.' Friends and acquaintances aware of her situation visited. Most came to offer friendship, others 'to gather material for common-room anecdotes'. She spoke of tears: of course there were tears. But however much others tittered, 'I found it crueller and crueller to present myself as a male.' She had started to look younger as the diethylstilbestrol and other hormones softened her skin and smoothed out incipient wrinkles. But the sheer amount of pharmaceuticals Morris had ingested was punishing. She estimated that between 1954 and 1972 she swallowed twelve thousand pills and absorbed up to fifty thousand milligrams of female matter. People began to notice changes, though Morris covered up her breasts (she had begun to hunch her shoulders too), and the rest was so gradual that nobody thought about it much. Mark wrote later that not until he was at Eton did his 'childish intuitions' of the fathers' cricket match variety 'start turning into concrete thoughts . . . I was simply old enough to notice that, however subtly, my father was bodily different from other fathers.' He went on, 'The whole family began to get used to James being less James and more Jan. This was an androgynous stage, during which the masculine appearance gradually slipped into something more nebulous . . . The change took place over such a long period of time that it began to seem natural.' In his final year, Mark was secretary of the Eton College Music Society. After a concert, the precentor (director of music) hosted a party. Mark and Jan entered together, one in tails and wing collar, the other in jeans and sweater. The precentor approached. 'Mark! You've arrived. Good. And this must be your brother?' Jan finally told Mark at home in Wales when he was eighteen.

> Night was about to fall. We were walking down the curving drive of our house. My father was clearly nervous. I was not exactly unprepared, and the rhododendron tree was in full flower in spite of the winter air . . . We discussed the impending change, the likely reactions of my brothers and sister, and my mother's feelings. I can remember that my father emphasised that the condition was not hereditary.

Morris asked the children to call her Jan. 'I remember saying,' Suki recalls (she was six in 1970), '"That's a girl's name." Mummy told us, "It can be either – in Scandinavia, Jan can be either a man's or a woman's name." Every time I said "Daddy", Jan refused to answer.' The adult Mark was instructed to introduce Jan to his friends as his aunt. As for the wider world, at any given time some people knew and some didn't. By 1970 it was no longer possible to conceal the physical transformation. At one of the Boxing Day parties, a neighbour's daughter asked her father, 'Why does Uncle James have boobies?' Other guests remember preparing their children in the car on the way to Trefan. David Holden was the correspondent who had taken over the *Times* job in Cairo and moved onto *Saphir*. 'I had seen his children grow from the nursery to near manhood,' he wrote,

> and then one day, some years ago, in advancing middle age, there we were in the street outside my home in London. My wife had just kissed him goodbye at the door, and I was directing him to the best shortcut out of town, when he stopped me rather diffidently and said, 'Can I tell you a secret?' 'Of course,' I said. 'Well, I think you ought to know that I'm going to be a woman.'

Many things fell into place for Holden at that moment: the youthful bloom, smooth skin and 'growing sense of elfin shyness, as of one who belongs to some other, secret world', and the way Morris hugged himself 'in round-shouldered intimacy' to cover budding breasts. '"It won't make any difference to you, will it?" he asked anxiously, and as I shook my head, still dumbstruck, his eyes filled with tears.'

People ogled and leered. Once, Twm complained that a man was staring at him, but Morris wrote, 'I knew he was staring at *me*.' When they ate out as a family, waitresses began giving the bill to Elizabeth. The critic John Gross said he arrived at a dinner party to find a flustered hostess: 'James Morris is coming as a woman and it's thrown the seating plan.' That story did the rounds for decades, as did hundreds like it. The satirical magazine *Private Eye* had begun to take notice, running one (feeble) piece 'revealing' that if Morris received an invitation stipulating 'dress informal', it meant she was to attend *en femme*. She got to the point where she was 'past caring', and she couldn't remember who knew and who didn't anyway. She went to see her godson Peter Breitmeyer – the role she had accepted on Everest – when he was at Eton and took him to the Cockpit café in a skirt. By 1971 she was living wholly as a woman bar what she called 'an epicene ambiguity in Wales'.

Some people were attracted to the new her. 'I'm having a very nice time,' she wrote to Elizabeth from Bermuda. 'The odd thing is that the changes occurring in me only seem to give me a better time – with men and women alike! I don't understand it but it's very enjoyable! – nothing, though, ever so enjoyable as you.' Morris was still in these embattled years crazily in love with her wife. In November 1968 she sent a postcard from Vancouver to say, 'What a perfectly splendid woman you are! The more I think about you the more I admire you – quite apart from being perfectly bonkers about you!!' Elizabeth was her anchor. Without her, she would have been adrift. The following year Morris mailed a last-minute card from Heathrow (it depicted a plane) as Elizabeth went into the Radcliffe Infirmary for a gynaecological procedure likely to hasten menopause. 'Just to wish you luck this morning and to say (as if you didn't know) how utterly I adore you – toothless, distraught or even at a pinch bald.' In 1970 she sent a telegram on 14 February *FROM YOUR TRUEST VALENTINE.*

Elizabeth was more isolated in Wales. She faced, to say the least, an uncertain future. As always, she did not complain. Her life, unlike Jan's, ironically, was rooted in place. She absorbed herself in the syncopated rhythm of school terms and the seasonal cycles of the Trefan grounds – no longer just a garden – and in the animals. She recorded both asinine and feline births and deaths in a second-hand Victorian birthday book ('Olaf kicked by Copper and died'), to which she also added the date she had lost her mother thirty years earlier. Elizabeth led her own life, and did have other special friends besides Johnnie Kerr. One was Hugh Boustead, lately Sir Hugh, the resident adviser in the Hadhramaut when James was working the Middle East beat – he was the one who would summon more haddock with a silver whistle. Still a bachelor (he had called off an engagement years earlier as he said he couldn't bear to forsake the Camel Corps), Boustead, almost thirty years Elizabeth's senior, had also been born in Ceylon; his grandfather had introduced tea to the island after blight did for the coffee. Besides climbing on Everest in 1933, the impressive Boustead had been a diplomat, a soldier, a friend to the Arabs, a writer and of course a spy, as well as an Olympic-standard pentathlete. Morris once said that he represented 'the spirit of Empire at its most beguiling'. Not only a knight, Boustead was CMG, DSO, MC and Bar, and more importantly was deeply compassionate, with a lyrical imagination fired by the desert sands. He had settled in the Emirates on retirement, looking after a sheikh's steeds on a stud farm 'where the broken violet ranges border on the red-gold sands of the Rub' al-Khali' – the fearsome Empty Quarter. Elizabeth addressed letters to 'The Royal Stables, Mezyad, Al Ain, Abu Dhabi'. Boustead died there in 1980.

The six years leading up to Casablanca coincided with almost constant movement. Morris had begun wearing female clothes on assignments, and the ambiguity of her situation suited solitary journeys and a secret life on the road; something in her unclenched when she was alone. In 1966 she visited Aden, Egypt, Kenya, Malawi, Ethiopia, Canada, Rhodesia, South Africa and the US – the latter increasingly absorbed, since American destroyers had returned fire after apparently coming under attack in the Gulf of Tonkin in August 1964, in the ten-year nightmare of Vietnam. She got used to being on her own. When she went to Suffolk with Gareth and Chris for Enid's eightieth birthday, she didn't stay in the same hotel as her brothers. (They both noticed how youthful she looked.) Six years later Enid had a stroke. She lost her speech almost completely as well as movement down one side. After several false starts she moved to Saxlingham Hall, a nursing home in Norfolk, where she adapted, as she always had, and entered this new phase of her life with fortitude.

Back at Trefan, Morris began the first draft of *Pax*. She had already decided to centre the book on Queen Victoria's Diamond Jubilee in 1897: that sumptuous event was to be its centripetal and centrifugal force. Centripetal, as the narrative always returns to it (like the desert engagement in *The Market of Seleukia*); centrifugal, because the action extends out from London to all points on the imperial globe. The aim of the volume, Morris said, was to recapture the Jubilee spirit and infuse its pages with the perfume of saddle oil and joss stick. She explained the genesis of the project in a long piece in the *New York Times*:

HALF A FREAK SHOW, HALF A MIRACLE

> In 1946 I was directed by the War Office to help dissolve the Empire, and I spent my twenty-first birthday on a train travelling from Egypt (where we were not wanted) to Palestine (which we did nōt want). For the next fifteen years I found myself vocationally engaged in the decline of my country ... I went to Everest in 1953 and realised that ours was the last of a line of imperial adventures bred by the discredited public-school spirit out of the disbanded Raj ... I decided that I would write a big, colourful, frank and affectionate book about the Empire and call it *Pax Britannica* ... a work of historical reportage.

She finished the draft in ten weeks. As she sat clacking, England faced Germany in the World Cup final (they won), Huddersfield-born Harold Wilson imposed another wage freeze to curb inflation (it failed), and the first Welsh nationalist MP took his seat in Westminster (his war had a long way to go). Morris then stopped for four months to travel again. Features and essays flowed – for the *Architectural Review*, *Encounter*, the BOAC magazine *Welcome Aboard*, *Life*, *Venture* and another American monthly, *Holiday* (not what it seems – actually a literary colour periodical with a million subscribers). Experimenting with dramatic form for the first time since the Shropshire Lads performed *This Is London*, Morris also dashed off a stage piece called *The Oxford Entertainment* for the Meadow Players, a local theatre troupe. Before Christmas the show had its first performance in Witney, Oxfordshire, in front of an audience of twelve.

On New Year's Day, the sky a brilliant blue, she sat down to tackle the second draft of what was to become *The Climax of an Empire*, the first volume of *Pax* to appear. The opening stayed the same: the old Queen Victoria in her black moiré dress with panels of pigeon grey, pressing an electric button in the telegraph room at Buckingham Palace to send a Jubilee message to her far pavilions. Morris reordered, tightened sentences, removed a few 'dazzles', added footnotes and retyped the whole thing, totting up the word count and keeping a running total in the margin. She took a further month off to travel between the second and third drafts and the whole thing was finished by the end of May.

'Half the difficulties and much of the fascination of writing *Pax*', she had continued in the *New York Times*, 'sprang from the fact that I am not a historian at all, but essentially a reporter – by instinct as by origin. I like to describe what I can see for myself.' She said she often felt the disadvantages of this background, notably 'my weakness in historical analyses'.

> A professional historian with aspirations like mine, I think, would have dealt with the Empire in the round, subject races equally with imperialists. I did not feel myself competent to this complex task. I decided to concentrate frankly on the British themselves, describing the imperial scene as they saw it when they gazed out supreme over palm and pine . . . this is an emotional approach to history.

The *Pax* appeal lies in its prioritisation of detail over theory and the narrative flair with which detail is delivered; the protean diversity of Morris's prose suited the subject matter in these respects. Thousands of Victorian families cherished imperial souvenirs, and Marcus Samuel imported coloured shells from Asia which customers could cement to their summerhouses in the Midlands. When Samuel, in Jubilee year, got round to founding a petroleum company, he called it Shell. The catalogue of Hemming's, the Bristol ironworks, offered Britons abroad a prefabricated hotel with a veranda and a 'substantial gothic-style church with tower . . . at £1000'. In 1837 the nine thousand residents of Tullaghobegley in County Donegal possessed between them ten beds and ninety-three chairs. These details, and hundreds like them, stud the Empire books like chips of translucent stone. Morris shifts the narrative round the globe through closely observed vignettes, conjuring scenes like a film-maker. Up in Shimla, the viceroy himself was to be glimpsed on Sunday mornings 'resplendently driving to church in his carriage, a weekly second coming'. The concept of *Pax* was masterly in this regard, years in advance of Merchant Ivory. Half a century after the trilogy appeared, an emeritus professor concluded a survey of imperial literature with the claim that, despite extensive scholarship, 'It was

HALF A FREAK SHOW, HALF A MIRACLE

however a journalist and popular author who truly pioneered the history of Empire.' He referred to Morris. She had seized the moment. The imperial enterprise had inflected the childhood of her peers – red slabs on the schoolroom wall, flags on Empire Day, heroics in fiction. When Enid and Walter had eloped from the Marches, the British Empire had stood at its territorial peak. Yet after India went just three decades later, according to another imperial historian, 'the Empire got tucked in an attic and Britain moved on'. The time was ripe to wheel it out again.

Study of the complex historical phenomenon some call the Pax Britannica had not yet been politicised.* The literature of imperial defensiveness that has flourished since barely existed when Morris sat down to type volume one of what would become her trilogy as bees buzzed at the open window of her study at Trefan. Nobody would have expected her to begin by making the point, which now seems obvious, that all empires exist for the benefit of the colonisers. 'Cruelty was rare', she wrote instead,

> and almost never official . . . Private Britons, trafficking in Asian labour or blazing themselves a trail in Africa, might do terrible things to their natives. Schooner captains commissioned to take indentured labourers home to their South Sea islands, at the end of their service in Australia, sometimes . . . dumped their passengers on the first available atoll. British private soldiers in India often behaved abominably towards Indians . . . But Britons in the civil service were horrified at such conduct. Physical violence was seldom to their taste, paternalism was their forte.

The books – this first, and the two to follow – sweep butchery and appropriation aside to the tune of a bugle reveille. Morris enjoyed the spectacle too much to allow unpleasantness to spoil a good story, and

---

* Although historians had started questioning the morality of the imperial project. The influential scholars Ronald Robinson and John Gallagher had first published in the field in Everest year. But when Morris produced *Pax*, revisionism was still more or less confined to the academy.

where she could she cleaved to the 'bad individual apples' narrative cited above. To her mind, 'In an Empire based on racial differences, it was inevitable that some people were treated as less than human.' In wide-angle mode, she acknowledged the primacy of greed. By the 1860s, 'the British government in India had lost much of its old humanity', she writes near the beginning of *Climax*, and she was prepared to assert that, 'Rightly or wrongly, the urge to profit lay at the root of the New Imperialism.' (The statement suggests that the East India Company that preceded the Raj had displayed humanitarian intent.) With her close-up lens, she toned down actual approbation. The second paragraph of *Climax* had begun hyperbolically in the initial draft: 'It was the greatest Empire in the history of the world,' before she changed 'greatest' to 'largest'. *Pax*, which does a great many things, never tackles Britons' belief in their own racial superiority, the conviction that lay at the heart of the whole project. Paul Scott tried: Ronald Merrick is the villain of *The Raj Quartet*, if there is one, but Scott did not make him unsympathetic. Many readers thought the character *kindly*, even *paternal*; the novels deal in psychological complexity, muddle and human failing. The imaginative orchestration of *Pax* is contingent on muffling the issue. Morris attracts the 'right-wing historian' tag for failing to see events through the eyes of colonised peoples. She never intended to: her aim was to 'concentrate frankly on the British themselves'. She wasn't left or right or even a historian, as she acknowledged: she did no primary research bar a stint at the British Library reading General Gordon's diary – she adored Chinese Gordon. She was *hors concours*, beyond the fray. It seems harsh to criticise an author for something she never tried to do. For that reason, and for her outstanding readability, in the twenty-first century historians tend to make their peace with her. The professor who called Morris a pioneer of Empire concludes, 'Though infused with a rather romantic tone and limited by failure to make connections with wider historiography, [Morris's] books were path-breaking, and subsequent cultural historians owe them a debt.'

She did not address legacies of Empire in colonised lands, as she had in *The World Bank* (the failure of the Indus irrigation system, for example). The subject did not interest her as a mature writer, and she had after all explicitly stated her intention to concentrate on the British. It is more surprising that Morris, previously so compelled by the past, did not investigate ways in which Empire had shaped modern Britain, particularly as the verb 'shaped' recurs in *Coast to Coast* when the author considers how the American past formed the United States as she observed them. (And particularly too given she had reported on the damage wreaked by imperial hegemonies in the Middle East.) She could ignore the professor's 'wider historiography' if she wanted, but what about the television news? She once wrote, 'I am not very multicultural,' and used the concept negatively in her journalism ('There turned out to be a darkly conspiratorial side to multiculturalism'). Yet her cherished Empire had created the phenomenon. After the 1948 British Nationality Act offered citizenship to everyone in the Empire, Britain became a multicultural society *because* it had been a multicultural Empire. Even in the decades after *Pax*, Morris did not write about the consequences of imperialism in her own radically altering society. Scholars and commentators had not yet framed the 'we are here because you were there' narrative, and the legacy of Empire was neither Morris's field nor a live topic, but you would think she might have made the connection.

Take Ireland – there is a lot about it in *Pax*. She had visited many times since publishing a long piece on Dublin in the fifties. On that first trip she had met Erskine Childers II, a future president of the republic, describing him later as 'my kind mentor in Irish politics'. Analysis of the violence of Britain's conduct, or moral comment on it, did not fall within Morris's self-imposed scope, even though she acknowledged in the trilogy, 'It was around the name of Ireland that the moral problems of imperialism first assembled.' As she was hammering out drafts of the first *Pax* volume in Wales, Northern Ireland was heading towards violent confrontation. In the *very month* she began writing, the first victim of what became known as the Troubles died from burns sustained when a petrol bomb had flown through the window seven weeks earlier. Morris was too immersed in the past and in herself to take an interest in any connection that might exist between her own flamboyantly evoked history and the stories humming out of the wireless as the government in London finally realised it had to take Ulster seriously.

Critics have often compared Morris in imperial mode with Edward Gibbon, the author whose *Decline and Fall* James devoured with such pleasure in the army. James Pope-Hennessy (grandson of a governor of Ceylon, another military intelligence man and among the few writers of that generation as idiosyncratic, romantic and enthusiastic as Morris) said in the *Financial Times* that *Pax Britannica* should be placed on the same shelf as Gibbon; a *Sunday Telegraph* reviewer concluded, 'Morris, like Gibbon, writes with an inspired gusto firmly rooted in erudition, which carries the book [*Climax*] into the realms of literature.' That was where she wanted to live: the realms of literature. The comparison with Gibbon rests chiefly on a tendency to combine narrative with evaluative prose, but that similarity only goes so far. It is subject matter – the trajectory of an empire – that draws the two authors together in people's minds across the 189 years that separate them. But Gibbon saw empire as inherently unstable and unproductive, whereas Morris perceived it, she wrote in *Climax*, as a 'development agency'. *Decline and Fall* is not an elegy for empire. In many ways *Pax* is. It was Gibbonian style that attracted Morris, not Gibbonian ideas, and in the trilogy one hears the rolling echoes of the master's measured sentences. Nonetheless, Victor Pritchett said Gibbon 'has a taste for the truth that is melancholy, for seeing life as a series of epitaphs'; that was her too.

She identified more closely with Forster's attitudes to empire. '*A Passage to India*', she explains in *Pax*, 'is not really about imperialism, but about human nature playing itself out against an imperial background, between people of different origins thrown together by the imperial chance.' She wanted *Pax* to be the same and deployed the novel in its pages to defend her overall position. Forster influenced them all: Scott, Lawrence, Morris, everyone. The Royal Society of Literature had made him a companion – its highest honour – the night they awarded Morris the Heinemann Award for *Venice*. In the image of the Club, Morris continues, Forster shows

> this was an ugly system, based as it was upon racial awareness and arrogance, but it was undeniably effective in sustaining the brazen bluff that lay at the heart of the Empire. Forster recognised this – 'We're not pleasant in India', as one of his characters says, 'We've something more important to do' – and in exposing the idea of the Club in its sadness and falseness, he did not frontally attack it.

She goes on, 'Nor did he attack imperialism in the abstract.' Even though Forster was in India shortly after the Jallianwala Bagh massacre, Morris says,

> still he was not repelled by the principle of Empire, the spectacle of one nation governing another, but by the personal implications of imperialism, the sham million alienations it fostered, the hypocrisies. *Perhaps Forster did not worry himself much about the political meaning of it. He was looking deeper* [my italics], and in his tentative, inconclusive way treated the imperial phenomenon as a Greek dramatist might handle a fourth Fate, as an ever-present imponderable decreeing and ensnaring the lives of human beings.

But Forster does show how the Raj created embittered nationalism. (And he did think that the horrors of Amritsar had destroyed any hope of rapprochement in India.) 'We may hate one another, but we hate you most,' Aziz declares in the final scene of *A Passage to India*. Forster evokes the unbridgeable gulf between Indians and the Anglos who ruled them; Morris too projects a gulf in *Pax*, but she does not give Indians a voice – again, she had never intended to, as she had stated at the outset. She was interested in drama and spectacle – 'this is an emotional approach to history' – from a British point of view. In years to come, after Welsh nationalism took hold, she defended herself with rearguard action. The professor emeritus cited writes deep in a source note, 'Morris once expressed her credo to me as being that [*sic*] the British Empire was a dreadful phenomenon only redeemed by its "style".'

The unrenovated section of the Big House had a ping-pong table, and it was there that Morris had revealed to Mark the perils of masturbation. 'Would you like a game of ping-pong?' she asked him. 'I was fifteen', he recalls, 'and remember the bit about nocturnal emissions making you blind. I burst out laughing and told her she was wrong and it was never mentioned again. She cleaved to old-fashioned values and had a prudish streak. She would criticise people who left their wives. She was conventional, especially when it came to families.' Mark also remembers Jan losing interest in politics. At sixteen he was eager to discuss the *soixante-huitards*. 'I tried to engage her and she changed the subject. The point when she lost interest in politics coincided with absorption in the drugs.'

By this time Morris had asked Faber for so many advances of funds that vice chairman Peter du Sautoy, always sharper than Monteith when it came to money, had told her *Faber are not a bank*. But she had to keep asking, writing at the beginning of 1969, 'The Westminster Bank Group celebrated the New Year by inviting me to reduce my overdraft, and halfway through this month I have to pay my triannual contribution to the expenses of the Wall Game' (a sport that originated at Eton). It was not just school fees: consultations and medication made for equally fearsome costs. Back in May 1965, hoping to boost her income, Morris had engaged a younger but more patrician man, Michael Sissons at A. D. Peters, as her first British literary agent. Like a figure out of a Surtees novel, Sissons would have gone down well with the Spearmen. 'I know that he [James] is feeling the pinch a bit at present,' he wrote to Monteith in July 1967. Backlist sales were robust if not spectacular: by that month, *Oxford* had sold 9,000 copies in cloth (hardback) in the UK and *Venice* 17,000 in cloth and 11,000 in paper. *The Presence of Spain* had clocked up 2,250 in the UK and far more in the US. Dutch and German editions of *Spain* had appeared. But the income streams did not meet the sums required.

HALF A FREAK SHOW, HALF A MIRACLE

As with the World Bank, something miraculously turned up. This time it presented itself in the unlikely form of the Port of New York Authority. It was Eugene Black, president of the World Bank, who had put Morris forward. The head of the port, Austin J. Tobin, one of the most powerful men in the US, took Morris out to dinner in London, leaning across the restaurant table over sherry trifle 'like an American buddha' to ask if she (in masculine guise that night) would write a book about the port. Morris signed a contract that summer – Tobin was prepared to wait until she had finished *Climax* – and cashed a huge cheque.

She already knew that the Empire project had swollen to a trilogy, and that *Climax* was to be the middle volume. 'Excellent idea, to make this the centrepiece of a triptych,' Monteith said when she told him. 'Rise, Midday, Decline.' But Morris had to get her finances on track first. 'I am now taking a year off the imperial subject to do my book about the Port of New York,' she told du Sautoy, 'but can hardly tell you how much I'm looking forward to getting back to it.' She had sheepishly, even shiftily, raised this anomalous Port volume with Monteith, pleading the expense of doing up Plas Trefan. Faber, still keen to demonstrate commitment, again complied and bought the book, though with a lower royalty than usual. In addition Sissons extracted an advance for the two future *Pax* volumes of £2,675 apiece. The wolf retreated from the door, for the moment.

Irish-American Brooklyn-born Tobin was thinking of his legacy, like Black of the Bank before him. Now in his sixties, he had started as a clerk at the port at the age of fourteen. It was not yet the Port Authority of New York and New Jersey when Morris got involved, though it was effectively already a bi-state enterprise with the legal status of a public agency. Its remit included airports, at that time LaGuardia and JFK (recently renamed from Idlewild), and great chunks of real estate: Tobin had personally overseen the twin-towered World Trade Center project from its inception, breaking ground on the west side of Lower Manhattan in 1966. (The Port Authority was to name the plaza between the towers after Tobin.) Morris heard his colleagues call the project 'Austin's Last Erection'. He was the highest-paid official in the US after the president, and Morris described him as a 'high romantic of Tennysonian sensibility', which indicated that she liked him. She set off for six weeks in October 1967. 'My own conception of the Port of New York was cast in a romantic-historical genre,' she noted at the outset. One wonders what she did not conceive of in this genre.

Morris travelled, dressed as a man, in Port helicopters and on its cutters and police launches and swept round the docks in the recesses of a Cadillac. In addition, she drove herself to Port outliers around potholed Brooklyn streets and over the still-new Verrazzano Bridge to Staten Island. Most of all she walked, walked and walked, noting the imminence of salt water at the end of every cross-town street. She lived at first in a Midtown hotel, pinning the organisation chart of the Port Authority on the wall. Morris had friends in the know. She had even confided in Tobin and his second wife, an indication of her emotional neediness in the late sixties, as Tobin was a professional patron. The kindly couple lent her their vast apartment on the Upper East Side when they were absent, and there 'the ghostly flicker of my neighbour's television faintly shining through my window' was Morris's only companion. The television was beaming images of anti-war demonstrations down in DC, and of Che Guevara's corpse. When Tobin was in town he took her to Gracie Mansion to meet mayor John Lindsay. She 'popped' a letter in to David Rockefeller's Manhattan residence and was invited over for tea on the implausible basis that Rockefeller's wife, Peggy, liked Morris's handwriting. During the visit Peggy called out to David through the drawing room door to say the White House was on the telephone. The following year, Rockefeller wrote saying he had not realised Morris was one and the same man who had written *The Road to Huddersfield*, which he had reviewed. 'It is an excellent book,' he said.

She took the last-ever Erie-Lackawanna Railroad ferry to Hoboken. To mark the sad occasion, crowds packed the dismal old Manhattan terminal with its 40-watt bulbs and overflowing litter bins, among them another writer taking notes. Morris had already met the fedora-wearing

Joseph Mitchell. He was a blue-eyed Southerner eighteen years her senior and a *New Yorker* staff writer who had published a book about the waterfront and co-founded, that very year, the South Street Seaport Museum. Mitchell was among the greatest writers of the mid-twentieth century. Both he and Morris were prodigies who had started in news and moved to magazines. Both were in love with the operatic drama of New York. Both favoured irony as a mode of expression. Finally, both had a nostalgic streak, found material in cemeteries and understood non-conformity, if it can be understood. The year they met, Mitchell had begun one of his periods of near-silence. He had not written anything since 1964 but went into the *New Yorker* offices every day for thirty-one years thereafter, leaving for lunch like everyone else and drawing a salary like everyone else; nobody knew what he did, but they agreed that he was, at his best, among the best. Mitchell and Morris both liked the half-forgotten New York of throaty chanting from basement synagogues and far-seeing, ancient Irish navvies. It was all, as Mitchell said in the soft accent of the Carolinas, 'tragedy and comedy balled up into the same thing'. He blurred the lines between fiction and non-fiction, a notable feature of a movement that would come to be termed the New Journalism. In the fall of 1965 his own magazine had serialised Truman Capote's *In Cold Blood*, always cited as the original so-called non-fiction novel. Direct speech, attitude, close third-person points of view and a subjective, distinctive authorial voice characterised the emerging genre – Tom Wolfe, its high priest, liked to criticise the 'beige narrators' of the past. Everything about the self-conscious New Journalism applied to Morris's prose. She believed, like the NJ apostles, that all non-fiction represents a subjective shaping of the facts; Mitchell had said one of his own stories was 'more truthful than factual' and Morris used the exact phrase to describe her own work. Mitchell had been ahead of the trend, and so, to a certain extent, had Morris. As John McPhee (another *New Yorker* staffer) said, when the New Journalists came ashore Joe Mitchell was there on the beach to greet them. McPhee could have added that Morris was behind Mitchell, waving.

The world was changing as she did. While she was in New York, anti-Vietnam War protests spread far beyond DC: thousands demonstrated in 'Stop the Draft' Week in thirty cities. A sense of doom hung on the damp air of the docks as marines were shipped home in body bags. The next year was to be the worst of the war (and the worst on the American domestic scene too, for the same and other reasons: Martin Luther King was assassinated in April, Robert Kennedy in June; the Democratic Convention in Chicago two months later was among the most violently confrontational in US history). News from Britain was also portentously gloomy. On the flickering television at the Tobins', Morris watched beleaguered prime minister Harold Wilson solemnly explaining why he had devalued the pound. The decision came after years of pressure on sterling, numerous band-aid austerity packages and countless economic crises. In the first draft of *Pax*, Morris had written about the decline of Britain as foreseen at the glorious Jubilee; fifty years on, her subalterns had detected it in Trieste; and now, in 1967, Wilson had to make his 'Pound in Your Pocket' speech to reassure the country. But things got worse, not better. Britain's diminishing global role was plain to see even as Wilson pulled on his pipe during the infamous fireside chat. The same month, de Gaulle once again vetoed Britain's application to join the Common Market.

In the New Year, Morris wrote to Hetherington in between correcting page proofs for 'vol 1 of the trilogy', promising to send him a copy

> to thank you for all the delightful assignments that enable me to write it . . . Boys gone back to school today, house as silent as the grave, except when the two smaller ones are murdering each other – Elizabeth and I sadly preparing a return to our usual term-time supper of claret and boiled eggs, instead of the steaks, pastas, lamb chops and enormous risottos to which we are succulently condemned in the holidays.

A month later she reported, 'I'm off to Spain tomorrow for a few days if I can get through the snow down to Southampton, then on March 10

Elizabeth and I soar away to Persia.' That year, 1968, she also visited Malta, Lebanon, the US and Canada, Turkey, Italy, France and Switzerland. At home she alternated between Nelson Street and Trefan, where a campaign she had started to defeat plans to build a holiday camp forced a public inquiry. She was opposed to mass tourism on her patch – what her confrère R. S. Thomas called 'Elsan culture' (the Elsan was a primitive chemical lavatory indigenous to the camping scene). She was too embarrassed now to swim in the Dwyfor behind the house – 'stripped of my clothes, I was a chimera, half-male, half-female, an object of wonder even to myself' – bathing instead in a secret lake in Snowdonia's Glyderau range, 'sedgy and serene'. Stillness came like a benediction then, in moments that were almost holy when Morris glimpsed the unity she craved.

On top of everything else, she had written the script for a *son et lumière* spectacle staged in July at her old college, Christ Church, in aid of her true alma mater, its Cathedral School. Auden had contributed a prologue, which was to be read by the actor John Gielgud. Comedy duo Michael Flanders and Donald Swann had been cast as Flanders & Swann. Auden and Morris had met in New York the previous year to discuss the show. 'The dean of Christ Church tells me you are in town,' Auden had written to her as she stalked the crime-ridden streets for *The Great Port*. 'I'm very anxious to see both you and the script of Son et Lumière.' Now that it had come off, Morris had bullied Faber into taking an ad in the programme, and Monteith, loyal as ever, sat through the event. The following month, Soviet tanks rolled into Prague, consolidating another empire.

Morris's US editor Helen Wolff was delighted when an adulatory full page in the *New York Review of Books* kicked off coverage of *Climax* stateside. Overall, US notices were less equivocal than their British counterparts. In the *TLS*, Anthony Sampson, who had already published one rewritten edition of his *Anatomy of Britain*, thought '[t]he Empire Builders get off very lightly for their treatment of their subject peoples', and 'nostalgia is a dangerous guide', before wondering if 'the author's highly descriptive style stands in the way between us and the subject'. So perhaps revisionism was edging its way out of academia. Another old familiar, Dennis Potter, wrote the most accurate review. He fidgeted about 'sympathetic collusion' but wasn't spoiling for a fight that day. 'Mr Morris enjoys his adjectives, and I do too: the occasional florid or over-crenelated paragraph is a small price to pay for the enjoyment of such a lively and colourful style. And the perpetual ambiguity of his attitudes – the camouflaged piety in disguised nostalgia – is here perfectly tailored to the subject.' Enoch Powell, a politician as famous as the prime minister, was more interested in his own agenda in the *Spectator* but allowed that 'proportion is the artistic as well as the historical challenge of a book like this, and to my own feeling, Morris has met it successfully'. One review was handwritten. It had been broadcast on the Sri Lanka Broadcasting Company's English National Service. The writer was Elizabeth's half-brother – the child Elizabeth's widowed father had had with her ayah; his first name was Austin, after his father. He was working as a journalist in Colombo.

As reviews poured in from her cuttings service, Morris seized the moment to pitch a lavish picture book on Empire – it was the pomp and splendour in the foreground that had caught her eye in the first place. Both Faber and Harcourt were slow to respond, or so she thought. On 14 November 1968 du Sautoy wrote to Wolff, 'With James in his present mood we shall not be able to wait until the three volumes are published before we tackle the proposed illustrated volume.' Wolff replied, 'James has been extremely unpleasant about the fact that we did not set [typeset] the book [*Climax*] ourselves . . . I know that J occasionally goes into this kind of mood and that you have suffered from it in other circumstances. It seems to be part of the publisher's profession to be made to bear the brunt of what fundamentally are an author's feelings of insecurity.' The following summer, Wolff wrote to du Sautoy, 'James seems to be wildly disappointed with our sales of *Pax* . . . I am afraid he has been in one of his irredentist moods sparked, I am sure, by his Welsh environment.' More likely it was the drugs. When Faber decided to delay publication of *The Great Port*, Morris exploded. 'I am willy-nilly pulling out of the journalism which has kept us all in comfort for so many years, and I can no longer afford to have books treated as fill-ins, in-betweens and off-the-cuffs, to be slotted into whichever seasonal list has a gap in it. If you don't want a book, say so.'

Happy interludes untainted by arguments or pharmaceutical regimes included the installation of a convict at Trefan. Dafydd Iwan, chair of Cymdeithas yr Iaith Gymraeg, the Welsh Language Society, and a protest singer, had served three weeks in Cardiff Prison for refusing to pay fines after defacing English-language road signs. A Llanystumdwy dramatist and garage-owner, W. S. Jones, known as Wil Sam, had made his house available, according to Iwan, 'as the meeting place for young people like us. When I was about to leave prison, I got a message from him saying he had a family offering accommodation.' The Forwards had just moved out of the Big House, and Iwan, his wife and their baby moved into the top floor. The two families had never met before. 'James and Elizabeth were lovely people,' Iwan remembers. 'They didn't interfere, they were one hundred per cent behind the campaign and glad to give us a home. They never asked for payment and always welcomed us when we knocked downstairs for a cup of sugar. It was an incredible episode, when I come to think of it.' Morris loved the whole business and said, many decades later, 'We found ourselves in a maelstrom of young Welsh patriots who were busy burning houses down. I was very taken with them. A stack of explosives was hidden in the Trefan pighouse.' (It was actually a duck house. Iwan was never involved in arson or with explosives.) Three decades later Iwan became chair of Plaid Cymru, the Welsh nationalist party. He had seen the Morrises over the years, and discussed the struggle with Jan. 'Her attitude to nationalism was not political,' he says. 'It was romantic. She told me Plaid should have as its main policy kindness and happiness. She became more Welsh as she grew older. So did Clough [Williams-Ellis]. Even R. S. did.' They all retreated into 'the old, old dream'.

*

Her time, as she wrote, was approaching. She remembered those last ambiguous years with tenderness, aware, as she noted in a radio interview much later, that others saw her as she saw herself, 'half a freak show, half a miracle'. Morris wrote later in *Vanity Fair* (in a piece on Boy George):

> Wherever I wandered ambiguously in the world of the late 1960s, people seemed to treat me with a curious sort of concern, as though I were something of fragile public interest. New York customs officials, security ladies in Pakistan, African headmen, London clubmen – all surprised me by their gentle mixture of kindness, curiosity, and something approaching complicity.

Of course, there was anxiety: unlike E. M. Forster's character Cyril Fielding, she did not travel light. She carried so much that was difficult in her head, was so eternally focused on herself. When she found out the *Mail* was on her case, she approached the editor of the *Evening Standard*, asking if she could write something, as naturally enough she wanted to control the narrative. By the end of 1968, Monteith and Goad at least were fully informed. 'Don't worry, I shall be very orthodoxly dressed,' Morris wrote when arranging a lunch. It was the diffident, reserved Monteith, the closeted All Souls man, who acted as the interface between Morris and his Faber colleagues during the transition; in fact, between her and the entire book trade. Morris was not, however, the only author to display a lack of convention in the sartorial department. When the pinstriped Monteith took two of his poets, Thom Gunn and Ted Hughes, to lunch at the Travellers Club, Gunn turned up in a leather jacket and a pair of leather chaps. (Had it not been bad enough when Kenneth Halliwell wore a beret to a meeting at the Imperial Hotel round the corner from the office?) Leather was too much for members, however well travelled, and many complained to the secretary, who reported the incident to the committee, who asked Monteith for an explanation. He flannelled about Californian habits – Gunn was living in the Golden State – and even blamed the innocent Hughes, on the grounds that 'he arrived so late that the opportunity for quick action was lost'. Gunn continued to show no mercy: when he won a literary award and was not in the UK for the ceremony, he made his editor read out an anecdote about mice in high heels. Monteith saw it as the price to be paid for trading in genius. He had recently approached a young poet from Northern Ireland, and in 1966 Faber published Seamus Heaney's first collection. The future Nobel Laureate never forgot his debt to Monteith. Nor did Morris, but she did forget to whom she had told her news. She turned up for a lunch appointment with her agent, who knew nothing, in a skirt. When Sissons's secretary went into his office after the engagement, he was rocking to and fro at his desk with his head in his hands.

Travels in 1969 and 1970 included a long African tour gathering material for *Pax* volume two, which was to be called *At Heaven's Command* (it soon dropped its preposition). Back in South Africa, Morris had come to hate Johannesburg. 'Terrible city,' she wrote from there, asking Elizabeth if she could join her in Greece. 'So long as I am with you – you are my mobile paradise! . . . So remember if you said you wanted to meet in Wolverhampton my heart would leap at the prospect.' But they reunited at Trefan, where Morris wrote the introduction to a large-format photographic book called *Persia*. It was not an introduction, really, it was an essay – a perfectly judged combination of history, geography, personal anecdote ('I was once stuck for a few hours in a blizzard on one of the Elburz passes') and a few jokes. She had absorbed so much about Persia: the years trailing round the roadless hinterland and foraging for information in Tehran had not been wasted, nor forgotten. 'I went to the tombs [inaccessible rock graves near Persepolis] one night', she wrote, 'when the greatest of full moons, bigger and richer and more golden than Europe ever saw, was rising like some nobly-fulfilled dowager behind the Qashqai hills.' In excavating the layers of Persian history she found 'fable blended with fact', a medium that ensnared her always, and which informed her own writing. She foresaw what was to come: 'The Shi'a mullahs thunder about the cities in their green head dresses and swinging cloaks, and off-stage many a successor to the Assassins doubtless cherishes the dream of a Persia dedicated to more ferocious ideals of Islam, where the faith will be enforced by fire or steel, and murder in the cause will be rewarded by certain if not instant transference to Paradise.'

Not only had she forgotten nothing. However overwrought she might be, she had not lost her touch. Staying on a *shikara* (houseboat) north of Srinagar for *Venture* magazine, Morris stopped at a market stall to buy 'something for my supper' which the cook would prepare. Game birds lay in monstrous piles, including 'a solitary grey heron all folded in on itself, its neck tucked beneath its belly, its legs crumpled below its rump'. Drugs had not affected her almost unmatchable gift for descriptive prose. 'Silently, silently trail the pickpockets,' she began a piece on Calcutta, 'and sometimes a sleeper stirs in the arcades of Wellesley Place, raises an arm and returns to the catacomb.' (She went up to see Sherpa Tenzing in Darjeeling on the same trip, though he didn't recognise her.) The theme of time passing and the changes it wrought ran like a thread through everything now.

Morris often refers to what she was reading. She had Jane Austen with her on the *shikara*. The novelist's 'porcelain comedies . . . perfectly correspond' with Morris's sensory response as '[t]he focus narrows, within the narrow frame of the Kashmiri water-life'. She seemed to be saying that the scale of Regency drawing rooms suited the parade of bridges over the Jhelum and twitchy feathers in kingfishers' wings. In Fiji she used Joseph Conrad to disdain the encomia of the travel brochure ('if like me you prefer your South Seas in Conradian mode') in favour of clattering tropical rain on corrugated-iron roofs and the 'steamy, mouldy, gourd-like fibrous smell that exudes from the forest when the sun comes out again'. In these essays from the late sixties and early seventies Morris often said she was seeking an aesthetic. In Wyoming it was cowboys who lent the landscape a genuine 'aesthetic'. The 'full-blooded aesthetic' of Fiji appears 'in Gauguin colours and theatrical outline'. The seaside-scene 'aesthetic' of the Second Empire dominates an essay on Trouville, and Morris traces its influence on Proust's fictional seaside Balbec. What did she mean by 'aesthetic'? With the word she sought to pin down the appearance of a place in order to reveal something of its essence. She was the writer–lepidopterist. Aesthetics were not merely the beauty of appearance. They were a beauty that stretched over a framework of meaning. The cowboys were 'guardians of lost identity: they alone . . . still seemed at ease with their environment'. During the whole process of *Pax*, from gestation, through composition, to the unending years of legacy, Morris referred constantly to the appeal of imperial 'aesthetics'. When the climate changed, she played the word 'aesthetic' like a get-out-of-jail-free card.

Her personal aesthetic remained ambiguous. People often did not know if she was a man or a woman and sometimes they asked her. When she replied to a Fijian taxi driver who did so, 'I am a respectable, rich, middle-aged widow,' he said, 'Good, just what I want,' and put his hand on her knee. (The detail does not appear in the *Venture* piece on Fiji, but Morris used it later to demonstrate how charming it was to be female, inciting rage in feminists far from Suva.) India, even if she was not emotionally attached to it, suited her enigmatic arrangement. At the end of the long 1970 trip, after flying from the subcontinent to Kenya, she wrote to Elizabeth from the Nairobi Hilton: 'I did enjoy it all, and received so many touching kindnesses there, baffled and curious about me though everyone was – I think in a country where one can wear absolutely anything, or nothing . . . I was about the only person thought worth staring at! Never mind, they never stared unkindly.'

A man walked on the moon but the white heat of Harold Wilson's technological revolution had apparently failed to produce a new Britain after all. Six weeks after the public unexpectedly voted Ted Heath and his piano into 10 Downing Street, and with the sterling crisis far from over, the Morrises temporarily exchanged houses with their friends the Griggs. John Grigg, formerly Lord Altrincham (he had renounced the title), was working on the first volume of his biography of David Lloyd George; he and his family lived in Blackheath in south-east London. From one side at least this switch was not a success. 'If there is one society I do not want to be member of', Morris wrote irritably to the baffled Monteith, 'it is that of the Span-housed, Katharine Whitehorn-inspired, progressively educated Young Marrieds who seem to infest Blackheath.' Low-cost, modernist Span flats were built by a company aiming to *span* the gap between suburban monotony and Georgian rectories. The inhabitants of these dwellings were the *Guardian* readers playwright Michael Frayn had characterised as Herbivores, or so Morris imagined. She was soon to find out that it was *Guardian* writer Katharine Whitehorn specifically and Herbivore herds in general who would publicly support her when she needed it.

10
1971–1974
BEING A STAR

Early in 1971 the Inland Revenue dispatched the steepest tax demand yet, and in a panic Morris decided to 'shelve' *Pax* until she had at least paid off her £7,000 overdraft, if not the tax bill, telling a horrified Wolff that volume two was to consist solely of articles already published elsewhere. Meanwhile, she signed up for a short book on America's Cascade mountains. She had already made one trip, motoring through the Douglas firs of the North-West coast and writing to Elizabeth from the Portland Hilton at the end.

> I've been travelling *en femme*, so to speak, which has given me quite a new perspective – except here, where I have people to see and don't want to confuse the issue any further than it's confused already. I'm constantly congratulated on my bravery – 'all alone'! ... or given what [*Times* journalist] B. [Bernard] Levin would call the old Noddy talk – 'My, won't you have a lot to tell the folks back home!' But alas the folks back home know it all already.

Elizabeth went into hospital again, this time for a full hysterectomy. She convalesced with the Kerrs at Holly Bank while Morris was in New Zealand (where the populace, 'stunned' by her 'ambiguous presence ... listen to my wildly fluctuating explanations of myself with bated breath and shining eyes'). When Elizabeth had made a full recovery they flew to the US on a fresh venture to the Cascades, travelling as two women for the first time (sisters-in-law, they said). For Morris it was 'the happiest [journey] of my life'.

The Cascades volume did not come off, nor did projected books on Eton or the Port of London, and Morris bailed out of an embarrassing Time-Life partwork on Empire and a bad television series that went with it. But she did sign up with Monteith for a book on the Venetian Empire. Faber gave her an advance of £3,500 in that cruel April of hovering tax collectors. Before she started, Morris set about collating a second anthology of her own work. Some of the essays she chose were enjoying their third outing: a piece on the Anglo-Irish Ascendancy had already been published in both *Encounter* and *Pax Britannica*. Faber heroically marketed the collection by referencing the rise in leisure air travel. 'Thanks to the jet airliner,' the flap copy trumpeted, 'journeys which a few years ago would have seemed great adventures, have now become ordinary holiday prospects.' We do not know how many readers of *Places* did in fact holiday in Swaziland, where Morris had met the king.

She used the foreword to mark another break, though really it was the same break announced in the review about being able to book a ticket to Kathmandu in Piccadilly or Cedar Rapids. The travel essay was 'a fading genre. Now that everyone who reads has been nearly everywhere, the travel writer finds his occupation gone, and turns to other forms . . . perhaps like me projecting his view of today into an evocation of yesterday . . . Anyway it was grossly overpaid.' She added – and this was the beginning of 1972 – 'it became clear to me that my dilettante days were over too, for the writing of travel essays could no longer be relied upon to provide a kind of private income. But I did not mind. I was becoming a different person anyway.' She was trying to manage her transition. Regarding her retirement as a travel writer, she was protesting too much, as scores more travel essays appeared. But she was probably right that the money had gone, substantially.

Meanwhile, Monteith felt they should make an Official Transition Announcement in-house, with Morris present. Goad organised this excruciating event. When it was over, Morris wrote to her: 'All went off harmlessly and usefully, I thought, and that I'm sure was largely due to you. I feel wonderfully liberated by the fact that it's no longer a secret, and I hope that if we can see the small children through all right we may all live happily ever after!' Suki turned eight in 1972. When more press coverage seeped out, Morris knew she had to make it official with Chris and Gareth too. In the second week of December, ahead of a trip to London, she wrote to them.

> Dear Gareth and Chris, I'm going to be at the Royal Commonwealth Society on the nights of Thursday and Friday next week: partly because I am seeing a lawyer about my future, and Elizabeth's and the children's. If either or both of you would care to meet me there, and I really think one of these days you must, unless you want to write me off from your lives (which I see is a perfectly feasible alternative!) would you care to drop me a card . . . I hope you will come: I would like to put you more fully in the picture, and demonstrate, I hope, that it needn't all be as ghastly as I think you fear – and is even, as most of my friends and colleagues seem to think, not without interest. Love to all.

Gareth and Chris met ahead of time so they could go in together; Gareth, always early, was pacing the Northumberland Avenue pavement when Chris arrived. The barman took their orders, and when Jan chose a gin and tonic he asked if she wanted ice and lemon. She enquired with a simper, 'Would that be a squeezy lemon?' Chris remembered that.

She no longer needed the house in Jericho, so Mark, now with long curly hair and sporting a cloak, lived there in his second year – he had gone up to Christ Church himself. Morris visited in a BMW with personalised plates (the motor company had given them to her). 'She was very flirtatious with men she liked. She used to pat them,' Mark's girlfriend Belinda Mitchell-Innes remembers. 'If Elizabeth came on her own it was lovely, but if Jan came with her, Elizabeth moved to the edge.'

Morris found time, that tense autumn, to write to congratulate two men on their books: Kingsley Amis, no longer a modish Movement writer, for his novel *Girl, 20*, and Henry Paget, 7th Marquess of Anglesey, her neighbour across the Menai Strait and a fixture of the Anglo-Welsh set. She had read with pleasure a book he had edited, and wrote to invite him to the Big House. 'I've just finished and sent off the first volume of my intensely boring history of the British cavalry from 1815 to 1919,' Anglesey ended his exuberant reply. 'It only goes up to 1850! Three more intensely boring volumes are projected.' In fact, seven more came. ('It reminds me of Patrick Leigh Fermor,' Morris wrote to him much later, 'so doggedly progressing towards Constantinople in his masterpiece.') From that day on, poems and cards flowed between Trefan and Plas Newydd, the ravishing Anglesey seat, until the 7th Marquess, four years Morris's senior, died in 2013.

The pair gossiped about their lives as authors. They were both aficionados of dash and detail, both pun-lovers. Anglesey accepted Morris's transition for what it really was. (The 5th Marquess had been a raving queen, so Henry was not on unfamiliar ground.) 'My very dear gurl,' he sometimes began his missives, ending them, 'love and kisses, dearest fabulist'. He had always been thin, a sixty-a-day man, and when he gave up smoking he grew rotund. He had a flirtatious relationship with Morris, and when he and his wife Shirley came to Trefan with their five children, he insisted on sitting next to Jan at table. The Morris children remember suppers in the forty-foot, narrow Plas Newydd dining room with its Rex Whistler mural. (Henry gave the estate to the National Trust in 1976.) Jan and Elizabeth were at his seventieth in Venice and his eightieth in Torcello and his ninetieth in Surrey, and at Shirley's eighty-fifth in a Wiltshire pub, and at another party in Nice – 'She and Elizabeth were always there,' recalls the Angleseys' son Alex Uxbridge, the 8th Marquess.

Others talked about her unkindly. In El Vino on Fleet Street hacks cackled over stories about Morris changing outfits in the lavatory on the train to London. And there was much worse. She was defiant. She raised flags, sent up balloons. When *The Times* reported on a new Olympic hair test to deal with the 'problem of sexual determinacy', Morris wrote a letter, which appeared in the paper, to say this test would not in fact solve the problem. It was merely a handy way of applying one obvious yardstick of sexual identity, chromosome analysis . . . It does not begin to measure far deeper sexual attributes and energies – in particular that perplexing new sense of gender which is already having so profound an effect upon our social structure, and seems to me a contemporary version of the idea of soul.

She wanted to write about that aspect of her life, that side of the divide – it had been a mute half for so long. All those other trans voices had spoken in the memoirs she had read. She was preparing to speak herself.

Before she did, she abandoned the plan to convert *Pax* volume two into an anthology, much to Wolff's relief. Morris was at her typewriter working through her first draft as the lights went on and off during the seven-week miners' strike and the country lurched from one official state of emergency to the next. What would they call the book? *Jingo* had support in Queen Square, where Faber had moved. At the end of March, Monteith wrote to say, 'We are all very happy to settle for your latest suggestion, *Rule Britannia*, subtitle, "The Theme of Empire". Excellent – and nice to have it settled.' Fortunately it was not settled. Daphne du Maurier published a novel with that dire title in 1974, and that scuppered the plan.

In April a story appeared in the *Spectator* announcing that Morris was to complete her transition in Casablanca. She published a denial, and Goad reported to the office, 'If he has an operation at all . . . he will most definitely have this in England.' In fact, Morris *had* decided on Casablanca. Bizarrely, two days before she actually left the UK on a passport stating she was male, she had celebrated the imminence of liberation with the unlikely figure of Alistair Horne. They had met seven years earlier when the historian, a former spy and foreign correspondent who had, like Morris, turned to books, had worked himself (and his publisher and agent) into a tremendous 'panic' over the fact that he too was writing an Empire book based on Queen Victoria's Jubilee. In an agitated letter, Horne suggested a meeting to see if there might be 'a practical way of dividing up the Empire', a neat case of art imitating life. They had mutual friends, Horne threw in as if it might help, such as Charles Breitmeyer, whose son Peter was Morris's godchild. In the end Horne, after a lot of *Sturm und Drang*, turned to another subject, and he and Morris exchanged chummy postcards and letters for decades. Morris felt safe with the unlikely figure of the reactionary Horne, and at the beginning of July they lunched at the Hole in the Wall in Bath. Two days later, Mark drove Morris to Heathrow.

In *Conundrum*, her trans memoir, Morris writes that when she arrived in Morocco she looked up the Clinique du Parc in the telephone book – at last a directory had a speaking part. She certainly did call on the British consul in case she died under the knife ('He did not seem surprised'). Then she hired a car to drive to Marrakech to get a piece out of it – 'had this lovely Stella (like beer)', she told Elizabeth. Their pedestrian intimacy was touching.

Her room at the clinic in rue Lapébie, a narrow street parallel to the palmy avenue du Général d'Amade, had floral curtains and a balcony looking onto the 'non-architecture' that had begun to blight urban Morocco. On the pavement directly outside, a knife-grinder played the flute. Fatima, Morris's kindly nurse, told her that patients in residence included a Greek, two Americans and a lecturer in sociology at the University of Lancaster. Georges Burou appeared on his rounds, affable and 'dressed for the corniche'. Born in the Hautes-Pyrénées in 1910, he had grown up in Algiers, where his French parents were teachers. He qualified and worked as a gynaecologist and obstetrician, and moved to Morocco in 1940 after being struck off in Algeria for performing illegal abortions. He was a keen waterskier, among the first to ski across the Strait of Gibraltar, as well as an enthusiastic golfer. His English was poor but his vocabulary in gynaecology and golf was strong. Unlike Harry Benjamin, Burou kept a low profile in professional circles, and only ever gave one clinical presentation, although he and his second wife did go on to pose for *Paris Match*. He had pioneered anteriorly pedicled penile skin flap inversion vaginoplasty, in which the skin of the penis is turned inside out to form a vagina. He left the prostate in if possible. Standing in the hard Maghreb sunlight slanting through the window, Burou ran through potential complications. The fearsome list included urethral stenosis, bowel perforation, fistula formation and much else including the big one: sepsis. Morris wasn't listening.

She had the operation on Saturday night, 8 July. Burou had performed his first male-to-female reassignment eighteen years previously and had clocked up many hundreds; by 1972 the procedure took only an hour. After Fatima wheeled Morris back to her room, she strapped her arms to the bed. A drain remained in place until Monday night. On Sunday, Morris slept, lulled back to dreamland if she woke in pain by the strains of the knife-grinder's flute. By Monday morning she was able to sit up and write – and that was what she first thought of: writing. 'It's over', she told Elizabeth, 'and I'm feeling better already though naturally a bit weak. It will make an excellent and not unentertaining piece of memoir!' On Tuesday her letter home began,

> My chief sensation now is one of liberation – free to live happily again without that blessed obsession and to make up I hope all the torments I've plagued you with over so many years. Darling I just don't know how to thank you for all your kindness to me . . . I feel now that it will be much less important to me what other people think I am, because I shall no longer be deceiving them, so to speak, with illicit organs! For what it's worth, or what it is! – I really am me!

Elizabeth sent roses – an enormous bouquet. On Wednesday, 'the clips came out – Burou is some sort of a genius, I suspect'. Work began with neovaginal retractors.

Casablanca nights were long. Ships hooted, like elephant grief. In the morning, the same hard light slanted onto the tiled floor. On Thursday, Morris looked at herself in the mirror above the sink for the first time. 'Not impressed,' she wrote in the daily missive to Elizabeth. 'You must expect to find me haggard . . . I'm sure the reason it's had so little mental effect on me is that it was, in my case, little more than a matter of form – I'd been so thoroughly feminised anyway.' She repeated this in another letter two days later: 'I don't feel I've undergone a <u>change</u> in any sense – merely the removal of some atrophied and unnecessary organs . . . the change came far more with the hormones over all those years.' On Saturday 15 July she reported, 'Slight complication this morning when the new orifice closed and had to be reopened.' Just as alarmingly, she read Erich Segal's *Love Story* twice. She had naturally brought her typewriter to the clinic. On the Tuesday she had written to Monteith:

> Just a line to let you know that I had that surgery on Saturday in Casa after all to get it over with . . . the chief sensation so curious an event has left in me is one of liberation – the blessed thing has tormented me for so long, and now I hope I shall be able to make it up to Elizabeth for all the wretched problems I've loaded on her. Do ring her if you have a moment.

The 'wretched problems' were not over. Morris had decided to sell the Big House. She no longer needed to express status through feudal Boxing Day parties. That phase at least really was over. They would never again have a family home where everyone could gather at Christmas. ('We were no longer allowed to *be* a family,' Mark says.) Elizabeth knew this upheaval lay ahead when Jan returned.

The second paragraph of Morris's first letter to Monteith from the clinic dealt with typesetting matters arising from *Heaven's Command*. 'I'm most fearsomely and embarrassingly bad at paying compliments,' the editor replied, 'but do please let me say how immensely I admire your courage and intelligence in having faced up to this problem.' He hastily moved on to *Heaven's Command*, the first two parts of which he had just read. 'I do think, quite honestly, that it's the best book you've written yet.' They had begun signing off letters 'with love'.

After two weeks in the clinic, Burou discharged her, all smiles, and Morris checked in to a hotel for another fortnight until she was well enough to fly, watching the dusty daily cycle of the Casablanca street from her window and typing up travel pieces. She had written to John Randell asking him to suggest a London doctor for a check-up as soon as she got back. Then she flew home. The operation had cost $4,000 – about £19,000 in today's money.

That autumn, she had two more procedures in England ('I would have gone through the whole cycle ten times over, if the alternative had been return to ambiguity or disguise'). In October she took Elizabeth and the two younger children to St Lucia. Morris read her mail lying on a chaise-longue at the Halcyon Beach Club. 'Torrential congratulations,' Monteith wrote again, having read the rest of *Heaven's Command*. The warm sea was sapphire blue on the Caribbean coast, and Morris lounged in satisfaction at her editor's reaction, and at everything.

At the end of November they exchanged contracts to sell the Big House. They had found a property in the Black Mountains in south-east Wales, where Elizabeth and the two younger children would live while Jan alternated between there and a rented flat in Bath, a short commute of under two hours. But it was not the end of Trefan: they kept the coach house and the derelict stables opposite, both granite-built and roofed with Welsh slate. They planned to convert them and, in time, move permanently back to Llanystumdwy. They also retained fishing rights on that stretch of the Dwyfor, for the romance of it. 'We got £37,500 for it [the Big House],' Morris told Monteith, 'which will with luck just about cover the cost of the new Abergavenny house and its extensions.' In fact, they had paid £12,000 for the new place. Mark suspects the whole move was 'a vague attempt at freedom. The squirely thing had to go because of the gender reassignment. She had to sell anyway as she needed the money.' Casablanca had not severed the psychological link between Jan and Elizabeth and there was no talk of permanent separation. Mark says, 'It's harder for a narcissist not to have a wife than to have one. A codependent wife is a good target.' How did Elizabeth feel about the move? Since the hysterectomy she had been experiencing periodic depressions and did not want to leave Plas

Trefan. When Suki asked why she stayed, she said, 'Because I made a vow to God.'

As for Morris, the 1972 Boxing Day party was 'my first as a woman, my last in the house. More people came than ever . . . I felt my personality changing almost as I walked among my guests.'

Trefan Bach (Little Trefan), as they renamed the new house, lay eight miles from Abergavenny in the crook of a hill at the head of a forty-mile valley through the Black Mountains, the eastern ridges of the Brecon Beacons. It had whitewashed stone walls and slate roofs, one sloping sharply, and inside it was dark. The donkeys made the move with them, taking up residency in the 'dacha', as Morris called an outbuilding close to a bank of the Grwyne Fawr. Elizabeth made friends with her neighbour Betty Jones, a Welsh-speaking sheep farmer's wife. Suki remembers, 'They were like two schoolgirls when Jan was away. But Mummy was never allowed to see Betty when Jan was there. Jan was like a guard dog.' The writer Elspeth Huxley was another neighbour who became a good friend to Elizabeth. When the roof had to come off Trefan Bach, the Morrises lived in the Huxleys' holiday cottage. At least Elizabeth had some inherited money. She was able to make financial decisions independently of her husband. In theory, she would have been free to go.

Suki went to three primary and four senior schools. 'I don't know why I kept moving. A teacher told Mummy I shouldn't move so much.' (In a piece she published in the press after Morris died, Suki noted, 'My brothers were sent to the finest schools in England.') She remembers, 'Jan was hard to me, and then she'd go and tell someone like the postman, "I've been mean to Suki", and he'd say, "Oh I'm sure it's fine", and she'd ring me up to say, "The postman said it was alright."' In the archetypal dysfunctional-family model, Suki was the scapegoat and Elizabeth the enabler.

Jan had changed her first name by statutory declaration five months before Casablanca (actually to Catharine Jan). 'It's very important', stated a company-wide Faber memo on 19 June 1972, 'that from now on all communications should be addressed to Jan Morris and <u>not</u> to James Morris.' But at the same time, *Places*, the latest anthology, was going through the publication process under 'James' as the author had requested, as it was under that name the essays had been written. In New York, Wolff like everyone else was confused. Volume two of *Pax* could surely not come out under a different name to volume one? Even Elizabeth got muddled with pronouns, sending a note to Monteith in July: 'J is away and will write when he [*sic*] comes back.' Of course she thought of her husband as a man. To add to the chaos, when Morris compiled autobiographical notes that Monteith had requested for a jacket in the October following Casablanca, she told him, 'They [the notes] are by necessity muffled – I have to lie rather low during the progress of our divorce action, Her Majesty's judges being unlikely to allow E and me a decree nisi if we made it publicly known that we were nuts about each other anyway, whatever our genders.' In April 1971, as a result of the April Ashley trial, the House of Commons had debated the issue the case raised: was a marriage legal if one party had a 'sex change'? Honourable Members, having got into a fine muddle themselves, upheld the *Corbett* v. *Corbett* verdict and left it open for the courts to decide how 'male' and 'female' were to be defined. Before the divorce reform enshrined in the Matrimonial Causes Act 1973 (still in the future when the Morrises sought their own divorce), guilt had to be affixed to one party or the other, and Elizabeth had cited desertion. From all points of view, it was advisable to 'lie low'. Regarding which name to use for publication, Morris had come up with a scheme to amalgamate old and new. 'I must confess', du Sautoy, now chairman of the firm, wrote to her, 'that I don't feel very happy with Jan James Morris as a writing name. It seems to me to create more problems than it solves.' His intervention did the trick. 'Thank goodness she's agreed to drop Jan James Morris,' Monteith wrote in an internal memo. 'It's all settled. *PB3* [they referred to the *Pax* books in-house by their initials, making them sound like cars] will be the last book by James Morris – also *The Hashemite Kings* reprint.

No need to do anything more unless and until Hussein is assassinated.' The Jordanian king died in his bed in 1999. He never knew he had been involved in this matter.

There was awkwardness. 'It is a perturbing experience', Morris said after she had gone shopping in Criciéth, 'to walk for the first time in skirts into a shop, say, whose people have known you as a male for many years.' An old friend spotted Morris on the Earls Court Road and remembers crossing to avoid her because he didn't know what to call her. Children asked why a family visitor in a skirt had a deep voice. Faber's young managing director, Matthew Evans, often mentioned Morris's five o'clock shadow; everyone else said the hands were the giveaway. Some people were kind. Austin Tobin, the now retired high Tennysonian of the Port of New York, and his wife Rosaleen sent a note when they read about the transition: 'Dear James/Jan – We love *you*.'

She gave Mark her Jaeger suits, which fitted, including the turquoise one. Now Morris had to find a style of her own. Mark remembers she 'started trying to look like the Queen'. Ten years later, Paul Theroux said she resembled Tootsie, the Dustin Hoffman character who favours female clothing. She continued to have her hair cut at Sissors and loved to wear jeans, but she never showed any interest in fashion. Whatever she wore, even after Casablanca had removed all trace of ambiguity, she was diffident about social events. In November that first year she asked Monteith if he would accompany her to the annual *Spectator* party. 'I want to go, but would rather like someone to go with!' On another occasion, at a lunch at the same magazine, an Australian sitting next to her said, 'I thought Jan Morris was a man. What happened? D'you change your sex or something?' It just went on and on.

Enid had heard the news of the gender reassignment on the radio. She was in her bedroom at Saxlingham. She was of sound mind and, as always, rose to the occasion with grace and empathy. She could not hold a pen steadily but was able to dictate a letter to Daphne, one of her carers. 'This is the first letter I have ever written to my daughter. I do hope you will like it when I call you my DAUGHTER. I am getting used to it at last and think it is very nice! I do feel so glad for you that you are so happy at last.' Even this she added to, scrawling on the back in her own barely legible hand, 'Much love from mummy.' If there are heroes in this story, Enid stands in the first rank. *I do feel so glad for you that you are so happy at last.*

'I began work on this', Morris wrote in the first notebook dedicated to what became *Conundrum*, 'in the Clinique du Parc, Casablanca, on July 12 1972, four days after being operated upon by Dr Burou for a change of gender role.' The very month Mark dropped her at Heathrow, she had signed a contract with Faber for a transition memoir in return for an advance of £10,000 (about £118,000 today), her largest to date. Why did she take it on? In one television interview she said she thought it was one way of making money while the going was good. Christine Jorgensen's memoir had sold 450,000 copies in the US when it appeared five years previously. 'It was a matter of survival,' the American had said of her surgery in *Christine Jorgensen: A Personal Autobiography*. 'I was merely searching for my own personal expression of human dignity.' (As inconsistent as the rest of us, she went on to try to sell nude pictures to *Playboy*.) Writing was an addiction for Morris anyway, and she was right about the money. Foreign publishers snapped up the rights. Faber scheduled the book for autumn 1973, then delayed it to the following spring, chiefly to avoid colliding with *Heaven's Command*. But now Morris had to write it. 'I am deep in *Conundrum*,' she wrote to Monteith in January 1973, 'and very conundrumical it is proving – I had no idea such tangles and enigmas lay within me.' Britain's formal accession to the European Economic Community that month raised her spirits.

The divorce came through in February. Nothing changed when they had an official piece of paper, and thirty-five years later Elizabeth told a journalist, 'It did not make any difference to me. We still had our family. We just carried on.' Morris always said they had never divorced spiritually. She continued in the robustly stereotypical male role she had always played, shunting all domestic labour onto Elizabeth. *Conundrum* revealed a certain irony, as in its pages Morris presents the concept of a woman in the framework of the stereotype – domestic, weak, inferior. She wrote of a man's 'feeling of unfluctuating control that women cannot share', and of women 'doing real things like bringing up children'. Her male body, she felt, had been 'made to push and initiate, [whereas] it is made now [as a woman] to yield and accept'. The transition had made her go a bit soft – that was apparently part of being a woman too. 'I had loved animals all my life but I felt closer to them now, and sometimes I even found myself talking to the garden flowers, wishing them a Happy Easter.' She enjoyed identifying with that kind of imaginary feminine type. But she never prepared three meals a day for six.

The month after the divorce came through, Morris had one final operation, then flew to Corfu to recuperate with Elizabeth and Suki. 'I'm getting better fast in the sunshine,' she told Monteith on a postcard of a castle. But money worries loomed again that spring, despite the *Conundrum* sums. Sissons appealed for a cash advance 'to assist in the purchase of a flat in Bath later this month' (Morris had been renting there until this point). The agent asked for the £2,500 due later that year for delivery of the memoir, £1,000 for the book they had cooked up on the Venetian Empire, and £668 for starting *PB3*. Faber paid up. So they were a bank after all.

In May she attended her first Everest anniversary reunion as a woman. Because it was the twentieth, more climbers than usual made the effort to get to Pen-y-Gwryd, Hillary among them. Morris took along Murray's *Story of Everest*, the book the others had read, one by one, over the tense last days at Base Camp, signing the flyleaf when they finished. Now they signed the battered volume again and posed for the reunion photograph – the first in colour – in the flagged yard, Morris clutching her handbag at the end of the back row. Meanwhile, the *Daily Mirror* yelled 'James of Everest is now a woman'.

Both Mark and Elizabeth read the first draft of *Conundrum*. 'It was something of a stream-of-consciousness ramble,' Mark says. 'My mother and I both provided notes and suggestions to give it a more objective hue.'

Morris sent a revised typescript to Monteith and, this being among the most newsworthy books of the decade if not the century, he circulated it for comment in-house. Dismay rolled over Queen Square like a tide. Morris had produced a book extolling the spirituality of transformation and the yearning for wholeness. Faber wanted practicalities, not metaphors. Even the loyal Goad suggested in a memo that the author ought to be 'more explicit about her actual sexual feelings', and she baulked at Morris's 'extreme self-absorption at the expense of her family'. (Everyone agreed there was too little about the wife and family.) Evans wanted more tension in the clinic before surgery and thought the book as it stood was not 'commercial'. Part of it was 'a natural for Pseuds Corner' (in *Private Eye*). All the Faber reports thought the book too 'purple' (a recurring word in Morrisian criticism), too superficial and too reticent about family reaction. The diffident Ulsterman Monteith went so far as to confess he was 'disappointed'. But Goad noted that Faber staff had all been discussing the book 'obsessively' in-house, so 'it's probably better than we at first thought'. Besides the general issue of content, the book was far too short.

The heroic Monteith was dispatched by train to Bath ('A long morning,' he reported to Wolff, who was anxiously brooding over the unsatisfactory material in Manhattan). Morris had to capitulate – too much money was at stake, and she was beginning to lose interest. She knuckled down, shuttling between Bath and Trefan Bach for the rest of the summer, irritated that she could not get her own way. Before autumn set in, it was over. *Conundrum* was ready. 'It was now', Morris summed up, 'a book specifically about the experience of sex change, with passages of reminiscence introduced only to illustrate this.' She was always to look back on it as a wasted opportunity: 'I think I failed to use it [transition] artistically in the way I might've used it,' she admitted later. 'I don't believe I've created a work of art around it.' Elsewhere she said, 'Perhaps I'm not a big enough writer.' But she owned the truth, she told Faber.

> This proposed book is <u>falser</u> than the last draft. Although the urge to change sex has been by far the most compelling instinct of my life, I

have never believed it to be the most <u>important</u> one, and its place in my scheme of things was better expressed last time. But since other people seem to think it more interesting than I do myself, *voilà*! I reserve the right to veil it all still in a little mystery and shall not pander to the more prurient curiosities.

The second draft was hardly any longer than the first (fewer than 150 pages). To keep Faber happy, she added descriptions of her sexual life, to the extent that she had never much cared for penetrative sex and 'I certainly did not feel myself to be homosexual.' As for marriage, 'Sex was subsidiary in our marriage. We have each had loves of our own.' No evidence of the latter was supplied beyond 'The men I have loved are married already, or dead, or far away, or indifferent.' The revised version included details of sexual experiences at Lancing ('nothing fitted'), and more detail (though not terribly much, and certainly not about the orifice closing) about Casablanca. After the event, 'orgasm was possible, because the erotic zones retained their sensitivity'. She increased the word count by adding 'conception was not'. She also added what she believed to be the total number of vaginoplasties performed, for context (600 in the US, 150 in the UK). On her main point she did not capitulate: 'It [the desire to transition] is not primarily a sexual quandary at all.' 'Transsexualism' is above all a spiritual matter, one that represents a quest for unity. She is convincing on this point, and when she says, three times, that suicide was for her the only alternative to surgery, the reader believes her. 'I regret', she concluded, 'the stolen years of completeness,' but there could be no misgivings. 'If I were trapped in that cage again . . . I would take a knife and do it myself.' Surgery as the summit of the journey, as *Conundrum* consistently suggests it is, asserts the primacy of the body. Morris catered to general perceptions of 'sex change' by presenting Casablanca as a culminating and terminating event.

When all is said and done (if only it could be), Morris used a facility with words to keep the reader at arm's length. The famous direct appeal ('Come with me . . .') was a tactic deployed to deflect, in this book and every other. Anguish is hard to convey on the page, and anyway it was a mystery. Suki, reading *Conundrum* as an adult, objected to many aspects of it, including the portrayal of baby Virginia's death. (Morris conjured a nightingale trilling, 'part elegy, part comfort, part farewell', the night her first daughter died. It was a movement in the emotional score of the book.) 'Jan refused to go into the hospital with Elizabeth to see Virginia. Mummy told me. The *Conundrum* account of the nightingale singing is a romantic thing. Shocking. There's no mention of Mummy's pain.' When Morris transitioned, as we have seen, the gender role she herself stereotyped did not change from masculine man to domestic woman. 'She did nothing at home,' Suki noted. 'She wanted to be a woman different to any other woman in the world.' Mark ('who knew the terrain as well as I did', according to the *Conundrum* acknowledgements) says, 'I took a lot of it with a pinch of salt,' including the fact that Morris got her father's death date wrong – she said she had lost Walter when she was eight, but in fact she was twelve. Mark feels this was a subconscious effort to shrink her father's role in the family. In the end, he concludes, 'Jan became in her own eyes what she wanted to be, a mythical figure.' It was *her* truth she owned. But what other truth is there turning inside each one of us?

Monteith broke off publication preparations to attend Auden's funeral in Austria. When Morris sent the deputising du Sautoy a revised jacket blurb, he told her,

> I would strongly suggest that the word 'ecstatically' should be removed from before the phrase 'happily married' in spite of the fact that I am sure it represents the truth. The two adverbs do not run very easily together and the result, it seems to me, jars rather than attracts. The blurb, after all, is the publisher speaking. We may have our own ecstasies, but we can't really know about yours.

In *Over the Sex Border*, which came out eleven years before *Conundrum*, Georgina Somerset, the dentist, challenged the notion that 'one was either wholly male . . . or wholly female'. Morris did the same in *Conundrum*, a little less explicitly. She wondered whether she might simply be ahead of her time, and she was – she foreshadowed the gender fluidity of the twenty-first century. It was not a new idea. It is hard to think of many older ones. Scholarship reveals that the binaries of sex and gender have always been unreliable. Some ethnic groups and first nations understood that people might be both masculine and feminine, hence 'two-spirit identities'. Yet challenges to the binary have come to frighten people, tapping into a fear of instability and ambiguity.

Exposing a curated image on paper facilitated privacy rather than betraying it. Now Morris had to wait to see if reviewers had bought her story.

Travelling in the calm months before *Conundrum* actually came out, Morris was, she said, happier than she had ever been. Writing from the Hong Kong Hilton on 24 November, she asked Monteith to airmail a copy of *Climax* to Sir Ronald Holmes. This individual, she explained, was 'the archetypal HK colonial civil servant, and I have fallen head over heels in love with him'. Many straight men found her exciting. Betty Cowell, to whom Morris had written from Cairo for advice on transition (she of the rising soufflé), said the same thing. 'When the story first broke I received 400 proposals, some of them of marriage. I could have had titles, money, the lot.' When one admirer wrote to Morris in praise of *Pax*, the correspondence led to lunch, and then many more lunches. Bill Gordon, twelve years her senior, was the kind of powerful, well-read, good-looking, roguish ex-army man Morris liked – another *beau idéal*. He had served in Palestine, and in the West African Frontier Force on the Gold Coast, both places Morris knew well. Gordon travelled round the country with his work and the two met regularly at the Walnut Tree at Llanddewi Skirrid, not far from Trefan Bach. Both liked a good lunch. Gordon told one of his daughters that he flirted with Morris and found her titillating ('Mum thought it was rum'). But when Morris wrote in *Conundrum* that she and Elizabeth 'each had loves of our own', it was wishful thinking on her part. In all her autobiographical fragments she subsumed her intimate life in suggestive fog. Privately, she told a friend that the men she attracted were fetishists, and that she didn't want to get involved with them. From India she reported to Elizabeth 'a sort of non-affair' with a Delhi travel agent 'which made me feel quite frigid'. The man had 'more or less picked me up . . . He says he is very fond of me but while he is always wanting to make physical advances I can't make out whether he really is or just wants to make love to me.' She felt guilty, she said, as 'he may think I've brushed him off because I'm too grand or something. What problems! I never had *these* before!' As a welcome distraction. Dom Moraes, the bibulous Indian poet last seen at the Eichmann trial, took her sightseeing. She had also arranged to meet her son Henry in Delhi. Aged nineteen, he had heard about the transition in Goa, where he was living. When he arrived at the Imperial he announced himself at reception as Henry Kissinger.

Heaven's Command came out, half a decade after *Climax*. Morris did not write the trilogy in chronological order: the second volume portrays the sixty-year period preceding the Jubilee. Discrete episodes include the Zulu Wars, the Irish Famine, Gordon at Khartoum, Thuggees and a brilliant set piece about the deeply weird John Hanning Speke which conjures 'the central saga of exploration in the imperial age'. (The Scramble for Africa both overall and in detail was 'a chronicle of squalor'.) In *Heaven's Command* Morris exploits, more than ever before, what an older travel writer had called 'her unteachable gift of readability'. In 1857 a thousand men on board the troopship *Transit*, stranded on a barren and blazing coral reef in the Java Sea, 'kept up their strength on a diet of chopped baboons cooked in a stew of salt pork and beans, each hoping, so a survivor recorded, that somebody else was eating the baboons'. On the uplifting side, in India 'three bottles of claret a day was normal for a man, and a bottle an evening quite customary for a healthy woman'. These jokes are foils to passages of great lyricism. In a chapter on 'The Humiliation of the Métis' (an indigenous nation of Canada) Morris writes,

It was a timeless tragedy, the intuitive protest of people whose manner of life was doomed by the no less instinctive progress of an empire: a gesture from that older, simpler world, impelled by airier aspirations, and worshipping more fragile gods, which it was so often the destiny of the British Empire to destroy.

In 1820s Tasmania, 'Bushrangers used to catch aborigines in man traps and use them for target practice. A man called Carrotts, desiring a native woman, decapitated her aboriginal husband, hung his head around her neck and drove her to his shack.' Yet, as in volume one, Morris cleaves to the 'cruelty was rare' line. In pages on the First War of Independence, also known as the Mutiny, she describes coverage at home in which every paper peddled an inflamed 'they raped our women' narrative. Indians did rape some white women, though not nearly as many as the press made out, and they could not touch the British in the scale of violence and murder in that rebellion or at any time. Similarly, Morris does not highlight disparities in the numbers of dead at the Battle of Omdurman: ten thousand Sudanese, forty-eight Britons. The story focuses instead on a single tear rolling down Kitchener's 'brown and flinchless cheek'.

As she was hammering out *Heaven's Command*, tens of thousands of terrified Ugandan Asians were landing at Heathrow. They were British passport holders on account of their colonial heritage, and now victims of a despot. Furious Little Englanders did not want the new arrivals and wrote to the papers to say so. Race had risen to the top of the national agenda, but again Morris did not connect it with the story she was telling. Links between past and present no longer compelled her. She was insulated against the world itself.

Still, as the *Sunday Times* reviewer asked, 'How many professional historians can write books that give so much pleasure?' Paul Scott himself wrote an adulatory review in *The Times*, revealing his own complicated feelings in a final paragraph on 'insular British indifference to . . . areas on the map for which [we] were responsible'. He went on to point out how 'curious' it was that 'we don't feel guilty at all'.

Just before Christmas, Monteith told Wolff, 'We are in the grip of a full-scale Emergency over here — and from the New Year printers and binders will be working only three days a week — so all our production programmes are likely to be knocked sideways.' On the first day of 1974, Prime Minister Ted Heath duly introduced the curtailed week. The cartel-engineered oil shock went on reverberating for years. In addition, the IRA had ramped up its bombing campaign on the mainland.

Another strike began on 5 February, and two days later Heath called his 'Who Governs?' election. (Three weeks later the nation answered his question and the piano went back where it had come from.) The public had endured five states of emergency in less than four years and Heath's incomes policy — the one he had pledged not to introduce — had failed, to disastrous effect. The shortened working week delayed the revised *Venice* as Monteith had feared. Perhaps it didn't matter: Morris had told her editor, 'The trouble is that I don't much like Venice anymore.' When Monteith suggested she add details about the campaign to prevent La Serenissima sinking into the lagoon, she said she didn't care one way or another. 'Whatever they do to it now, it will never again give off the particular amalgam of sensations and evocations I loved.' She softened her comments in a note when she mailed the final revise: 'I don't think I'm prepared to tone it down any further . . . but as you will see I no longer actually say that I hope it [Venice] sinks!' A proud Monteith then sent a dummy of the revised book. 'I loathe the jacket,' she reported back. She was in high dudgeon too about alterations to the opening of *Heaven's Command*, as well as 'the mingy format proposed for *Conundrum*' (the book she had refused to expand significantly). Furthermore, she had hated the design of a Faber book she had just reviewed. 'Happy 1974!' she ended the missive, which was dated 1 January. 'PS I would welcome a talk on this and allied subjects, finding myself a bit unhappy about my publishing affairs.' She couldn't take it out on the M4 eastbound either, as the government had imposed a fifty-mile-an-hour limit to conserve the nation's diminishing reservoirs of fuel. Three months later she was still at it. 'Can't Faber ever get a blurb right?' she wrote on a sulphurous postcard depicting the Pump Room in Bath, which did indeed dispense sulphurous water. 'Now they've gone and left out a comma at the end of the *Conundrum* one . . . it's enough to make the blood boil.'

The new Bath flat in 9 Marlborough Buildings was at one end of the Royal Crescent, the street Jim had pasted into his childhood gazetteer. It was not a Span home, like those in Blackheath. It was Georgian, in a row of thirty-three spacious and gracious five- and six-floor houses dating from the late 1790s. Bath Spa had echoes of childhood visits, shopping or listening to a concert with Enid while Walter waited in his taxi and Haile Selassie in his train carriage. 'If I am having trouble with a recalcitrant paragraph,' wrote the middle-aged Morris, 'I simply go outside and wander through the town for half an hour: and the proportions of the place, the green interventions, the honey stone and the gentle faces soon put my adjectives in order and calm my restless cadences.' She corrected manuscripts over 'fairly muddy' coffee in the Pump Room depicted on the card, where on weekday mornings a resident trio played songs from *Oklahoma!* or *Perchance to Dream*. She liked the city with reservations, expressing ambivalence, if not at the beginning of her tenure, at least towards the end. When her nephew Paul visited she told him, 'Bath isn't really good at anything.' Morris supported a conservation campaign by contributing a sixteen-page historical essay to a new architectural guide. In it she criticised 'planners' *naïveté*, developers' greed and architects' sterility'. (One hears the voice of Portmeirion's Clough Williams-Ellis.) Faber published the guide, which was scheduled to coincide with a festival, and when the firm delayed it Morris dispatched a furious letter to Monteith, threatening to withdraw all her own books: 'If it [the guide] turns out to be ugly as well as late, then it's goodbye from me.' The Two Ronnies had not toiled in vain.

Architectural conservation, like *Pax* (increasingly, as the trilogy wore on), appealed to the nostalgic escapism of 1970s Britain. The trend looked back to a national past that was glorious if not idealised and certainly distant from oil sheikhs and union men in donkey jackets shouting

Top left: Enid at the piano in Trafalgar, the Payne villa in Monmouth, with her father, Charles, and brother, Geraint, 1902.

Top right: James and Chris, Clevedon, 1927 or 1928.

Bottom left: Walter, Gareth and James, on the front path at home at 1 Herbert Road, Clevedon, Somerset, in the 1930s.

Bottom right: 1 Herbert Road, where Morris was born in 1926 – an event now commemorated with a plaque.

Left: Morris preserved this battered snap, taken in Clevedon, for more than eighty years. With a telescope one saw close up, from a distance.

Below: Morris at eleven.

Above: With Chris (right) in Piccadilly, London, in the winter of 1947–8, when James had just left the army.

Right: Chris in the organ loft in St George's, Hanover Square.

Top: Morris (right) and the giant Martin Busk, slogging it out on Occupation Duty in Venice, 1946.

Bottom left: Morris's military ID card. He was so keen to join up that he lied about his age.

Bottom right: Lieutenant Morris, Intelligence Officer in the 9th Queen's Royal Lancers, Palestine, 1947.

Top left: Paignton, 1949. A union that endured for seventy-one years, 'for better, for worse'.

Top right: Baby Mark looking pleased with himself after meeting his father for the first time at Heathrow in 1952.

Bottom: Morris's scrapbook records assignments as *The Times*'s Middle East correspondent in the turbulent fifties.

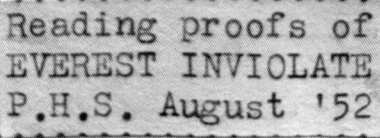

Top left: Morris wrote background pieces on Everest the year before John Hunt's expedition set off. The one he is reading here in Printing House Square (PHS – *The Times*'s offices) actually appeared in July 1952, not August.

Top right: Nepal, March 1953.

Bottom: On the slopes with Sherpas.

Above: Morris shakes hands with a triumphant Ed Hillary in the hours after Everest is climbed.

Right: Morris and Ed Hillary on an Everest lecture tour in the US at the end of 1953. This picture was taken in DC, where the climbers met President Eisenhower.

Left: Companies – in this case Pye Telecommunications – were quick to capitalise on British success on Everest. This ad appeared in *The Times*.

Top: Morris, Mark, Henry and Elizabeth, 1953 or 1954.

Bottom: (left) Morris and family with the first Rolls, in the French Alps, 1955. He was about to leave for Suez; *(right)* Morris and Henry, c.1957.

Top: Morris, Elizabeth, Mark and Henry in Venice, 1959.

Centre left: Morris with Mark, Twm (then Tom) and Henry, 1961. The latest telescope stands ready for action.

Bottom left: Suki (then Susan) and friends in front of Plas Trefan ('the Big House') in the late sixties.

Below: Plas Trefan: 'For me it will always be the most beautiful house in the world.'

Top left: 1970; *Top right*: 1971.

Bottom: Morris appeared on ABC's *Dick Cavett Show* in 1974, when her trans memoir *Conundrum* came out. The broadcast was less gruelling than its British counterpart.

Left: Charles Monteith, a new editor at Faber, approached Morris after reading the Everest despatches. Theirs was to be one of the great editor-writer partnerships.

Centre: After suffering a stroke, Enid had to dictate correspondence. When she heard about Morris's transition she told her, 'I do feel so glad for you that you are so happy at last', adding a PS sending love in her own hand.

Below (left): Newsstand poster advertising the serialisation of *Conundrum* in *The Sunday Times*, 1974. Morris agreed to appear in the television ads, as long as she didn't have to speak. (*right*) When *Conundrum* appeared, every news outlet in the world wanted photographs.

Right: Christopher Isherwood's partner Don Bachardy sketched Morris when she visited the couple at their home in the Santa Monica hills in 1975. She never mentioned the picture, and it has never previously been published.

Below: *Pax Britannica*. The third volume of the trilogy, *Farewell the Trumpets*, came out in 1978. Morris called her history of the British Empire 'the centrepiece of my life'.

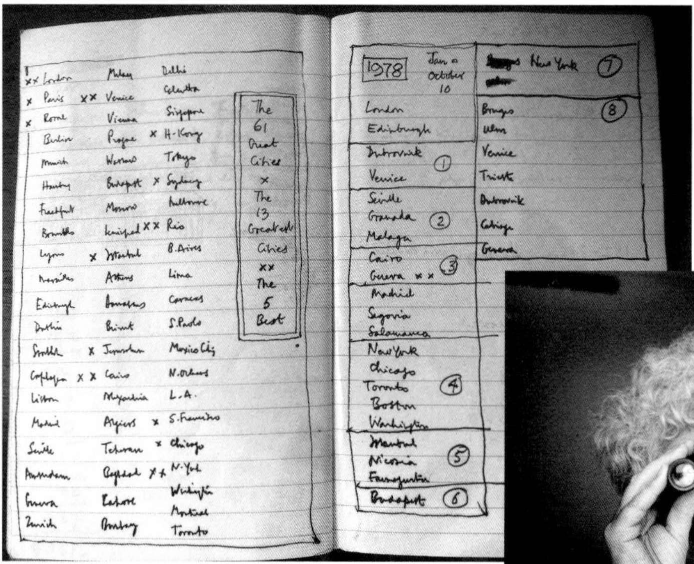

xx London | Milan | Delhi
x Paris | xx Venice | Calcutta
x Rome | Vienna | Singapore
Berlin | Prague | x H-Kong
Munich | Warsaw | Tokyo
Hamburg | Budapest | x Sydney
Frankfurt | Moscow | Melbourne
Brussels | Leningrad xx | Rio
Lyons | x Istanbul | B.Aires
Marseilles | Athens | Lima
Edinburgh | Damascus | Caracas
Dublin | Beirut | S.Paolo
Stockholm | x Jerusalem | Mexico City
Copenhagen | x x Cairo | N.Orleans
Lisbon | Alexandria | L.A.
Madrid | Algiers | x S.Francisco
Seville | Teheran | x Chicago
Amsterdam | Baghdad | xx N.York
Geneva | Lahore | Washington
Zurich | Bombay | Montreal
 | | Toronto

The 61 Great Cities
x The 13 Greatest Cities
xx The 5 Best

1978 Jan — October 10
London
Edinburgh
Dubrovnik ①
Venice
Seville
Granada ②
Malaga
Cairo ③
Geneva x x
Madrid
Segovia
Salamanca
New York
Chicago
Toronto ④
Boston
Washington
Montreal
Nicosia ⑤
Famagusta
Budapest ⑥
[illegible] New York ⑦
Bruges ⑧
Ulm
Venice
Trieste
Dubrovnik
Cetinje
Geneva

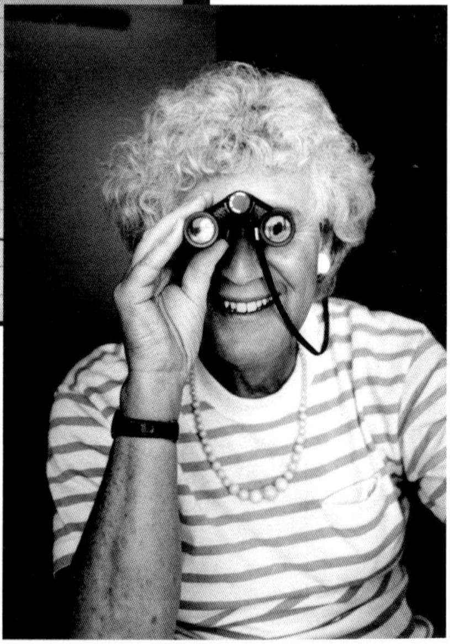

Above: Morris listed places visited each year in a series of notebooks. The right-hand side shows her record for 1978 ('BEST YEAR OF MY LIFE', she wrote on the next page). The left side ranks her sixty-one top cities ever visited, with one asterisk for 'greatest' and two asterixes for 'best'.

Right: Always on the lookout. 1988.

Below: Morris and Twm in the garden at Trefan Morys, 1994.

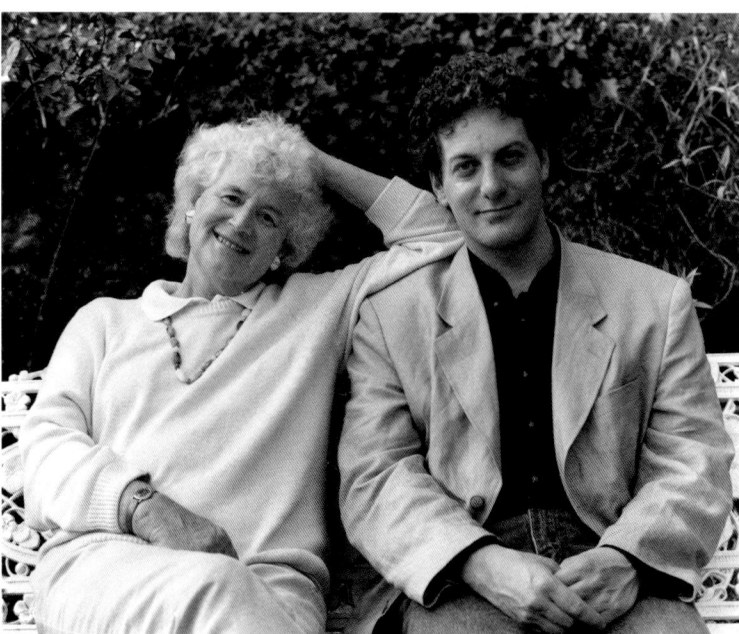

Above: Twm, Elizabeth and Mark, Trefan Bach, 2003.

Left: Welsh Nationalist meets monarch at an event celebrating the fiftieth anniversary of the ascent of Everest in 2003.

Trefan Morys.

Right: All visitors got the Jacky Fisher treatment in later years. Morris had written a slim biography of the admiral, and pinned a poster of him in her wardrobe. Leading the unsuspecting guest upstairs, she would fling open the louvred wardrobe door and announce that she intended to have an affair with Fisher 'in the afterlife'.

Above: The National Portrait Gallery commissioned this image by Arturo di Stefano in 2004. Through the windows one sees the Manhattan skyline, Everest, the Gulf of Trieste, a Porthmadog schooner and the Trefan sycamore. Ibsen sits at Morris's feet.

Left: Elizabeth in 2012.

Jan and Elizabeth with children, grandchildren and great-grandchildren, 2012.

The last profile. The *Observer* commissioned Antonio Olmos to take this picture in 2020. Later that year, Morris died. She was 94.

But then a cloud moves across the sun, and the meaning of it all once again escapes me.

through megaphones. People were not nostalgic for Empire. They were nostalgic for an imaginary past that was not like now. *The Pallisers* and *Upstairs, Downstairs* were on the box, *The Country Diary of an Edwardian Lady* topped the bestseller charts and Laura Ashley florals edged tie-dyes and miniskirts off the high street. Clough's daughter Susan Williams-Ellis tapped into the nostalgia and 'heritage' craze when she introduced the wildly popular Botanic Garden collection to the Portmeirion pottery ranges in 1972. *The only thing to look forward to is the past.*

In early 1974 the *Conundrum* campaign was underway, with restless cadences of its own. It ran in parallel with the general election campaign, a weary Harold Wilson tramping rain-sodden streets as if he had already lost. John Bodley was handling publicity at Faber and he commissioned Lord Snowdon (Tony Armstrong-Jones, the Queen's brother-in-law, then at the zenith of his fame as a society portraitist) to take photographs. On 12 March Morris wrote to Bodley from Bath, 'It will be a very good thing when all this rumpus is over: it is having a very bad effect upon me, and making me preposterously self-important.' In other moods, with characteristic ambiguity, she saw the dark side. 'She is clearly very much in two minds', Monteith told colleagues in a memo, 'about the wisdom of appearing on TV at all over here . . . She is alarmed at the thought of being pointed at in the supermarket.' Morris declined to appear on Russell Harty's chat show. Ashley had been on the previous year and had said, to camera, 'I long to get away from that April Ashley image.' Morris too did not want *in any way* to be associated with that image, or indeed with Ashley. She did agree to appear in television ads for the *Sunday Times* serialisation, providing she didn't have to talk in them. Editor Harry Evans persuaded her over lunch, having paid 'a very large sum' for rights. The paper produced a two-colour poster for the newsstands, trailing *The Strange and Beautiful Story of a Man's Journey into Womanhood*. The *Melbourne Age* and *Sydney Morning Herald* were to run the extracts simultaneously. The *Bookseller* reported unprecedented advance interest. Wilson returned to Downing Street after all.

Le tout Londres attended the launch at the Faber offices, including Valerie Eliot, widow of the poet, who talked to Elizabeth about the new–old government, a topic easier to handle than the subject of the book they were jointly celebrating. Someone asked Mark's girlfriend Belinda what it was like having two mothers-in-law. It turned out that Morris's misgivings had been well founded. Shortly after the party she appeared in one of the most vulgar exchanges ever shown on prime-time television. The bowtie- and heavy-spectacle-wearing Robin Day was among the most familiar interviewers in the land, so famous for his abrasive style that he was known as the Grand Inquisitor. Morris had known him at university. When the cameras began rolling on Day's BBC1 show *Talk-In To Day*, the interviewer looked his prey in the eye and cited Germaine Greer's review of *Conundrum*: 'Jan Morris is still to me a man who has eaten a great many pills.' 'What do you think of that, Jan?' Day asked, his bowtie immobile but his eyelids flickering. Morris was wearing a demure cream two-piece. A second of silence clogged the airwaves. 'What do you expect me to say?' she replied. Day's glasses seemed to scowl on their own. He showed her a clip of herself as James from a 1958 *Panorama* and asked how she felt when she saw it. He then asked her about her sexual function. 'Would you ask Catherine Storr that?' Morris replied, referring to one of the four-strong panel invited to contribute to the discussion. 'She hasn't written a book,' countered Day. Leo Abse was also on the panel. The Labour MP for Pontypool in South Wales, Abse had sponsored a bill to enact a watered-down version of the findings of the Wolfenden Report by decriminalising male homosexuality in England and Wales; in 1967 the Sexual Offences Act had passed into law by one vote. Abse was an odd champion. 'Those of us who are possessed of the normality which makes us look with revulsion at homosexual conduct', he pontificated in the House during the passage of his bill, 'must surely want an end to this continuing public discussion.' That night, he was the most snarling of Morris's denigrators. She responded on air, 'It's arrogant for anybody to think they know what anybody else feels like'; she had described only what *she* felt like and what she wanted to feel like. The only member of the panel to express empathy was journalist Katharine Whitehorn.

Day himself said later that it was 'probably the most unnerving interview where I've been totally lost for words for a few seconds . . . I had known him as a very virile undergraduate'.

Morris had asked Mark to go with her to the studios for moral support. 'She was dreading it,' he wrote in an unpublished memoir, and who can wonder. They stayed at the Hilton and sat watching the programme when it went out later that night with a picnic supper on their knees. Towards the end, one of them spotted a stranger's toothbrush, and they realised they had mistakenly settled in someone else's room.

Morris formally complained to the BBC. Managing director Huw Wheldon waffled a reply. 'The publication of your book . . . such immense public attention that I thought . . . both sensible and seemly to respond to it . . .' Then it turned out that the corporation had paid Morris £20 and the panel £35 each. Morris wrote to Whitehorn (the source of the fee leak) from Trefan Bach 'to thank you for your kindness during that traumatic exposure the other night . . . If I had a *shattered* air to me it was because I had been invited merely "to take part in a discussion about sex & gender, & about the advantages and disadvantages of being a woman".' She said she had no idea it was to be a discussion specifically about *her*, or that 'Robin would be anxious to know the details of my sexual excitations!' In a postscript she added, 'You may perhaps wonder why I did that show at all. It was because Elizabeth and I thought that by showing myself to a larger audience I might convince sceptics that I was something other than a mere exhibitionist nut. Alas, I fear it may have had the opposite effect!' It did rather.

When she thanked Bodley, her Faber publicist, for attending the filming, she again used the word 'shattered' to describe the effect the programme had had on her. Then she flew to the US to do it all again, though this time she was so fearful that she stayed in Julian Bach's stucco-fronted row house in Turtle Bay Gardens rather than in a hotel. ABC's *Dick Cavett Show* turned out to be far more dignified than *Talk-In To Day*.

Ten years younger than Morris and once the gymnastics champion of Nebraska, Cavett, though still new to ABC, was, like Robin Day, virtually a household name. Like Morris he could be playful and serious at the same time – unusual on American television. He and the network had dispensed with their usual studio audience, and there was no savaging panel. In their affable talk, Morris repeated a trope she had used about her children in *Conundrum* ('I see them as a patron admiring a work of art') and was happy to admit, when quizzed, that she had 'no single rational explanation' for her transformation. That was what everybody wanted: the thing *explained*. But it was inexplicable. The truth is more complicated than language allows and Morris, who wrote on place with such style, had shown in *Conundrum* that the most foreign country is within.

Meanwhile, literary nabobs and the highest-paid among the fourth estate queued to review the book. Journalist Nora Ephron's piece in *Rolling Stone* reflected the tone of many.

> Jan Morris is perfectly awful at being a woman; what she has become instead is exactly what James Morris wanted to become those many years ago. A girl, and worse, a forty-seven-year-old girl . . . It is a truism of the women's movement that exaggerated concepts of femininity and masculinity have done their fair share to make a great many people unhappy, but nowhere is this more evident than in Jan Morris's mawkish and embarrassing book . . . so giddy and relentlessly cheerful that her book has almost no dignity at all.

Greer's review in the *Standard*, headlined 'THE BOOK EVERYONE IS TALKING ABOUT', was not as brutal as Day had indicated. The author of *The Female Eunuch* (published four years earlier) began, 'You cannot help liking Jan Morris.' She found the book 'a bit purplish and hazy', noting, 'she [Morris] does so love such an excuse to go on about herself'. Greer mentioned Morris's 'enduring contempt for genitality [a little-used word] in men or women' and ended by writing about Elizabeth: 'Her unbroken silence is the truest measure of Jan Morris's enduring masculinity.' Victor Pritchett, whose rejected Spanish commission had gone to Morris, announced after a complimentary introduction, 'essentially Jan is an invented woman'. *Conundrum* was 'evasive' and 'really asserts an impenetrable egoism'. VSP did not understand 'why he [Morris] did not opt for homosexuality or the life of a transvestite. Self-love is snobbish; the whole tone of the book is intensely narcissistic.' (VSP was right, though, when he wrote, 'The scene in Casablanca is very briefly presented as musical comedy; the dread and doubts are not there.') Again like many, Pritchett noted 'the strange egoism that empurples the tale'. Bernard Levin, the journalist Morris had cited in her letter to Elizabeth from the Cascades, brought decorum to proceedings. 'As a communication of the incommunicable *Conundrum* is very good indeed . . . On every aspect of the conundrum itself, she is consistently brilliant.' But literary grande dame Rebecca West, in a long review in the *New York Times* (she started by saying Morris is 'perhaps the finest descriptive writer of our time, of the watercolor variety'), said she used to understand every word Morris wrote as a man but 'now that we are both women he mystifies me'. Morris writes, West felt, 'as if he had had to make the change from man to woman against a host of opposition . . . But I do not see any sign that Mr Morris has been persecuted, and I cannot see why the proceedings are fraught for him with such emotion.' This was wilfully obtuse. Then West bizarrely revealed that she herself would have liked to become a man 'at the age of just under fifty' and would have found it 'amusing' rather than fraught. In a private notebook entry on the topic the same day, she added, fantastically, 'most women do become men as they get older, only the clever ones conceal it'. Like Ephron, West considered that Morris had conjured in *Conundrum* 'a man's idea of a woman', and that 'by her own account she is trivial' in her depiction of womanhood. That was more or less true. 'At the end,' she concludes the review, changing back to the masculine pronoun, 'he does not seem to me to have got what he was trying to buy.'* That was going to turn out to be true too.

---

* Later, West insisted elsewhere, 'the he was a better writer than the she'. Auberon Waugh took to the *New York Times Book Review* to say the opposite. Everyone had a view.

The coverage paints a rather unsatisfactory picture from every point of view. The celebrated *Cosmo* agony aunt Irma Kurtz wrote to *The Sunday Times* after publication of its third extract, which was headed 'The Sheer Fun of Being Female', pointing out that for many women it was no fun at all. Sloshed old right-wingers were delighted with the feminist response to *Conundrum*, as the fuss somehow 'proved' the whole movement was a dud, as of course they already knew. One of their number announced gleefully in the *Guardian*, 'No matter what tortures his [Morris's] female soul might have had, you cannot help but feel he has made a bum choice joining that shower.'

In the whole farrago of reaction and counter-reaction, no trans voices were heard. But hundreds spoke, in sacks of letters the postman brought from all over the world. Many correspondents had never before heard their own story told. Some begged, *Please, Miss Morris, can you recommend a doctor?* Several from Pakistan asked for a full breakdown of costs. Letters arrived in French. Some people pinned their hopes on the Charing Cross clinic. A Welshman described the anguish he felt when his grown-up children refused to have anything to do with him. Many spoke of praying every day to be a girl. One man listed the particular problems presented by his spina bifida. Teenagers wrote in whispers, their parents downstairs. Some used capital letters. One actually wrote in green ink. Many had led lives of quiet desperation, pain and above all loneliness. One said 'sex change' was 'a poor phrase – it was more a realisation of what was already there'. This was more accurate, and truer, than anything reviewers came out with. Several included sheaves of poetry they had written 'through the lonely years'. Many others told Morris, 'I feel as though I know you' – she had already heard this from fans. Quite a few referred to the Day show. 'As I have colour,' one viewer revealed, 'you looked really nice.' David, a Canadian cameraman, said, 'Leo Abse can boil his head.' A man from Devon described the programme as Morris's 'Gethsemane'. Letters poured in from women who pointed out that they were happily married but wanted to say how wonderful they thought she was on television for her kindness, honesty, sincerity and belief in all-encompassing love. 'I have never heard of you,' one said, 'but I am now looking out for your work in the Reader's Digest condensed books' (where some indeed appeared). A beautician in New York wrote to say she had given electrolysis to two hundred transsexuals before and after their operations. A neighbour of the French-born writer Anaïs Nin in the same city wrote to say that Nin loved *Conundrum* and thought it had two heroines, the other being Elizabeth. Many felt that way, and many still do. The correspondence never really ended. A woman from Northamptonshire thanked Morris for *Conundrum* years later: 'When I was ready . . . to become what I am, that I was willing to set out, and as unfearful as I found myself surprisingly to be, was in no small measure due to the long-term leavening of your example.' The correspondent ended by expressing gratitude to Morris, 'not for your books alone, but for all that you have been to me over many years, all that you have helped bring about in my life, and all that you have helped me to make of myself. For this last, most of all, I thank you from the bottom of my heart.' The cache of mail represents the most moving body of correspondence any author has ever received. Morris gave people hope.

Ephron had attributed Morris's claim to an 'idyllic marriage' to 'creeping Harold-and-Vitaism'. This was a reference to the happy union of homosexuals Sir Harold Nicolson and Vita Sackville-West, the diarist who had expressed fury over the 'conquest' of Everest. Their son Nigel Nicolson had written to Morris from Sissinghurst, the family seat.

> Your own experience is most moving, and I quite see what you mean in drawing a parallel between it and my parents' marriage. [Morris had made the comparison in a letter to Nicolson. His book *Portrait of a Marriage* was about to appear.] There is so much emphasis on the sexual side of marriage, that people have forgotten that it contributes no more than 10 per cent to its success, and they usually make a mess of the 90 per cent. In my parents' case, there was not even 10 per cent, but they made of the 90 per cent a greater success than any other

relationship that I had ever heard of, until you told me of your own. What a triumph for you both!

Elizabeth did speak in public. She wrote to the *Standard*: 'In her bigoted review of Jan Morris's *Conundrum*, which gets so many facts wrong, Germaine Greer describes me as a silent and anguished figure. I am not very silent, and certainly not anguished. The children and I not only love Jan dearly, but are also very proud of her.' The 'wretched problems' Jan had acknowledged to Monteith were a private matter. Kate Murray-Brown, daughter of Jan's *Panorama* producer, Jeremy, and his wife, Joan, was a regular visitor in these years. 'It wasn't Jan who was the strong one, it was Elizabeth. My love was always for Elizabeth. She was a woman of incredible strength and courage.'

Conundrum turned out to be a landmark in the trans memoir genre: other accounts are placed 'before' or 'after'. Morris had moved the topic of gender reassignment into the realm of literature where a reviewer had said *Pax* belonged. But the accusations levelled by Ephron and West – that the book reinforced gender stereotypes – never went away. Trans women themselves criticised *Conundrum* for that reason even at the time it came out. In addition, the book fuelled a perception among radical feminists that trans women were bandits on their patch, an idea powerfully expressed in Janice Raymond's *The Transsexual Empire*, which came out five years after *Conundrum* and became a classic of its (admittedly limited) kind. One trans woman Raymond targeted wrote a riposte called *The Empire Strikes Back*, and began it with a passage from *Conundrum*. Then and ever after, Morris did not engage. She didn't even notice. Many years later a distinguished female biographer had a drink with Morris and two other writers at a book festival. Morris talked about the joy of handbags, at length, leaving the appalled biographer with the impression that, in Morris's opinion, being a woman was about handbags.

Conundrum also left its mark on an issue still live more than half a century on. Morris began the book, famously, with the assertion, 'I was three or perhaps four years old when I realised that I had been born into the wrong body.' Critics have disputed that a child of that age could have such intimations. Furthermore, gender-critical writers reject the childhood-realisation narrative as a misleading interpretation of what it is to be trans. A blogpost after Morris died referred to *Conundrum* in this regard as peddling 'the usual ret-conned narrative'. The opposition cite studies in gender dysphoria that support the commonality of Morris's remembered experience. The debate was well underway in Morris's final two decades, and she continued to ignore it though she knew it raged on. 'Half a lifetime of diligent craftsmanship seemed to have done less for my reputation than a simple change of sex!' she said. She didn't mind, not really. Of the period around publication of *Conundrum* she wrote wistfully, 'It was like being a star.' In April Ashley's rather brilliant autobiography, co-written with Duncan Fallowell, Ashley revealed, 'One of the problems of my newspaper exposure was that I became a sex change first and anything else second . . .' She also wrote, or Fallowell did, 'Most people all their life are the dupe of their self-image.' Isn't that the truth.

As for the wider public: David Holden's piece about his friendship with Morris, and her revelation in front of his house, appeared in the *New York Times* in the same month as *Conundrum*. It attracted correspondents, few of whom had any sense of history. It seemed 'the Gray Lady' didn't either. Its Letters editor gave a whacking thirty column inches to a missive from a Nantucket woman – 'I felt emboldened to share a similar story of my own' – describing a friend, Sandy, who thought she was a horse and had set about transitioning, eventually travelling abroad to have a tail grafted onto her bottom and subsequently undergoing a hoof transplant. Her husband had been understanding, the children brave, Sandy was writing a book, etc. The correspondent – anonymous, like all brave persons – thought she herself was tremendously clever and funny ('Did her teeth look longer or was it my imagination?'). Mrs Nantucket ended the feeble spoof with a PS: 'I have tried and tried to decide whether your story [Holden's feature about Morris] was in earnest. Or was it a put-on? If it really is true, it should have been subtitled, "Is there any limit to human folly?"' Even the priggish *Times* judged it acceptable to ridicule a transsexual openly with schoolboy joking. Did nobody realise that history and myth show men turning themselves into women since the dawn of time?

Conundrum's appeal extends beyond matters of gender. Morris's exposition of her conundrum reveals an extraordinary gift for eliciting a response in readers to profound themes in their own lives: the search for identity, body image, spiritual yearning, unexpressed sexuality – characteristics with universal application. It was the gift of a popular writer, and she worked the same magic in the other books, or in most of them. If she hadn't, why would they together have sold in their hundreds of thousands? It is not enough to be a fine descriptive writer, if you want to sell copies. Counterintuitively, Morris's gift of showing readers the world and themselves in her prose is most obvious in *Conundrum*. Some of us might even glimpse a version of ourselves in the cartoonish 'if we can see the small children through all right we may all live happily ever after!' – we only manage to parent by ignoring or denying our own failings. Even the writer's love affair with the reader – 'Come with me . . .' – expresses the human desire to communicate rather than live silently, though in the end we do live silently, as Morris knew. She was the most individual of people, yet in her prose she is able to make everything universal. It is a kind of complicity – again, she is Everyman. As she tirelessly said, her work is superficial; but through it she guides the reader to gaze deep.

Faber – exhausted themselves – suggested a complete break after the brouhaha. In May, Jan and Elizabeth retreated to a hotel on Lake Geneva. The day Morris arrived back at Trefan Bach, she went through her post and wrote to Blackwell's bookshop in Oxford to say she was disappointed not to find *Conundrum* in their spring catalogue. George Bernard Shaw's biographer once wrote of his subject's 'Everest of vanity'. Fame was Morris's second Everest. She was, like Shaw, addicted to public attention as well as to writing.

BEING A STAR

She was off travelling for most of the rest of that year and the next for *PB3*, which she funded as usual with commissions. Her forty-eighth birthday, she told Monteith, 'entailed falling deliciously in love with a diplomat'. But men continued to pose hazards. On a trip to the Dardanelles in which she was caught in a forbidden military zone, trapped on a ferry alongside a distressed Liberian tanker and later stranded with a puncture, she wrote on a postcard to Elizabeth, 'I have seldom been so frightened in my life and was all ready to throw myself into the water,' continuing two days later in a letter, 'and the least of it was when a tyre burst and the garage man who fixed it put his hand up my skirt... I think you must admit that only a born traveller would have enjoyed it all as much as I did.'

Morris's idea of being a woman remains unsettling. Few women 'enjoy' a stranger putting his hand up their skirt. As far back as 1961 Morris had implied that women travel writers were airheads. Reviewing Mora Dickson's *Baghdad and Beyond*, she had written, 'All too often, the lady chroniclers of the Middle East fall into an irritating feminism, laced with coy whimsy.' There were exceptions: 'But then, the Starks and the Bells are more than just women. They are artists too, and human beings of wise and inexhaustible depth.' *Baghdad and Beyond* was 'a nice enough book, but heavy with womanliness, sisterliness, wifeliness'. The 'but' makes it clear that these are not desirable characteristics. Morris ended the review, 'Writing is still a craft, not a kind of mail-order agency for the acquisition of pin money.' It was hardly fair to suggest that only frivolous women wrote travel material except for Freya Stark and Gertrude Bell, who had the good fortune to be 'human beings' rather than women. (They had private incomes too.)

She had told Bodley, after the tides of *Conundrum* publicity had finally receded, 'I think we're home and dry now, don't you? Oddly enough, despite a few bumps and scars, what I overwhelmingly feel is a sort of glow of gratitude for all the love and friendship I've been shown.' The glow never dimmed. Morris never regretted any aspect of her transition. When she wrote about her gender change over the many decades to come – always briefly, even fleetingly – she never wavered in the conviction that she had had no choice. 'Transsexualism', she had said in *Conundrum*, 'is a passionate, lifelong, ineradicable conviction, and no true transsexual has ever been disabused of it.' Mark agrees there were no regrets, though he wonders 'if transition brought all the rewards she was expecting in the long term. I don't think it did. I think she expected more of being a woman. Removal of maleness was achieved, yes. But I think she expected something she didn't get. Full-blown romance, for example. But not just that.' Some other yearning lingered, beyond gender.

Morris basked in a deep sense of fulfilment, her torments removed at last. But she was no longer interested in the journey that had peaked in Casablanca. She had again carried the message on the downward slope, but once *Conundrum* had appeared she was, as she said, home and dry. She never again involved herself in gender issues – neither as a spokeswoman, nor a patron, nor a trustee – not even as a flag-waver. The children agree that she wanted 'to move on'. Mark says, 'It was onwards to Wales and Welshness.'

11
1975–1979
MON DIEU

In her account of imperial debacle and the indigenous peoples of Canada, Morris advised, in *Heaven's Command*, 'For parallel cross-purposes, misunderstandings, streaks of pathos and stubborn innocence, I recommend the study of the Welsh Nationalist movement in the 1970s.' Whilst it was the ineptitude of the campaign that had left the most vivid impression, the struggle drew her now. She had not forgotten the heady days of Dafydd Iwan holding court on the top floor of the Big House, where Welsh housemaids had once scurried to answer bells pulled by English hands. Freshly purged by the publication of *Conundrum*, Morris drew closer to the young Welshmen committed to the removal of the despised coloniser. Monteith thought he had heard it all when she asked him to send a copy of *Climax* to Prisoner 0353 John Jenkins Esq. in Albany jail on the Isle of Wight ('He's not allowed to receive books direct from me, so perhaps you'll just put an anonymous compliments slip in. He'll know!'). Jenkins was a British army soldier who had led Mudiad Amddiffyn Cymru (Movement for the Defence of Wales) from 1964 until his conviction on bombing-related charges in 1969. Morris cast him and his ilk as heroes, and she did perceive Wales as the cradle of a culture in peril (as well as an enchanted land where the battles were fought in the twelfth century). She did not fancy committee meetings in draughty village halls, but nationalism offered the chance to achieve personal union with the people she had adopted as her own, especially as Britain roiled in decline. She wanted to bathe in Celtic Twilight. When a twentieth-century fight did approach, she took it on with gaiety. 'Miss Jan Morris needs to have £150 in travellers' cheques,' she scribbled on a note to the Cricieth postmistress as a devolution referendum loomed, '+ hopes you will all be voting YES in the referendum.' Political nuts and bolts were as alien to her as the bank manager's ledger. She operated by instinct. But although Morris had a tendency to romanticise everything, and Wales was ripe for treatment, she really believed in independence. She wrote to Faber about a big book on Wales and took a *cwrs carlam*, crash course, in Welsh.

She was not Welsh, but her father's people had roots almost exclusively in English-speaking Wales. 'I always admired the Law of the Return', Morris once wrote, 'in the early days of Israel, which declared that anyone who journeyed to the country and said, "I am a Jew", *was* a Jew. The same should go for Wales.' She often repeated this theory, sometimes bolstering her argument with a choice example: 'Lloyd George, the typical Welshman, was born in Manchester.' And why not? Work gave her life meaning, and the misty Welsh hinterland suited the allusive style that had replaced engagement, so she merged them. The idealism of *The Outriders* had vanished as Britain sank into unrest and gloom; the fault lay in Whitehall, not Cricieth or Cardiff, and Morris was no longer prepared to sit at her typewriter and bang out proposals for change. She now shrank from specifics. 'I found my reportage and travel writing metamorphosing more and more into impressionism,' she said, 'perhaps because nothing in the world seemed to me so clear cut as it used to.' The shift from engagement to evocation is both a virtue and a fault of the *Pax* trilogy. But as Helen Wolff had written in the note, 'What matter empires fall, so long as authors rise.'

Mark was not part of this Welsh renaissance. He felt that Jan didn't need him anymore. In 1976 he married his American girlfriend at her family home in Missouri. He invited his parents, but they didn't go. When he later asked Jan for a loan for a deposit on a modest house, she said no. 'My father wasn't a parent,' Mark says, 'and Elizabeth couldn't be a parent because Jan made the rules. Jan was a narcissist in her inability to empathise.'

*

Morris conceived her most significant Wales book as a biography of Owain Glyndŵr, whom she called the last free prince of Wales; through that giant of history, she would win over doubters with a powerful nationalist polemic. When Monteith tried the idea out on Faber colleagues, they asked if Morris could do Robert Baden-Powell or King Farouk instead. Someone suggested a Scottish figure was likely to have 'a larger sales potential' than a Welsh one, revealing how little Morris was associated with Wales and reflecting the strong performance of the Scottish Nationalists in the recent election. Du Sautoy noted on Monteith's memo, 'I wonder if I am right in thinking the public interest in JM has largely evaporated?' Monteith added a line below that note: 'Peter is right, I think that interest in James Morris is waning, almost as though he [sic] were dead.' But he fought on for Jan, his author.

Britain in the seventies was enough to drive anyone into the friendly arms of Plaid. Inflation and the balance-of-payments deficit were running at unsustainable levels, unemployment was surging, everyone was still on strike and over in Northern Ireland blood ran in the Bogside. But the clouds parted, at least in Llanystumdwy, when an editor from *Rolling Stone* rang out of the blue from San Francisco. The magazine was, Morris wrote as Welsh nationalism receded into Welsh fog, 'the most thrilling phenomenon of contemporary American journalism'. The biweekly newsprint magazine certainly stood at its cultish peak. Its offices on Third Street were still at the heart of West Coast counterculture, but *Rolling Stone* had 2.9 million readers and sold many pages of advertising. Co-founder Jann Wenner was twenty years Morris's junior. He wore a pageboy haircut and button-down shirts and drove a Porsche convertible, and he had anointed politics the rock 'n' roll of the seventies. New York-born Wenner had just hired Kennedy and Johnson speechwriter Dick Goodwin to run the Washington office as political editor. It was Goodwin who had suggested Morris as a contributor. 'I took her over,' says Wenner. 'We first cooked up the idea of a series on former colonial capitals, kind of her overall perception of the British Empire. [This concept evolved.] She looked schoolmarmish when I met her over here, but she was funny and charming and flirtatious. I had the feeling she might have been interested if I'd opened that up.' When they were having lunch in San Francisco, Morris admired the restaurant's rattan chairs. Wenner 'instantly' snapped his fingers at the waiter and ordered him to have a couple sent to Morris in Wales. This was style, and Morris liked it. Wenner recalls, 'America was a dream to her and *Rolling Stone* was the essence of that dream. We were broadening our range when she came in. By 1974 we'd reached a plateau. We'd done Hunter [S. Thompson, the magazine's star writer] and covered the [1972] presidential campaign.' In that election Wenner and his editors had practically become part of Democratic candidate George McGovern's team.

Morris was prepared to overlook the unpleasant *Conundrum* review the magazine had run. She called Wenner 'a journalistic genius' and lapped up *Rolling Stone*'s mix of glamour, authenticity and success; it was an inverted image of what she described in *Pax* as 'the mystic sheen of tradition'. Ambiguous sexuality was in fashion, so the staff enjoyed watching her, in twinset and (fake) pearls, glide about the office, where a plastic marijuana plant and a picture of Mickey Mouse shooting heroin greeted guests amid fugs of dope and the clickety-clack of IBM Selectrics. So Morris began at the 'thrilling phenomenon', as she put it, 'tempering the *Rolling Stone* cutting edge with a few thousand words of moss'. Her first piece was on the Watergate trial. (Thompson's postscript on Watergate, 'The Scum Also Rises', also appeared that year.) As she noted, Eisenhower had occupied the White House when she first visited America. Now Gerald Ford was installed, and DC, where she landed, festered 'in the aftermath of nightmare'. In the essay, Morris brought light relief to the saga with attempts to solve puzzles in an airline magazine and an application for a Diners Club credit card under the name Ethelreda B. Goering. The ritual trawl through the phone book on the first night in her hotel revealed that the mayor's name was actually Washington and that the treasurer of the White House Correspondents' Association was Mr Edgar A. Poe. During a lunchtime recess at the opening of the trial, defendant John Ehrlichman, former White House counsel and the foreman of the Plumbers, the covert White House leak-busting unit, held the door open for her. He was walking hand-in-hand with his wife. 'Against all my better instincts, for in me, the urges of the investigative reporter are not simply atrophied, they are actually reversed,' Morris wrote,

> I decided to follow the couple down Constitution Avenue. At first a small pack of photographers pursued them like seagulls following the trawler... Standing trial for one of the most shattering political crimes of the century: only a few weeks before, he'd been one of the most powerful men in America... I was oddly touched, sentimentalist that I am, by the sight of that fated couple waiting for the traffic lights to change.

When she reported the episode to friends, they said Ehrlichman was 'a bad, bad man... Hand-in-hand is the oldest cliché in the game.'

Rolling Stone gave her more space, literally and figuratively. (Wenner remembers, 'She didn't need editing.') On 1 July 1976, the magazine trailed her 'LA Turnoff: Driving Through the Days of Future Past' on the cover, next to an image of an elongated Paul Simon in a white suit. For the first time Morris stayed in Los Angeles more than a few days – and she stayed at the Chateau Marmont overlooking Sunset Boulevard. A dirigible advertising Goodyear famously floated over Tinseltown in those months and Morris tried to go up in it, but the Goodyear PR person had never heard of her. The city, she found, was 'of the forties and fifties... one is constantly plucked back to that simpler world'. When she went to Burbank Studios, Truman Capote and David Niven failed to impress her ('I am antipathetic to the famous'). But she relished the company of writer Christopher Isherwood and his partner, the painter Don Bachardy, whom she visited at their home in the Santa Monica hills. 'It might seem a house for cultivated indolence,' she wrote piously, surveying the view of the Pacific and the shrubberies of the canyon. 'Not at all. "We are working people," Isherwood says. And so they literally are, each in his own end of the house, each with his art, the one surrounded by his books, the other by his brushes and pictures. Carefully and skilfully, they work through the day, friends and fellow labourers. I very much like all this.' Starstruck at last, she returned to the industrious pair later in the essay, and 'Isherwood, showing me the view from his window, remembered the days when Stravinsky, Schönberg, Brecht and Aldous Huxley had all lived in the city out there' – the seductive forties and fifties again. The Englishman – playwright, screenwriter, novelist – stood at the pinnacle of an ideal for Morris. It was all about going beyond self for Christopher and his kind, and Morris deeply admired that endeavour even though she was not able to cross her own border 'beyond self', not internally, notwithstanding the fact that she had done the hardest thing. Bachardy drew her while she was at the house above Santa Monica, and she signed the image, but she left that out of the accounts. Perhaps she didn't like the picture.

After the piece appeared, writer and LA resident John Gregory Dunne, whom Morris knew, wrote a fan letter. 'I am – we are,' wrote Dunne, co-opting his wife Joan Didion, 'astonished by your piece on Los Angeles. To say it is the best piece ever done on LA is to do you disservice. I doubt if there is a city in civilization that has been written about as badly so often. In a way it is disheartening to have someone do in ten days what we have been trying to do for ten years. In other words, get Los Angeles right.'

Morris and Tom Wolfe both appeared in a television documentary about *Rolling Stone*. After it went out, Wenner wrote her a long letter. 'Between Tom and you,' he said, 'hands are joined across the Atlantic by the best journalist in each country, on the subject of dear old *RS* . . . It's making me blush.' Wolfe and Thompson had pioneered a form of the New Journalism known as 'gonzo'. It was not quite Morris, but she circled it with her first-person involvement, subjectivity ('I very much like all this'), humour (Ethelreda B. Goering), exaggeration and occasional and bogus self-satire (failing at airline puzzles). It all came out in her piece on Panama, in which she appealed for the withdrawal of US forces and a timetable for transfer of the Canal to Panamanians. Point of view was king at *Rolling Stone*. The essay appeared with the cover strapline

'Late Classic of the Imperial Form'; the image below featured the rock band Jefferson Starship. 'Let the Bicentennialists have their party,' the editorial flagging Morris's piece proclaimed. George McGovern sent her a congratulatory note and circulated a cutting.

Rolling Stone dollars furnished the opportunity for a nose job back at home. 'She took advantage of so much changing', Mark says, 'to change that too. She had never liked her nose. I think one per cent of her feared everyone would find her lacking as a woman.' The purely aesthetic rhinoplasty spoke to that one per cent – to the doubt. But she carried on. Essays continued to finance travel as well as cosmetic surgery and she found friends at the magazines. Her relationship with Arthur Crook at the *TLS* had been fond and familiar for many years. A protégé of Stanley Morison, the Catholic Marxist typographer who had spotted Morris as an undergraduate, Crook had commissioned her even before he took the editor's chair in 1959. 'A marvellous day up here,' Morris had written from the Big House in a cover note to a review, 'the sea from my window looks like Venice, all still and misty, and the mountains are white with snow and look like Nepal, and everything else looks delectably Welsh. I could think of nowhere lovelier to come home to, and only wish I could be as enthusiastic about this book.' Crook had written touchingly when Morris alerted him to unwelcome press speculation in December 1971. After expressing sorrow 'that you have been burdened by the complications inevitably created when this kind of thing happens', Crook wrote, 'You will not need to be told that a friendship of twenty years' standing will not be affected in the slightest.'

Morris had told Monteith, 'I am tentatively calling *Pax 3* "*Farewell the Trumpets: An Imperial Resignation*".' *Rolling Stone* had seriously hindered progress, but she had not got this far by crumbling under pressure, and at the end of January 1975 she set out 'on the last of my big imperial journeys'. (It was to be no such thing.) She began in a troubled India: opposition to Prime Minister Indira Gandhi's regime, and to her domination of the Congress Party, was gathering momentum. Morris's schedule took in Gallipoli, Delhi – where she wrote an essay for *Rolling*

Stone, trying to keep both the magazine and the book on the boil – and Gujarat, where the previous year reformists had forced the closure of the state legislature. From there she proceeded to Bombay, where she sent Faber's John Bodley a letter from the Taj Hotel. 'I am giving myself a day off in the best hotel in Asia if not the world after a particularly gruesome journey to Dandi, the place on the Gujarat coast where Gandhi ended his Salt March in 1930, and thus threw his gauntlet in the face of the Empire. The things I do for Art – and Faber!'*

In June, invoking the constitution and citing threats to internal security, Mrs Gandhi declared a state of emergency (which lasted twenty-one months). But Morris was gone. On the way home she stopped in Mauritius, writing on a card to Elizabeth, *Whatever you wish us/ Don't wish us Mauritius/ I'd rather vacation in Kalamazoo.*

Back in Bath, *PB3*, the big Welsh book, *Rolling Stone* and all the rest notwithstanding, she suggested a third collection of essays. To squeeze out cash when she couldn't fit in more trips, she had sometimes picked themes rather than places – a feature on guidebooks or a biographical essay on Ibn Battuta – and she included them in the new volume, which was to be called *Travels*. She identified with Battuta, the fourteenth-century Maghreb traveller and scholar ('he wandered as a way of life'). His memoir, she wrote, 'If it is not always true in the detail, it is certainly true in the sweep.' She often returned to this theme – that what mattered was truth 'in the sweep'. In a short review of the collection, *The Economist* astutely summed up 'one of the most carefully honed prose styles in the business. It is a sort of intellectual hopscotch with squares for anecdotes, squares for historical irony, squares for little jokes and squares for *lacrimae rerum*, with the author, nimble-footed, touching down each time clear of the lines.'

In July, in the middle of the fearsome 1976 heatwave, she wrote to du Sautoy from Bath. She faced, she said, 'another of my perennial financial

---

* I contemplated writing to the firm when I was in Dandi, to say the same thing.

crises, and wonder if Faber can do anything to help me... I quite thought that selling Nelson St [the Oxford house] would get me off the eternal treadmill, but in fact the cash I got for that has all been swallowed up in inflation.' This latter had reached 30 per cent the previous year, so she was not exaggerating. In addition, Heath had introduced value added tax in 1973, which meant more contact with pernicious accountants, and income tax rates had risen yet again. Morris was not in the 83 per cent bracket, but the tax burden bred resentment in her, as it did in many. She thought of moving to Ireland to take advantage of the writer's tax-free status. Bitterness at the rapacious welfare state followed, fostering suspicion of 'spongers' eagerly fed by the Tory press, along with much hand-wringing about the decline of the traditional family. Morris followed public opinion in this regard. She saw herself in a separate category from all those others who eschewed the 'traditional family'. Partly in response to the squeeze, self-government was moving up the political agenda in the smaller countries of the United Kingdom. Bodley reported to his team, 'Jan sets great store by this big Welsh book and thinks the devolution issue will make her fortune.'

As that sweltering summer cooled, she sold the Marlborough Buildings flat (at the price she had bought it for, because she liked the purchaser). On her fiftieth birthday she drove back to Wales from Bath for the last time. 'All being well,' she wrote to Monteith, 'work should start on the conversion of the old Trefan stables after Christmas. A new age begins! What fun!' Fun for some. Welsh mists were all well and good but Elizabeth needed some certainty. Besides, she loved the Black Mountains. She and Betty Jones had grown closer with Jan away so much, especially after Betty's husband died. (He shot himself. Elizabeth had found him bleeding in his Land Rover.) Nonetheless, as always Elizabeth loyally took over Morris's voluminous correspondence when the latter was abroad, even if that meant complaining on her behalf. Jan had 'often despaired' over Faber, Elizabeth wrote to Monteith, 'and only because of you, Charles, has she turned down the idea of leaving in the same way as she desperately wants to leave Harcourt Brace and would do so but for Helen [Wolff]!'

Faber were finding it hard to balance their own books. Printing costs rose 30 per cent in a year and distribution prices also soared as sterling collapsed along with Harold Wilson's Social Contract. (Wilson himself had also gone, replaced in the spring of 1976 by the more stable Jim Callaghan.) Publishers wanted shorter books, not more *Pax* or *Encyclopædia Britannica*s – weighty volumes were speeding to the remainder shops that had sprung up as warehouse fees skyrocketed. Faber had begun printing books without prices, stickering the volumes instead to keep up with rises. Callaghan might have been stable but the pound was not. Late in the autumn of 1976, Britain went to the International Monetary Fund for a bailout. Something had ended. Though many economic historians say something had begun.

In April 1975 Morris had received a letter from Oxford University Press asking if she would edit an anthology celebrating the firm's five hundredth anniversary. She knew the material and needed the money, so, as Faber didn't mind, she accepted, assembling *The Oxford Book of Oxford* in the first half of 1977, juggling spring days selecting pictures for *Farewell*. The book appeared unexpectedly on the *Sunday Times* bestseller list in the summer of 1978, and as a result OUP brought out the revised paperback of Morris's *Oxford*, which Faber had turned down. The two books marked the beginning of a new publishing relationship, and the opportunity Morris had been looking for to slip the Faber shackles. 'What nice people you all seem to be!' she wrote after lunch with the Oxford team. Impulsively, she offered them the big Welsh book, and they took it. Hurt staff at Faber took comfort in the fact that Morris's prose had – they thought – 'become girlie' since transition. Even the loyal Monteith said she had lost her edge. It was the whimsy some people couldn't stand.

America held up. Few travel writers enjoyed her success there. In October 1977 a telegram arrived in the Black Mountains from the Bach Agency: *ROLLING STONE INTERESTED VIENNA TRIESTE GREECE AUSTRALIA TREMENDOUSLY INTERESTED LAGOS WOULD ASSIGN AUSTRALIA SOME LATER TRIP*

MON DIEU

COULD ASSIGN LAGOS SEPARATE TRIPS OR IF YOU WISH HOMEWARD FROM MEDITERRANEAN VIENNA FIRST CHOICE OUTWARD BOUND EVENTUALLY WANT ALL FIVE PIECES STOP. Not long after, another one came: *CONFIRM VIENNA NOW EXPENSES TO 500 AND CAIRO ALL EXPENSES 2000 FEE EACH ARTICLE.* Morris was also contributing to the American *Horizon*, a high-quality hardback periodical covering the arts and history. In one squibbish piece for it, called 'Good-by to Britain, Good-by British', she announced that 'Britain' was 'an imperial word . . . now it is outmoded, discredited, imprecise, and often rather silly'. She wanted the word expunged, 'partly because I am a fierce Welsh patriot'. That was the self she most believed in now, and her association with *Rolling Stone* had given her the confidence to express it.

Not only was imperialism outmoded; Britain itself had gone to the dogs. Whenever Morris passed through Heathrow she witnessed endemic decline – queues, ill-dressed people, surly staff and public transport worse than in any former colony. She filed a piece on London for *Rolling Stone* in 1978, 'during one of Britain's periods of socialist government'. (Non-Labour hacks tossed around the phrase 'full-blown state socialism' to frighten the horses.) 'The thirty years since World War 2 have been rotten years for London,' she wrote. 'Rich or poor, this city is no longer the greatest capital of the world, just as the pound sterling is no longer the world's criterion of security.' She described class breakdown, the new international status of the capital (a bad thing), 'a strong flavour of takeover or possession' and the rise of xenophobia. She battled traffic when she drove to London, filthy trains when she went by rail. It was impossible, almost, to get anything done. Graffiti blazed across walls and plastic bags cartwheeled through streets, and London's light industry, such as the manufacture of car parts, had followed the collapsing trajectory of heavy industry in the Midlands. Surveying the square mile of the City, Morris concludes the *Rolling Stone* essay, 'it is not a nice scene. There is something vicious to it. Every street is full to its attics with money-men, bankers, stockbrokers, agents, accountants, exchange specialists, economists, financial journalists and entrepreneurs.' She had already written in the same magazine about 'vast sums of Arabian money subsidising the transformation of Cairo', but now she saw it happening in London. *Private Eye* had depicted a sheikh offering the prime minister cash to buy the whole country. Morris had written a fan letter to Kingsley Amis, but it was his son Martin whose novels revealed the reality of England in the second half of the seventies: shabby, morally degenerate and generally shocking.

When Monteith told her *The Presence of Spain* was going out of print, she suggested a new edition without the expensive Hofer photographs – Franco was dead; the phoenix was rising. Faber agreed, offering an advance for the updates of £500. 'She may want more,' Matthew Evans wrote, 'but as she has quite a bit of our money already I hope we will resist this.' Evans had little truck with Morris. He didn't like Monteith either, regarding the two of them as 'a pair of old queens'. But Monteith was not queenish and Evans was wrong to lump the pair together. In a BBC *Woman of Action* radio programme at the time of the revised *Spain*, Morris described her 'idea of heaven' as 'bowling across Castille in my Rolls-Royce of the day with the roof open, Mendelssohn's Violin Concerto on the radio and my Abyssinian cat beside me on the front seat'. When a press cutting circulated at Faber, Monteith wrote on it in pencil, '*Mon dieu*.'

In the notebook listing places visited in 1978, she wrote, 'BEST YEAR OF MY LIFE', and she expressed the same feeling to Monteith. There was no longer a secret existence on the road. She was herself, all the time. She had feared she might see places she had loved differently through female eyes and not like them as much; but she didn't, and noted her relief on a trip to Cairo, which she had visited for *Rolling Stone* while the new *Spain* was underway. It was after Egyptian president Anwar Sadat had visited Israel, the first Arab leader to do so: the city was, Morris felt, 'about to explode'. Cairo was still 'one of the half-dozen supercapitals – capitals that are bigger than themselves or their countries'. She was prescient, warning: 'Many places pass through a period of this pre-eminence, to be left forlorn when history passes on.' She herself had history there, but since her day the baton had been passed, and 'the British Embassy, once the true centre of power in this capital, is now hardly more than an agreeable museum'. *Saphir* too had sunk. So she sat on the frayed sofas in El Fishawi's, sipping mint tea and observing what she took to be 'plotters', and 'I felt in my bones, as old reporters do, that in this cauldron of a city some fresh revolutionary substance was simmering.'

The English writer Jonathan Raban was in Cairo researching a book on Arabia – it was to begin with the same phenomenon of the Arabian takeover of London that Morris had noted. The two met among clouds of mosquitoes at an open-air café on the Nile to drink the Stella beer Morris had discovered in Marrakech the day before she vanished into the clinic. They knew one another, as travel writers tend to, and had exchanged amiable letters, gossiping about their recalcitrant typescripts and complaining about the trials of the writer's life. Raban signed off one missive by reporting a scaffolder's van parked outside promising 'A Good Erection Every Time'. Now, batting away the Cairene mosquitoes, she told him, 'I'm so frightened of going back to places and finding that I liked them better as I was than I do as I am.' Raban asked how she was finding Cairo this time. 'It was such a relief this morning,' she replied. 'I walked across from the hotel and climbed up a bit of the pyramid of Cheops. I got exactly the same feeling that I remembered – and I had been dreading that it would look all wrong.' When he asked her if the city had changed, she said, 'I've changed so much more than Cairo has that it's really rather hard to tell.'

'Jan Morris was quick and crisp,' Raban wrote.

> She was a proper traveller with the traveller's gift for swimming in the stream without drowning in it . . . sensible jeans and sensible blouse, a sensible headscarf . . . She spoke in an eager alto, with a trace of dry rust around its edges, leaping from emphasis to emphasis, alighting for a second on a word in italics, like a chalk-hill blue in a meadow of

dogroses . . . I felt sincere, unstinting admiration for the careless, artful style with which she had made herself at home in this singular and alien landscape.

Morris typed up the Cairo essay on the balcony of her room overlooking the Pyramids. But there too menace lurked: 'I could sense a miasma of horror that attended them [the Pyramids], swirling down to the Sphinx in its bunker over the ridge.' The piece ended with further warnings about the rise of Islamic fundamentalism, 'the puritan extremists of the faith . . . riding in from Fustat to sweep the money-changers from the mosques and the belly dancers from the nightclubs'. (She was right about the explosion, though it was three years before a fatwa-mandated assault rifle finished off Sadat.) Foreboding also hangs over the feature on Istanbul she wrote that year for *Rolling Stone*. The flanks of the city's hills, Morris felt, were 'festering in the shadows', and everywhere she noticed 'sensations of unrest and uncertainty'. She liked to stay at the Pera Palace on Galata Hill, 'a haven of potted plants, iron cage elevators, ample baths with eagle feet'. It was there that Morris proved that a good reporter can get a story anywhere. In those years she performed a morning yoga routine. When she lay on the floor, 'Lo, from the deep recess beneath my double bed an authentic fragrance of the Ottomans reached me, dismissing the years and the vacuum cleaners alike: an antique smell of omelettes and cigars, slightly sweetened with what I took to be attar of roses.'

Three years after she had written the first line, the concluding volume of *Pax* appeared. *Farewell the Trumpets* covers the period from the Jubilee through the First World War, the post-war build-up which led to Jallianwala Bagh, and Partition. The book pays out a thread of decline: the same catalogues that had advertised flat-packed houses with verandas and chapels now offered mourning warehouses as 'across the world the graveyards spread'. Morris reaches again for vocabulary she deployed to conjure a rotten Empire in the Middle East books (not to mention the essays on Britain) – 'impoverished', 'dwindling', 'second-rate'. The Suez crisis, she says, 'powerfully influenced me in the writing of this book'.

Detail and set pieces bring the pages alive as they did in *Climax* and *Heaven's Command*: in 1956 King Ibn Saud ordered a picnic lunch for 1,200 at the same Bombay hotel where Morris had written to Bodley after the martyrdom of her own Salt March. The wireless, 'a transforming agency for the Empire', excited many: Freya Stark reported from a mission liturgy in Persia in 1934 that the preacher had likened the Lord Himself to a radio receiving station, while back in Lambeth the Archbishop of Canterbury wondered if he needed to leave the palace windows open to receive signals. A favourite word reached its apotheosis when Gandhi appeared in a loincloth in front of King George and Queen Mary, the meeting that had impinged on young Jim when he heard about it on the wireless in Clevedon. 'The king had enough on for both of us,' the mahatma said afterwards when reporters asked him if he had been cold, and Morris wrote gleefully, 'This was a pungent engagement.' She does not care for Gandhi – she smelled something fake in the fakir. In *Farewell* she says that Churchill, 'a seer among imperialists, instantly recognised the truth of [Gandhi]. He was revolted, he [Churchill] said, "by the nauseating and humiliating spectacle of this one-time Inner Temple lawyer striding half-naked up the steps of the Viceroy's Palace".' Over the decades, Morris was quiet on the Bulldog himself, despite the fact that he was in many ways her type – an emotional romantic who cried easily and an aesthetic imperialist, as she thought of it, who perceived Empire as a grand narrative. As for the Britons who went out to lead, she is kind in *Farewell* because, as she repeats, *they* were kind, on the whole, and she had, as we have seen, set out to paint an 'affectionate' portrait: she is tolerant of Victor Hope, 2nd Marquess of Linlithgow, and Archibald Wavell, the last viceroys but three and two, while acknowledging the uselessness of both – Linlithgow was so removed from the Indian experience that he gormlessly admitted he had never seen a rupee.

The *Farewell* set pieces reach a climax with Gallipoli. The scent of thyme and cordite, the silence, the corner of the foreign field – those pages are hard to read ('boats full of dead men drifted away from the beach, or lay slowly tilting in the water, and a crimson stain of blood spread out to sea'). With this disaster, imperialists had second thoughts, or so Morris imagined, to some benign degree retrofitting motivation to human progress. 'Gradually it occurred to them [the British] that . . . the very conception of one race having the right to rule another was unjust.' She briefly wonders, 'had it all been a colossal mistake?' It wasn't as if the aftermath had brought benefits to mankind. Many if not most of the countries she had visited after independence had not followed a democratic path – she had seen it for herself. Tyrants like Idi Amin thrived across the Global South while deported Ugandan Asians had to cope with a strange and broken-down Britain. Yet as Morris relates the demise of the Raj, she again does not follow its consequences through to the times in which she lived. The convulsions of 1947 had never ended. The most potent consequences of Partition might be yet to come, in nuclear form.

The present was looking (almost) as shoddy as the past when *Farewell* piled up in the bookshops. The IRA went on a murder spree. A book called *Pox Britannica* had done well (note the 'o'). But the record shows that Morris was in step with her times. Only a year or two after *Farewell* appeared, Eton College began giving all first-year boys a personal copy of *The Climax of an Empire*, along with extracts from the other two volumes. (Five out of the ten twentieth-century viceroys of India were Etonians.) The work had a powerful effect on thirteen-year-old minds: 'It was *Heaven's Command* by Jan Morris', says sometime politician Jacob Rees-Mogg, 'that sparked my interest in history.' But one of the Etonian recipients, literary critic James Wood, came to question the gesture. 'Now I wonder', he wrote in 2019, 'at the school's reflexive turn towards Britain's imperial past and its choice of this glittering nostalgic text. Morris doesn't exactly hide the racism and genocidal violence of the imperial enterprise, but they're somehow swept up in the sheer mad gusto of the narrative.'

Morris had severed relations with A. D. Peters and taken on Hilary Rubinstein as her agent at rival firm A. P. Watt. (They represented Julia

Grant, about to become the most famous trans person on television.) Rubinstein had warned Morris against the flight to OUP, but by the time *Farewell* came out she had committed two more books to the Press, including *Owain Glyndŵr*. But, keen to maintain links with Faber, she suggested to them the book on Cairo she had punted years before. 'So all appears to be sweetness and light again,' Monteith wrote to Goad. Morris had to keep thinking up new projects – she was working flat out, but it was not enough to stave off another financial crisis, even with *Rolling Stone* dollars and OUP advanced funds. In desperation she had applied for an Arts Council grant, but she didn't get it. Faber again agreed to make payments ahead of schedule. But when she suggested the anthology of *Rolling Stone* pieces, they actually turned it down. *Places* had performed poorly (2,014 out of 6,600 sold), and an internal memo described *Travels* as 'a disaster' (1,826 out of 3,500 sold, though fire had destroyed a thousand). She had finally found Faber's limit. Monteith said he regretted that the decision 'further weakens the links between you and Faber. I needn't tell you, need I, that I hope from the bottom of my heart that it won't lead to their total severance.' The previous year, he had become chairman of the firm.

Life in the UK deteriorated further after Morris had published her bleak *Rolling Stone* London piece. Prime Minister Jim Callaghan, famously in retrospect, did not call an election in the autumn of that year, and the Winter of Discontent that followed brought his administration to an undignified close. January 1979 was the coldest since the last really cold one (1963) and the snowy peak of Yr Wyddfa blended into the foothills and fields around Trefan. A farmer shot three pickets outside a flour mill not far from Trefan Bach. In England a strike at the Ford motor plant triggered the public-sector disputes that resulted in hummocks of splitting rubbish bags on the streets. On 3 May 1979 Margaret Thatcher entered Downing Street. But at least OUP agreed to publish the *Rolling Stone* anthology, jointly with the books arm of the magazine: the firm was turning out to be as compliant as Faber had once been, and Rubinstein's misgivings had apparently been misplaced. At the party to launch *Destinations* at the magazine offices on Fifth Avenue (it had moved to New York in 1977), Morris had expected the Oxford University Press co-publishers to arrive in suits and the *Rolling Stone* crowd in tie-dye T-shirts, but it was the other way round.

The first of the ten essays, the one about the Watergate trial, had already appeared in *Travels* four years earlier. But overall *Destinations* is the stronger of the two collections. The pieces are longer, conceived with more thought and structured with internal logic. Robust essays on Panama, Cairo, Trieste and Istanbul mark a shift: not thousand-worders churned out for a European magazine, but something longer and sharper. The reader catches a whiff of *Rolling Stone* urbanity after Morris is left alone in Manuel Noriega's bunker in El Chorrillo during the colonel's tenure as chief of security for the Panamanian National Guard. Noriega fails to turn up for their meeting, so Morris pokes around among the security screens, the death manuals, the outsize picture of the chief parachuting out of a plane, the well-stocked cocktail cabinet, the guns.

> And gradually there overcame me a feeling of despair, familiar to any student of the ends of Empires. Those adolescent symbols of manhood and virility! Those second-rate pictures! Those manuals of violence and repression! We are ruled by children, I thought, and all the agonies of state and ideology are only games for little soldiers.

When she was writing *Farewell*, Morris had asked Lord Mountbatten, the last viceroy of India, if she might interview him. The 1st Earl had agreed, but the meeting had never happened. Now she sent him a copy of the published book. She had appreciated, of course, 'the style' Mountbatten had brought to the viceregal role – like her, Dickie loved flash and dash. (Grotesquely, in *Farewell*, Morris describes Partition as 'like Dunkirk, a failure, dashingly achieved'.) Just under eight weeks after Mountbatten wrote to thank her, an IRA bomb blew him to bits. Seven and a half years after Bloody Sunday, the cycle of sectarian violence continued beyond Northern Ireland, with balaclavas and pickaxes both in the Republic and on the mainland. Three months after the murder, Mountbatten's estate approached Morris regarding the authorised biography (though the job never came off). In one of the many reissues of *Farewell* she added a footnote exonerating herself for her emollient treatment of the former admiral of the fleet. After acknowledging that Mountbatten's policy had subsequently 'been much criticised', she fudged: 'My account of his Viceroyalty is subject to my own preferences for colour, panache and decision.'

Morris might have lost interest in her own gender change, but, through *Conundrum*, she had introduced transition to the mainstream. In 1979 nine million Britons watched the first episode of the BBC2 documentary *A Change of Sex*. It told the story of a young Lancastrian working as a hospital catering supervisor while navigating a route to become Julia Grant. According to the 2018 collection *Trans Britain: Our Journey from the Shadows*, while *Conundrum*, with its 'degree of exoticism', broke new ground, it also encouraged less literary voices to speak. 'Surgery in far-off Casablanca', one clinician wrote, 'seemed beyond the reach of ordinary mortals – whereas Julia [Grant] was immediately relatable.' (The series 'showed the way forward for many', according to a trans woman who lived through the seventies.) Morris had facilitated engagement, and at intervals of many years the BBC screened four more parts of *Julia's Story*, as it retitled the series. There will never be a more dignified television portrayal of the transition experience. When Grant moved into her public housing flat, a hater posted a burning T-shirt through the letterbox. 'It's not bad all the time, though,' she says to camera. Grant's two volumes of memoir tell a fuller and to a certain extent different story ('I spent the next five weeks in Strangeways [Prison], and they were most enjoyable'). Regarding the TV series, she concludes, 'I wanted the films to educate the public and give other transsexuals confidence.' And they did. After the first episode went out, Grant received five hundred letters, of which only two were negative, and gender referrals surged. Morris made no public comment. But she, in her own way, had achieved Grant's aims.

12
1980–1984
THE MATTER OF WALES

It was the perfect subject for Morris: the Venetian Empire was all about *energy*. In the eponymous book, which she had been discussing with Faber for a decade, she pursues the conquering armies and their attendant merchants from the Grand Canal to Constantinople – in the fifteenth century the sailor could travel all the way to the Levant via ports under Venetian control. Passages read like a film treatment, sailors 'yelling into the wind from the deck of a galley', 'the slap slap of the water on the rocks', and set pieces involve thousands of oarsmen. Researching in Crete, Morris had sailed from Elounda to Spinalonga with a single figure at the helm of a motorboat. '"Back in half an hour," the boatman told me darkly as we parted at the jetty. "Or there will be problems." All seemed bitterly haunted and oppressive.' She climbed to the summit.

> And there suddenly a grand excitement seized me. It was as though the island had sprung to life again – and I saw the trireme galleys foaming past the island, and heard the trumpets from the redan below, and felt the very slap of the rope on the flagstaff above my head, where the winged lion streaked still, all afire in the sunshine, in the dry, hard, Cretan wind.
>
> 'Time to go!' cried a voice far below me. 'Time to go!'

A third revised edition of *Venice*, which came out alongside *The Venetian Empire*, sold out, and Morris then plundered her extensive Venetian library again to write the lovely *Venetian Bestiary*, 'a mighty menagerie of fact and fantasy'. But she desperately wanted to get down to her Welsh project. That commanded her imagination now, not Venice. There was always something in the way, like the agreeable Venetian fillers, and in addition she felt she had to capitalise on emerging commercial trends while she had the chance. With technology on the march, publishers were able to bring out reasonably priced picture books like *Bestiary*, and Morris spotted a gap for further repurposing – she could repackage her backlist by adding illustrations. Monteith had said no to a *Sultan in Oman* with pictures, and to an illustrated *Coast to Coast*. But he agreed to a new large-format book, using recycled material, to be called *The Spectacle of Empire* and subtitled *Style, Effect and the Pax Britannica*. In 1982 she finished it after revising *Venice*, writing *Bestiary*, making a television programme on Wales, editing a second anthology on the country, visiting New York and Florida and supplying text to a photographic book on Wales by Paul Wakefield.

Amid the gleaming gubernatorial teak and fluttering scarlet pennants, a few of the archive photographs selected for inclusion in *Spectacle* reveal a rather different reality. A white man with a towel round his waist reads a newspaper on a veranda while a brown man in a turban does something to his toes; shackled convicts who are all ribs work a treadmill as a white man in a hat, holding a cane, looks at the camera. Evicted Irish peasants crouch with their meagre possessions beside them on a path, the battering ram that has evicted them still in position. Sudanese dead lie on stony ground, thin legs like zigzags, fingers spread. A spectacle of empire indeed. Aware that the subject was bottomless, Morris had earlier approached Faber about an even more ambitious illustrated Empire book, but now said she was 'bored of India'. There had been talk too of a second volume of *Conundrum*: 'something deeper [she wrote to Monteith]: the development of ideas, spiritual and evolutionary, which has occurred as a result of the *Conundrum* experience'. Essentially this was the book she had wanted to write in the first place. But she had lost interest in that subject too. Wales was taking over.

Further distractions included a BBC *Late Show* special about travel writing in which Morris appeared alongside Bruce Chatwin and Paul

Theroux. She had met Chatwin several years previously, and they saw one another in the Black Mountains when Chatwin was working on his novel *On the Black Hill*. They had also become postcard buddies. In a letter to a friend, Chatwin said, 'I confess to a sneaking pleasure by [*sic*] a card I got yesterday from Jan Morris saying that my description of the Welsh in Patagonia [in his 1977 book *In Patagonia*] actually moved him/her to tears.' Chatwin enjoyed making a meal of the pronouns: he found it hard to accept or understand Morris's hard-won gender reassignment. It was often people who presented themselves as smart progressives, like Chatwin, who mocked Morris behind her back. Older, apparently reactionary conservatives like Henry Anglesey or *TLS* editor Arthur Crook were able to see and respect Morris for what she was. After *The Late Show*, Chatwin wrote a letter to a friend describing 'Jan Morris, in his/her twinset and pearls. Going back to London in a taxi she/he said, "I was so interested in what you said about the dangers of travel. You see, having travelled all over the world, both as a male and a female, I can safely say it's far safer to travel as a female."' She detected his distaste. 'As a person,' she wrote long after Chatwin's death,

> he was decidedly too much for me. Snobbism, equally camp and genuine; showy connoisseurship of the quirky kind . . . sexual ambiguity of the Strength Through Joy kind. (I can see him now, riding his bicycle blonde and bare-backed through Powys [the largest county in Wales], for all the world like a Hitler Youth . . .) Some of his own books turn me off as he tended to turn me off.

Theroux had empathy Chatwin could not feel. He visited the converted Trefan stables shortly after Jan and Elizabeth moved there in the spring of 1982. 'Everyone else was talking about the Falklands,' Theroux remembered. They had first met the previous year at a literary event in London. 'I needed her to give me a sense of place in Wales, and she did. She went on about the ugliness of static caravans.' This was the Elsan culture R. S. was so keen on denigrating. Theroux's *The Kingdom by the Sea* was coming out the following year, and Morris later sketched its cover in the Trefan visitors' book alongside Theroux's name. It was a practice of hers in these years: she cherished the visitors' books, which nobody was allowed to sign more than once, no matter how many times they visited. The next entry after Theroux was Arthur Meggers, a VAT inspector. In *Kingdom*, Theroux recalls Morris's voice. 'The maleness that still trembled in it made it sultry and attractive.' He said she was kind, reckless and intelligent, and that he had 'a queer thrill when saying goodbye at Porthmadog station'. Theroux says now, 'She did influence me.'

> She teaches you how to see. She was a model professional writer. I really admired her. You can only repurpose if you do it well. I remember her quality of listening. She had the gaze of a descriptive writer.

OUP had reissued the *Destinations* anthology, under the impression that they were now her main house, and went on to pick up some of the earlier collections when rights reverted. But four years after Morris had told the team at OUP what nice people they were, the honeymoon ended, as Rubinstein had warned it would. She had already expressed misgivings about the firm's stewardship of the big Wales book, now proceeding at full tilt. In July 1981 she cancelled the contract. 'I thought I was joining a confident and expanding general publishing house,' she wrote to the OUP chairman himself,

> in which a lot of money was to be invested in publishing and promoting books like mine. Instead, I find I am signed up with a small and apparently contracting general publishing house with no money at all. I don't want just to be an appendage to a clutch of academics.

She woke the next morning and scrawled an apologetic postcard reinstating the contract. But gradually all the complaints she had levelled at Faber were to be hurled at OUP: poor jacket design, poor blurbs, poor sales. 'I hope I'm not going to have any trouble about House Styles, I don't recognise them,' she once threatened a new copyeditor at the Press, 'and I shall insist on my own punctuation, commas in particular.'

*

When Morris and Elizabeth moved permanently into the stables, they called their new home Trefan Morys. The original builder had cut a hole in the roof to let barn owls in and out, and the Morrises had to evict the birds. It made them sad, so they had an inscription engraved on a pane: *er cof am y tylluanod* – 'in memory of the owls'. But the descendants of the evictees hooted retribution, even in daytime. At least part of a timber beam bearing a hoof mark had made its way into an upstairs windowsill – Morris said that was 'a reminder of the constancy of things'. A forty-foot room took up most of the two floors, and Morris's library filled both. She had commissioned bookshelves like the ones in the Vatican, she said, stepped out to allow sidestacks. The dominance of the library at Trefan Morys reflected both her priorities and her grip on family decisions. Suki remembers, 'Mummy said Jan wasn't interested in anything except literature.' They had to sleep somewhere, so Jan had a small bedroom and bathroom off one end of the first floor, and Elizabeth an en suite off the kitchen below. Stairs linked the floors at both ends; at the kitchen end they were spiral. Outside, to the right of the front (Dutch, or double-hung) stable door, steps webbed with toadflax led to the first floor directly from the yard where they parked their cars, and round the corner to the left Jan's bedroom opened onto a flat roof. Elizabeth planted hydrangea in the front and vegetables in beds at the back accessed through an archway (she put honeysuckle in there too), as well as ferns in the shady spots.

The design of the house reflected Morris's curiously detached view of her family: there were no spare rooms. Even when the children visited, she could be less than welcoming. Suki has what she calls 'a foundation memory' of arriving at Trefan in her late teens. 'I've always struggled with my weight, and Jan opened the door and said, "My, Suki, you're very substantial." She was judgemental about my appearance.' Morris had written in *The Outriders*, 'if you dye your beard blue . . . you are honourably welcome to do so', but when Suki got a nose ring she did mind ('I have nothing but utter contempt'), soliciting advice from third parties about whether the hole would close up if the ring were removed and telephoning Suki to relay the news. As for chubby people – Morris was always averse to them. 'It is her fatness I chiefly notice,' she wrote of someone in *Rolling Stone*. When a cold-blooded American magazine editor sent her to cover the Paris fashion shows, however, people were too thin, not too fat. She didn't mind the models, but couldn't stand 'the unbelievably ugly high priestesses of American fashion journalism . . . red-taloned, emaciated to the point of grotesquerie'.

Morris appeared not to notice when her reactionary right-wing views offended family sensibilities. When a new waitress appeared in a Criccieth café and failed to meet the usual standards, Morris said in front of Suki, who was visiting, 'I bet she's a single mother.' Suki herself was a single mother at that point. Higher taxes and rising unemployment continued to breed resentment in Britain, and Morris was still gunning for perceived spongers. In other areas too she could be oddly tone-deaf, emotionally. The adult Peter né Breitmeyer (he had changed his last name to Carew) wrote once to reconnect: she was his godparent; they had last met when she'd taken him out to the Cockpit café as an Eton schoolboy. Morris replied now saying she had no knowledge of being his godmother. Peter wrote back enclosing a copy of Elizabeth's proxy acceptance letter, written in 1953. He never heard from Morris again.

In 1981 Enid had died. She was ninety-five, and had outlived Walter by forty-three years. They buried her in the family plot at St Andrew's in Clevedon, on a cliff overlooking the Bristol Channel where Jim had watched the colliers. The others repaired to the Walton Park Hotel for luncheon, but Morris left after the service. *Another one done.* When Chris's daughter Sallie got married, Morris was pleased when Chris did not recognise her at the reception ('Have we met?' Chris asked). Sallie's brother Paul remembers, 'Dad was mortified, but I think Jan was pleased – she didn't want to look like James.'

Another couple got married the year Enid died. Morris wrote to *The Times* to complain about the publicly funded expense of the nuptials of Charles, Prince of Wales, and Lady Diana Spencer, and on the day organised a rival event, a picnic (in the rain, as it turned out) on the possible site of Mynydd Carn, an eleventh-century battle, the damp participants 'exchanging mutually self-congratulatory seditious sentiments'. Resuming hostilities six years later, Morris published an imaginary interview with Prince Charles in the Welsh magazine *Planet*. 'Nobody', she began by informing His Royal Highness, 'need employ me, but we can't get rid of you.'

She immersed herself in Welsh projects, compiling anthologies and submitting features. The Welsh Language Act of 1967 had granted Welsh equal status with English, known to some as the thin language. Road signs had gone bilingual and in 1977 the BBC had launched the Welsh-language Radio Cymru; a subsequent television channel triggered a thunderous row, as stakeholders fought over the number of hours allotted to the non-thin language. 'I believe', Morris once wrote, 'that political power is necessary to secure the cultural integrity of a people,' and she believed too that language is power. Her vision of that power, cultural and political, was vested in a federal Europe with Wales in it as an independent nation. She strove for unity. But she never fully engaged with the practicalities of independence or self-determination. It was the cultural nationalism Plaid Cymru had struggled to achieve in its early decades that attracted her.

As we have seen, Plaid and the Welsh nationalists also furnished an escape from the political gloom she had documented. Although the recession was global – oil prices trebled in two years – it had hit Britain hardest, and day after day front pages tolled bells of decline amid reports of a calamitously high pound. The extreme-right National Front was flourishing, and Morris had documented an encounter with a group of its goons. Race riots had convulsed the country in 1981. Morris's friends Theroux and Raban both drew a shocking picture of the UK during this period, and Chatwin too, returning to Britain in 1984, found the country 'in a soupy, pre-Fascist condition'; Geoffrey Moorhouse, another writer pal, joined the threnody with powerful state-of-the-nation journalism. Between 1979 and 1987, manufacturing jobs in Wales fell by 34 per cent, and not just in the industrial south.

In Flint, fifty miles from Cricieth, when British Steel and the textile firm Courtaulds slashed jobs, unemployment reached 32 per cent. Long public housing waiting lists were getting longer. Widespread English ownership of Welsh cottages – 7,500 in Gwynedd alone at that time – hardened into a symbol of cultural drift. The famous protest fires blazed on the Llŷn Peninsula in December 1979, when arsonists torched a home in Nefyn on the 'anniversary' of the murder of Llywelyn ap Gruffudd by English forces in the thirteenth century. Before the conflagration was cold, another flared in Llanbedrog, also in Llŷn. Over the following years, nationalists torched two hundred English-owned houses, estate agencies and Conservative Party offices, most of them in the north of the country. Theroux said that on his tour of Wales he did not meet anyone who didn't support the burnings. This was the climate in which Morris wrote her Welsh books at a desk looking out at Eryri, the geography that had played such a significant role in Welsh history. She told a journalist that, while she wasn't going out with a box of matches, she didn't think there was anything sacrosanct about property.

Morris's dawning understanding of Welsh oppression realigned her imperial views. It was personal – the 'emotional approach to history' she had pioneered in *Pax* had come home. It was this realignment that led to her private comment that Empire was 'a dreadful phenomenon redeemed by its style'. One is bound to note that the idea of celebrating her Welshness or even of being Welsh hadn't occurred to Morris before she turned fifty. J. E. Jones, Plaid general secretary and trailblazing television gardener, had planted a metaphorical seed twenty years before, when he wrote from Glamorgan to say she ought to be writing about the land of her fathers. 'I was much moved', Morris remembered, 'by this unexpected call.' Quizzed on the BBC about her allegiance in 1983, she said that 'about ten years ago it [Welshness] gradually grew on me'. That dated it to the year after Casablanca.

Morris expressed the deepest meaning of her new Welsh identity in text accompanying Wakefield's photographs. In *Wales: The First Place*, after repeating what by now was an accepted truth – that her father had been Welsh – Morris wrote that her love of Wales was partly 'an insatiable dream, a never-to-be-fulfilled conviction that out there somewhere another country is concealed . . . And some hidden key to the understanding of things is waiting to be turned.' It was of a piece with her other longing, to cross the gender threshold. Morris goes on to acknowledge a desire for 'something indefinable, perhaps unattainable'; the national struggle, like her own, was 'a fight that can never be won'. At the end of *The First Place*, Morris writes of her yearning for 'that metaphysical image of otherness'. Wales did not represent 'physical unity . . . for Gwynedd people are very different from the people of Dyfed . . . It is the unity rather of the otherness itself.'

In later years she and her friend Sir Simon Jenkins, former editor of *The Times* and a frequent guest at Trefan (his father was Welsh and he had a house on the southern edge of Snowdonia), often discussed what he calls her 'aggressively romantic view of her compatriots'. Jenkins wrote,

> she placed great store behind the myths and legends of a glorious Welsh past. When I protested that myths cannot be treated as history, she disagreed. Myths, she said, were facts, just as history was facts. I should never underrate the role of myths in the nation's identity. They could be among its most potent 'facts'.

Myth was antithetical to the bank-manager approach to history: that was stolid and materialistic, whereas myth was incorporeal and ambiguous. But it was not all sprites and misty glamour in Wales: Morris was asked to present the prizes at the local sheepdog trials. (The owners got the prizes.) She herself had become part of the legend. Mark says, 'She found she had more of that mythical status she sought in Wales . . . She was a kind of prophet there.' She had even acquired vatic significance abroad: admirers from foreign lands regularly made the pilgrimage to Llanystumdwy, and if they wrote ahead she invited them for tea. If nobody had arranged to come, and Morris spotted a tourist peering at the house from the lane, she invited them in. That suited her, as the visitor never stayed long. When a guest wrote thanking her for the hospitality and adding that next time he would stay the night, she wrote back, No you won't. She was sociable at the surface level that word implies. 'Could you exist on a desert island?' Roy Plomley had asked her on *Desert Island Discs*. 'No! I get lonely after a weekend!'*

She had repackaged herself, as she had her books, changing the parameters of her life by shifting to Wales and withdrawing from the circular-drive stakes. A Welsh identity conferred a structure for the self, for herself. It replaced the identity of the squire holding court in the Big House on Boxing Day. Both in their turn replaced an intimate life. Wales was a means of expressing otherness, as transition had been in its way.

In a piece for *Life* magazine ten years earlier, Morris had used the third person for the Welsh – 'they', not 'we'. By 1976 she was writing 'us Welsh' (for example in *Rolling Stone*). Now, finishing the 'big' book, she was in full Welsh throat, and had cast aside postures she once derided in print as 'the dottiest ambitions of Welsh nationalism'. Her conception of Wales yielded order and pattern, replacing the now unreliable security of the imperial ideal, and the book underway had therefore expanded in scope: it was no longer a biography of Glyndŵr. Morris used him as a narrative device instead, 'looking at the country always not so much through his eyes as in his company. He is present throughout the work, even when I do not mention him.' (A group called Meibion Glyndŵr – Sons of Glendower – allegedly lay behind the arson campaign.) *The Matter of Wales*, when it finally emerged, was a romanticised portrait of 'the lonely magic rowans of the Welsh memory' reaching back to the half-truths of the Dark Ages. A section on English-sponsored child labour in the ironworks and coal mines would turn anyone into a cottage-burner. 'I have been below [in Plymouth Mines, Merthyr] six or eight months,' said Susan Reece, aged six, in 1849. 'And I don't like it much. I come here at six in the morning and leave at six at night.' Righteous indignation

---

* She enjoyed picking up hitchhikers for short bouts of companionship. Once, in the Black Mountains, she gave a lift to a young man wearing a T-shirt printed with the famous Korda image of Che Guevara. 'I once met that young man on your shirt,' Morris said with a smile. 'Oh?' said the hitchhiker. 'Who is it?'

infuses the prose, an indignation not evident in the conquests of *Pax Britannica*. Morris had moved to the side of the oppressed.

The Matter of Wales is not an insightful book, and it tails off at the end, but it is informative, entertaining and elegantly expressed. 'I am all Wales in one!' the author concludes in a sort of apotheosis – 'I know myself at one, ecstatically, with the winds and the wild creatures ... The country I have celebrated in this book is not just a country on the map, or even in the mind: it is a country of the heart, and all of us have some small country there.'

Literary editors telephoned biddable Welsh reviewers. Most said they enjoyed the book without persuading readers that they had. Torey Hayden in the *New York Times* broke rank. *The Matter of Wales*, she proclaimed, was 'riddled with minor mistakes, mostly geographical', and its author 'suffers from a *Dungeons and Dragons* infatuation'. Hayden thought Morris's 'passion, sustained at a fever pitch for more than 400 pages, turns the prose purple', and that the author failed to throw light on the real paradox of Welshness, presenting instead 'the poetic view only'. Conceived as a rocket, the book had landed as a squib. Morris knew she had failed to pull it off, telling Rubinstein that she herself found the volume 'very boring'.

The roundabout continued to spin. In 1984 Morris returned to Venice as American *Vogue*'s new columnist (a short-lived post), flew to Toronto for its sesquicentennial and visited Manhattan twice for a new book. She was still dependent on American magazines, even if fees had gone down. Travels for short pieces included a road trip from Red River on the Oklahoma state line to Rio Grande at the Mexican frontier, risking the hostility of readers of *Texas Monthly* with the assertion 'there is more beautiful scenery within five miles of Llanystumdwy than there is down the length of US 281'. In 'Not So Far: A European Journey' she motors from Wales to Montenegro in a BMW, blaring Mozart from the cassette deck in brilliant light. But the most significant trip of the early eighties was China. Morris had been trying to get a visa for years, and once the country had rejoined the world economy in 1978, setting out on the most spectacular growth story in history, she finally succeeded. She went in by river from Hong Kong, her steamship threading among abandoned sampans and flotillas of trawlers. China might have embarked on mighty expansion, but Morris noted in Shanghai, 'There are virtually no private cars in this city of 11 million.' She didn't respond to the country because she didn't understand it, and postcards home resorted to irony: 'Yum yum! I'm eating the Weight Watchers salad at the Holiday Inn. China at last!' She told the *Paris Review*, 'Beijing was too big for me.' This was imaginative failure of a kind. Morris knew she had finally lost momentum, and the significance of the China journey lay in its sense of an ending. 'Beijing and Shanghai were my last great cities,' she concluded soon after she returned. 'I may go upstream now instead.' Her heart wasn't in the *Rolling Stone* essay which emerged from the journey; she was coming to the end of what she could deliver for the magazine as well. It had changed, anyway. '*Rolling Stone* didn't matter anymore,' according to Wenner's biographer. The visions rock culture had once delivered 'had morphed into the Me Decade, and the Me Decade had turned into Me *Decades*, and finally the falcon could no longer hear the falconer, not even in the pages of *Rolling Stone*'. That was a bit allegorical even for Morris.

13
1985–1989
WHAT'S BECOME OF WARING

'After half a lifetime of urban wandering,' Morris said, announcing her only novel, *Last Letters from Hav*, 'I've been asked so often to describe my favourite city that in the end I made one up.' She admitted, as sixty loomed, that, over the years,

> I seldom knew what I was writing about, and I did not truly understand the multitudinous forces . . . that worked away beneath the forces of all societies . . . At the same time societies themselves were becoming ever more complex and obfuscatory . . . So, having failed to master so many real places, I invented one to emblemise this new confusion of the peoples.

The narrator of the novel, travel writer Jan Morris, finds the city of Hav impossible to pin down, 'like one of those threadbare exhausting dreams that have you groping through an impenetrable tangle of time, space and meaning, looking for your car keys'. Menace lurks, and the story ends on a note of unspecified foreboding. Nuclear Armageddon was on everyone's mind when Morris was cooking up *Hav*: membership of the Campaign for Nuclear Disarmament had surged, and when, in February 1982, an eighth Welsh council declared itself a nuclear-free zone, daffodil-touting campaigners including the poet R. S. proclaimed Wales the first nuclear-free country in Europe.

The concept of shifting identity preoccupied Morris in these mid-to-late years, and in *Hav* she landed on novelist Anthony Powell's character Waring as a symbol of brooding dislocation; at one point the narrator sits in the stern of a launch 'like Waring'. Powell's prototype was itself an invention of the poet Robert Browning, and Morris, who first deployed Waring as far back as *The Market of Seleukia*, was not the only other writer to co-opt him. When Burgess and Maclean vanished, all sorts of literary-minded journalists reached for Browning's lines (*What's become of Waring/ Since he gave us all the slip*). The character particularly suited Morris, as in Powell's fifth novel he appears as a travel writer who had never been to the places he chronicled. Called *What's Become of Waring*, Powell's book came out in 1939, a brooding enough year. (Morris knew the author and had visited him at The Chantry, his Somerset home.) Waring was her perfect symbol of doppelgängerish evasion. Fabulism played an important role in her art – and in who she was.

The new editorial director at Faber, Robert McCrum, wore jeans rather than Monteithian pinstripes and had arrived 'determined to turn up the wattage'. He got to know Morris while shepherding the backlist and became immensely fond of her, but, new broom in hand, he was not prepared to countenance 'new novels from the second division . . . I thought Jan was a very good writer, but essentially a reporter.' Rival publisher Viking pounced on *Hav*, and much sheepishness followed at Queen Square when the title appeared on the Booker Prize shortlist. Doris Lessing, Iris Murdoch and Peter Carey were among the other shortlisted authors that year. When critics and journalists suggested *Hav* did not deserve its place, Morris agreed. (New Zealander Keri Hulme won, for *The Bone People*.) Meanwhile, in letter after letter, correspondents begged her to tell them where Hav actually was – they had got the atlas down but couldn't find it. A custodian at the Royal Geographical Society declared that he had ransacked the Map Room in vain. Morris had fooled them all.

Her only novel was bound to be about a city. 'I am an aficionado of urbanism,' she said once, and she seldom wrote about the rural environment or the natural world. Suki remembers that, when they went for family walks, Elizabeth took an interest in nature whereas Jan only went for the exercise. To express her devotion to the built environment,

Morris talked OUP New York into a collection called *Among the Cities*, which would come out in 1985. It was to be a selection from the five already published – an anthology of the anthologies. She wrote in the preface that, years ago, 'observing that nobody in the history of man had ever seen and described the entire urban world, I resolved to do it myself; and in 1983, standing at last in the great square of Tiananmen ... I felt this perhaps jejune ambition to have been fulfilled'. This was enjoyable Gibbonesque parody, rolling cadences included ('It was at Rome,' the author of the Roman *Pax* famously wrote, 'as I sat musing amidst the ruins of the Capitol, while the barefooted friars were singing vespers in the Temple of Jupiter, that the idea of writing the decline and fall of the city first started to my mind.') Morris had chosen pieces, she said, which would 'illustrate the shifting responses of a single mind, faced with the slow unfolding of the planet'. It is a dazzling book in places, offering the reader 'skeletons of monks tied together like asparagus' in Lima, the 'potato world' of Eastern Europe after the Curtain clanged down, Morris herself eating lychees in the sun as she floats down the Li amid the humped green mountains of Guangxi (in a postcard to Elizabeth she said the Li was 'the Dwyfor of China'). She had made a few changes as the essays migrated. When a Moscow feature had first appeared in *The Times* in 1957, Stalin lay next to Lenin in the mausoleum. When she collected the essay in book form six years later, Stalin had exited the tomb, so Morris removed him from the story too. In *Among the Cities* she put Joseph Vissarionovich back on his slab in the service of historical accuracy, as the account carried a date at the end. She said she hoped that the Soviets never did the same thing.

When Mark's first marriage had ended he had moved to Canada, where he did a PhD in creative writing and published *Domesday Revisited: A Traveller's Guide*. A few years later he began teaching at the University of Alberta, where he was to receive a Faculty of Arts Teaching Award, and where he remains an adjunct professor. He went on to write a second, highly regarded book on twentieth-century composers. A gulf had opened between Morris and her eldest son. She had publicly acknowledged the intimacy between them when she thanked Mark in *Conundrum*; she never acknowledged the decades of strange near-silence that followed. It was as if she wanted to close a door. When Mark married again, his parents did not attend the second wedding, just as they had not attended the first.

Twm had taken over as Morris's primary support long before Mark emigrated. He had wandered over the hills around Trefan Bach with a guitar, a curly-haired troubadour, a Payne and a Morris and a Bourne, and as a young man he had hitchhiked to Germany to play his harp in the *Marktplätze* (it was a smallish harp). He was committed to the Welsh struggle and the authenticity of his passion greatly appealed to Morris. 'I became Jan's batman,' Twm says. 'We toured as a duo. I helped her write about Wales.' She often brought him into the books, and they translated Welsh poems together for inclusion at the end of *The First Place*. Like all nationalists, Twm objected to the imposition of a foreign prince. At a ceremonial occasion in the early eighties involving Charles, Prince of Wales, police arrested Twm for obstructing the law. When he appeared in court, he insisted on speaking in Welsh. Twm's explanation of his actions – that prior to the imposition of Charles the office had been unoccupied since the thirteenth century – was rendered by the court translator, 'There hasn't been a Prince of Wales since the last one.' 'Everyone laughed at that,' Twm remembers.

These were hard times for Elizabeth. She worried about the children far more now they were adults. In addition, Suki always felt the Stables, unlike Trefan Bach in the Black Mountains, 'was Jan's house'. (Elizabeth had written her name in one book out of seven thousand in the library.) When Mark had asked his mother about the move, Elizabeth had replied, 'It's what Jan wants.' She unburdened herself to their former neighbour, the writer Elspeth Huxley, who replied with a postcard sent inside an envelope. Huxley knew everything, and urged Elizabeth on.

> I hope Trefan Bach is up for sale together with your North Wales rural oubliette [Trefan Morys] and that you're off to Tokyo, New York and Los Angeles without further delay, lusting for life, fizzing like a bomb. What nonsense you do talk! If your arrival in the celestial city of your dreams coincides with a garbage men's strike, a power cut, an outbreak of smog, a monumental traffic jam and minimum price of £100 for a meal, I can only sympathise.

Besides Huxley, Elizabeth confided in her friend Joan Murray-Brown, the former wife of Morris's *Panorama* producer, Jeremy.

> Dearest Joan, what a splendid person you are, and I want to thank you <u>so much</u> for taking <u>so much</u> trouble for me. Things have changed so much more than I have realised! Life seems to get more and more complicated. So, dear friend, stay single and enjoy your <u>own</u> life with <u>friends</u>.

Both Jan and Elizabeth had become part of the landscape around Llanystumdwy. The farm adjacent to Trefan had been in the same family for several generations, and Twm remembers the farmer, Geraint Parry, 'talking for hours' with Jan. Later, in the next century, Morris herself wrote of the Parry van going by: by then it was young John at the wheel. There were no Boxing Day parties, but carollers came from the village and took refreshments around the kitchen table. The immediate surroundings – a seascape sometimes, as that part of the Llŷn Peninsula called Eifionydd stands in one of the wettest corners of Europe – were a fixed centre for both Morrises as the rest of the world blew by. Jan was part of a community in Llanystumdwy, for the first time since Christ Church School and the army. People accepted her. 'When I did the unimaginable and went through what is vulgarly known as a change of sex,' she wrote, neighbours 'took it all easily in their stride, and from that day to this have kindly pretended that nothing ever happened.'

*

Saturday Night magazine in Toronto had asked if she would write a series of essays on Canadian cities, and Morris rarely refused a commission. She saw Mark briefly in Banff, though turned him into a 'friend' in the ensuing essay. The rest of the trip turned out to be mixed. 'Exasperated by the self-control, the moderation, the logic of everything,' she wrote during her sixth visit to Vancouver, '... I pined for the dingy, the neglected, and the disregarded old.' When she walked on Grouse Mountain a ptarmigan attacked her, 'uttering sinister gurgles and prancing around me in so crazed a way that I was obliged to beat it off with my handbag'. What a film it would make.

New York beckoned again, especially after Canada. Morris had visited Manhattan annually since 1953, and for years had longed to write a book to follow *The Great Port*, which nobody read. When she set about planning one, in 1979, the city had been experiencing one of its crime waves just as the country at large was suffering economically: two oil crises, a weak stock market, a loss of manufacturing jobs in major industries such as automobiles and steel, and a rocketing mortgage rate (it passed 13 per cent in 1981). So Morris turned to the past, and the bit of it she liked best, she said, as she had said before, was the idea of Manhattan in the 1940s or, more specifically, in the decade between 1935 and 1945. It was the same 'simpler world' of 1940s Los Angeles she had already celebrated in *Rolling Stone*, and Morris embalmed it in *Manhattan '45*, a portrait between hard covers of a city eight years before she walked down the gangplank of the *Mauretania*. She began to write in 1984 and delivered a typescript to Monteith, working now as a consultant at Faber, at the start of 1986 – the first book they had done together since the OUP break. 'It's like old times,' Morris told him. So it was: a fortnight later she erupted like a volcano about the jacket of the book, its price, and Faber's inability to sell any copies of anything. The next day she rang back to say she was sorry they had quarrelled. She was at her most incontinently human when contrite.

Like *Venice*, the set-piece opening of *Manhattan '45* involves the arrival of a ship, this time the *Queen Mary*, bringing GIs home. Old

Glories fluttered, tickertape flickered and water sparkled – just the kind of spectacle Morris liked.

> 'We Made It Mom' . . . everything that America seemed to represent in a world of loss and ruin . . . town of all towns, and this was a culminating moment in its history . . . Battered and impoverished London, humiliated Paris, shattered Berlin, discredited Rome, the capitals which, before the war, Americans had so often looked at with sensations of diffident inferiority . . .

It is an affecting portrait. The East 35th Street police house was lit by gas, and only four police cars and one motorcycle in the whole of Manhattan had two-way radios. Mayor Fiorello La Guardia had dictated that no navels were to be shown on stage. In the communal changing rooms of clothing stores (70 per cent of all American women's clothing was made on the island of Manhattan) signs in English, Italian and Yiddish read: 'DO NOT DISGRACE YOUR FAMILY. THE PUNISHMENT FOR STEALING IS JAIL.' The US annual quota for Chinese immigrants was 105. The book does have longueurs ('celebrities were the pillars of Café Society'), but not many. The 'On Movement' chapter vividly evokes a period in which 'the railway age was at its glorious zenith': one gilded couple maintained a private suite at Grand Central with its own pipe organ. As for the five-foot-two-inch, Stetson-wearing La Guardia, an anomalous Republican New Dealer, he was in the last months of his revolutionary mayoralty. (Shortly after unveiling Arshile Gorky's murals at Newark Airport to welcome the new Air Age, he said, 'If this is art, then I'm a horse's ass.') Morris dedicated the book to nine GIs who had not come back on the *Queen Mary* because they were dead. When the book came out, the widow of one of the nine sent a letter expressing her gratitude.

'The skyline was not so dense in those days,' Morris wrote, 'so that one could more often see the gleam of water at the end of a street – Cheever's "river light".' Morris did not generally let light of any kind shine on rival writers, but John Cheever is a presiding spirit of *Manhattan*

'45; besides quoting him ('a long-lost world when the city of New York was still filled with river light ... and almost everybody wore a hat'), she acknowledges that he 'would one day be the laureate of Manhattan'. Morris wrote elsewhere of Cheever's habit of scrunching up reviews of his books and tossing them in the wastebasket, only to fish them out again, confessing that she did the same. She would have been wise not to retrieve the notices of *Manhattan '45*. Critics thought the book lacked substance, which is inapt as it was never supposed to be substantive: it aims to capture the spirit of an idea. Some attributed its perceived weaknesses to post-transition decline. Everything she saw, fulminated the *Literary Review*, was 'distorted through the pink prism of gender. Her exaggerated femininity embarrasses the reader on every page ... For reasons we should probably never know this once vigorous, intelligent writer has decided to adopt the persona of a Silly Old Bag.'

At home in Britain the Thatcher government had pushed on through its second term, enabled in part by the fact that the Labour opposition had appointed Michael Foot as its leader. In *The Times*, Morris's supporter Bernard Levin said Foot couldn't blow his nose without his trousers falling down. In the first half of the eighties, the 'victory' of the elite forces that had ended the Iranian embassy siege in London had stiffened national resolve, and two years later, just as economic recovery was glimmering on the horizon, the Falklands War had boosted a populist brand of patriotic pride and transformed Thatcher's reputation at home and abroad. But in May 1984 – the year after a Tory landslide – images of striking coal miners and police facing off at Orgreave coking plant in Yorkshire had appeared on the front pages for days and burned off the Falklands shine. Morris's generation had grown up with the expectation of social progress; some said, now, that it had stalled. Something humane had unravelled in Britain. A few months after Orgreave, Jan and Elizabeth had switched on morning television (itself a recent arrival) to see Secretary of State Norman Tebbit being stretchered out of Brighton's bombed Grand Hotel during the Conservative Party conference.

Morris continued to add her voice to those expressing frustration at the English invasion of cottage-owners and Elsan-users. A piece of hers ran with the headline 'Sick of the Tourist Rollercoaster', and she called another 'Save Wales for the Welsh'. When she addressed Welsh societies of one sort or another she told them she believed there would be a place for an independent Wales in a federated Europe. The EU had approved the Single European Act in 1985 and it came into force in 1987, the first significant revision of the Treaty of Rome twenty-eight years earlier and a step towards meaningful European unity of the kind for which Morris yearned. The problem was, as she recognised, foreshadowing the trauma to come, 'the English ... had always viewed the prospect of a more integrated Europe, still more a federated Europe, with suspicion and distaste ... Continental trickery, the profoundest national conviction seemed to say, would gang up to humiliate them.' That, and the fact that poll after poll revealed that nobody cared very much, if at all, about Europe.

Mikhail Gorbachev had taken office as general secretary of the Communist Party of the Soviet Union two years before *Manhattan '45* came out, and in 1986 he used the word *glasnost* for the first time. His admirer Thatcher announced that the Cold War was over. Surely, Morris believed, about as passionately as she ever believed anything, it was Europe's time.

Old Bag or not, she kept up with technology. She always had: long ago she had installed a telex machine in the Big House, and neighbours were still talking about its impromptu eructations years later. She had begun to collect Betamax videos as soon as they appeared in Criccieth, and had recently embraced the fax. When a copy of a Payne coat of arms Gareth had mischievously adapted juddered out of the Trefan fax machine, Morris managed to send an image back of her own hand making a V-sign (not the Victory one). She had subsequently acquired an Amstrad computer. She enjoyed tech, as she liked structure and compartmentalisation, and after *Manhattan '45* came out she bought a Toshiba T1850 and was so thrilled that she drew it in the visitors' book, as she did each new car. Friends remembered her zestfully offering advice on which machine to purchase. 'I finally acquired my computer, though not the one you urged me to get,' wrote a disobedient Geoffrey Moorhouse. Morris eventually bought a laptop that synced with the one stabled on her desk, and life on the road was never quite the same again. She whipped the machine out if ever forty-five minutes opened up, and once, in a lobby of the Frankfurter Hof, a crowd gathered as people mistook her for a Toshiba sales agent giving a demonstration.

Back in September 1981, Faber's Matthew Evans had sent Morris a letter. (He became chairman of the firm that year, taking over from Monteith, who was about to retire permanently.) 'Somebody speaking on behalf of the Hong Kong government', Evans revealed enigmatically, 'has asked me if you would be at all interested in writing a book about the New Territories for a lot of money, all expenses paid, etc., etc. There would be no editorial interference at all.' She was overcommitted for the next two or three years, but the book's inscrutable sponsors were happy to wait. The British lease on the archipelago fell due in 1997, and, ideally, they wanted a portrait of the colony as it sailed into its last decade.

Morris flew to Hong Kong on 22 February 1986, twenty-eight years after she had first landed at Kai Tak in a Comet. She had visited often in the interim. Just the year before, she had told readers of American *Vogue*, 'Hong Kong seems to me at this moment the most truly enthralling place in the world.' This time she spent a month in a suite at the Mandarin on Connaught Road, writing notes to Gareth joshing about elitism on headed paper printed with her name. Every morning she walked the four-kilometre (two-and-a-half-mile) Peak perimeter, trying to concentrate on panoramic views which didn't enthral her. She loitered on the waterfronts to watch the lights of the ships or eat fried chicken on a bench in the gathering dark, and she visited the junk-building yards on Cheung Chau where oxyacetylene flashed or a vessel was winched out of the water to have its hull cleaned. By the time she checked out of the Mandarin, Morris had a draft of *Hong Kong: Xianggang*.

It is hardly surprising, therefore, that it is a weak book. The history is 'slapdash', as a reviewer had noted of an earlier work. Morris lifted almost all the sections about nineteenth-century Hong Kong piecemeal from *Pax*, taking little care to ensure that the finished product at least looked like an organic unity. Even the Second World War episodes are culled from published memoirs, despite the fact that protagonists were still living on the archipelago and she could have spoken to them. The majority Chinese are silent actors. You sense an author treading water; her ten-page piece on Hong Kong in *Encounter* in 1974 is better than the book. Cliché and generalisation seep onto the page ('These were the early years of a fateful confrontation between East and West'), as well as uncharacteristically clumsy phrasing ('a general sense of having a good time is shared by all races'). She reached instinctively for the present immediate – 'Here come three Japanese businessmen' – a trusted formula, but the passages appear as just that: formulaic. In a footnote she records meeting the lawyer Martin Lee at the Hong Kong Club. Lee, who incarnated democracy in Hong Kong for a generation, gets one line. To Morris, taipans were just Monmouth bank managers transported to Asia.

Still, the book was *popular*. Governor Chris Patten wrote from his official residence facing the Peak: 'I read your excellent book before I came out here. It remains the best book I have read on the territory.' Morris repaid her debt to the Mandarin ('repeatedly nominated the best hotel in the world') in three embarrassing pages. She had booked a room for the handover in 1997, or so she said.

The failure of *Hong Kong*, both as a work of history and as a travelogue, represented the end of a road. Morris had thrived on the double-purposed narrative, but the love affair had run its course. At this point, therefore – there being no alternative to non-stop writing – she embarked on another volume of memoir, a slender and somewhat pointless rehash she called *Pleasures of a Tangled Life*. After dismissing travel as a 'debased' personal addiction, Morris acknowledged that she had never believed in trying to experience foreign cultures from the inside. 'Far better to regard the great world as a kind of show, a tragicomedy, kindly put on for my fascination.' As a perspicacious reviewer pointed out, to some extent the claim also suggests the limitations of her attitude to life at large. But it had not always been so. A strong sense of aesthetic value had driven the earlier works; in *Venice*, *Pax* and *Trieste*, the world had not been reduced to a show.

Morris had recently dismissed questions about her gender change in a radio interview, using a travel analogy, as she was to do in *Pleasures*: 'I truly don't think about this subject from one year to the next . . . over the years I gradually swam from one side of the barrier to the other.' In a chapter called 'As to Sex' she cracked a joke she often deployed to disarm, about belonging to two clubs in the ambiguous period, one as a man and one as a woman. She used to change her outfit in a taxi, she said, as she travelled between the two. But one odd new theme appeared in that chapter. Morris proclaimed, 'Blood love is the purest of loves,' and that 'all the best sex, in my view, aspires to the condition of incest'. When Mark came to that part of the book, he threw it against a wall – he had just returned from a residential workshop in Alberta with adult victims of childhood abuse. A *New York Times* review of *Pleasures* concluded, reasonably enough, that Morris 'enjoys shocking her reader . . . But then she pulls in her horns by saying that she and the partner she has lived with for nearly forty years, namely the former Mrs James Morris, have achieved a bond so deep it might be that of brothers – or sisters. It is all very confusing.'

Many years earlier, shortly after Casablanca, Morris had commissioned the engraving of a slate headstone reading:

> *Yma mae dwy ffrind,*
> *Jan & Elizabeth Morris,*
> *Ar derfyn un bywyd.*
> *Here are two friends,*
> *Jan & Elizabeth Morris,*
> *At the end of one life.*

It had been resting ever since against the stepped bookcases downstairs. Morris fetishised this object and pointed it out to every journalist who made the pilgrimage to Llanystumdwy. It was to stand, eventually (she said), with their mingled ashes on the islet in the Dwyfor close to the steep bank called Gallt y Widdan, Witch's Slope. Morris was determined to orchestrate her own ending.

Elizabeth, very much alive, accepted even her partner's wilder indulgences. (When Morris imported a bevy of fantailed doves for the Trefan roof, they flew straight home to Gloucestershire.) She worried instead about Jan's health, and about the children's assorted travails. In addition, her friend Betty Jones, the dead farmer's wife, was seriously depressed and had twice come to stay at Trefan for a week when Morris was away. 'So the year ended,' Elizabeth recorded bleakly on the last day of December 1989. 'What next?'

At least they escaped regularly to London, where both of them were devoted to Durrants, a small hotel near Nottingham Place, where they had met on the boarding house stairs in 1948. Morris liked the brass and mahogany furnishings, as they made the long, narrow hotel look like a ship. She also joined the Academy Club, a raffish authors' bar and restaurant in Beak Street which offered up the Dickensian boho Morris liked in small, hitchhiker-sized doses. She took other writers under her wing, at the club and elsewhere, the attraction usually based on intellectual kinship, though she also went for flamboyance and outsider status. Sometimes she never met her protégés, conducting friendships for decades by post and on the telephone, reaching out in a way she could not to her family. She had built her life around such exchanges. At the turn of the millennium, Roger Lewis was working on a biography of the writer Anthony Burgess. On the phone Morris regaled him with stories about Burgess in Moscow, including his vanishing act on the theatre steps. The next day she sent Lewis a postcard: 'Not that Burgess.'

Writing postcards was a form of companionship in itself. On the road she marked cards to Elizabeth with pinholes to indicate the location of her room. When at home she sent letters to other authors correcting their work. In 1993 she wrote to David McCullough, 'America's historian', congratulating him on his Pulitzer-winning *Truman*, recalling the time she had sat with Harry in his Missouri study. She then set right errors she had spotted in McCullough's biography, supplying page numbers.

In 1989 Morris had gone on contract as a book reviewer at the *Independent*, where literary editor Robert Winder soon became a friend. He offered her four or five books a month, and she picked one.

> We barely edited Jan at the *Indie*, ever. We had a joke on the desk when her copy came in – 'Oh dear, one word over. We'll have to redo the page.' She was a generous reviewer but could be waspish. It was an attractive combination, trenchant yet light – in her playful manner she was disarming. She never wrote a mean-minded review and wouldn't tackle subjects she hadn't walked around. She was the horse's mouth as far as I was concerned.

Winder enjoyed what he calls Morris's 'anti-received-wisdom stance – she was a little against the grain. Once I told her I had been to Venice and complained about the cruise ships and she said, "I like the cruise ships – they are very Venetian." She was like a ship herself, dissolving into the mist – she always gave the impression that she knew something you didn't.' (A few years later she told a journalist, 'The doges would have loved cruise ships! Showy, moneymaking, marvellous engineering!') Winder also noted a Waring-esque tendency. 'She loved giving everyone the slip.' As for her own books, 'I think her reputation is much too low. It's the sweep of history that she does so well, and that gives her such influence. I would put her very high on the list of twentieth-century British writers.'

Wales: The First Place had sold out its 10,000-copy run and reprinted, so photographer Paul Wakefield suggested *Ireland: Your Only Place* as a follow-up. Morris's emotional involvement with the Welsh struggle had softened her views on Ireland. It was, she wrote, 'The most pungently individualistic part of all Europe – it seems to me the constancy of perpetual unfulfilment.' Ireland, like Wales, was her.

14
1990–1995
ON THE BRINK

In the middle of the *Saturday Night* Canadian city tour, Morris flew down to San Francisco to write a piece gauging public mood in the run-up to Operation Desert Storm, the US-led Gulf War mission to liberate Kuwait from Iraq. She had never liked Fog City as much as she did Los Angeles and was depressed thinking about the imminent conflict in the country from which she had once reported, albeit on sheikhly hawking expeditions rather than Nighthawk bombing raids. Another thing oppressed her. In the closing pages of *Your Only Place* she had written again of her fear of every country 'becoming much like all other countries', and now she felt it in Northern California. This was the theme of almost everything she wrote during this period: the depersonalisation and alienation that homogeneity tows in its wake.

Some places weren't the same as everywhere else, though. Viking in London had agreed to publish a book on Sydney in which Morris would reflect on changes that had taken place since she first insulted the citizens in 1962. She had returned several times and went again, specifically for the new *Sydney*, in 1991, polishing off the whole project the same year. That first series of articles for the *Guardian* (Sydney was 'no more than a harbour surrounded by suburbs', and much worse) had brought condemnation raining down, or up, from the southern hemisphere. 'It was a full five years before the last letter of complaint reached me,' Morris wrote, though she had not learned her lesson, regaling readers of *Farewell the Trumpets* with talk of 'virile postures' Down Under and general inanity which she exemplified with choice anecdotes. She attributed her earlier comments, delivered *de haut en bas*, to youthful arrogance: nowadays, 'I thought a little less of myself.' This turned out not to be the case.

While she was in Sydney she did what she always did: walked the streets and poked around in cemeteries, at home in unobserved communion with the past. When it came to recording her observations, she was like a record stuck in a groove. 'Most of the world's great cities have something inevitable about them,' she wrote, 'as though God decreed them come what may. In Sydney, even now I catch myself feeling sometimes that the place never need have come into being in the first place.' She took a knife and fork to the dinner-party class, even though they graciously included her in their soirées.

> There is still no denying a predatory character to the Sydney élite . . . among the upper crust here the art of conversation is mostly the art of competitive monologue . . . I was proudly introduced one evening to a woman descended from one of the oldest and most eminent Sydney families, and never in my life have I encountered such an overbearing, loud-mouthed, overdressed, sozzled and insensitive old hag.

Having little to say, Morris even harped on the convict trope – 'manacles to millionaires' – noting furthermore that 'a sizeable proportion [of the bourgeoisie] is homosexual'. In a limp attempt to fend off a second furore, she tacked on qualifying clauses ('Still, when all is said, on the whole, this is a naturally sociable and egalitarian city'). The reader might be surprised, only a few lines after the appearance of the sozzled hag, to learn, 'There is something undeniably attractive about Sydney's high society.' Weak observational underlay betrays speedy composition. Obliged to comment on the Vietnamese community, Morris reports 'smells of Asian cooking'. The *Guardian* reviewer correctly identified a 'flavourless advertorial style . . . a travel book crossed with a tourist board memorandum'. But, confirming Morris's assessment of a national inability to discern, *The Australian* judged the book 'a winner'.

In the first months of 1993 she revised *Venice* again and wrote a new foreword. The city never went away. She visited most years, was the go-to whenever anyone wanted a piece, and wrote an amiable essay on 'Turner, Venice, the Generals and Me' for a book accompanying the *Turner and Venice* show at the Tate. She had even written the introduction to a Harry's Bar cookbook.

Everest too was never far off, in all the sixty-seven years Morris lived after leaping out of the tent that morning when the wireless crackled to life. When she had congratulated Harry Evans on his appointment as editor of *The Times* in 1981, he had sent the handwritten reply, 'Dear Jan, What fun! Feel like climbing Everest again? Love, Harry.' It was the assignment that had made her famous. She didn't mind that it kept coming up – she was still punting the big Everest book after thirty years. She never missed an anniversary reunion at Pen-y-Gwryd unless she really had to on account of her schedule. In October 1992 she sent a postcard to Robert Winder to say, 'I'm working up to an Alpine state of mind owing to next year's fortieth anniversary . . . which promises to be a marvellously sentimental splurge of nostalgia and self-congratulation.' When the date duly came around, her contemporary the Queen joined the team for a do at the Royal Geographical Society. Hunt usually sent a postcard to mark the day of the ascent. But he died in 1998. One by one, each smiling face vanished from the reunion photographs.

The month Morris celebrated with Her Majesty, Freya Stark died. She was one hundred. It was thirty-eight years since Morris had bought *Baghdad Sketches* actually in Baghdad, and thirty-three since Stark had told her *Venice* was 'better than *The Hashemites* because you have lived yourself into it'. Morris had picked her out as one of the few female travellers who were 'more than just women'; Stark had the good fortune, Morris asserted in a review, to be a 'human being' as well. When she was living in Venice, Morris had visited the grande dame at home in Asolo, eighty kilometres (fifty miles) away, and after news broke of Casablanca the older woman had written kindly.

> I am glad to welcome you among all our little feminine secrets because of your courage in wanting to be yourself – I can so well understand

this urge and am always surprised at how few there are to follow it. I must say I wouldn't be a man for anything so I do hope you will be happy this side of the border.

Stark's ex-husband, the confirmed bachelor Stewart Perowne with whom Morris had run around Lebanon and Jerusalem with such pleasure, had died four years previously. A month or so before Stark joined him, Morris reviewed a biography of her by another old friend – Molly Izzard, wife of Ralph of tennis-shoe fame. The new book, Morris thought, made too much of Stark's 'petty failings and trivial peccadilloes – the naughtiest of which, concerning the illicit sale of a car in Tehran, strikes me as an excellent wheeze'. Morris continued with what might be the closest description of herself she ever gave. It was

> the very theatricality of Freya Stark that makes her so fascinating. Of course she is self-created – that is the whole point of her. Every facet of her personality, as of her life and of her art, is studied. She has been determined to inhabit her own chosen self, not a self imposed upon her by history or heredity, and has been frank enough about the impulse – indeed as she once wrote: 'I am always surprised how few there are to follow it.'

Few indeed, but Morris was one. Stark was right about the importance of 'courage in wanting to be yourself'.

After Hilary Rubinstein retired, Derek Johns took over as Morris's literary agent; in the US, Julian Bach had also stepped down (he had represented Morris for thirty years, weathering many tempests), and Johns now handled Morris worldwide. But it was Monteith who had done the most to support her when it counted, and she was sad when he died of a heart attack in May 1995 in his London flat. Monteith had not made her, as Bill Golding said he had made him ('There is a way in which I am as a writer at least partly your creation,' Golding wrote after winning the Booker, and Monteith accompanied the novelist to Stockholm when he got the Nobel). No editor ever transformed a Morris typescript. She barely even discussed her work with anyone: it came out fully formed – often, in later years, to the detriment of her reputation. Monteith had played the role of midwife, getting books out of her safely. She was twenty-seven when he approached her, and it was he who had protected her against the world during the transition years. She was sorry – they all were – that Monteith, the man with an ironclad sense of decorum, had weathered a sexual-identity storm himself. In 1979 a disaffected author (another Ulsterman, as it turned out) had appeared outside the Faber offices in Queen Square wearing a sandwich board advertising Monteith's homosexuality. Having gained entrance, he threw a bulky piece of telephone equipment at Matthew Evans. (Golding's biographer wrote that Evans was 'apparently the only Faber representative deemed able-bodied enough to tackle him'.) The man then launched a hate-mail campaign. *Private Eye* weighed in. It must have been agonising for the dignified, deeply private Monteith. He was essentially an ascetic; there was something of the saint about him, though perhaps that was only in comparison with his authors.

In the eighties and nineties the Morrises saw a lot of Morfydd and Arthur Roberts, a couple who lived in Pwllheli just along the coast. 'Sometimes', Arthur remembers, 'we bumped into them on the prom at Cricieth, other times we walked along the Dwyfor with them. I don't know who their other friends were. We thought they were pretty lonely. They were a natural couple. We never saw any tension or unhappiness.' Jan and Elizabeth often went to the Robertses' house. Arthur continues,

> Once she [Jan] sent us a note thanking us for 'exquisitely unfrenchified victuals'. Another afternoon Morfydd asked her what sort of tea she wanted and she said, 'Not Earl Grey!' On the other hand she took us to the Michelin-starred Plas Bodegroes near here. It was the only time I ever saw her look twice at a bill. If she was presented with a wine list, she told us once, she always picked the second-most expensive.

In 1993 Arthur, a Methodist minister, responded to an appeal for Welsh-speaking priests to watch the flock in Argentinian Patagonia – the

Y Wladfa community descended from nineteenth-century colonists. (Chatwin's descriptions of them, as Morris had told him on one of her postcards, had moved her 'to tears'.) During his first period in Chubut province, Morris appeared. She had flown down from Santiago and stayed in what Roberts called 'the best hotel' (a relative term). The next day she moved on in a hire car. Arthur recalled, 'She only reluctantly agreed to meet the Welsh community. I don't think she was interested in Welsh culture in Patagonia. She didn't have an awful lot of Welsh and nobody spoke English so I had to translate.' In print, Morris made the encounter more of a Welsh experience. As she chatted to a farmer on the outskirts of Trevelin (she wrote), the man's horse inevitably tied to a post, 'his cloth cap tilted on his head, his hands in his pockets, that Welshman of South America touched my heart not with melancholy at all, but with grateful pride to be Welsh myself'.

Other long-haul trips in the mid-1990s included a cruise to French Guiana during which a high swell prevented a scheduled landing on Devil's Island, where the French authorities had put Alfred Dreyfus. Historically minded passengers threatened to sue the tour company for false advertising, and Morris reported gleefully that conditions had not prevented customs officials risking the trip in their own launch and enjoying a hearty lunch in the ship's top dining room. When she went back to Hong Kong, in part to revise her book, she met up with William Kerr, son of her old friends Johnnie and Isabel. He had moved there, and the two of them enjoyed reminiscing over gin and tonics at the Mandarin or the Hong Kong Club. 'She was enormous fun,' Kerr remembers, 'as she had been in my childhood, doggerel included. She made it clear she wasn't going to engage with Hong Kong after the handover – she was interested in its past, not its future.'

Summing up these years, Morris wrote, 'I enjoyed almost every minute of the journeys – to be travelling alone on a job, all my antennae out, thinking about nothing but the work in hand, seemed to me one of life's greatest pleasures.' (This was before it became 'a debased addiction'.) When she had turned sixty she had stopped flying economy (she still paid for her own travel), but it was testament to her robust spirit that she was able to relish 'almost every minute' despite the illness that meant she sometimes had to cut trips short. Side effects of the drugs she still had to take included headaches, dizzy spells, irregularities in her gastrointestinal tract, hallucinations and more. She told one epistolary friend that she had woken up that morning screaming, 'Get me out of this terrible hotel!' – despite the fact that she was in her own bed. Everyone still asked her about her transition, even though, two decades on, she insisted that there was nothing left to say. After Winder left the *Independent* for Granta, he asked her to write *Conundrum 2*, the volume she had once longed to publish. She said no. That was all long gone.

She had, however, not abandoned a passion cherished for forty years for Admiral Lord John 'Jacky' Fisher, the first sea lord who had introduced the revolutionary HMS *Dreadnought*, the world's fastest battleship. Bulky majesties steaming across painted oceans had exercised a grip on Morris's imagination since Clevedon, and Fisher, with his 'weakness for grand style', came to represent the whole Royal Navy in maritime synecdoche. That institution, like the technology that had always drawn her, offered structure and compartmentalisation; so did Welsh nationalism, and the life of a squire – they all laid down a pattern and imposed order on an otherwise runaway world. Morris had stuck the poster immortalising Fisher in 1881 inside her wardrobe, flinging the door open to reveal Jacky to visitors subjected to a tour of the house, at least if the tombstone on the floor below hadn't finished them off. Fisher is not entirely likeable in Morris's slim biography, *Fisher's Face*, which came out in 1995. He wasn't as exceptional as she made out, and she failed to note that his disruptive 'modernising' methods were hastily conceived and executed. He did, though (as she said), improve conditions for ratings, introducing knives and forks to the mess deck. The biography was anyway, Morris said – aware of naval historians sharpening knives of the metaphorical variety – 'a *jeu d'amour*'. This was nicely put, but she overworked the joke. In a rebarbative counterfactual passage she imagines Fisher on the bridge of his flagship, 'with the ships of a terrible enemy visible through the haze and gunsmoke', and as Jacky prepares to die like Nelson she herself bends over him, 'kissing his forehead with a tear'. The *Journal of Military History* referred to 'moments of self-indulgence' in *Fisher's Face*, criticism which was itself pretty indulgent.

Morris had been in Berlin when the Wall came down; of course she had. She could remember it going up, not long after she had persuaded the *Guardian* to let her out of Jerusalem, leaving the banality of Eichmann's evil in the courtroom. A piece she wrote for *The Times* to close 1990 contemplated the rebirth of Eastern Europe following the collapse of Communism.

> One by one, the half-dead states . . . came to life again and terrific old cities such as Prague and Budapest rejoined the civilised community. The Soviet Union turned out to be not an enigma at all, but an all too fallible association of human beings, like the rest of us . . . The end of the Cold War seemed, like the discovery that the world was round, to discredit many other hidebound mis-assumptions . . .

As she realised even at the time, other forces were moving in to fill the new vacuum. 'Like one of those pale mornings that are at once tremulous and preternaturally exact, [the immediate post-Wall period] was too beautiful to last. Even as August moved into September, I began to feel the window closing once again and the options clenching.' Her old stamping grounds in Czechoslovakia, Hungary and Poland had become 'Central Europe' as they moved into the embrace of Western liberal democracies. She hurried back to the Czech Republic in its first year of existence after the 'velvet divorce' from Slovakia, tracing the outlines of old empires, as she liked to do – not just Austro-Hungarian, but Russian, German and Ottoman too. These were the palimpsests that attracted her, had always, and she was again in on the creation of a new layer. Was it 'the return of history', as ethnic revivalists advertised? In part. But options were 'clenching', as Morris noted, and the newly liberated peoples had yet to reckon with the encumbering legacies of Communism.

Welshness at least never clenched. 'It represents', she once wrote, 'an old, instinctive *hiraeth* for a better place, where better people with better values live, love, sing and cherish nature.' She even acknowledged that the political situation was 'frequently plastered over by romantic interpretations of history', aware that she herself had gone in for a spot of plastering from time to time. But she remained a member of Plaid Cymru and thundered in the Thunderer about poor representation, among other things: the Tories governed, but only six of thirty-eight MPs representing Welsh constituencies were Conservative, meaning in effect that Wales was 'a non-nation'. Her gift, her contribution to the struggle, was the ability to yoke a romantic vision to political goals.

In 1993 the Gorsedd Beirdd Ynys Prydain (Society of the Bards of the Island of Britain), an institution dedicated to the Welsh language, public life and the arts, elected Morris to its White order, the highest of three, its members known as Druids. Admission required honourees to take a special name, and Morris chose Jan Trefan. She said that, when she first put on the regalia, 'it was one of the proudest moments of my life'. Describing the annual Eisteddfod which she attended thereafter when she could (it moves to a different location each year), she wrote, 'I am myself a Druid on these occasions.' It made her feel part of a syncretic whole. She finally accepted an honorary doctorate from the University College of North Wales (now Bangor University), having earlier turned down an honorary professorship there on the grounds that her taste was 'unreliable or even unscholarly'. Further accolades included the Glyndŵr Award for Outstanding Contribution to the Arts in Wales, an honorary fellowship at RIBA for contribution to architectural writing, and an honorary studentship at her alma mater. *The Times* named her the 'fifteenth greatest British writer since the war', an honour with a Pythonesque flavour. National-treasure status had come to pass. But she felt old, and one of the dizzy episodes involved a hospital visit.

The year after the Gorsedd honour, and as if in homage to it, Morris came out with *A Machynlleth Triad*, a novel which Twm translated into Welsh. The regrettable volume evokes the past, present and future of

Machynlleth, a defenceless market town on the Dyfi in Powys. In the 'future' section the place has become the capital of an independent Welsh republic. 'Wales is essentially a centrifugal state, in the Celtic tradition,' Morris wrote, possibly a case of wishful thinking. *Triad* was the only one of her works that failed to elicit a single reader's letter. At a speaking event in the US, a member of the audience asked if she was embarrassed about any of her books. She wouldn't go so far as to call it 'real embarrassment' (she replied), but there was one volume in which she had let her passion for the theme overwhelm her usual standards of measured distance. Twm, who was there, thought she was referring to *Triad*.

She was beginning to wonder, in fact, if the solution was really as simple as she had once dreamed. She told a Plaid comrade that she recognised the resurgence of what looked awfully like fascism all over the continent, as well as in Britain itself. Now, travels in Bosnia-Herzegovina in the aftermath of the bitter tragedy of the Balkan Wars led her to question the perils and limits of nationalism directly. In 1996 Morris toured the region she had blithely visited when it was Yugoslavia, stopping in, among other places, Zagreb, Mostar and Medjugorje, and, once again, she was at the epicentre of events at a key juncture of European history. At the end of the tour she was supposed to fly out of Sarajevo, the city only recently released from its 1,425-day siege, but snow had closed the airport, so she and an assortment of others had to travel by road to the Adriatic coast. This time Morris was not gliding in a car with Mozart on the deck but lurching along smashed-up highways in a freezing minibus. The snow was deep, the roadblocks frightening, and 'the awful gorges through the mountains loomed dark and dangerous'. She wrote, 'These were not the usual ruins of war' but of 'particular and personal hatred. It seemed such a spiteful sort of destruction. Bosnia had been ravaged, it appeared, not by ignorant conscript armies clashing, but by groups of citizens expressing their true emotions.' She reflected on the single-arched packhorse bridge over the Taf in Wales, and on the bombed-out Turkish one over the Neretva separating the Christians and Muslims of Mostar in southern Bosnia-Herzegovina. 'Would we be very different, I wondered, if it had all happened to us?'

It was far from certain that a Welsh republic was sure to come as she predicted it would, but in 1997 the people of Wales did vote for a measure of devolution. The Government of Wales Act duly granted the formation of the National Assembly for Wales – the first since Glyndŵr had proclaimed *his* assembly in Machynlleth. This, Morris wrote (optimistically, as it turned out), 'changed everything'. It had been the tightest of votes – as she reflected, Wales had come within less than one percentage point of abolishing itself (and that was on a 50 per cent turnout). But Wales had got there. In one respect. Events inevitably triggered a revised edition of *The Matter of Wales*. She renamed it *Wales: Epic Views of a Small Country*, and in a new prologue banished her doubts and heralded 'a portent of a truly federal Britain to come . . . the dream of a new Europe in which Wales would play a properly equal part in the making of history'. She included, in Further Reading, the *Rough Guide to Wales*. This was the Morris of *Outriders*, robust, determined, impassioned. The new material largely revealed how much worse everything had become, in terms of 'The Neighbour', as she called the penultimate chapter. She tried to remain positive, inserting into the last sentence of the prologue the claim that Wales stood 'on the brink of a new fulfilment'. But she knew the longed-for Welsh Parliament was impotent, and wrote to Dafydd Iwan after one protest campaign, 'Congratulations on what you do. I admire your style, but I fear the world will win in the end.' She would come to describe herself as a Welsh culturalist, more concerned with the erosion of *Cymraeg* than with the machinery of domestic politics. 'I long ago came to think of the Raj', she had written in 1972, 'chiefly as a grand aesthetic, not a political structure at all'; this was how she began to perceive Wales. The Welsh writings from now on hold a magnifying glass to the spiritual journey, that universal yearning to be reunited with something from which we feel cut off, every reader's *hiraeth* to be on the inside of a door hitherto only glimpsed from the outside.

Anxieties about nationalism, and what she called 'this first faint hope of an independent Wales at last', meant she was increasingly fixated on the notion of a federal Europe, a state of affairs she imagined would mitigate 'the dross of Anglo-American culture' overlaying Welsh values and confine fascism to the sidings. Ever since Black Wednesday on 16 September 1992, when the UK had been forced to leave the Exchange Rate Mechanism, Europe had dominated Editorial and Opinion pages. As the millennium loomed, Morris determined to write 'an enormous book about my lifetime association with Europe'.

15
1996–2001
JESTER IN CAMELOT

On 27 April 1994, Morris boarded a ferry for Kirkenes in north-eastern Norway, primed and exuberant as she set off on the first journey specifically for *Europe*. Over the next three years, the book – always described by her as 'big', like the Welsh one – took her almost everywhere. She made a performance of booking herself onto Eurostar almost as soon as the Channel Tunnel opened. 'It was like treading on a step that wasn't there,' she said on emerging in continental Europe for the first time without seeing water (a fine analogy). While she was working on the book Morris wrote and presented two forty-nine-minute films for BBC Wales in which she reflected on cities that had influenced her. The first begins in Trefan: a Morris voiceover explains the urge to get away from what the director sets up as a scene of domestic harmony – Elizabeth sewing by the wood-burning stove, a curled cat, the Dwyfor burbling outside. The camera proceeds to follow Morris around Trieste, Cairo, Manhattan, Darjeeling and Sydney before returning to Wales, where the camera pans up to Elizabeth, still on the sofa. 'I am now in my seventieth year,' says Morris, 'and this [coming home] is still the best moment of my life.'

She had filmed the New York segment in October and held a joint birthday party in Manhattan with Twm – her seventieth, his thirty-fifth. At home in Wales, Suki was looking forward to a big trip herself. 'At lunch at the Walnut Tree Jan had said she would take me to Hong Kong for the handover as a birthday present. I was so looking forward to it. Three weeks before we were due to go, Jan rang and said it was too expensive. She liked to dangle treats and withdraw them."*

The British press worked itself into a lather over Hong Kong that June, casting the ceremony as a last rite. Morris flew out – alone – for London's *Evening Standard* (she said it was her final exercise in reportage) and installed herself at the Peninsula, so perhaps she had booked a room all those years ago.

Fifty Years of Europe: An Album amounts to a third volume of autobiography, and to a certain extent it is the most successful of the three. It is a rich, funny, melancholy and deeply satisfying book which captures the lurching vicissitudes of a long life as well as its most filmic moments. A troop train pulls into Lausanne in 1946, smiling Swiss ladies 'waiting for us with cisterns of hot coffee, buns, sandwiches – miraculous sandwiches of white Swiss bread, light and crusty, like manna after several years of our brownish wartime kind'. As the train began to move off again,

> while I hung out of the window, I caught the eye of a small well-dressed man standing indecisively on the platform. Shyly smiling, he hastened towards me. The train gathered speed. The man burst into a trot. The train went faster. The man lost his smile and ran. He held out his hand to me. I held mine out in return. The train got into its swing. The man panted anxiously. I stretched as far as I could out of my window. Our hands touched, just in time, and there passed from one to the other a small Swiss silver coin. As a token it was priceless.

In a Valletta courtroom in the late 1980s, she writes in *Fifty Years*,

> The case concerned heroin-trafficking, and, the small court being rather full, I sat in the front row, occupied otherwise only by a single

---

* After Morris died, Suki published a sensational critique in a Sunday newspaper. 'She was a lousy parent', the last line read, 'who damaged all four of her living children one way or another.' Suki told me unequivocally, before that piece appeared, that gender didn't come into it. 'Transition doesn't mean a cost has to be paid by others. If she'd been nice to us, there wouldn't have been a cost.'

man. All was remarkably informal, but I was puzzled to see no sign of the accused. When I left the court and asked a policeman where the prisoner's dock was, he told me I had been sitting in it, together with the day's villain (who got five years. I saw it in *The Times of Malta* the next day).

As she tells it, and as the reader is by now aware, over her half-century as an adult her own country had lost its edge.

> By the 1980s the English *had* no national characteristics . . . They had been taught to be ashamed of their lost Empire . . . In foreign policy as in social attitudes, slavishly the English tracked the footsteps of the Americans – whom, at the same time, in a grotesque echo of old supremacies, they all too often professed to despise . . . it could actually be said that they were suffering from an inferiority complex – who would have believed it possible when I was young?

Morris herself despised not Americans but the insularity that was her birthright and the nationalism she observed festering everywhere. Her views had shifted on actual republicanism, both in Britain and in a federated Europe. In a conversation with a Plaid supporter she discussed the problems of nostalgia and rewritten history common to the generation – hers – who remembered the last war, reflecting on the dangers as nationalism coalesced in new forms.

But she tethered the new book to reality. Climbing Mouseion Hill in Athens one spring day, she recounts in the book, 'my mind full of Hellenic glories', a flasher sprang from a bush. 'Were they [the Greeks] not the fathers of poetry?' she barked. 'To find a representative of this noble race flashing his cock to innocent tourists was a sad disillusionment.' She had seen so much come and go – regimes, dictatorships, utopian projects, cock-flashers: *Fifty Years* has real sweep. Morris wrote from memory (mostly), facilitating an effect of spontaneity which seems laboured in the endless 'Come with me now' tropes of other books – here it comes off as atmospheric brio. She remembered the drive from Wales to Montenegro, when the light was always brilliant, her BMW always ran smoothly and the locals, when she stopped, were always the most handsome in Europe. 'I used to be happy and hopeful driving down the Dalmatia Highway,' she wrote. When a magazine commissioned her to repeat the journey in an Alfa Romeo, she jumped at it. But they couldn't get insurance on account of her age. Morris herself had become an allegory.

She maintained her Stakhanovite work rate. While she was preparing the new *Wales* in the spring of 1998, she was also writing fresh introductions to all three volumes of *Pax*. A note of apology entered the prose. 'If my book seems to display a certain sympathy for them [the Empire builders] it is because I am a child of my times' (*Heaven's Command*). 'Mine is an aesthetic view of Empire' (*Farewell the Trumpets*). But she did not address the question the zeitgeist was asking: was it acceptable, morally, to look at only that one aspect of the imperial project?

On the personal front there was much to be gloomy about. Chris's wife Ruth had died the previous year. Morris had been trying unsuccessfully to get her own blood pressure down and feared she might be next. In addition, she had been laid low by an emotional crisis afflicting one of the children, something which, she told Winder, 'greatly depresses and debilitates me. Children's troubles are, in my experience, infinitely worse than any of one's own, especially when they are no longer children at all.' She who saw irony everywhere did not detect it in personal events.

She now 'hated' the *Guardian*, chiefly because she found its identity politics 'distasteful'; the hatred carried a faint, bitter tinge of regret that she had not held on to the glory of those glamorous days at the forefront of international reportage. She told any journalist who asked that she only read car magazines. It was a joke designed to shock, as she admitted in private, but cars did engross her, and she loved to put her foot down as well as read about enhanced crankshafts. She still addressed letters for publication to *The Times*, even though she considered it 'a rag'. One had appeared on 1 September 1997, the day after Princess Diana died.

> Sir, At San Francisco a fortnight ago the immigration officer who checked my passport asked if I was connected with the press. I mumbled that I was, sort of. 'In that case,' said he, 'I want to make a request. Please lay off Diana . . . we hate to see her hassled.' 'Well,' I retorted, 'God knew she often asked for it.' He looked at me with sad reproach then, and today I'm sorry I said it.

Morris had met the young Queen, now the late Diana's beleaguered mother-in-law, in June 1953, as we have seen, receiving the Everest medal at Buckingham Palace. On that occasion, Her Majesty had recalled receiving the news of the ascent the night before her coronation, and the tanned and suited James Morris had described the trajectory of the message from his tent to her palace. In 1999 Morris returned to the royal residence to attend a reception to celebrate National Book Day. As footmen handed round platters of cheese footballs,* Morris took the opportunity to approach the Queen again on the Everest topic. Yes, of course I remember, said HRH when Morris asked if she recalled getting the message that evening in 1953. 'I was the person who brought the news back,' said the middle-aged frump wearing plastic beads. 'Her eyes went cold,' Morris noted. (Apparently nobody had explained Morris's transformation to Her Majesty at the fortieth-anniversary celebration a few years earlier.)

The Queen did not hold it against her, as later that year she offered Morris a CBE (Commander of the Order of the British Empire) for services to literature. R. S. had scrunched up his own letter proposing an honour and tossed it into the bin. With so much shouting about republicanism, Morris recognised it might be awkward to accept an enemy tribute. At Twm's suggestion, she consulted the Archdruid. The oracle of ancient Celtic wisdom concluded that, as there was no Welsh equivalent of the honour, she was free to accept. When the news broke, nobody mentioned hypocrisy. Morris was like Teflon in this regard.

---

* This is hard to believe. Cheese footballs had not been seen in public since 1972. But I was there.

She and Elizabeth celebrated with Gareth and his wife Trish at the Walnut Tree, while the *Liverpool Daily Post* led with 'SEX CHANGE WRITER'S CBE'.

Beyond family, Henry Anglesey was first off the block with a letter. 'Well earned ole gal! By George, not only pop stars and footballers!' (He had been sending her cards addressed to 'The Rt Hon Jan Morris DCVO' – Dame Commander of the Royal Victorian Order – since 1982.) The Kerrs, the Skeets, Leader of Her Majesty's Opposition William Hague, Lancing College, the Parrys across the way, the staff at NatWest bank in Cricieth – all sent heartfelt congratulations.

Tony Blair had won the 1997 election, and Morris was cynical about his decision to rebrand his party New Labour. She found the government's 'Cool Britannia' slogan excruciating, as did many. In an email to Faber correcting a spelling mistake in publicity copy, she added, 'I hope you like this kind of input from your authors. It is cool [the correction was to the word "Britannica"] and related to the "inclusiveness" so dear to Mr Blair. It should make you feel like The People's Publisher.' (Blair's team had anointed the late Diana 'The People's Princess'.) New Labour had attracted literary courtiers, but by now Morris was a jester in Camelot. Alun Michael, Blair's Secretary of State for Wales, in his congratulatory CBE letter addressed her as 'Mr Morris'. The Right Honourable Member duly received a proper birthday-honours reprimand from Jan in the next post.

In the fall of 1998 Morris had spent three weeks in the eastern United States tracking Abraham Lincoln, as she had decided to write his biography. It was a bad idea from the start. Not only did she do no primary research; this time she didn't even do much serious reading. But she did draw conclusions: 'Lincoln was essentially a nice man.' As in *Fisher* and *Hong Kong*, the reader is left with the sense that the author decided on a thesis and jemmied in material to fit. 'In this book, it's not only Lincoln that Morris fails to understand; it's an entire culture,' wrote the *Publishers Weekly* critic, though Canada's *Globe and Mail* fearlessly declared *Lincoln* 'the best book ever written by a trans-sexual historian'.

Derek Johns noticed that she was depressed by the reviews – hurt, even. But she cheered up when a four-man crew representing the American TV channel CBS motored up to Trefan to film a piece on *Lincoln*. The camera panned over the ground floor, alighting on the gravestone before climbing the stairs for the Jacky Fisher routine. When they all came back down, Morris poured herself a large drink and they went outside. Cameraman Nicholas Turner remembers that 'Elizabeth was there, but she was in the shadows.' After they had finished shooting the segment, and to Turner's alarm, Morris tried to snog him. She put her tongue in his mouth.

The hoof mark on the Trefan windowsill had faded, a reminder now of the inconstancy of things, not its opposite. Sycamore, ash, hollies, hazels and horse chestnut had grown tall in the yard, and the narrow gate through to the vegetable garden was almost impassable in summer now, rampant with honeysuckle and wild ferns.

Letters still poured in – that never changed. Correspondents set down memories of sitting on the pavement in the early morning of 2 June 1953: 'cold, wet and miserable, we were thrilled just after dawn to hear the newspaper sellers shouting, "Everest conquered!"' Readers of Welsh birth wrote from Seattle battling, they said, their demon *hiraeth*. The boy whose father had taken them all out for a cream tea when he and Jim got the choral scholarships in 1935 wrote from Colorado. Old enemies stepped up before it was too late. Christopher Ricks responded to an amiable letter she sent him, thirty years on, folded within a copy of a new edition of *Oxford*. (It was he who had poorly reviewed it as a young don.) He too had not forgotten. 'How wittily generous of you,' Ricks wrote, 'forgiveness of a sort, and coals of fire upon my bald head.' Hundreds of men and women took up a pen, as they had for decades, 'to thank you for the pleasure you have given me'. The body of correspondence at Trefan testifies to the intimacy Morris had created with her readers. Many said they felt she had reached out 'and taken [me] by the hand'. It was the key to her popularity, or one of them.

Beyond the connection with readers, her personal life revolved around telephone calls to old pals, and to Gareth. But most of the interior drama played out at the keyboard, where she wanted it to remain. 'I have not dined in someone else's house for several years,' she wrote in 2001, though it could have been any year, 'and I would stay in the scruffiest hotel in Zagazig rather than accept the offer of a room for the night from the dearest of friends.' She avoided formal dinners at almost any cost, mingling at the drinks then absconding into the night. Displays of affection repelled her, and she could not stand anyone touching her, ever. Her niece Catharine remembers Morris picking her up in the car 'and I made the mistake of hugging her. She just shrank away.'

But of course there was something else, the central pillar holding her life up. Morris wrote to Elizabeth even when they were both in the house. In February 2000 she composed a poem ending, *On this as on every St Valentine's Day/ My poor little present is always the same:/ My dearest Elizabeth* – je t'aime!

Morris published a late-career triumph in her mid-seventies – a book intended to illuminate and summarise her life and work. To a large extent it did. It took some time, however, for the concept of *Trieste* to mature. The first book off the press in the new millennium was *Our First Leader: A Welsh Fable*. Morris had cooked it up with Twm, who translated it as *Ein Llyw Cyntaf*. A counterfactual fantasy, the story unfolds after Germany has won the Second World War and established a protectorate in Britain called Germania; Churchill is in exile in Ottawa, while at home Eryri has become an 'inner shrine of Welshness, a sort of Valhalla'. Special trains and barbed wire make poor comic material. In a notably tin-eared passage, Hitler himself urges the gauleiter of Great Britain to 'make the most of' his Welsh 'swine' as 'Jews are getting a bit short already'. Most outlets ignored the book, the kindest approach. The *TLS* felt obliged to acknowledge it, and its reviewer cringed, 'For no amount of *hiraeth* could justify the tropes of genocide used to light satiric purpose.'

Morris had written a more sensible outline for a book on Ivan Bunin, the Nobel-winning, Voronezh-born exile and novelist. But she couldn't see it through – he was too good a writer for her to unpick – and dropped the project in favour of a book on Trieste. The city was Bunin in bricks and limestone, a symbol of exile in itself, deprived of its hinterland by a plateau. It had haunted her since she had skylarked with Bill Norman and the others half a century earlier; she had often returned, riding the ferry to Muggia, where descendants of cats she had known still lingered at portside trattorias, and she had written about Trieste again and again. (When she finished *Hav*, she said she realised that 'between every line Trieste was lurking'.) The city was beyond topography. It provided a springboard for the contemplation of ethnic confusions, frontier mazes, enclaves, minorities, anomalies and political fragmentation – and it had become an emblem of fluid identity.

> Trieste is also a perfect place to disappear into, and sometimes over the years, as my Britishness has refined itself into Welshness . . . I have been tempted to disappear here myself . . . for what would race, frontier and nation mean in such a condition of liberty? I would be escaping from . . . the arbitrary sham of the lines that criss-cross the continent.

That was gender to her now: 'arbitrary sham'. Trieste suited her mood, and in the summer of 2000 she did disappear there, staying until October, the month she turned seventy-four. She still worked in notebooks bought in Criccieth (they had rocketed to forty-nine pence) and began number 3 of the Triestino series with a boxhead, 'Meaning', and after it she wrote, 'Nowhere!' She had her title. *Trieste and the Meaning of Nowhere* is a beguilingly incorporeal book, a sequence of anecdotes loosely linked by diaphanous themes – ones that a less confident writer would feel obliged to smuggle in within a plot or structure. That said, overt autobiographical detail is close to the surface: boarding school, army trucks breaking crusts of snow, Otto Thwaites. The landscape glimmers faintly as it always does on a Morrisian page, whether a tug labouring across a harbour, a listless flag or a solitary angler hunched on a quay. The Karst, the lizardy limestone plateau brooding behind the city, turns representational, a symbol of the wild side. The book is purged of the matronly jollity of many of its predecessors as Morris responds to the genius loci by thinking sad thoughts about age, doubt and disillusion. Approaching the conclusion of what she has declared in the prologue to be her last book, Morris veers to the eschatological: 'What a nightmare hiatus we all pass through, on the way from birth to death. Surely the only logical response would be to stand on a bridge and scream? But no, self-deception sees us through.'

The unease of *Trieste* – its intimation of an unknown future and unredeemed present – was millennial, and readers lapped up the tension between the book's egregiously colloquial tone ('Which way are we going? Search me.') and the graceful dignity of the ideas it expressed. Stan Barstow sent a fan letter from Pontardawe: 'There is wonderful writing throughout *Trieste*, but page sixty-one quite took my breath away.' Barstow's 1960 novel *A Kind of Loving* had reflected the preoccupations of the kitchen-sinkers, notably in its focus on the nostalgia of the working class (endemic domestic violence included). The page the playwright referred to conjures in lilac prose the return of Franz Ferdinand's corpse to the Molo San Carlo. Of the thousands waiting in the silent crowd, Morris asks, 'Did some of them guess that the saddest of angel messengers was passing by, foretelling the world's tragedy, the empire's humiliation and their own proud city's long decline?' This was the sentiment the once angry young man wrote to admire. Morris had waited for him and his peers, like the crowd waiting for the coffin, and they had caught up with her.

Editorial assistants escorted Morris to publicity events, and several mentioned the flirtatious persona she adopted as they sat in the back of a car heading to literary festivals. One remembered that Morris's live performances were revelatory – she seemed to embody her work in a way that was both charismatic and scripted. Monteith's author Philip Larkin hated book tours: he said the experience was like pretending to be yourself, but that came easily to Morris as it was what she did all the time. When she said, as she often did, that she was 'not a literary sort of person', Morris meant that she hated not tours but the appurtenances of the literary world involving other people, which included festivals, committees, judging panels and the like. When a journalist asked her whom she would invite if she were to host a literary dinner, she said, 'Nothing on earth would induce me to host a literary dinner.' She hammed up the last-book claim at every opportunity when *Trieste* came out, recognising the critical and commercial appeal of the valedictory. Nobody who knew anything about literature, writers or her believed it for a moment. 'Your last? Ha Ha!' Anglesey said.

She might have been polite to her publishers in later years, but Morris never minded treating formal interlocutors with disdain; they were not part of her team, so she did not need to foster good relations. When a member of the Travellers Club introduced her before a talk, she stood up and told the audience, 'That was all straight from Wikipedia!'

She had been away in *Trieste* publication week, returning to Trefan on 10 September. The next day, she and Elizabeth turned on the television to see images of the cratered Austin J. Tobin Plaza, named for the friend who had been kind when Morris needed it most. It was he who had authorised the construction of the Twin Towers in his capacity as chairman of the Port Authority – 'Austin's Last Erection'. On the Sunday after the attack the *New York Times* published a special supplement on the city. For the introductory piece they took lines from *Manhattan '45* and ran them below an apocalyptic photograph of the destroyed cityscape: 'The Manhattan skyline shimmered in the imaginations of all the nations and people everywhere cherished the ambition, however unattainable, of landing one day upon that legendary foreshore.' There was a sense that Morris spoke for everyone; for the silent majority. She was in on it again.

World events were converging to derail her wistful search for unity. 'If race is a fraud,' she had written, 'as I often think in Trieste, then nationality is a cruel pretence. There is nothing organic to it.' The situation in Wales deteriorated. Two weeks after 9/11, Morris's open letter to First Minister Rhodri Morgan appeared in *Cambria* magazine. She was disillusioned with his leadership; in fact, 'after a year of the National Assembly most of us are too bored to follow your discussions... I suppose most people now accept that Welsh devolution in its present impotent form has been a flop.' To make up for it, she wanted the A470 renamed Ffordd Cymru.

When a fifty-year-old chemistry graduate from Cardiff read her *Cambria* piece, he agreed: Morgan had done nothing for Wales. So the ex-chemist sent the first minister a packet of anthrax. (Post-World Trade Center panic had triggered global alarm about biological weaponry in general and anthrax in particular.) The maverick said in court that he had wanted to make a political statement in the wake of 9/11. In an odd confirmation of status, one that made headlines, Morris too received a packet. When the judge asked the accused why he had sent poison to Morris when he *agreed* with her, he said he wasn't sure. At any rate it was not really anthrax, it was flour, and after mailing the envelopes the chemist got cold feet and called the police, who intercepted all the farinaceous packages.

Trieste and *Trieste* reflect aspects of Morris's life she felt to be significant. Duality, firstly. 'Historically,' she wrote, 'Trieste has been decidedly ambivalent.' Secondly, 'Like my life, it [Trieste] still gives me a waiting feeling, as if something big but unspecified is always about to happen.' This, then, was the bittersweet yearning of *hiraeth* once more – a longing, first experienced when the biplane flew over to Cardiff, for something that is not there, has never been there, will never be there. Morris wrote of a 'fragrant sense of might-have-been', evoking 'nostalgia for a place and condition I have never known'. Her fantasies of Europe 'before the convulsions of the twentieth century' were of a 'cohesive whole' – she had glimpsed it, she thought, in 1946. Now she realised it had all been 'a fake'. Mark, who had lived through so much, feels that *Trieste* expresses Morris's admission that transition never really fulfilled the gnawing at the core – nothing ever could. Just as Christmases away from home had not derailed the chorister Jim, loss and its elegiac undertow did not agitate the adult Morris, on the threshold now of old age. Emotional privation was part of being human. She started telling interviewers that she had been searching for something she now knew to be illusory – not in her transition, but in something that went far beyond it. The words 'unfulfilled', 'haunting', 'sadness', 'tragedy', 'limbo', 'melancholy' ring through the pages of *Trieste*; they tolled for her.

Thirdly, city and writer shared a kind of detachment. Morris wrote of Trieste's 'conscious sense of separateness', a condition with which she identified, 'outsider that I am'. Trieste was 'a geographical and historical anomaly, Italian by sovereignty but in temperament more or less alone', and so are we all in the end, as she knew by now. The following year she told the BBC, 'I can't pretend I'm one thing or the other. Nor can Trieste.' The word *irredentismo* 'entered the vocabulary' when Triestinos 'found themselves caught in Garibaldi's spell' – the condition of being unredeemed. And now here she was, an irredentist herself, marooned on the shores of the twenty-first century.

16
2002–2012
ANCIENT MARINER

The strongest of the many introductions, forewords, prologues and prefaces Morris wrote to other people's books appeared in these later years. It was her métier to look at a subject from a great height and distil the view – one of the functions of a fresh introduction to a classic or a foreword to a new book – and she had more time for it now. In 2003 she took on two of the best in her own field. Her introductory essay on Sybille Bedford's *Pleasures and Landscapes* began with the assertion that the collection 'comes straight from the heart – the source, to my mind, not only of the best art but the best reporting too'. She does notice Bedford's unctuous pretensions over 'limpid' olive oil and fine wine: those passages drove her, Morris, 'to the deep-freeze Ocean Pie'. (On a tour of Burgundy vineyards, Morris had called a vintage 'a bit Range Rovery'. Bedford would have fainted clean away.) Introducing a reissue of Rose Macaulay's *Towers of Trebizond*, the sort of half-fiction hybrid which so often attracted Morris, she praised 'the irony, the self-amusement, the historical awareness, the mingled tolerance and command that had been the hallmarks of the best English travel writing since Alexander Kinglake's *Eothen*'. The *Trebizond* narrator remains, until the end of the story, ambiguous – neither male nor female; the whole book is a metaphor for unbelonging, really, so no wonder Morris liked it.

For leisure reading, Morris sped through the early Martin Amis, noting that one character's badge of honour is never to have been to the US, a reversal of that country's allure when Morris was a young writer. Reading had always deeply informed her prose. Sometimes – not often, but more than occasionally — she drops in a reference to a writer of canon status. The mentions came instinctively. She did not sprinkle them on for effect, like glitter. In *Last Letters from Hav* she had invented a line of Chekhov dialogue: 'Why must you always be talking of Hav? Isn't our town good enough for you?' Morris never went to the theatre (a waste of time), but she consulted her eight volumes of Chekhov more than any other books in her library (she said; it shows). The habit reflected appreciation — an identification, really. There is no 'other' in Chekhov, in either the stories or the plays. Morris liked to think that she too took everyone's side — she once said she was 'everyone's patriot'. She *was* mostly able to see all sides, Sydney being a notable exception, and like Chekhov she knew the world to be unintelligible; at least, she did now. As for Dickens: she said once that she had 'consciously modelled' the opening of an essay on a paragraph of his. Dickens's use of humour, in particular his comic characters, had had an impact on her from the beginning, and the sophisticated structure of the later novels influenced the composition of *Pax*. But Morris appreciated Dickens with her head, not her heart — the opposite of the Bedford approach. Similarly Jane Austen, who pops up in Kashmir and elsewhere — both authors, Dickens and Austen, Morris acknowledges, 'have sometimes beaten me'. Proust, on the other hand, worked on her heart. When a journalist asked her to pick the six most influential books of her life, her selection included *In Search of Lost Time*; she said she had spent a whole year reading Proust once, and that he offered a glimpse of the reconciliation she had sought, one 'where will and destiny merged, squalor could be apotheosized into beauty, and time itself might achieve a final unity'. (Wales delivered that kind of ending too: a fleeting spiritual redemption she had not been able to find in the surface swagger of Empire.) Proust sort of falls into her sentences — the pageboys in Trouville remind her of the ones he put in Balbec.

In June 2002 she performed on *Desert Island Discs* for the second time. She was waspish with presenter Sue Lawley — the deference she had shown to Lawley's predecessor Roy Plomley was long gone. This time she picked eight records written by Irving Berlin. Chat started with *Trieste*, just out. 'All my books are terribly self-indulgent but luckily people often don't realise it. *Trieste* was ego biography. [The city in 1946] was limbo. I think I was wrong to say I found an identity.' It was here that she went on to say, 'I can't pretend I'm one thing or the other. Nor can Trieste.' After Morris had run through her childhood conviction that she was a girl, Lawley piped up: 'It's almost perverse that you should marry. Almost as if you were affirming your maleness.' 'It didn't feel like that,' Morris said. 'I'm not enjoying this bit. You seem to see the whole thing far more in black and white than we [Elizabeth and I] ever did.' When they reached Cairo, Lawley said, 'So you were happy there.' 'Yes, you got it right at last.' Questioned about Casablanca, Morris said, 'There is something romantic about it, isn't there?' It was hard to associate vaginoplasty with romance. 'It brought you relief,' said an unflustered Lawley, 'didn't it?' 'Of course. I thought of it as a spiritual and metaphysical thing.' Record five was Gwynedd-born baritone Bryn Terfel singing Berlin's 'White Christmas'. 'Wales is much more important than this sex-change business,' an irritable Morris said after Terfel had finished. A journalist who made a film with her at about this time said she had reached pantomime-dame status but had such style that she could carry it off. 'I am a hybrid in all things,' she declares in the film. She was always ambiguous – part old-fashioned literary star, part camp and racy flirt. The tension between parts was unresolved. That was the conundrum, or part of it.

Nothing beat her, no matter how many conundrums gathered mass on the horizon. When *National Geographic* offered the whopping fee of $50,000 for a book about her house, Morris told an audience you had to be an old pro to write five thousand words about your lavatory. That is what she was: an old pro. She begins *A Writer's House in Wales* with the statement that Trefan Morys is the 'essence . . . of all I love about my country', before embarking on the familiar anti-English peroration, Owain Glyndŵr and the assorted cast of sprites lining up alongside the 'exceedingly vulgar royal wedding' and the seditious picnic at Mynydd Carn. With the sentiments expressed in *Trieste* on the perils of nationalism still fresh, she wrote, 'I have come to think of myself as a minority patriot, a cultural patriot, perhaps,' conceding even that the 'alien power – England – [is] itself nowadays hardly more than an agent for the even more monstrous forces of English-speaking globalisation'. Carollers seldom knocked at Christmas, and children never asked for New Year pennies like they used to, because, as she said, 'the old customs are dying now, even here'. Bats, however, were still regular callers – Morris said she had observed ninety pipistrelles swooping out of holes above the kitchen door at dusk, and forty-six at one time flying about in an upstairs room. She had covered her bedroom window with wire mesh to keep them out and played 'loud hi-fi music close to bat haunts' to dissuade them from settling. Twm says she liked them really.

The little book found a market, and translations appeared in German, Japanese, Dutch, Spanish and Mandarin. The novelist Penelope Lively referred in a review to 'a whiff of the Ancient Mariner' as Morris piloted the reader round Trefan ('sit down, take a look at this').

During the Hong Kong handover, Indian journalist Rahul Jacob had interviewed Morris for *Time*. He had read her *Rolling Stone* essay on Delhi and admired her approach: 'Fifty-odd years after she wrote that, the de facto feudalism of India's absurdly hierarchical bureaucracy holds true. She captures it perfectly.' Jacob recalls, 'When we had got to know one another, I suggested in a review of her work that on the other hand she didn't get the business or economic aspect of a place in *any* book, certainly not *Hong Kong*. You can't write about the colonial project without understanding economics. It is not enough, as a defence, to say the style is "impressionistic".' Despite that, and as Jacob suggested, 'Mrs Gupta Never Called', the *Rolling Stone* essay, 'is an analysis of Delhi that would have saved multinationals investing in India hundreds of millions if only their executives had read it'. (The piece, and Mrs Gupta, popped up in editorials for years as a cipher of paralysing Indian bureaucracy.) Morris knew Jacob was right about economic lacunae. An *Economist* reviewer had made the same observation about *The World Bank* forty years earlier. When the *Financial Times* in London appointed Jacob travel, food and drink editor in 2003, Morris was the first writer he approached, offering her £400 for each travel piece, which she refused: it was £1,000 or nothing.

Morris's seven-year relationship with the *FT* was a happy one. Jacob used to meet her and Elizabeth for breakfast or dinner at Durrants, their small Marylebone hotel. 'She had a unique sense of playfulness,' he notes, together with

> a kind of Janus tendency, looking back and forward. She left voicemails as if she were talking to you. 'Chuck it in the bin if it's no good, no charge for failure!' I spent most of my time laughing. I would happily have organised the fanciest hotel, but she didn't want to write about fashionable places. She was a reporter.

Her *FT* stories varied: the best included a rail journey across Europe, 'rim to rim', starting a few miles from home on the Rheilffordd Ffestiniog and ending with a plunge from the Carso to the Adriatic on the Ferrovia Elettrica Trieste–Opicina. Other efforts were tepid. She had nothing much to say about Slovenia; Elizabeth's diary is more revealing. They had visited Venice and Trieste on the way.

> Much had changed [Elizabeth wrote]. There are no longer cats in Venice – only two left in the gardens by Harry's Bar. Very, very sad. BUT redemption was at hand: on our last night here we went to Harry's Bar where we were received as long-lost friends – with Alan Whicker and his wife, we are the oldest clients there. Quite a claim. At the house [where they had lived in Venice] though things seemed much as they were thank goodness except for the cats. Glad to leave the crowds. Train next day to Trieste – usual big hotel shut so stay at Duchi d'Aosta and stroll to a bookshop to buy yet more books.

They drove into south-western Slovenia; the car was automatic and they couldn't start it again after a coffee stop. Elizabeth's diary continues,

'Arrived Postojna. The Predjama Castle was of great interest. There are plenty of cats too – all sorts!'

It was a gloomy time for Morris, and for everyone. 'For years and years,' she told a journalist, 'I've sneered at the old farts who say the world is going to the dogs, and now I realise they're right.' She withdrew instead even further into the fastness of Eryri. Besides proselytising for the creed of *kindness*, she started repeating her insistence on 'culturalism' in place of the 'nationalism that has soured on me'. She said, 'I'm very depressed . . . I don't awfully like the human race.' She was feeling mortal. She cancelled an appearance in San Francisco ('only the second time in my life'), experiencing, as she emailed Faber, 'a sort of permanent state of jet-laggedness, coupled with incipient immobility and a profound mental and physical lethargy'. With her mind on her legacy, she donated the first tranche of her papers to the National Library of Wales in Aberystwyth. (Seven years later she handed over a second batch. Both bequests were haphazard. Most letters stayed at Trefan, tucked into books and motoring manuals or wedged in boxes under the stairs.) As for the house itself: she wanted it to become a literary centre after her death. She had considered gifting it to the National Trust. Simon Jenkins was chair of the organisation at the time, and he talked her out of it.

Her ambition extended beyond the grave. While organising her legacy, she was also writing a posthumous volume. The title was to be *Allegorizings*. 'Nothing is what it seems,' she declared, preparing the ground. She warned the children that they would not approve of the book, hinting that it contained some hitherto concealed fact ('We were primed for an explosion'). Morris wanted to suggest, to the children and to everyone, that *she* was not as she seemed. Death preoccupied her, like Prospero. Both Mark and Suki are convinced Jan had planned a double suicide: that she and Elizabeth would die together by their own hands. Morris returned obsessively to the topic of the Crawshay-Williamses, the couple who had ended their lives that way. The two siblings believe this was what lay behind the gravestone Morris had commissioned. 'It was part of her personal mythology,' Mark says. 'Making things how she wanted them to be.' When she knew she couldn't emulate the Crawshay-Williamses, she wrote a book to take control of death's mystery. Writing made sense of her life. At first it had ordered her experience, and it still did, but the process had become mechanical.

Two things cheered her up in 2003: the fifty-year Everest reunion, and Twm winning a great honour. Al Alvarez, the young man with whom the Morrises had toured New England in 1954, now a distinguished writer himself, sent an anniversary card. 'With Everest 50 coming up,' he wrote from his home in London, 'I've been thinking about you . . . Christ, we were young!' He included a signed pamphlet of his poetry. In an epilogue to the anniversary reissue of *Coronation Everest*, Morris called the ascent 'one of the most honourable and innocent of the great adventures'. Alvarez reviewed the new edition and noted, 'So, too, was hers.'

On 29 May the Queen attended a Royal Gala Celebration called 'Endeavour on Everest' followed by a reception at Spencer House at which Morris made a magnificent speech.

> Now I have to tell you here, with affectionate respect to everyone present, hoping I won't get my head cut off – I am a Welsh republican. But just as I was an aesthetic imperialist, so I was an aesthetic monarchist too. Of course I responded to the poetical, Shakespearean side of it all, and I was moved by the thought of the young Queen and her sailor husband clip-clopping across London in their gilded coach. And I thought to myself, if I could bring together these two fascinating abstractions, on the one side a grand old empire fading, on the other a rejuvenated monarchy, to revive the confidence of the nation and bring pleasure to the world – well, that would be more than a scoop, it would be a historical allegory.

Just three months later, forty-two-year-old Twm won the National Eisteddfod bard's chair. His winning ode was about 'the crisis in the rural heartlands of the Welsh language'. Bardic members of the Druidical Order in their special white robes left the stage to greet the victor and accompany him back through an applauding crowd, television cameras whirring in the gantries and an organ thundering. Morris was among the party, and she said it was one of the happiest days of her life. Twm had a Welsh authenticity she lacked. 'He is much more Welsh than I am,' she said. 'He doesn't have any feeling for that sense of stately order that I like about England.' She repeated her conviction that she was 'a born hybrid'. Twm says, 'She could never really become one of the tribe. But I could.'

Many of the later books reveal the onset of whimsy as publishing conventions fell away, conventions that had once dictated formality and the appearance of objectivity. As a result, some of the mature work is more like juvenilia (though not Morris's actual juvenilia) than the early material. In 1961 she had criticised female travel writers for their 'coy whimsy'; now she was at it herself, joshing about stealing face flannels from five-star hotels. The predominant tone of these years, however, was one of disillusion; the whimsy was a hedge against gloom. Reminiscing about halcyon days lolling on rattan chairs with Jann Wenner, she said, 'I liked young Americans of that generation – I thought they were decent people, interesting and clever. Now they've all matured and got a bit more ordinary.' For her, as for many, the US had once represented hope and limitless possibility. But now – what was there to hope for now? It was age and experience that changed Morris's prose style, not gender transition.

She continued public speaking but would not sit on a panel, and never had, as in a group she would not be in control. At the Hay Festival once, the organisers had included her in a literary roundtable after her individual event and she had not spotted it on her schedule. She fled before it convened. But solo talks piled up in these later years, in 2004 alone at the Galway Festival, a Jacky Fisher centennial conference, the opening of a garden in Pennal, Meirionnydd, where in 1406 Owain Glyndŵr wrote a famous letter asking Charles VI of France for help defeating the English (Simon Jenkins says there is no evidence that the

Pennal church was Glyndŵr's chapel royal. 'It's not even a legend,' he told Morris. 'It is now,' she replied), and the Cricieth Festival, where she delivered the Lloyd George Memorial Lecture in an overflowing Capel Moreia. But her star turn that year was at Faber's seventy-fifth anniversary celebration at London's Royal Festival Hall. She read from *Trieste*, and made jokes: she always pretended there was gin in the water glass, expressing surprise after taking a sip in the first minute or two. Everyone present said she stole the show – and it was a starry show, to the extent that the literary world can be. But halfway through the drinks reception, Morris had vanished into the Waterloo sunset.

When she wrote a new introduction to a 2002 edition of *Conundrum*, Morris acknowledged that the book had established itself as a classic. Others agreed. The volume was, according to Christine Burns, editor of *Trans Britain*, 'The first British mainstream trans autobiography . . . It is hard to convey nowadays the importance of that book to so many people.' Addressing the legacy of *Conundrum*, Morris wrote that the 'fundamental attitudes' of the book 'have not in the least altered'.

> I never did think that my own conundrum was a matter either of science or of social convention. I thought it was a matter of the spirit, a kind of divine allegory, and that explanations of it were not very important anyway. What was important was the liberty of us all to live as we wished to live, to love however we wanted to love, and to know ourselves, however peculiar, disconcerting or unclassifiable, at one with the gods and angels.

It would be hard to disagree that the liberty to live freely is important. But once the trans debate began to acquire nuance in the first two decades of a new century, some noted again the exclusionary literary aspect of *Conundrum*, and therefore the book's limitations. 'It is very much the tale of someone with privileges,' an activist wrote two years before Morris died. But, notwithstanding the exclusion some felt, *Conundrum* had still been, according to another trans campaigner, 'an early hint that trans people's stories might be something else – something more than just titillation . . . an articulate professional [was] prepared to take readers beyond the veneer of "sex change" as shock headline and invite them to examine what her journey contributed to our understanding of the human condition'. Morris had become a talisman in her own lifetime, and *Conundrum* a foundation text for the generations. *The Times* chose it as one of the '100 Key Books of Our Time'. As *New Scientist* had said when it first came out, 'Nobody who reads her story can ever again think of the trans-sexualist as a mere freak or lunatic, to be dismissed with scorn, or mockery, or heartless pity.' But this was the only quotation Morris asked Faber not to include on the jacket of the new edition. She did not want to be a pioneering 'trans-sexualist'. She didn't even want to be 'a trans woman'. She wanted to be a woman.

She did change her mind about one thing. In a piece about Victorian lady travellers she wrote,

> For better or worse I am one of those persons who by some hormonal misunderstanding began life in the male gender and moved on to the female. I lived adventurously as a man, and like everyone else, I used to suppose that this was because I had been subconsciously trying to prove my masculinity. I have lately reached a different conclusion. I think now that when in those days I deliberately courted danger or discomfort, I was obeying not the masculine in me but the feminine. I have come to think that the female is intuitively more adventurous than the male. I now believe that the most courageous, original and thoughtful adventurers have generally been women.

So it was the woman in her that had propelled her up the Khumbu icefall. Elsewhere she extolled the opportunities afforded to women on the road. '[During my own travelling years] the female traveller has had it easier than the male,' she had written in an essay to accompany an exhibition celebrating that tweed-skirted tribe. Morris had taken to trotting this out – she had said it to Chatwin in the taxi. (The assertion is true in the narrow sense, in that people tend not to perceive the woman traveller as a threat.) She was not particularly interested in the issue either way. But she saw the funny side, as she almost always did. She had expressed the same opinion about women travellers earlier in a preface to a biography of Isabella Bird, one of the stars of Victorian lady-adventuring. (The preface was itself adapted from an essay in *Gourmet* magazine – there was no end to the recycling.) After Bird got married she put her suitcases away, and when a friend commiserated about a cancelled trip, she replied – and Morris cites this – 'New Guinea was not the sort of place you could take a man to.'

She was aware, of course, that she had become a historical monument in the trans field. On 25 May 2004, when the Gender Recognition Bill was crawling through Parliament, an Honourable Member pointed out in the House, 'This is certainly not a new issue. Jan Morris wrote *Conundrum* well over thirty years ago.' The legislation, which received royal assent two months later and was implemented in April 2005, recognised 'acquired gender'. The passing of the Gender Recognition Act had taken years of grinding campaigning as well as legal rulings in Europe. It was flawed – for example, a statutory instrument was added concerning disclosure of a person's transsexual status for legal and medical purposes. But it was the best trans-rights law in the world at the time, and the best that could have been achieved under the circumstances. 'The government had finally grasped', as one campaigning Parliamentarian put it, 'that being trans was not a mental health condition.' The act stipulated that trans people who were heterosexually married could only obtain full gender recognition by first divorcing their spouse. Just as Randell had threatened Morris forty years earlier: only if you divorce first.

Unlike Everest, however, this was not a topic Morris welcomed – she was only prepared to write a new introduction to her famous book because it benefited her. And anyway, 'She was so ambivalent about the sex change by the end', Mark says, 'that she never embraced it, and was irritated when it came up. Certainly she never went out of her way to help anyone else in the position she had been in. It annoyed us, after what we had been through – she had made such a huge thing about publicising it, we thought, you can't drop it now! But she did. She pulled the ladder up behind her.' When one of Bill Norman's daughters wrote a novel about a transgender journey, Bill rang to ask if Morris wanted a copy. 'No,' she said. 'I've had too much of that kind of thing.' She told an interviewer that 'people try to define something which is indefinable, that's partly why I don't like talking about it'. And of course she herself was – is – indefinable.

Jan and Elizabeth spent Christmas 2004 in Venice and met Alan Whicker by chance again in Harry's Bar, where they had their Yuletide dinner. 'We saw her and Elizabeth from behind,' Valerie Kleeman, Whicker's partner, remembers. 'They were bent close, engrossed in conversation. Alan said, "That can't be them, nobody's heads are that close together after fifty years of marriage."' They told Alan and Valerie they had come to get away from the children. Two months later they were in London for Patrick Leigh Fermor's ninetieth at the Mandarin Oriental. Leigh Fermor was fond of Morris: the only crime in his book was to be boring. They had known one another for many years. Leigh Fermor had once sent her a four-page German poem, copied in his own hand and translated by him on the facing page. Not only was he fond of her – he told a friend privately, 'I admire her very much.' Both, as writers, were above all stylists. She had long considered him 'beyond cavil the greatest of living travel writers' – though, characteristically, she was not afraid of pointing out weakness, especially if she scented an obsequious attitude to toffery: in her review of *Between the Woods and the Water* she wrote, 'Mr Fermor is perhaps more fascinated by the ways of the lost Austro-Hungarian aristocracy than most of us are; and in this as in other pursuits he is led very nearly into self-parody.' In the early summer of 2004 he had sent her a postcard from his home in Greece.

> I wish you could simply stroll in here, as you did ages ago about noon (and then frustratingly evaporated as soon as lunchtime neared). I'm writing this on the table on the other side. The little cat ('Tiny Tot') is now in a better world, mousing above the clouds. Two dolphins swam

across the middle distance a few minutes ago, rare visitors now – rare enough to make me want to tell someone hence this P.C.

The year of the ninetieth party she wrote introductions to reissues of two of Leigh Fermor's books – his 'imperishable picture of life among the toffs of Mitteleuropa before catastrophe fell upon them'. She enjoyed the voluptuous romance of Leigh Fermor's inter-war walk through Europe, its central figure 'so fresh and hopeful set against the doomed majesty of an ancient continent'. In *A Time of Gifts* she wrote, very wonderfully indeed, Leigh Fermor is 'not only remembering himself, he is looking at himself too, as in one of those Cubist paintings in which we see profile and front face at the same time'. Morris was shrewd in her comments to and about other authors, just as she was shrewd in her book reviews. Three years after the ninetieth she was at the Travellers to celebrate the launch of another Leigh Fermor book. Guests noted she was full of bounce, and she went round telling everyone that she was the club's only Lady Card Holder.

'The past is a foreign country,' she had written in *Trieste*, 'but so is old age, and as you enter it you feel you are treading unknown territory.' She started lecturing on cruise ships rather than striking out on assignments alone. Elizabeth usually accompanied her. One ship appeared in print as the *Geriatrica*, its first onboard lecture – Morris claimed – 'Facing up to Rheumatism'. In between cruises, she spent more time at Trefan, and in the summer of 2005 had what she referred to as a 'cosmetic face transformation' to fend off the hazards of the road ahead. Suki says, 'Mummy told me it was worse having her at home – things had been better when Jan was on her travels.' But Elizabeth wrote to Jan fondly, just as Jan wrote to her. On their wedding anniversary Elizabeth sent a card – depicting a cat, as usual – to say, 'We've been together for fifty-eight years . . . no wonder you need a new pair of slippers! All my love as always your very loving E.' The same year, her birthday card read, 'To my very special Jan with so much love and thanks for all the past and looking forward to all the future. Ibsen joins me.' (A moratorium had been declared on Abyssinian names, because Ibsen was a Norwegian hunting cat. Morris said it stared at her with 'the look of an equal'.) It was unusual to include the incumbent feline. It usually sent a card of its own.

When Morris fell in the street, passers-by helped her into a supermarket, where in-house first-aiders took over. She had appeared in a documentary on BBC Wales the night before, 'and when passing customers saw me in the hands of the first-aid folk, my blood streaming all over the place, my clothes torn, my face ghastly with pallor, "Enjoyed the programme", was all most of them said as they proceeded towards the checkout'. A fortnight before Christmas she collapsed in her bedroom and lost consciousness. 'It was thought to be a stroke,' Elizabeth wrote in a letter some weeks later,

> but after a head scan she was immediately taken to Liverpool for an operation to drain her head of a clot of blood. She came back here for Christmas and was recovering well when once again she fainted and was taken to Bangor and the whole thing was repeated. She is now back home but I am kept busy with work cancellations, looking after all Jan's business as well as the house, the cooking etc etc.

Morris recovered and was not down. Twenty years after *Last Letters from Hav* she wrote a coda she called *Hav of the Myrmidons*, which Faber published bound in with a fresh printing of *Last Letters*. 'I don't think much of it,' she told Mark in an email. That didn't particularly matter to her. Something was more important. Morris had randomly noted in *Pleasures of a Tangled Life* a comment by the Russian author Mikhail Saltykov-Shchedrin. 'Finding himself in his last years without a magazine to write for,' Morris recorded, he 'said he had lost the one person he had ever loved: his reader'. She would evade that fate, at almost any cost.

In the pages of *Myrmidons*, Morris looks back over the decades in which she tried to make sense of it all and concludes that historical pattern and meaning is illusory. Whereas she had written *Last Letters* in the mid-eighties as 'multiculturalism was blurring old loyalties and senses of identity', in *Myrmidons* 'the confusions are clarified rather: religion has assumed new meanings, the hostility between East and West is franker, there are new ethnic tensions, but everything is subsumed anyway by the universal corrupting energy of global capitalism'. In the *TLS* review of the first *Hav*, the critic had said Morris wasn't the Argentinian master Jorge Luis Borges, a case of praising with faint damnation; in the same periodical another writer, reviewing the double volume twenty-one years later, noted that 'the 2006 Hav is nostalgic for the 1985 Hav, and 1985 Hav was filled with nostalgia for many earlier eras'. This was astute: if Morris were writing today, she would be nostalgic for 2003. The loyal reader was now far from *Pax*. Its geographically and culturally fragmented world at least had a central core of meaning. The Hav-place is a vacuum.

To Morris's astonishment, the double *Hav* was shortlisted for the Arthur C. Clarke Award for 'best science fiction novel' of the year. She had not even thought it belonged to that genre. But to a certain extent it did. The king of sci-fi, J. G. Ballard (almost the same vintage as Morris), had once suggested that a valid version of reality exists in the mind; that the world at large does not acknowledge this indeterminate inner reality and crowds it out; and that fiction does allow it (the inner reality) to flourish or at least breathe. Morris was not Ballard but she also believed that; she believed it applied to all books, one way or another. She knew very well that a valid version of reality exists in the mind. In addition, there is an argument – and Ballard made it – that only science fiction could express the craziness of the twentieth century (the twenty-first was proving even crazier).

In the Book of the Week slot in the *Guardian*, Ursula K. Le Guin – queen of sci-fi to Ballard's king – was in no doubt. In by far the most perceptive review, she said of the double volume,

> Probably Morris, certainly her publisher, will not thank me for saying that *Hav* is in fact science fiction, of a perfectly recognisable type and superb quality. *Hav* exists as a mirror held up to several millennia of

pan-Mediterranean history, customs and politics. Where have we been, where are we going? Serious science fiction is a mode of realism, not of fantasy; and *Hav* is a splendid example of the uses of an alternate geography.

Morris had said in the epilogue that *Hav* is (of course) an allegory. 'I don't take it as an allegory at all,' said Le Guin. 'I read it as a brilliant description of the crossroads of the West and East in two recent eras, viewed by a woman who has truly seen the world, and who lives in it with twice the intensity of most of us. It is a very good guidebook, I think, to the early twenty-first century.'

Morris had won the Thomas Cook Travel Book Award for Outstanding Contribution to Travel Writing and a Golden PEN Award for a Lifetime's Distinguished Service to Literature (the slab of glass went under the stairs along with the boxes of letters and the fax machine). She would have won the David Cohen Prize too, a £40,000 biennial honour for a body of work, as a judge in 2009 argued strongly for her, but the panel chair dismissed her candidacy by saying she was just a travel writer. (Seamus Heaney won the David Cohen that year – another author the young Monteith had spotted.) The chairman's opinion reflected a view in the literary community that the label demeans real writers. (When one of Chatwin's titles was shortlisted for the Thomas Cook Travel Book Award, he insisted on its withdrawal.) Morris herself had come to believe that the term 'travel writer' diminished her gifts. 'I seem to spend half my life trying to persuade people I am not a travel writer,' she had written, 'but I seldom succeed, and I suppose I've got to live with the definition and die with it too.'

As proof that she had become a monument, the National Portrait Gallery commissioned a likeness. Director Sandy Nairne invited her in to discuss the project. 'I'm not really a person,' Morris told him. 'I'm a set of places.' She went on to set down 'two stipulations'. One, her calves should appear in the picture, and two, so should Ibsen. *Calves?* Did she fear trouserish intent on the artist's part? Nairne had no idea. At any rate, it was agreed, and some weeks later Morris sat to Huddersfield-born Arturo di Stefano in his studio in London's East End wearing a rope of plastic white beads, a butter-yellow sweater and a black skirt; she expressed disappointment, when she first saw the blank canvas on the easel, that it was so small. In the finished portrait Ibsen duly lies curled at the sitter's feet staring ferociously at the viewer, and di Stefano incorporated Morris's 'places' through a series of windows looking onto the Manhattan skyline, Everest, the Bay of Trieste, a Porthmadog schooner and the Trefan sycamore. At about the same time, friends and acolytes produced an endearing festschrift to mark her eightieth. Besides these signposts of status, new editions of Morris's backlist appeared and Faber reissued *Fifty Years* with a better title: *Europe: An Intimate Journey*. The subject matter had not lost its relevance. One reviewer, first time round, had called Morris 'a cheery old cracker'. She had outlived that moniker, as she had outlived so much else.

Pax, the centrepiece of her life, stood the test of time even as the climate changed. Historian Tom Holland, no reactionary, said in 2005 that the *Pax Britannica* trilogy 'evokes the swagger and self-doubt of Empire so perfectly that it is worthy to stand beside *Kim* as one of the few great works of literature inspired by Britain's imperial adventures'.[*] Two years after Holland's encomium, at Christ Church, Morris met Professor Nigel Biggar, mitigator of the imperial dark side, and he too came out as an admirer, writing to Trefan wanting to know about her shift to Welsh nationalism. So she had it both ways. Neither Morris nor *Pax* fitted the reductive binary nature of the debate that raged in her mature years, which is why no side could co-opt her. The British Empire might have been 'a dreadful phenomenon', but style and spectacle still won through as far as she was concerned, and nobody disagreed particularly loudly.

---

[*] Some years later, Holland met Morris over the morning buffet at a hotel in Sweden, where the pair bonded over the baffling display of herring dishes. 'Among the most meaningful breakfasts of my life,' reports Holland.

Morris was neither chameleon nor Zelig: her readership was both. As late as 1997 she mounted a robust defence of the imperial enterprise, trumpeting in a full-page piece in the *Mail*, 'The British Empire was a tremendous development agency. It was an instrument of education and enlightenment ... its own interests came first – of course they did – but by the standards of most empires its methods were humane.' She refused to submit: she liked what she liked. 'The Empire is dead, thank God,' she ended the piece. 'Long live the Empire!'

The reader might have thought that by 1997, the year Hong Kong went and *Pathfinder* landed on Mars, the glorification of imperialism as a civilising mission was dead in its own salty water. But, again, Morris was in tune with her times: the *Mail* article was written to mark the founding of a museum devoted to 'the British Empire and Commonwealth', the planning and execution of which was underway in one of Brunel's train sheds in Bristol. Morris was a trustee and had been an early supporter. Even in 2014, a YouGov poll revealed that fifty-nine per cent of Britons thought Empire was something to be proud of. The imperial project still shone, in other words, but, like an old star, nobody including Morris could agree on when it had burned out. The public certainly had no interest in the non-Briton's experience of Empire. They might have responded positively to a poll, but ultimately they weren't proud enough to keep the museum afloat. It closed after six years, and in a scandal involving the alleged 'disappearance' of artefacts a New Zealand gallery director publicly asked, 'Is this the arse-end of colonialism?'

Morris's fondness for the flashing epaulette, the gleaming gunboat and the trickle of sweat from the pith helmet was in many ways nostalgia *tout court*. But she knew, and showed in *Hav of the Myrmidons*, that nostalgia itself shifts with the wind. She saw the Empire with the perspective of the ages in these years, just as she had traded the telescope for binoculars. (She rarely used the expensive scope at Trefan anymore but never left on assignment without her bins.) In a review of Niall Ferguson's *Empire: How Britain Made the Modern World*, Morris judged that the young academic 'has succeeded better than anyone else' in fashioning a one-volume narrative on the imperial topic. There is a hint of feline disparagement in the superficially laudatory review – she calls Ferguson 'the Professor' all the way through – and a touch of Penelope Lively's Ancient Mariner too: 'sometimes he is a little simplistic, in the [Simon] Schama manner – on both world wars, for instance, on the character of George Nathaniel Curzon, on the Suez crisis of 1956'. But she, the elder stateswoman, could take the long view. 'If there is one true historical truism, it is the one about history repeating itself. The Pax Britannica was only one of mankind's perennial attempts to bring order to the world, generally in the reformer's own image.' In the final chapter of his book, and in the television series that went with it, Ferguson draws parallels between the British Empire and the American hegemony that followed. Morris could not have agreed more. 'Time and again as I read this book,' she wrote, 'I was reminded of almost exact analogies between the two world dominions' – in Sudan in the 1880s it had been the Mahdi, in New York in 2001 bin Laden. America was reviled across the world 'in the lurid glow of its hubris' at the time she was writing, just as Britain had been after the fall of Khartoum. But, as Morris said, 'The contrast is irrelevant anyway. Sooner or later, humiliation will abase the one as it abolished the other.'

On 14 February 2007, Jan and Elizabeth, on their way to Cricieth, switched on the car radio and heard Radio 3 playing a Tchaikovsky flute solo. 'I bet that's Gareth,' they both said at the same time. And it was. They got back to Trefan that afternoon to an email from Trish to say Gareth had died. He was eighty-six. His last postcard to Jan had commemorated the hundred and twelfth birthday of Aunt Fanny, who had taken them for penny buns on Clevedon Pier. Morris delivered the eulogy at the funeral in Bristol Cathedral. 'Whenever I have felt a bit dismal,' she said, 'I have given him a call on the telephone, knowing that he would cheer me up.' Gareth's daughter Catharine says, 'They had a bond and an intuitive understanding.' Gareth was an uplifting character. 'He was born with a gift for happiness,' Morris said. 'He was a truly great artist.' She had told him so privately. 'No, alas, we're not really quits,' she had once said in an email. 'Your book [he had published a volume on flute technique] was written by a great artist on the side. My books are all I can do.'

Chris broke the tension at Gareth's funeral. 'Imagine,' he said, 'if Elizabeth died and we were Indian I would have to marry Jan.'

Elizabeth had a minor operation and to allow her to convalesce they went to Lake Lucerne for a week ('which I'm hoping to pay for with an essay about the marvellous paddle steamers on the lake', Morris said). Then Jan got shingles. It took a long time to recover. When she did, Betty, Elizabeth's Trefan Bach friend, told Suki, 'If only Jan had died, your mum would have been free to lead a little bit of life.' Both of them were just about all right by December, and they enjoyed a 'glorious' Christmas in Oxford with a Lebanese lunch and carols in the cathedral, sacred of memory, which were 'divine, however abject the Dean's sermon'. At the beginning of January the New Zealand government flew the two of them in for Ed Hillary's state funeral. In a tribute in *The Times*, Morris turned Sir Ed into something other than ashes – 'I prefer to consider him as allegory.'

She headed almost immediately to Manhattan, where she recorded a promotional video to be shown posthumously whenever *Allegorizings* appeared. She liked her editor at Norton, and for the last two decades of her life Bob Weil provided affectionate bonhomie and professional reassurance. He knew what she liked – lunch on the thirty-fifth floor of the Mandarin Oriental on Columbus Circle, or at the Four Seasons in the Seagram Building, where maître d's fawned and chefs came out to hug her. It was lunch as theatre. As for the promotional film: it was excruciating. The eighty-two-year-old Morris sat in a brown sweater and a different rope of beads, bored to tears in front of a Norton bookcase displaying her work face-out, running through the usual topics, from the gravestone to the importance of kindness. 'Do you want to tell us about Elizabeth?' asked an unseen Weil. 'No.' 'What message do you want readers to take from this book?' 'Keep smiling!' 'What's the meaning of the *Allegorizings* volume?' 'Not being a literary person myself, I don't think about it much. I've always considered myself a superficial writer. The thing is, I don't intellectualise things, I do things by instinct.' As the Norton film drew to a close, Weil asked her why, when journalists had wanted her to name her least favourite city, she had always said it was Indianapolis. She said she couldn't remember. 'I must have gone there fifty years ago and something bad happened to me. But the word runs off the tongue, doesn't it?' Any regrets? 'I would have embarked on a career of fiction writing. I thought I was going to. I thought the way into fiction was journalism, partly because of Steinbeck and Hemingway.' It was now, when the interview finished, that she said, off-camera, 'I've never heard such a lot of balls propounded.'

She was back in the UK in April for Hillary's memorial service in St George's Chapel, Windsor Castle. And still it went on. Two years later she delivered the Sir Edmund Hillary Memorial Lecture at the Royal Geographical Society. She called the talk 'An Outsider on Everest'. It was brilliantly entertaining, as usual. She began by setting foreign news reports in context. 'During the Napoleonic Wars, *The Times* had its own sailing cutter to scud across the English Channel with the news from the continent; its master leapt ashore on Dover Beach to hand the day's dispatches to a courier waiting there, his horse champing at the bit, to gallop instantly up the Dover Road to Printing House Square.' 'Scud', 'leap', 'champ', 'gallop': verbs of movement and action. An old pro indeed, still holding an audience, eyes blazing.

On 15 April 2008, four years after the Civil Partnership Act passed into law, Jan and Elizabeth formalised their union for a second time. Morfydd and Arthur Roberts were the only witnesses; Jan wore a red skirt suit and the registrar at Pwllheli gave the four of them tea and biscuits following the brief ceremony. Morris told a friend over dinner at Portmeirion, 'I thought I'd make an honest woman of her.' Two months later she went to Corfu to talk at the Durrell School Summer Symposium. Mark was a board member and was helping out on the island that year. 'After the talk,' he says, 'she ignored me and everyone else. Landscape didn't interest her, but she went round Corfu Old Town with the curiosity of a detective, looking for material. She loved ruins, things people had made. That was when I realised she was addicted to writing. When we did finally sit down at a café, a *Daily Mail* reporter came up and asked about the civil partnership. Jan hadn't told me!' Mark had co-written a song cycle based on Morris's novel, called 'Songs of Hav'. 'I sent them to her, and she never made a single comment. She perceived it as a threat, I think.' Nobody had told Mark about the brain bleed either. He had been teaching for some years at the university in Edmonton, Alberta, and when, just before Covid, he came over from Canada and booked into a Cricieth bed and breakfast, Morris made arrangements to tour a local vineyard without him the morning he was due at Trefan. Suki, meanwhile, had become a schoolteacher. 'Jan said at the dinner table once, in front of my kids, "Those who can, do, those who can't, teach."' As far as both brother and sister were concerned, as Elizabeth got more frail Morris took on a gatekeeping role. 'In the last ten years or so of Jan's life,' Mark says, 'it became very hard for me to speak to my mother when I rang from Canada.' Twm sees things differently. He was based opposite in the coach house and lived with them, effectively, for many years, and he thinks that he would have known if his mother was unhappy. As for Henry, the brother between Mark and Twm, resident now in Spain, when a writer asked him to sum up his relationship with Jan, he wrote in an email, 'We were introduced, but we never actually got to know each other.'

On the fiftieth anniversary of *Venice* she idly picked the *Rough Guide* to the city from a hotel bookshelf and read that her own volume was 'insufferably fey and self-indulgent'. She didn't mind: as she said, the book had provided her with a modest private income ever since it had come out. She still went to Venice most years. The door at Harry's was a revolving one now, not the swing one the other officers had pushed her through when she was nineteen. It was increasingly difficult, however, for Morris to travel anywhere alone, as Elizabeth, showing signs of cognitive decline, had begun to wander off if left at Trefan. (She vanished even when Morris was there sometimes, and visitors found Jan pacing the lane, huffing ferociously.) So they took holidays together at the Beau-Rivage on Lake Geneva, where they had sought refuge from the maelstrom of *Conundrum* publicity all those years before.

Morris had kept up the forewords and introductions. Of a reissue of Robert Byron's *Europe in the Looking Glass: Reflections of a Motor Drive from Grimsby to Athens*, first published the year she was born, she wrote that the author had been 'pioneering a new kind of travel writing'. Byron was a giant in travel literature (still is). *Looking Glass* was his first book (he was twenty-one) and, 'faux incompetence', 'pretensions' and 'adolescent dogmatism' aside, 'some phrases stop one suddenly in one's patronising tracks'. Morris acknowledged, 'Many of us feel that we have been liberated by Byron's example from the curse of the travelogue – the stigma that used to imply that travel writing did not qualify as literature.' (Her failure to get the David Cohen Prize showed we are not yet entirely liberated.) And, just as she used introductions to jemmy travel writing into what she considered its appropriate literary position, she also used them to address the troubled theme of invention. Laurie Lee's *A Moment of War* led the way in this department. A classic evocation of the miseries of war set in 1937 Spain (Lee said the country was 'stretched dead on a slab'), *A Moment* was the third in an autobiographical series, and critics said the author had not even been at the Battle of Teruel. 'For myself,' Morris wrote in an essay that prefaced a new edition, 'I doubt the literal truth of it all – but I accept its more profound reality as another sort of truth.' As she had written years ago of Ibn Battuta, the story was 'true in the sweep', and like Lee and all the best writers she understood that truth cannot be reached by facts alone. She was invested in the idea, as much of her own work was contingent on it. Morris was happiest in that porous borderland between fiction and non-fiction – in its ambiguity it was like the Marches, where she came from, and it was like her.

This singular writer who produced cogent assessments of modern classics could also submit fatuous copy. When the editors of *Four-Letter*

Word: Original Love Letters asked if she would contribute, she composed a paean to Elizabeth, imagining herself behind the wheel, racing back to a reunion at Trefan. 'Oh my love, my light, my glory! I am coming! You are waiting! Up the bumpy lane (my heart bumping too . . .)'

In the early English summer of 2011, Leigh Fermor died. *Must go, don't know where;/ I am astonished I am so cheerful*, he had written about death in *A Time of Gifts*. The *Observer* commissioned a tribute from Morris, and she positioned her old friend as 'the last of a line that began with Alexander Kinglake'. She mentioned the dolphins he had described to her, and noted that Leigh Fermor was 'especially good at relating modern to ancient worlds', which was what she did in her imagination automatically and tried to do on the page. 'One of the great prose stylists of our time,' she had written, 'he had no rivals, and so stands beyond envy.' At the reception at the Travellers after the memorial service, guests noticed she was gloomy – she gave the impression, one said, that everything happening in the news and in her life was miserable. Another, who had been at Paddy's ninetieth, said, 'The fizz was gone.'

Elizabeth, meanwhile, worried about the children. 'ESCAPE ESCAPE,' she wrote in her diary when she and Jan had the chance of a break. 'We ran away for Christmas,' she recorded in the last days of 2012, 'and came back from a beautiful time at The Old Bank Hotel in Oxford.' She wrote an anguished note to a friend venting the same worries and urging herself on to keep the peace, 'anything to stop Jan worrying . . . burn this please'.

17
2013–2020
BOTH

Elizabeth was admitted to hospital. When she was discharged after six months she returned to Trefan and she and Jan struggled on, two Zimmer frames parked at the Dutch door ready for the next journey.

In March 2013 George Lowe died. He was the Kiwi who had given the thumbs-up on the Lhotse. Morris was the only one left. A sixtieth-anniversary 'reunion' went ahead at Pen-y-Gwryd, as relatives had begun attending *in loco montanorum*. Morris took the battered Murray they had all signed at Base Camp, now bound in leather, and children and grandchildren added their names.

Shortly after Lowe, Alan Whicker died. Morris read the eulogy at his memorial service wearing a canary-yellow cardigan. Valerie Kleeman, Whicker's partner, says, 'Jan was always the first to ring after a transmission of *Whicker's World* [Alan's wildly successful television series]. Alan admired her hugely, and, as a reporter, would often turn down a subject if Jan had covered it, believing that she would have done it better.' The two had been friends since they'd shared a billet in the Canal Zone and Morris had noted the dapper Whicker's beard. They were intimate, or as intimate as Morris was with anyone. She once rang Whicker to ask if he could get one of her children a job in television 'after all I've put them through', a rare acknowledgement that she had put anyone through anything. When the *Spectator* attacked Whicker, Morris defended him in print. 'Both Alan and Jan put their life force into their work,' Kleeman continues. 'Alan had the splinter of ice and I suspect

Jan did too.' Morris rang Valerie every year on the anniversary of Alan's death. 'Most people had forgotten me.'

On 23 November 2014, Chris died. They had had a happy time celebrating his ninetieth two years previously. Chris, like Gareth, had been an optimist. And now he was gone.

Books kept her going. She was still able to put her hand on a Houston almanac to see when the sun set on a particular day, or on a tides timetable for the Florida Keys. She had been buying books for approaching seventy years, and the library brought order and pattern to her interior life. She never annotated but had no scruples about scrawling in her name, the date and, usually, where she had bought the book, often with a Sharpie. She had inked her name and 'Marlborough 1959' in a 1904 edition of Carlyle's *The French Revolution*. Morris had collected verse, even though Twm says she didn't like good poetry, she liked bad poetry – doggerel – and she turned again now to Housman ('Ismailia 1952'), Betjeman ('Bogotá 1961') or a signed 1937 hardback of Auden and MacNeice's *Letters from Iceland*.

She was discovering authors new to her in the mutable field of narrative non-fiction until the year she died: she knew who was really good and who was just good, and she never got it wrong. The late discovery of Maeve Brennan's 1969 *The Long-Winded Lady*, which 'brilliantly' observes 'the endless spectacle' of Manhattan, 'made me very envious'. (A writer not envious of Brennan has much to learn.) Reflecting now, at the end, on the difference between fact and fiction, Morris said the two were 'irrevocably mingled in my own work, and to one degree or another, I suspect, in most other writers' work too. The thing is, truth is not absolute.' She harped on this theme, telling the BBC, 'Everything in *Venice* is true, which you can't say about my later books. I've come to think there's nothing different between truth and the imagination – it's a central tenet of my art now.' As for Venice the city, as opposed to the book, it still stood as an expressive symbol of her love of the past and its buildings. It was a Ruskinian attitude – Morris loved Ruskin and had edited a new edition of his *Stones of Venice*. She was a Romantic in that way; hers was the kind of Romanticism that believes the memory of a swagger can conquer time, or at least tame it, rather than the Keatsian variety that sings of oneness with field and fell.

She put music on more frequently and bought an electronic keyboard to share with visiting grandchildren. 'Though I came from an intensely musical family,' she had once written, 'for many years I took little pleasure in listening to music.' In her work, music had featured mostly when she listed cassettes and then CDs she put on in the car – she appeared in *Private Eye*'s Pseuds Corner for saying she 'played *Tosca* when crossing the Severn Bridge'. Undaunted at eighty-eight, she had another book out. The quality of the late output had been mixed, but Morris was not yet finished as a writer. When asked by a magazine to pick her favourite painting, she had once nominated Carpaccio's *Vision of St Augustine*; she had always loved the Renaissance artist's brio and puckish humour. In 2014 Morris published the small-format *Ciao, Carpaccio! An Infatuation*, the strongest of her *jeux d'esprit* and an enchanting volume in every sense. The pictures were old friends. The hats! The animals! The tights! She didn't mind that every art historian knew many images in the book were not by Carpaccio. It was the spirit of the thing that counted.

Auden had addressed loneliness in a poem: *Routine is the one technique/ I know of that enables/ Your host to ignore you now*. For most people, 'routine' meant having the same breakfast at the same hour and doing the laundry every Monday. For Morris it had meant customs forms and a travel kettle: those were the things that had kept loneliness at bay. She adapted some of the old routines, visiting Venice in her eighty-ninth year with Twm alongside her; she said she took him to stop her falling out of a boat. She had never done her own laundry anyway. (Though breakfast did play a role. Morris had always packed a supply of marmalade for the road, and at home had seven jars lined up in the kitchen, one for each day of the week.) Her Welsh had gone completely when she had her brain bleed, but she still told off anyone who wrote 'North Wales' in her address, on the basis that the descriptor was divisive. When her friend Mike Parker stood for Plaid in Ceredigion in the 2015 general election, the day before the polls opened she sent him a message: 'Praying that you win, for all our sakes!' (He didn't.) She and Elizabeth met Plaid leader Leanne Wood in Porthmadog that year. In a handwritten letter sent afterwards, Wood told Morris she was 'such a great ambassador for our country . . . I want you to know how much you are valued', and enclosed a photograph of the three of them, revealing that when she had posted it on Facebook 'it attracted hundreds of people'.

Morris had lost her pal Henry Anglesey. He was ninety when he died: he had been a constant presence, in person or in his letters, for four decades, always cheerful, always punning, always slightly flirtatious. The light seemed to dim after he went.

When the 2010 Equality Act included transgender status as a protected characteristic, in theory it gave trans people, or some of them, a new level of security. Literature on the topic references 'the trans community'. Morris had never been part of such a thing, though since *Conundrum* she had been a figurehead in spite of herself – a mane of white on the ship's prow. (When she walked into Dylan's on the Criccieth seafront for lunch with the *New York Times* when she was ninety-two, the reporter wrote, 'she materialises from what, due to a trick of the light, looks to be the ocean itself'.) Morris had never been interested in the relationship between sex and politics, but in her tenth decade her position aligned with that of a new cohort fighting gender wars: why must a person be one or the other? She had already called herself 'a born hybrid'. To a certain extent the 2004 Gender Recognition Act had *reinforced* the entrenched binary system, and, in the years that followed, activists had begun calling this out. Morris had come to believe the universe might be non-binary, and she told journalists who came to profile her in these later years, 'I haven't gone from one sex to the other. I'm both now.' To one, she added, 'Of course I had this feeling that I was in the wrong sex and I had to get out of it. But it didn't occur to me then that the ultimate object might be to be both.' The zeitgeist had caught up with her. She said, 'I think more and more people will move to my condition.' They did. A non-binary identity had come to her naturally. 'She became more and more androgynous as she got older,' one family member said, 'in the sense that she was just a person.' As Morris had written about Freya Stark, 'She has been determined to inhabit her chosen self, not a self imposed on her by history or heredity.'

Her literary agent, Derek Johns, retired. He had become fond of his client, and she of him. 'She was one of the most egotistical people I've ever met,' he says, 'but she combined it with charm. She created a carapace about her – you only have to go to the house to see she was an unapologetic egotist. She imposed herself on everything.' He had noticed that she evaded censure for what could be perceived as imperial apologia. 'She was an escape artist – always in flight.' Johns was writing a memoir about her, and he and editor Angus Cargill drove to Wales for lunch with the subject herself at Y Plu, The Feathers, the pub in Llanystumdwy which the community had taken over as a co-op; Morris and Twm were shareholders. On the way there from Trefan, where they had picked her up, she commended the locally made marmalade sold at the pub. 'I'll buy you some,' she promised Cargill. At the bar, Morris said, 'I want two jars of marmalade.' 'I only have one left,' the barman replied, and when he produced it Morris slipped it into her handbag to keep it for herself. Johns went on to publish his memoir, *Ariel*, which Morris told the family she didn't like, even though it was effusively nice about her (she told Johns she liked it) and even though she had curated the facts herself. In 1956 she had said categorically that she left *The Times* 'because they won't let me write the books I want to write'. But now she told Johns she had resigned out of principle because editor William Haley had condoned Suez. A heroic resignation had entered her personal mythology, and it became an accepted truth. Nobody ever challenged her – she had become an impregnable institution, even a kind of oracle who spoke for everyone. There were hurts; there always had been, since she'd taken the plunge. A new biography of Hillary retailed a crass anecdote about Sir Ed not recognising Morris once when she approached him *en femme*. A former OUP editor described, in a literary memoir, Morris turning mannish during an argument at the office, legs akimbo and beefy forefinger wagging. Morris wrote to the author, expressing her distress. But there was usually something to make up for it. Rahul Jacob, her former editor at the *Financial Times*, visited Trefan one spring. 'I never felt there was a generation between us,' Jacob said. They went to Dylan's and talked about Hong Kong. Jacob said the halfway house was the worst outcome. 'She replied, "Is it really the worst?" And of course in the light of what happened, she was right.'

On her own ninetieth birthday Morris accepted the Medal of the Honourable Society of Cymmrodorion for services to Wales. Two weeks later, the Llanbedrog arts centre put on a special day in her honour, producing a bilingual colour brochure which proclaimed: 'Jan is a precious jewel in our community.' Dafydd Iwan was there, the ex-prisoner she and Elizabeth had taken in forty-six years earlier. Twm and his partner Gwyneth Glyn sang a song about kindness and marmalade, and Twm chaired a Q and A session. He enquired, in a question he asked himself, if she remembered taking in the patriot Iwan. Yes, she said, and she would do the same today, if someone came knocking, to shelter one of those 'so-called villains from' – she searched for the words, which she had heard on the television news – 'the Jungle at Calais'. The BBC had got in on the act. Earlier in the year they dispatched Michael Palin up to Trefan to make a film to mark Morris's nonagenarian status. She had written a foreword to the American edition of Palin's *Around the World in 80 Days* – they had never met, and Palin, who had read *Venice* as a young man and compares the experience to 'a flower opening', 'wondered why she did such a kind thing'. During filming, Morris took a fancy to the director, noting 'that very handsome young man' in email exchanges with the production company. In the genial documentary, which went out the week of her birthday, Palin asked her how far she had got up Everest. 'It gets higher every time!' she replied. It was a joke she had been making for years. Palin also asked about her meeting with Che; she mentioned that he'd been a bank manager at that point, not a revolutionary, but by now she had forgotten that she hated bank managers. 'She was warm and responsive company, pretending to be naïve about how TV works,' Palin says. 'I got the feeling that she'd thought about how to play it.' Like everything she had ever done, it was her show. 'She ran things while trying to give the appearance of being scatty,' Palin continues. 'She shuffled a bit, but was hale – it was like visiting some ancient deity in her Welsh cave.' Twm had taught her how to use social media. When Palin's television programme went out, she said, 'I eagerly turned to Twitter in search of favourable comments.'

During the day, she and Elizabeth visited their regular cafés. Morris still drove ferociously fast along the Welsh lanes, and when they parked on Cricieth seafront she accosted strangers to ask if they knew the second half of a song she couldn't get out of her head. Their twelve-year-old Honda had 106,000 miles on the clock as well as a faded European car sticker on the back next to a Welsh one. But Morris got flustered easily, and fell victim to a scammer who pried bank account details from her. There was a sense of partial withdrawal, even if handsome young men caught her eye. When an editor rang with an assignment, she said, 'It's very kind of you to think of me but to be honest I can't be bothered.' She said she was like Ovid, exiled from Rome by Emperor Augustus. 'I have entered a sort of temporary exile myself, incapacitated by sickness, overwhelmed by worries material, familial and philosophical. I have declared myself *hors de combat* for the time being, declining commissions, fighting off visitors and going nowhere.' For much of Morris's life, an assiduously cultivated public image had deliberately obscured an entirely separate private one. By this stage the two were no longer very separate.

Elizabeth moved out of reach. In 2017 Morris wrote, 'that subtle demon of our time, Dementia, [was] coming between us'. It was hard, as a carer. 'I, the mere partner of the affliction, am the one the more insidiously affected.' They carried on. One day, when the Honda was at the garage, she and Elizabeth inadvertently locked themselves *inside* their courtesy

Citroën in a garden centre car park. Without a phone, they were obliged to gesticulate to visitors getting out of another car; the baffled strangers eventually opened the Citroën doors from the outside. When Jan and Elizabeth emerged from the garden centre, they could not get the vehicle started. And so it went on. At night they had supermarket ready-meals – perhaps Ocean Pie – in front of *Mrs Brown's Boys*. Morris listened keenly for news reports about Elon Musk's ventures in electric cars and space travel, telling a journalist that he, Musk, was the most interesting man alive. The wood-burning stove in the middle of the first floor glowed in the darkness of winter evenings, vying with the annunciatory radiance of the television, and both lights weaved on the walls of books. Once in bed next door, Morris heard the owls hooting in the sycamore.

For many years bills had given her a reason to immolate herself in work. She no longer owed money anywhere, but she still had to fill the void. In 2018 she published a short book on a Japanese battleship scuttled by its captain (another strong and lovely effort, essentially a meditation on death), and the BBC produced a specially extended edition of the poet Ian McMillan's Radio 3 programme *The Verb*. At the recording, Morris repeatedly insisted on the centripetal nature of her work – that it was all about her. 'I'd have been a better writer if I weren't so self-obsessed,' she said; most authors would have accepted McMillan's suggestion that other factors were at play. The interview had a farcical tone, like the Norton film. McMillan battled to get a sense of process out of her. When he admired 'cultural and social resonances', she said, 'I do it instinctively rather than intellectually, because I'm not an intellectual writer.' 'Was Wallace Stevens an influence on you?' 'No.' 'What about encountering The Other?' 'I'm generally only encountering myself.' The valiant McMillan did succeed in eliciting the reflection that, 'When I die, people will say that I've written a whole lot of books about one person responding to the world at one moment in history.' It would be a fair assessment. 'You want to draw us in,' McMillan continued. 'Yes, I like you [the reader] and I want you to be on my side.' Respite was brief. 'Is there a moral purpose to all your books taken as a whole?' 'No.'

Two months later, a more successful radio documentary set out to reveal ways in which her feelings on imperialism had shifted. Morris chose eleven pieces of music to illustrate the theme, *Desert Island Discs*-style. The clue was in the programme's title: *The British Empire: An Equivocation*. She started, the musky voice tired now and a touch slurred, 'A pretty equivocal sort of subject these days, is it not?' She picked 'Waltzing Matilda' as one of her tunes. 'The astonishing effrontery of it [the Empire]', she said as the song faded out, 'had a romance of its own.' She was used to dealing with what 'for so long now has been the epitome of political incorrectness. I've insisted there was much to be proud of too. If ever Britons get over their perpetual condition of self-denigration, perhaps they'll be able to look at their imperial postures with a bit of pride and amusement.' This cued in Gilbert and Sullivan's 'I Am the Very Model of a Modern Major-General'. Morris laughed. 'Who knows whether the good things or the bad will be remembered longest? I'm in two minds about it still.' With that, the Cowbridge Male Voice Choir launched into 'The Day Thou Gavest, Lord, Is Ended'.

But it had not ended. 'Having for the moment nothing much else to write', Morris, the writing addict, began a diary column for the *Financial Times*. She had always enjoyed reading published diaries. She had John Evelyn (four volumes, 1879 edition, bought in Marlborough in 1959 for 55 shillings); all of Pepys in the 1899 edition; all of the politician Alan Clark; and three volumes of Victor Klemperer, purchased in Bristol in 1999. Her column focused on daily life (Morris asks Siri what millennials are, and afterwards says 'Thank you' to her phone) as well as the world at large. She mixes the trivial with the serious, and aims at the spontaneity of an actual diary. 'What is it with the birds?' Morris asks after her daily walk of 'a thousand paces', wondering how warblers remember migratory routes. Faber published the pieces, spliced with columns that had appeared in the Welsh-language *O'r Pedwar Gwynt*, as a 188-day 'thought diary' called *In My Mind's Eye*, its cover depicting Morris gurning in front of a blue Morris Minor. The volume includes poems and trivia – 'We all talk to our dogs, cats and horses, do we not?' – as well as complaints about a malfunctioning bedside lamp and familiar Morrisian sermons on the importance of kindness. Retrospectively, she liked to say she had learned the value of that virtue from the Christ Church canons. In reality, the idea of kindness as a life principle had moved in to fill the void left by engagement.

Even she ran out of steam sometimes. She is at her most winning when she can't even fake a diary entry.

> *Not feeling terribly bright,*
> *I lost all compunction to write.*
> *Without more inquiry*
> *I shut up my diary*
> *And read P. G. Wodehouse all night.*

Her capacity for doggerel, limericks included, was undimmed at ninety. The *ubi sunt* thoughts on life's fragility that run through the diary are more characteristic of old age. Morris laments the 'squalor and disillusion' under which the beautiful world has sunk. 'Every single piece of news that reaches me', she wrote from the desk at the foot of the back stairs '. . . speaks of conflict, disaster, deceit, tragedy, sadness, pathos.' Even the remembered past had become a foreign country: 'I cherish the memory of Manhattan before the rot set in'; the Arabs among whom she spent so many mostly happy years have been 'coarsened, cheapened and betrayed'. But she mourned Britain most deeply. Reading about Prime Minister Theresa May setting off for a summit, Morris notes, 'Gone is the charisma that would have attended her predecessors . . . in the days when we thought of ourselves as pioneers and champions of democracy.'[*] Between the elegiac mesto she strives, mostly valiantly, to sound upbeat notes. She urges bonhomie all round, including upwards to a deity she doesn't believe in. 'Goodnight God!' she ends one entry. 'Goodnight, and

---

[*] She knew it was not just charisma that had gone. In 1997, when Morris published *Fifty Years of Europe*, British GDP was greater than China's and India's combined. By 2020, when *In My Mind's Eye* appeared, the two economies together were six times larger.

good luck to you!' But *In My Mind's Eye* topples into the embarrassing zone. Morris includes letters to *The Times* that the paper understandably declined to publish, including one in which she expressed the desire to marry her cat. She recorded new symptoms of decrepitude: 'In the middle of the night I awoke with the need to have a shit.' This was not Pepys, nor even Alan Clark.

The BBC chose *In My Mind's Eye* as its Book of the Week on Radio 4. When Suki heard Janet Suzman reading its perorations on kindness, 'I screamed at the radio.'

Royalties came to about £50,000 a year, and new editions generated a modest income stream of their own. For the first time, a government-owned Chinese house bought the rights to translate *Pax* into Mandarin, semaphoring imperial ambition. Letters from readers also still flowed. The spidery hands of old soldiers might have woven their last web, but a gap-year student wrote a six-page missive after an art history course in Venice, ending, 'and thank you most of all for making me feel that there is someone, somewhere who just understands perfectly'. *Conundrum* continued to give succour. An eighteen-year-old Scottish Catholic, D., was starting out on gender reassignment treatment ('I have had to go private as my uncle is the family doctor'). D.'s girlfriend, who was in on it, had bought a swimming costume as a gift, as they went to a lake to bathe in private sometimes. 'You are my heroine,' D. told Morris. A man wrote from St John's in Canada; he had lately read *Conundrum* and had a lot to say. But it was too late for him: 'my emotional needs have been a lifelong hunger that will now follow me alone to my grave'. A doctor contacted Morris from New Zealand to say he had loaned the book to an 'extremely conservative older colleague' and it had caused 'a major change in attitude'. A Swede working as an assistant air traffic controller sent a photograph of Fatima, the nurse at the Clinique du Parc, 'to bring back happy memories'. The correspondent had been in Morris's room.

She was popular as a writer if she was anything, but as a person never a populist. Morris had lived through sixteen presidents, Coolidge to

Trump, and eighteen British prime ministers, Baldwin to Johnson, so she had seen too much to embrace the populist belief, gaining ground, that individuals fell into two groups, real ones and manipulative elite ones. But Trump – whose power lay in the dissemination of that idea – was unavoidable on the radio news.

> I have always rather liked his political style, as against his personal ideals, which are almost grotesquely crude. It is an All-American way: America First! Make America Great Again! As one with a sneaking sympathy for patriotism, whatever flag it flies, I respond to this approach as instinctively as any redneck bigot.
>
> Then again, although I loathe Trump's attitude to women, I think there is something forgivably childlike in his behaviour, like the sulks and outbursts of a spoilt schoolboy.

The published diaries (a second volume had followed) catch the rhythm of these years; but they were thin. Critical response was respectful. In private, one friend, hearing them read on the radio, said they were wretched. Some below-the-line comments in the serialised extracts were unkind – though the hate brigade were policing everyone by then, and the response to anything Morris wrote or had ever written had, in some quarters, changed forever. But she had to go on writing. Mark says, 'She kept control until the end.'

Lockdowns made everything worse. Facing the unknowability of Covid-19, Llŷn people talked over farm gates about the English, certain to move to Wales to distance themselves from their overpopulated land in times of plague – they saw them doing so, as cottage after cottage fell into nasty English hands. Elizabeth went into hospital again as the pandemic raged. In November, when all the leaves had fallen from the Trefan sycamore, the same hospital admitted Morris. She had a private room, not a bed on a ward like Elizabeth. Twm read to her from *The Welsh Fairy Book*, the first volume the boy Jim had bought with his own money back in Clevedon. When regulations did not permit visitors,

BOTH

Twm took things in. One day she asked for wine. The weather remained overcast. Twm wrote messages on sheets of paper, and on 9 November sent in a note reminding her of a dream he had had, in which she had said, 'You are me and I am you forever.' He wrote to her, 'One edge of me has long since merged with you.' Eleven days later, she died.

> Sometimes down by the river I almost think I have discovered the real purpose of my pilgrimage, the last solution to my conundrum. But then the light changes, the wind shifts, a cloud moves across the sun, and the meaning of it all once again escapes me.

AFTERWORD

Twm scattered her ashes on the Island of the Pool of the Cliff of the Enchantress in the Dwyfor. When Elizabeth died four years after Jan, in 2024, half her ashes went there too; the other half joined Virginia in the Saxon churchyard in Waterperry. The slate headstone still leans against the stepped bookcases in the Trefan library.

'I want to be remembered as Jan "Empire" Morris,' she often said. 'But the headlines will read, "Sex Change Author Dies".' Many more or less did, but the obituaries were respectful, and they appeared all over the world, in every country she had skewered on the page. The *Allegorizings* collection appeared posthumously, as Morris had planned. It included a six-page fantasy about the 'reassuringly common' Princess Diana. Despite the warnings to the children, in the end whimsy had taken over, and there was nothing to shock in the pages of Morris's final book.

The Clevedon Civic Society unveiled a Blue Plaque on the house at 1 Herbert Road, Clevedon, and after the ceremony Twm sang a song in the front garden, on the path where the boy Jim had set out with his telescope. Trefan Morys, under the aegis of a trust, is to become a writer's house, set in its own 'woodland grotto'.

Long before there was any talk of Morris's biography, I heard a radio interview with Tom Hooper, director of the Hollywood movie *The Danish Girl*, which told the story of Lili Elbe, one of the first people to have gender reassignment surgery. The film had just been nominated for four Oscars. Hooper said *Conundrum* had inspired him. Morris was in her ninetieth year then, and still a pioneer. When I came to write this book, I realised she had died at the exact moment when transgender issues took on unexpected cultural and social urgency. The debate grew toxic immediately: the Royal Society of Literature, where the lecture at which

I had introduced Morris took place all those years ago, became embroiled in a rancorous public dispute over the obituary which appeared in its magazine. (One national newspaper headline ran 'INSTITUTION CAUGHT UP IN "GENDER CENSORING" ROW'.) Perhaps one can detect the irony that Morris was always quick to observe herself.

I said in chapter 17 that after Morris had concluded she was 'both now' she wondered if more people might acknowledge a sense of gender fluidity. Although they did, as she predicted, the binary nature of sex remains contentious. In 2025 the UK Supreme Court ruled that in the 2010 Equality Act 'sex' means 'biological sex', and the same year, on his first day in office, President Trump signed an executive order declaring there are only two biological sexes. Were Morris alive now, she might be denied entry to her beloved Manhattan, as information in her passport would differ from the sex assigned on her birth certificate in Clevedon in 1926. The storm rages on, but *Conundrum* remains a landmark of trans history. It was the first literary trans memoir, the first to flourish in the cultural mainstream and the first to gain traction all over the world. I meet people almost every day who remember reading it, either back in the seventies or last week – people who are themselves neither trans nor invested in one side or another of the current polarised debate. Almost everyone uses the word 'moving' to describe the reading experience.

What of the book's legacy among trans women and men? Three months after Morris died, a trans poet concluded a critical appreciation in the *Paris Review*, '*Conundrum* belongs near the headwaters of a great and nourishing river of Western trans self-representation.' Although young trans people now have a wide range of material to digest, multiple blogs and thousands of comments indicate that many still turn to Morris's memoir. But as the movement has fragmented and deepened, the issues mentioned in chapter 15 have taken on fresh salience. Two ideas in particular that Morris established in *Conundrum* have metamorphosed into points of ferocious dispute. First, the notion, also discussed in chapter 10, that a trans individual knows from a young age that they have been born into the wrong body. Second, the assertion that surgery

AFTERWORD

is the summit of the journey – that the body has primacy. Even in the introduction to a beautifully produced fiftieth-anniversary edition of *Conundrum* (one of several), a trans writer accuses Morris of 'closed-minded sophistry' for packaging the story too neatly, 'almost sanctifying her [own] experience' and eschewing polemic. They wonder how Morris could 'show so little curiosity about the social and political meanings of traditional gender roles' – the same critique feminists levelled first time round, applied now to a transformed social landscape. Perhaps most significantly, Morris always said that being trans was not central to her identity, and many today resent that attitude.

Since the trans community became visible, it has spoken in diverse voices. Morris enabled that polyphony. Historical revisionism is anyway as unavoidable as the grave, and debates will continue to gain nuance and complexity. But she'll be part of them.

Peter Fleming once said Morris was 'with but not of Sir John Hunt's expedition', and similarly, she remains a detached figure in the gender wars. I do think, though, that future readers looking for reassurance that they are not alone will find it in *Conundrum*. As Morris wrote about her experience of other trans memoirs, 'If they [the authors] did not quite share my riddle, at least they would have understood it.'

As for Empire: even as the zeitgeist shifts, historians and pundits accept the ambiguities of *Pax*. In a radio documentary immediately after Morris died, the historian Sathnam Sanghera, author of *Empireland*, said of Morris, 'She comes across as fundamentally humane [in *Pax*]. She's not a culture warrior ... everyone's so bloody angry now, and she had nuance, that rare thing when it comes to Empire.' Her prestige in the field has not only weathered the cultural climate but risen above it to thinner air. It is hard to imagine that *Pax* will not be read in a hundred years. Sanghera continued, 'If I had to give one book to someone to understand Empire, it would be *Pax*.'

I have not mentioned every title Morris published in these pages, because this is an attempt at a life story, not a bibliography. There are still more questions than answers, with and without all those books. It remains hard to reconcile the two pictures of Elizabeth: strong woman and codependent victim. I have let the gaps in the record speak for themselves, but I do know that none of the volumes could have been written without Elizabeth. She carried the domestic burden, and some of the emotional one too. The blanks in Morris's own story – why she was unkind to people she loved, and much more – are themselves part of her, unknowable. Does the life overshadow the work? Sometimes. Are the two mutually dependent? Yes, but I have not laboured the theme. Could I, the lowly biographer, modulate the space between the narcissist and the Funny Girl? Probably not. As she said of her own understanding of the conundrum, it was like the clouds moving on and off the surface of the Dwyfor, intermittently obscuring the sun.

That essay on the Triestino wharf marked the start of a lifelong nostalgia for something that didn't exist – relief from the agony of the human condition itself. It was one of the themes that made Morris's work popular. There was no actual relief in life, except temporarily, at the keyboard, or stroking a cat. Yet the yearning remained, beyond gender; in Trieste and forever, Morris longed to be on the inside of that door she had only glimpsed from the outside. She cherished a numinous, indefinable unity which, by the end, she accepted was unattainable. We all have to accept it, sooner or later.

I once heard a wise practitioner say that the older you get as a biographer, the less you are prepared to tick anyone off for their failings. No biography tells the whole story about anything or anyone, and a biographer's role is neither to judge nor to side with her subject, just as a writer should never side with herself. I think Morris's strongest books will stand the test of time. As a descriptive writer I believe she will always be up there among the best. And I still think she lived an almost insanely interesting life. She *was* the twentieth century.

Her friend Paul Theroux once wrote to her fondly to say, 'Wherever I go, you have been there first.' I feel the same. The Ota River estuary, the Gare du Nord in pre-dawn cold, the medieval rookeries of Cairo – those places belong to her now. So perhaps the biographical subject exacts revenge in the end.

At the finish line I have accepted the tensions that exist within any presentation of Morris that seeks 'truth'. The gulf between the monster and the humane, lovable companion on and off the page is one that cannot be bridged – I only hope I have shown, in this book, a few currents of desire, thought and energy that might connect the two. 'Do you like her?' is the question I am most often asked. But it's not like that. I am human. So was she.

SOURCE NOTES

Guide to Notes
All books published in London unless otherwise indicated.

ARCHIVAL SOURCES
FA Faber & Faber Archive
FC Family Collection
GA Guardian Archive, John Rylands Research Institute and Library, University of Manchester
NUKA News UK Archive at Rainham, Essex
NLW National Library of Wales
OUPA Oxford University Press Archive

ABBREVIATIONS
JM James/Jan Morris
EM Elizabeth Morris
MM Mark Morris
SM Suki Morys
TM Twm Morys

MG *Manchester Guardian*
NYT *New York Times*
RS *Rolling Stone*
TLS *Times Literary Supplement*

ABBREVIATIONS OF BOOKS BY JM
50 Yrs Fifty Years of Europe: An Album, 1997
ATC Among the Cities, 1985
AWHiW A Writer's House in Wales, Washington DC, 2002
AWW A Writer's World, 2003; *The World: Life and Travel* in the US
CE Coronation Everest, 1958
Climax The Climax of an Empire, Vol. 2 of *Pax Britannica*, 1968
CtC Coast to Coast, 1956; *As I Saw the USA* in the US
FTT Farewell the Trumpets, Vol. 3 of *Pax Britannica*, 1978
HC Heaven's Command, Vol. 1 of *Pax Britannica*, 1973
IMME In My Mind's Eye, 2018
Last Letters Last Letters from Hav, 1985
PoaTL Pleasures of a Tangled Life, 1989

SiO Sultan in Oman, 1957
TA Thinking Again, 2020
THK The Hashemite Kings, 1959
TMoS The Market of Seleukia, 1957; *Islam Inflamed* in the US
TMoW The Matter of Wales, Oxford, 1984
Trieste Trieste and the Meaning of Nowhere, 2001

All quotes from MM/SM/TM from interviews with the author unless indicated.
All letters from JM to EM, and all extracts from Elizabeth's diary, in private Family Collection.

Notes

vii *What a nightmare hiatus* Trieste

INTRODUCTION

3 *silly like us* W. H. Auden, 'In Memory of W. B. Yeats', 1939
3 *union . . . has given nobility* Conundrum, 1974
5 *I think it could* JM to Bob Weil, book proposal, 21 Jul 2001, courtesy Bob Weil
6 *ambiguous epic* IMME
6 *the centrepiece of my* TA
6 *the recollections of a* Foreword, Leslie Glass, *The Changing of Kings: Memories of Burma 1934–1949*, 1985
6 *I've never heard such* courtesy W. W. Norton & Company
7 *the grave sound of* 50 Yrs
7 *Come with me now* e.g. 7/8 Nov 2009, FT

I TWENTY-EIGHT KNOTS FOR SANDY HOOK

9 *one of the longest* 27 May 1910, *Monmouthshire Beacon*
11 *Oh, she had heard* 23 Sep 1995, *Independent*
11 *It is ripping of* 29 Nov 1914, FC
12 *We are having a* 3 Mar 1915, FC
13 *full of the Welsh* Trish Morris to SW
13 *The record of the* Apr 1915, *Monmouth and Over Monnow Parish Magazine*, courtesy Monmouth Museum
14 *conventions of the day, et seq.* Conundrum
15 *My mother, who preferred* PoaTL
15 *Another one done, Wally* Trish Morris to SW
16 *the horrible fashion . . . attacking each note of* 1 Jul 1929, *Musical Times*
17 *an exemplar of dingy* 50 Yrs
17 *sitting alone, pale, dark-eyed* AWW
17 *Gandhi was sixty-two, I* FTT

18 *Only a grassy hill . . . I can see those . . . irrational surge of pride* PoaTL
18 *most prized possession except* ibid.
19 *identifying passing ships for* ibid.
19 *gave private insight into* Conundrum
19 *seemed to me more* Trieste
19 *I could always see . . . A lumbering old* ibid.
19 *the restrained mysticism of* TA
19 *Quaker strain* PoaTL
19 *no land stood between* ibid.
20 *tantalising visions of Manhattan's* ibid.
20 *grown up . . . great ships . . . I pored over their* Trieste
20 *CHRIS SUCCESSFUL PLEASE MEET* FC
21 *I was born just* HC, Intro to 1998 edn
21 *I can myself remember* JM, *The World Bank*, 1963
21 *A lost England made* Trieste
21 *great symbol of our* The Baldwin Age, ed. John Raymond, 1960
22 *In his dreams the* TA
22 *Everything Victorian was generally* PoaTL
22 *low dishonest decade* W. H. Auden, 'September 1, 1939', 1939
22 *This is the midnight* Rudyard Kipling, 'The Storm Cone', 1932
22 *Exile was mine when* Trieste
23 *Everyone was happier there* Desert Island Discs, 1 Apr 1983, BBC Radio 4
23 *We lived medievally, a* Conundrum
23 *sometimes passed rather comically* ibid.
23 *Three big chestnuts grew* ibid.
23 *my first intimations of . . . beyond my telescope's range* ibid.
23 *The style of it . . . left a mark on* 19 Dec 2016, 'A Very Embodiment of Simple Goodness', *The American Scholar*
24 *the one true spiritual* JM, *Contact!*, 2009
24 *grubby and malodorous in* Richard Davenport-Hines, *History in the House*, 2024
24 *beyond all dogma* Contact!
24 *How tall the candles* Conundrum
24 *I spent a string . . . On the contrary, those* TA
25 *I was raised on* PoaTL
25 *This is the best* FC
26 *I hardly knew my* TA
26 *All hearts seem open* Raymond, *The Baldwin Age*
26 *Waves of anger and* W. H. Auden, 'September 1, 1939'
26 *He was the most . . . seemed to pick up . . . made me feel gauche* PoaTL
27 *Even in the 1930s* ibid.
28 *flint-girt fortress* The Diaries of Evelyn Waugh, ed. Michael Davie, 1976
28 *The old hierarchical structure* B. W. Johnson, 'The Ludlow Years', Papers of B. W. Johnson, Lancing College Archives

SOURCE NOTES TO PAGES 29–41

29 *Dear mum, Thanks for* n.d., FC
29 *I was beaten more . . . not really unhappy . . . I was habitually frightened . . . Conundrum*
29 *When I thrilled to* ibid.
29 *nothing fitted . . . not the clumsy embraces* ibid.
30 *If any institution could* ibid.
30 *You won't need those . . . Though everything went wrong* Lancing College Magazine, Lent Term 1943, Lancing College Archives
31 *The works of Aeschylus* Johnson, 'The Ludlow Years'
31 *He was renowned for . . . he left to undergo* Lancing College Magazine, Summer Term 1943, Lancing College Archives
31 *Miss Morris, is music* Desert Island Discs, 1 Apr 1983
32 *There's such a sound . . . huge . . . Thanks so much for, et seq.* 'Music in Air Force Blue', 29 Aug 2005, BBC Radio 4
32 *I was a young* TA
33 *The English stage is* 28 Dec 1943, Western Daily Press
33 *The soldier musicians of . . . and in that very* PoaTL
33 *singing in a very* ibid.
34 *I learned that when* JM, *Allegorizings*, 2021
34 *Canteen packed with troops* Noël Coward, *Future Indefinite*, 1954
35 *at the very moment . . . All around us were* Contact!
35 *The only authority I've* PoaTL
35 *In the army of* 6 Oct 2006, Guardian
36 *resplendent in Sam Browne . . . and as I remember* PoaTL

2 SOLDIERING

38 *I was entering a* Conundrum
38 *Morris was rather better* Alan Whicker, in *Jan Morris: Around the World in Eighty Years*, ed. Paul Clements, Bridgend, 2006
38 *half-empty, lonely, defeated* Bookclub, 5 Jun 2008, BBC Radio 4
38 *In the evenings especially* 50 Yrs
38 *desolately impotent in the, et seq.* JM, in Ian Warrell, *Turner and Venice*, 2003
39 *and I remember still* Conundrum
39 *Giorgione's 'La Tempesta' began* PoaTL
39 *drinking grappa, practising our, et seq.* Conundrum
39 *all but uncontrollably down, et seq.* 3 May 1996, Guardian
40 *a grand office in* Alan Whicker, *Whicker's War*, 2005
40 *belonging to an exclusive* ibid.
40 *I loved it from, et seq.* TA
40 *I liked the lean* Conundrum
40 *glitter and club-like exclusivity* ibid.
40 *for if there was* ibid.
40 *Among the officers there, et seq.* ibid.
40 *James had made great* Bill Norman to SW
41 *impostor* Conundrum

SOURCE NOTES TO PAGES 41–52

41 *and told me commiseratingly* 50 Yrs
41 *I watched the shifting* ibid.
41 *Getting to know Venice* ibid.
41 *smoky looking, hooded-eyed, tweedy* Contact!
41 *In a very short* Winston Churchill, *Triumph and Tragedy* (Vol. VI, *The Second World War*), 1953
42 *the subalterns of my* 50 Yrs
42 *James was good at* Bill Norman to SW
43 *Europe distilled – the civilised* Trieste
44 *Rhine wine after all* Conundrum
44 *of particular gentleness of . . . Without a pause, apparently* Climax
45 *I remember going swanning* Bill Norman to SW
45 *we sampled the society* Conundrum
45 *licence to wander far* ibid.
46 *James was very competent* Bill Norman to SW
46 *Our job was to* ibid.
46 *It was awkward . . . We made promises we* ibid.
46 *They were on the* Tom Segev, 'Origins of the Israel–Palestine Conflict', *Empire* podcast, ep. 40
46 *The most fervent apologists* 19 Mar 1971, *Times*
47 *magnificently civilian, even Bohemian . . . the first official of* PoaTL
47 *Every blue-eyed Arab was* FTT
47 *one of the grand originals* Conundrum
47 *full of saturnine charm* ibid.
47 *deliberately outrageous* JM, 'One of a Kind', Darlith Goffa Flynyddol Lloyd George / Annual Lloyd George Memorial Lecture, Cricieth, 2004
47 *teaching me tricks of* Conundrum
47 *we were being driven . . . the sky looks so* ibid.
48 *I loved him* ibid.
48 *represented the greatest danger* James Barr, *Lords of the Desert*, 2018
49 *new Studebakers that looked* JM, *Manhattan '45*, 1987
49 *in an idiosyncratic and* JM, 18 Jun 1999, *Independent*
49 *only nominally prose* Andrew Taylor, *God's Fugitive*, 1999
49 *the soil of Arabia . . . gaunt untrodden mountain rocks . . . the glassiness of this* ibid.
50 *I developed in the* Conundrum
50 *first admitted impotence* FTT
50 *tryst with destiny* from Nehru's speech on the eve of independence, 14 Aug 1947
50 *the centrepiece of my* TA
51 *for the first time* FTT
51 *We got fed up* Bill Norman to SW
51 *I felt myself to be . . . totally separate and distinct* Conundrum
52 *Far from making a* ibid.
52 *confirmed my intuition that . . . My own libidinous fancies* ibid.

3 BRONZED HERO

54 *Darling sis Betty* n.d., FC
54 *a blur of shade* JM, *Fisher's Face*, 1995
54 *lofty and cool and* Climax
54 *Oh if only I . . . DARLING MARGARET DIED FRIDAY . . . My darling baba, Granny* FC
55 *My life has been* SM to SW
56 *Dear Tuppence, I've got* JM to EM, 24 Mar 1948
57 *I'm spending a miserable* JM to EM, 22 Apr 1948
57 *There are really very* JM to EM, 11 Feb 1949
57 *Don't expect a bronzed* JM to EM, 20 Aug 1948
57 *I've got a boil* JM to EM, 24 Aug 1948
59 *performed with disrespect on* Climax
59 *You cannot read the* Peter Hennessy, *Never Again*, 1992
59 *opened the way to* E. H. Carr, cited in Richard Davenport-Hines, *Enemies Within*, 2018
59 *Coca-Colonization* TMoS
60 *immense and sinister Woolworth's* W. H. Auden, *Prose*, Vol. 1, Princeton, 1997
60 *I was happy working . . . My friends were mostly* Conundrum
61 *Just saving a bit* Contact!
62 *PLEASE MARRY ME STOP* NLW
62 *sexual ambiguities* Conundrum
62 *ANSWER AS OVER TELEPHONE . . . SHALL I MAKE ENGAGEMENT* FC
62 *She's really rather awful* JM to EM, 11 Feb 1949
63 *fathomless* Conundrum
63 *from a magnificent steamship . . . a place of incessant . . . Scarcely an hour went* NLW
64 *is to keep the* Tony Judt, *Postwar*, 2005
64 *profound consternation . . . it was considered highly* 28 Jul 1950, *Spectator*
64 *Must go and make* EM to Enid Morris, 18 Nov 1949, FC
65 *a mature and able* Christ Church Archive
65 *You can't believe how* Hugh Trevor-Roper to Charles Stuart, in Adam Sisman, *Hugh Trevor-Roper*, 2010
65 *There is no pretending, et seq.* Intro to 1982 edn, Alexander Kinglake, *Eothen* (1844)
65 *poseur that he was* 18 Jun 1999, *Independent*
66 *I am no writer* 5 Jun 1976, *Spectator*
66 *I believe T. E. Lawrence* ibid.
67 *make something new out* Intro to Kinglake, *Eothen*
67 *Morison . . . invited me up, et seq.* Nicolas Barker papers, Cambridge University Library
68 *had not had their* Jean Monnet, *Memoirs*, 1978
68 *Graduated from the* Cherwell Christ Church Archive
68 *Could go deeper* ibid.
68 *covering the chief aspects* Donald Tyerman to JM, 31 May 1951, NUKA
68 *quite out of the, et seq.* Tyerman memo, 17 May 1951, NUKA
69 *the old firm* Nicholas Shakespeare, *Ian Fleming: The Complete Man*, 2023

69 *affected my attitudes forever* PoaTL
69 *god-like specialist writers* Peregrine Worsthorne, *Tricks of Memory*, 1993
69 *a high-risk activity, requiring* Worsthorne, in Clements, *Jan Morris: Around the World in Eighty Years*
70 *The lunches never varied* Louis Heren, *Memories of Times Past*, 1988
70 *bangers and mash . . . chippy* Worsthorne, *Tricks of Memory*
71 *In those days, James . . . to scruffy bohemians busily* Worsthorne, in Clements, *Jan Morris: Around the World in Eighty Years*
71 *At no point was* ibid.
71 *that daily tapestry of* FTT
71 *You will have had* J. I. M. Stewart to JM, 17 Jul 1951, FC
71 *What's become of Waring* Robert Browning, 'Waring', 1842
72 *Quilliam was most friendly, et seq.* JM to EM, 20 Dec 1951
72 *The Foreign Office has* Cyril Quilliam, 15 Oct 1951, cited in Iverach McDonald, *Struggles in War and Peace* (Vol. V, *The History of* The Times), 1984
73 *No true incompatibility divides* 30 Apr 1951, *Times*
73 *The British gave me* Ernest A. Gross, 2 Oct 1951, Foreign Relations of the United States, 1952–1954, Iran, Vol. X, history.state.gov
73 *British Task in the* 28 Dec 1951, *Times*
73 *particularly nice . . . David Walker, et seq.* JM to EM, 23 Dec 1951
73 *Christmas Day was ghastly . . . The 9th Lancers was* JM to EM, 26 Dec 1951
74 *Alan Whicker of Exchange* JM to EM, 30 Dec 1951
74 *I'm afraid I got* JM to EM, n.d.
74 *MANY THANKS FOR EXCELLENT* William Casey to JM, 25 Jan 1952, NUKA
74 *is doing much more* Tyerman to Francis Mathew, 23 Dec 1951, NUKA
74 *The chief of staff* JM to EM, 16 Jan 1952
74 *I'm sent flowers and* EM, diary, n.d. Jan 1952
75 *When the British Council* Barr, *Lords of the Desert*
75 *Poor time here, and* JM to EM, 9 Feb 1952
75 *beau idéal of the* 14 Dec 1992, *Independent*
75 *Living here is really* JM to EM, 29 Feb 1952
75 *transformed* JM to EM, 5 Mar 1952
75 *They are absolutely splendid* JM to EM, 20 Apr 1952
76 *It is difficult to* Ralph Deakin to JM, 27 Feb 1952, NUKA
76 *a rocket* JM to EM, 23 Mar 1952
76 *I tell everyone about* ibid.
76 *Thanks for the kindness . . . As you can imagine* EM to Deakin, 27 Mar 1952, NUKA
76 *I just can't wait, et seq.* EM to JM, 2 Apr 1952
77 *PLEASE COME HOME SOON* Deakin to JM, 23 Apr 1952, NUKA
78 *I was born of* John Berger, 'Self-Portrait 1914–18', *Collected Poems*, Thirsk, North Yorkshire, 2014
78 *until finally, one winter* Conundrum

4 KNOCKING THE BASTARD OFF

80 *Sport was now a, et seq.* CE, Introductory to 2003 edn
81 *whether some of the ... They would prefer greatly* Larry Kirwan to Deakin, 11 Oct 1952, NUKA
81 *I know so little* JM to McDonald, 19 Jan 1953, NUKA
82 *if only to keep ... have twenty-six-year-old ... he is tough and* Gerald Norman to Arthur Hutchinson, 4 Feb 1953, NUKA
82 *I was horribly ambitious* 28 May 1978, *Times*
82 *I wish Morris didn't* JM, 'Reporting the Conquest of Mount Everest', Sep 1953, *Times House Journal*
83 *summoned up a wan* CE, Introductory to 2003 edn
83 *utterly inexperienced and physically* David Holden, 17 Mar 1974, *NYT*
83 *Eggs and bacon in* JM to EM, 23 Mar 1953
83 *Everything is less strange ... rather a common girl* JM to EM, n.d.
84 *The embassy people in* JM to EM, 25 Mar 1953
84 *not only brave and* 14 Dec 2002, *Independent*
84 *In his cups had* Hutchinson to Norman, 19 May 1953, NUKA
84 *I have been having* John Hunt to Norman, 10 Mar 1953, NUKA
84 *He has a rather* JM to EM, 28 Mar 1953
84 *The squalor in Kathmandu* JM to EM, 4 Apr 1953
85 *passwords passed from hand ... instinct with the spirit* CE
85 *Give my love most* JM to EM, 4 Apr 1953
85 *Sahib! Sahib! One frog* 'Reporting the Conquest', *Times House Journal*
85 *outside a Buddhist temple* JM to EM, 4 Apr 1953
85 *There's an audience around ... The further one goes, et seq.* JM to EM, 4 Apr 1953
86 *My dearest darling just ... Easter day's [march] was a, et seq.* JM to EM, 6 Apr 1953
86 *a sombre bulletin from* CE
86 *We get to Namche, et seq.* JM to EM, 16 Apr 1953
87 *too dead and aloof ... odious* CE
87 *I can see the* JM to EM, 20 Apr 1953
87 *in time for the* ibid.
87 *One new major problem, et seq.* JM to 'Fletcher', 22 Apr 1953, NUKA
88 *Everything, thank you John* CE
88 *My tent is far* JM to EM, 8 May 1953
88 *so I'm feeling rather* JM to EM, 3 May 1953
89 *ghastly with glacier cream* CE
89 *I know who the* JM to EM, 8 May 1953
89 *uncomfortable bedmates* CE
89 *authority and responsibility* ibid.
89 *PS Congratulations on your, et seq.* JM to EM, 23 May 1953
90 *I could have done* Harriet Tuckey, *Everest: The First Ascent*, 2013
90 *big and bold* 14 Jan 2009, *Times*
90 *movement between tents is, et seq.* Hunt to JM, 27 May 1953, NUKA

SOURCE NOTES TO PAGES 90–101

90 *Terribly rushed now, et seq.* JM to EM, 29 May 1953
90 *his high shanty tent* CE
90 *going strongly up the* ibid.
91 *as tense as a* ibid.
91 *Agency messages confirm that* ibid.
91 *There they are!* ibid.
91 *Well George, we knocked* Wilfrid Noyce, *South Col*, 1954
91 *oozing icebog* CE
92 *loathsome, decaying wilderness* ibid.
92 *stiff as ramrods . . . I extracted my typewriter* ibid.
92 *He was going to* Allegorizings
92 *so he did – just* ibid.
92 *the jackals of fame* CE
92 *A moment of fumbling* ibid.
93 *Climbed 29 May Hillary* NUKA
94 *the splendid trophy brought* 2 Jun 1953, *Times*
94 *The British nation was* Foreword, George Lowe, *Letters from Everest*, 2013
94 *marched . . . in the hope of, et seq.* JM to EM, 14 Jun 1953
94 *like converging scavengers, to* CE
95 *HAVE BEEN OFFERED VARIOUS* JM to Norman, 15 Jun 1953, NUKA
95 *YES DISASTROUS* Norman to JM, 16 Jun 1953, NUKA
95 *Morris has returned, and* Norman to Hutchinson, 13 Jul 1953, NUKA
95 *Furious about this* Victoria Glendinning, *Vita*, 1983
96 *Do you want me* JM to EM, 31 Mar 1953
96 *The Sherpas set off, et seq.* *The Conquest of Everest*, 1953
97 *A weir of whirling* Louis MacNeice, *Autumn Sequel*, *Collected Poems*, 2016
97 *We all admired his* John Hunt, *The Ascent of Everest*, 1953
97 *Can you help me . . . I shall never have* JM to McDonald, 13 Sep 1953, NUKA

5 PERPETUAL THEATRE

98 *The dining car coach* JM to EM, 11 Oct 1953
98 *still the stormy, husky* CtC
98 *650 dollars, it has* JM to EM, 28 Oct 1953
98 *The combination of Commonwealth* JM to Norman, 31 Oct 1953, NUKA
98 *common* JM to EM, n.d.
99 *devices that change the* CtC
99 *Some motels provide coffee* ibid.
100 *We have been staying* EM to Betty Bourne, n.d. Feb 1954, FC
100 *went to great trouble* Contact!
100 *a caricature of a* CtC
101 *It's a lot of* ibid.
101 *The melting pot has . . . there emerges the familiar* ibid.
101 *teeming nation of nations* Walt Whitman, Preface, *Leaves of Grass*, New York, 1855
101 *America changed my life* Al Alvarez, *Where Did It All Go Right?*, 1999

365

101 *absolutely brilliant* Norman to JM, 7 Dec 1953, NUKA
101 *so we can get* Norman to JM, 30 Sep 1954, FC
102 *no hope ... All I* Monteith to JM, 26 Feb 1954, FA
102 *I don't know if* JM to Charles Monteith, 24 Oct 1954, FA
103 *Rubbish & dull. Pointless* Toby Faber, *Faber & Faber*, 2019
103 *I wanted to be* Allegorizings
103 *profoundly disconcerting* CtC
103 *abuse so theatrical and, et seq.* ibid.
103 *the whole performance, et seq.* PoaTL
103 *The American Way is* CtC
104 *Coca-Cola is the Danzig* 29 Mar 1950, *Le Monde*
104 *essence of capitalism* Richard F. Kuisel, 'Coca-Cola and the Cold War', *French Historical Studies*, Vol. 17, No. 1, Spring 1991
104 *the great greyness* Dennis Potter, *The Glittering Coffin*, 1960
105 *the supreme event* 11 May 1953, House of Commons
105 *the most glamorous room, et seq.* PoaTL
106 *The din of a* Kinglake, *Eothen*, 1844
107 *almost the last demonstration* AWW
107 *Circassians in long black, et seq.* TMoS
107 *and the Assyrians were* FTT
107 *multiple rivalries which were* 1 Mar 2014, *Daily Telegraph*
107 *diplomats and countless intelligence* ibid.
108 *still very much a* TMoS
108 *I hope you will* Wilfrid Noyce to JM, n.d., FC
108 *a very parfit* Noyce, *South Col*, 1954
108 *We had a simply* EM to Norman, 19 Nov 1955, NUKA
109 *a crippling backlog of* TMoS
109 *that noble amateur of* ibid.
109 *The air of get-rich-quick, et seq.* ibid.
109 *separatist ambitions* SiO
110 *concerned essentially with oil* SiO, Intro to 2008 edn
110 *protected the Sultan's domains, et seq.* SiO
110 *a certain niggling timidity, et seq.* ibid.
110 *The soft scent of* SiO, Intro to 2008 edn
110 *The sultanate of Muscat* ibid.
111 *like two ends of* Fleming, Intro to *SiO*
111 *Well, we've been on* W. H. Auden & Christopher Isherwood, *Journey to a War*, 1939
111 *He went into the* Tom Pocock, *East and West of Suez*, 1986
111 *He is such fun* JM to EM, 14 Dec 1955
111 *[o]ne of the great* Shakespeare, *Ian Fleming*
111 *it was almost as* 11 Nov 1974, *Times*
112 *roared* SiO
112 *how cordial their smiles* ibid.

112 *Colonel Fleming has told, et seq.* Norman to Mr Parks, 5 Jan 1956, NUKA
113 *That is why you* Sir John E. Hugh Boustead, *The Wind of Morning*, 1971
113 *this of course his* Norman to Mr Woods, 15 Jan 1956, NUKA
113 *resolved to hold out* Alan McGregor to Norman, 23 May 1955, NUKA
113 *a thousand congratulations* Monteith to JM, 8 Mar 1956, FA
113 *beautiful wife... The family had made* Pocock, *East and West of Suez*
114 *the mystic conviction that* Desert Island Discs, 1 Apr 1983
114 *When my first soufflé* Roberta Cowell, *Roberta Cowell's Story by Herself*, 1954
115 *WE LOVE YOU MORE* Christine Jorgensen, *A Personal Autobiography*, New York, 1967
115 *BRONX GI BECOMES A* ibid.
115 *riddle... that I was born* Conundrum
115 *and as I groped* ibid.
116 *His article in last* Stewart Perowne to Norman, 3 Mar 1956, NUKA
116 *the perpetual theatre of* Foreword to *Places*, 1972
116 *first-rate, and put* Norman to JM, 19 Mar 1956, NUKA
116 *I was extremely depressed* JM to Norman, 7 Mar 1956, NUKA
116 *its handsome dust jacket* PoaTL
117 *And if, one summer* CtC
117 *projecting my view of* Foreword, *Places*
117 *the American strain of* CtC
117 *Hawaiians seem to me* ibid.
117 *No. With best wishes* Mathew to JM, 13 Mar 1956, NUKA
117 *I'd much rather stay* JM to McDonald, 13 Apr 1956, NUKA
118 *I don't know yet... I might try spending* JM to Norman, 13 Apr 1956, NUKA
118 *I have the best* EM to Norman, 19 Jun 1956, NUKA
118 *modest Cairo house that, et seq.* Contact!

6 NOT WHAT I AM

119 *I never thought human* John Lahr, *Prick Up Your Ears*, 1978
119 *flair rather than taste* Faber, *Faber & Faber*
120 *middle-aged since I* Andrew Kerr to SW
120 *On the French side* Contact!
121 *immediately* Alastair Hetherington to JM, 15 May 1956, GA
122 *The Anglo-French ultimatum to* 31 Oct 1956, MG
122 *What do you think* EM to Monteith, 5 Nov 1956, FA
123 *A rainbow appeared this* AWW
123 *was struck by the* 20 Nov 1956, MG
123 *killing time while awaiting* Alan Rusbridger, 10 Jul 2006, *Guardian*
123 *seasoned in the Algerian* 27 Jul 1991, *Independent*
123 *They told me quite* Rusbridger, 10 Jul 2006, *Guardian*
123 *FRENCH COLLUSION WITH ISRAEL... French aircraft flown by* 20 Nov 1956, MG
124 *Well, I suppose I* Rusbridger, 10 Jul 2006, *Guardian*
124 *Big Lie: the pretence* 27 Jul 1991, *Independent*

124 *a sorry tale about* ibid.
124 *always thought the government's* JM to Hetherington, 20 Jan 1957, GA
124 *there are Union Jacks* AWW
124 *The decline of Empires . . . all these portentous movements* ibid.
125 *shameful . . . swift decline into* 27 Jul 1991, *Independent*
125 *Europe will be your* Konrad Adenauer to Guy Mollet, 6 Nov 1956, cited in Judt, *Postwar*
125 *The Nasty Affair at* The Goon Show, 4 Oct 1956, BBC Home Service
125 *and we woke up* 28 Dec 1956, *MG*
126 *I got tired of* Desert Island Discs, 21 Jun 2002, BBC Radio 4
126 *I thought I could* Conundrum
126 *to a window seat . . . it had given him* Alastair Hetherington, *Guardian Years*, 1981
126 *Sheikhs innumerable and indescribable* SiO
127 *I had seen it* ibid.
127 *an appalling hole* ibid.
127 *The transition between values* ibid.
127 *one of the more* Fred Halliday, 'The Case of Oman', in *The Media in British Politics*, ed. Jean Seaton & Ben Pimlott, Farnham, 1987
127 *a little backward paradise* SiO
127 *he had a fine . . .* Sultan *has since been* Geoffrey Taylor, *Changing Faces*, 1993
128 *Things seemed to be . . . manned the barricades against* JM, *South African Winter*, 1958
128 *shrinking from the ordeal* EM to Monteith, 22 May 1957, FA
128 *In a wire compound* 25 May 1957, *MG*
128 *to enjoy a metamorphosis . . . But don't be alarmed* JM to Hetherington, 24 Jun 1957, GA
128 *the dottiest ambitions of South African Winter*
129 *clumped . . . I shall never forget* TMoS
129 *eyes of porcelain* ibid.
129 *the Ovaltiney talk . . . semi-nationalists . . . the Queen's Arabs* ibid.
129 *one of the best books* Orville Prescott, 6 Sep 1957, *NYT*
129 *Shuttered* TMoS
129 *impoverished . . . dwindling hegemony . . . ageing* ibid.
130 *We dedicate this little, et seq. Reflections in a Village: Kent*, 3 Apr 1960, BBC Television, now available on BBC Arts
130 *My Dear Rosemary, Well . . . he will only get* EM to Rosemary Goad, 5 Mar 1958, FA
130 *A marvellous way to* JM to Enid Morris, n.d., FC
130 *I wore it at* EM to Goad, 5 May 1958, FA
131 *Two porters had to* CE
131 *Your sugsugsugsug! Your switchabubblebubble!* ibid.
131 *a very funny, very, et seq.* Peter Fleming, 28 Mar 1958, *Spectator*
131 *Halfway there, Randolph suddenly* Fisher's Face
132 *an otherwise totally unobtainable* Conundrum
132 *They are only the* THK
133 *that rambling and materially, et seq.* 'Reflections on Tokyo', BBC *Panorama*, 1958

SOURCE NOTES TO PAGES 133–43

133 *hollow men . . . skull-like emptiness* AWW
134 *everything movable was filched, et seq.* JM, *Venice*, 1960
134 *one of the world's* ibid.
134 *I just can't make* EM to Goad, 7 Feb 1959, FA
134 *Here you are, the* JM to Monteith, 24 Jan 1959, FA
134 *looked down from an* Venice
135 *And when I criticise* draft, THK, NLW
135 *affection* THK
135 *with clean hands* ibid.
135 *In its early stages* ibid.
135 *lifting the telephone . . . like a muddy flood* ibid.
135 *tasselled riding-camels* ibid.
135 *[a] book as brilliant* 22 Nov 1959, *Sunday Times*
135 *only a modicum of . . . no pretensions to scholarship* THK
136 *I am a very* Desert Island Discs, 1 Apr 1983
136 *which, by the way* JM to Monteith, 11 May 1957, FA
136 *Be careful! The water* Andrew Kerr to SW
136 *immense talent for doggerel* William Kerr to SW
136 *sailing up the Adriatic . . . gusts pungent with the* Venice
136 *I was a foreign . . . highly subjective, romantic, impressionist* Venice, Foreword to 1993 edn
136 *hazy and debatable . . . legend though is always* Venice
137 *It is not a* Venice, Foreword to 1993 edn
137 *curiously interwoven* Venice
137 *If you look through* ibid.
137 *The Venetians have never . . . a wistful sense of* ibid.
137 *In Venice the Orient . . . the frontiers of East* ibid.
138 *sensibly adjusted to her* JM, *Cities*, 1963
138 *I don't think I* JM to EM, Good Friday 1958
138 *and the older I* Conundrum

7 VEIL OVER LIPSTICK

139 *magpie-style . . . embedding passages* Venice, 1993 edn
139 *the more the better* Hetherington to JM, 21 Aug 1959, GA
140 *leaden burden* Cities
140 *the whole blighted concept* ibid.
140 *Ah, a psychological novel* PoaTL
140 *My mind is turning* JM to Monteith, n.d. Jan 1960, FA
141 *The writer of travel* 17 Apr 1959, *TLS*
141 *I shall now have* JM to Monteith, 28 Oct 1959, FA
141 *He has just bought* n.d., FA
142 *he was obviously frightened* AWW
142 *confided in me, as* PoaTL
142 *I could not help . . . We arranged to meet* AWW
143 *a gleam of smooth . . . sprawling and pouting* ibid.

369

143 *Everyone there, barmen and* ibid.
143 *live on television, as* ibid.
143 *the long humiliation of* Cities
143 *One of the sad* ibid.
143 *stood as a microcosm* ibid.
143 *torn between the old* ibid.
143 *Cairo is a half-way, et seq.* ibid.
144 *The best-flogged horse in* ibid.
144 *camel beside Cadillac, veil* ibid.
144 *It is very enjoyable* Freya Stark to JM, 18 Oct 1960, FC
144 *Dear Sir, Your book* Nancy Mitford to JM, n.d. 1960, NLW
144 *At worst, his comments* 12 Mar 1960, TLS
144 *When you got there* Michael Palin to SW
145 *Reading and then publishing* Monteith to JM, 17 Jul 1990, FC
145 *The Morrises were just* Andrew Kerr to SW
146 *Is James really going . . . James told me yesterday* Johnnie Kerr to EM, n.d., FC
147 *I was never a Contact!*
147 *I have come to . . . an arrangement which is, et seq.* JM to Hetherington, 3 Apr 1961, GA
147 *The elements I craved* Conundrum
148 *I love you more . . . Thank you for twelve* JM to EM, 22 Mar 1961
148 *fascinating though usually a* JM to EM, n.d. Apr 1961
148 *The hotel is full . . . Susan somebody, et seq.* JM to EM, 7 Apr 1961
149 *even eddying around the* AWW
149 *made me sound (just* ibid.
149 *Cuzco and Machu Picchu* JM to EM, 1 Jul 1961
149 *What a journey it* JM to EM, 19 Jul 1961
149 *You'll be pleased to* JM to EM, 26 Nov 1961
149 *I've been having nosebleeds* JM to EM, 6 Dec 1961
150 *I resent the laboured* AWW
150 *the beeriness of life* ibid.
150 *I LOVE YOU* JM to EM, 3 Jul 1962
150 *Australia strikes me as* JM to EM, 9 Jul 1962
150 *the women in particular* ibid.
150 *pallid or frigid at, et seq.* AWW
151 *My position now approaches* JM to Monteith, 20 Aug 1962, FA
151 *more horrid stories . . . How* internal memo, n.d., FA
152 *had great ideas for* EM to Goad, 5 Mar 1958, FA
153 *the technical revolution . . . that* The World Bank
153 *huge red slabs* ibid.
153 *vacuums and anxieties* ibid.
153 *Nowhere did the end* ibid.
153 *partly natural, partly political* ibid.
153 *This is an imperial* ibid.

154 *[t]he final effect of* 1 Jun 1963, *Economist*
154 *What a many-sided* 21 Jun 1963, *TLS*
154 *May a Liberal suggest . . . Our time hasn't come* 12 Oct 1964, *Times*
155 *I believe in style* JM to Hetherington, 14 Apr 1962, GA
155 *a single brisk volume* JM to Hetherington, n.d. May 1962, GA
155 *they won't tie themselves* ibid.
155 *We are the outriders* JM, *The Outriders*, 1963
156 *It must be among . . . dye your beard blue, et seq.* ibid.
156 *Morally there is no* ibid.
156 *Most of our people* Harold Macmillan, speech at political rally, 20 Jul 1957
156 *For James, with anxiety* FC
156 *an over-insistent manliness* Norman Shrapnel, 5 Jul 1963, *TLS*
157 *Stoop-shouldered and greasy-haired Cities*
157 *I was cultivating impotence Conundrum*
158 *I collect the boys* EM to Goad, 11 Dec 1961, FA
158 *more than twice any* JM to Monteith, 17 May 1960, FA
159 *as though I know* FC

8 TREFAN

160 *the long, well-beaten, expensive Conundrum*
160 *I learnt what my* ibid.
161 *Without you, probably none* Jorgensen, *A Personal Autobiography*
161 *existential terror* Lucy Sante, *I Heard Her Call My Name*, New York, 2024
161 *complex dance of knowledge* ibid.
161 *By my mid-thirties, my Conundrum*
161 *You just go from Sex Change?*, 21 Nov 1966, BBC
163 *my ideal historian – you* Jonathan Gathorne-Hardy, *The Interior Castle: A Life of Gerald Brenan*, 1992
163 *stands apart because she* JM, *The Presence of Spain*, 1964
163 *the magnificent balefulness, et seq. Spain* (formerly *The Presence of Spain*), Intro to 2008 edn
164 *Nobody could have been* ibid.
164 *TORRENTIAL CONGRATULATIONS . . . CARAMBA INDEED!* n.d. Mar 1963, FA
164 *As you foresaw, I* JM to Hetherington, 4 Jan 1963, GA
164 *Do send the ms* Hetherington to JM, 7 Jan 1963, GA
165 *What matter empires fall* n.d., NLW
165 *though unlike Wolff he* Bob Weil to SW
165 *the beginning of history, et seq. The Presence of Spain*
165 *Perhaps the best general* copy sent by Goad to JM, 21 Apr 1964, FA
165 *one of those very* Orville Prescott, 27 Nov 1964, *NYT*
166 *Franco died in 1975* Intro to *Spain*, 2008
166 *Dinner jacket Sundays in* University College SCR, Notes for Guidance, Sep 1963, NLW
166 *with three men who . . . I sometimes used to* JM, *Oxford*, Oxford, 1965
166 *I think they made* Petra Lewis to SW

167 *the ten years of . . . unity of vision, unity of, et seq.* Cities
167 *Quite the most <u>indigestible</u>* 10 Oct 1962, FA
167 *I may be giving* JM to Monteith, 13 Nov 1963, FA
168 *The essays display the . . . that gave the Bond, et seq.* Thrilling Cities, Intro to 2013 edn
168 *When I caught myself* Cities
168 *the vague intuition that . . . I had been selected, et seq.* MM, Nov 1984, *Esquire*
169 *lure* Clough Williams-Ellis to JM, 23 Mar 1964, NLW
169 *folly-village* 10 Apr 1978, *Times*
169 *a last bastion of* Foreword, Keith Bowen, *Snowdon Shepherd*, 1991 edn
170 *to a lady who* n.d. JM to Monteith, FA
170 *it will always be . . . with its climbing magnolia, et seq.* Conundrum
171 *Trefan is paradise* JM to Monteith, 29 Jul 1965, FA
171 *feline by nature* IMME
171 *I'm convinced that cats . . . When I lost a . . . Oh no, she's perfectly* 17 Sep 1988, *Daily Telegraph*
172 *a holiday retreat for . . . living folly* Jonah Jones, *Clough Williams-Ellis*, Bridgend, 1996
173 *Clough was his own* 10 Apr 1978, *Times*
174 *I think I understood* Allegorizings
174 *gets more and more* JM to Hetherington, n.d., GA
174 *We are in the* JM to Hetherington, 5 May 1965, GA
175 *I went to Matugama* JM to EM, 12 Oct 1962
175 *1 lakh: 100,000 . . . The gears seem to, et seq.* NLW
176 *To hell with the* Paul Scott, 24 Nov 1975, *Times*
176 *It was in India* Climax
176 *Take this tea to* TM to SW
177 *the new industrial towns . . . Another England has emerged, et seq.* Oxford
178 *Ding Dong Dismally on . . . If* Dennis Potter, 21 Oct 1965, *New Society*
178 *James Morris's Oxford is . . . transcend the limitations of* Christopher Ricks, Dec 1965, *Encounter*
178 *It's a terrible thing* JM to Ricks, 20 Nov 1965, NLW
178 *I have little room . . . after all, when all* Ricks to JM, 22 Nov 1965, NLW
178 *has been rightly praised* 6 Jan 1966, *Listener*
179 *a mixture of rhapsody* A. J. P. Taylor, 15 Oct 1965, *New Statesman*
179 *agreeable* Evelyn Waugh, 7 Nov 1965, *Sunday Times*
179 *more at ease in* Harold Kurtz, 26 Oct 1965, *Financial Times*
179 *It is sure to* Ricks, *Encounter*
179 *I know how the* JM to Monteith, 14 Oct 1965, FA
179 *Oxford is a dangerous place, et seq.* Oxford, 1968 edn
179 *I had a world at* Conundrum
179 *the worst period of* ibid.

9 HALF A FREAK SHOW, HALF A MIRACLE

181 *I don't like it* A Change of Sex, 1979, BBC2
181 *He was talking down* Julia Grant, *George and Julia*, 1980

SOURCE NOTES TO PAGES 181–91

181 *be able to be* J. B. Randell, *Sexual Variations*, 1973
181 *I think if they're* J. B. Randell, 'Indications for Sex Reassignment Surgery', *Archives of Sexual Behavior*, 1:2, 1971
181 *More than any other* Dave King & Richard Ekins, 'Pioneers of Transgendering: John Randell', University of Ulster Gender Dysphoria Conference, 2002
182 *Trans people had nowhere* Christine Burns, in *Trans Britain*, ed. Christine Burns, 2018
182 *The division between transvestite* ibid.
182 *I don't change men* 21 Jan 1974, *Time*
182 *I didn't know what* Duncan Fallowell & April Ashley, *April Ashley's Odyssey*, 1982
182 *I merely wanted to* ibid.
183 *surprisingly civilised* JM to EM, 23 Dec 1951
183 *As a result of* Fallowell & Ashley, *April Ashley's Odyssey*
183 *You move one mountain* ibid.
183 *The judge's ruling is* ibid.
183 *Is it the function* ibid.
183 *Psychiatry has nothing to* Jorgensen, *A Personal Autobiography*
184 *tended to pathologize that* *Trans Britain*
184 *to rebalance my mind* ibid.
184 *last witnesses to the* *Oxford*
184 *I felt myself to* *Conundrum*
184 *to gather material for* ibid.
184 *I found it crueller* ibid.
185 *childish intuitions . . . start turning, et seq.* MM, Nov 1984, *Esquire*
185 *Mark! You've arrived. Good* ibid.
185 *Night was about to . . . We discussed the impending* ibid.
185 *Why does uncle James* Sir Michael Williams to SW, 2005
186 *I had seen his . . . growing sense of elfin, et seq.* David Holden, 17 Mar 1974, *NYT*
186 *I knew he was* *Conundrum*
186 *James Morris is coming* Ricks to SW, 23 Sep 2024
186 *past caring* *Conundrum*
186 *an epicene ambiguity in* ibid.
186 *I'm having a very* JM to EM, n.d. May
187 *What a perfectly splendid* JM to EM, 14 Nov 1968
187 *Just to wish you* JM to EM, 5 May 1969
187 *FROM YOUR TRUEST VALENTINE* JM to EM, 14 Feb 1970
187 *the spirit of Empire* PoaTL
188 *where the broken violet* Boustead, *The Wind of Morning*
189 *In 1946 I was* 8 Sep 1968, *NYT*
190 *Half the difficulties and* ibid.
190 *substantial gothic-style church with* *Climax*
190 *resplendently driving to church* ibid.
190 *It was however a* John M. MacKenzie, *A Cultural History of the British Empire*, 2022
191 *the Empire got tucked* William Dalrymple, *Empire* podcast, ep. 1

191 *Cruelty was rare and, et seq. Climax*
191 *In an Empire based* ibid.
192 *the British government in* ibid.
192 *Rightly or wrongly, the* ibid.
192 *It was the greatest* draft, *Climax*, NLW
192 *largest Climax*
192 *concentrate frankly on the* 8 Sep 1968, *NYT*
192 *Though infused with a* MacKenzie, *Cultural History of the British Empire*
193 *I am not very* ATC
193 *There turned out to* JM, *O Canada!*, 1992
193 *my kind mentor in* FTT
193 *It was around the Climax*
194 *Morris, like Gibbon, writes* Worsthorne, 15 Jun 1978, *Sunday Telegraph*
194 *development agency Climax*
194 *has a taste for* Jeremy Treglown, *V. S. Pritchett: A Working Life*, 2005
194 *A Passage to India . . . this was an ugly . . . Nor did he attack . . . still he was not* FTT
195 *We may hate one* E. M. Forster, *A Passage to India*, 1924
195 *this is an emotional* 8 Sep 1968, *NYT*
195 *Morris once expressed her* MacKenzie, *Cultural History of the British Empire*
196 *The Westminster Bank Group* JM to Monteith, 6 Jan 1969, FA
196 *I know that he* Michael Sissons to Monteith, 19 Jul 1967, FA
197 *like an American buddha* JM, *The Great Port*, 1970
197 *Excellent idea, to make* Monteith to JM, 5 Apr 1967, FA
197 *I am now taking* JM to Peter du Sautoy, 12 Jun 1967, FA
197 *Austin's Last Erection* AWW
198 *high romantic of Tennysonian* PoaTL
198 *My own conception of The Great Port*
198 *the ghostly flicker of* ibid.
198 *popped* PoaTL
198 *It is an excellent* David Rockefeller to JM, 10 Aug 1968, FC
199 *tragedy and comedy balled* Thomas Kunkel, *Man in Profile*, New York, 2015
199 *beige narrators* Tom Wolfe, 23 Aug 1976, *New York* magazine
199 *more truthful than factual* Kunkel, *Man in Profile*
200 *Pound in Your Pocket* Harold Wilson, address to the nation, 19 Nov 1967
200 *vol 1 of the trilogy, et seq.* JM to Hetherington, 11 Jan 1968, GA
200 *I'm off to Spain* JM to Monteith, 6 Feb 1968, FA
201 *Elsan culture* Byron Rogers, *The Man Who Went into the West: The Life of R. S. Thomas*, 2007
201 *stripped of my clothes . . . sedgy and serene Conundrum*
201 *The dean of Christ* 9 Nov n.d., W. H. Auden to JM, FC
201 *[t]he Empire Builders get off, et seq.* Anthony Sampson, 7 Nov 1968, *TLS*
202 *sympathetic collusion . . . Mr Morris enjoys his adjectives* Dennis Potter, 19 Oct 1968, *Times*

SOURCE NOTES TO PAGES 202–13

202 *proportion is the artistic* Enoch Powell, 7 Mar 1969, *Spectator*
202 *With James in his* du Sautoy to Helen Wolff, 14 Nov 1968, FA
202 *James has been extremely . . . I know that J* Wolff to du Sautoy, 18 Nov 1968, FA
202 *James seems to be . . . I am afraid he* Wolff to du Sautoy, 3 Jul 1969, FA
202 *I am willy-nilly pulling* JM to Monteith, 8 Oct 1969, FA
203 *as the meeting place . . . James and Elizabeth were lovely* Dafydd Iwan to SW
203 *We found ourselves in* Travels Round My House, 12 May 2013, BBC Radio 3
203 *Her attitude to nationalism . . . the old, old dream* Iwan to SW
204 *half a freak show* Travels Round My House, BBC Radio 3
204 *Wherever I wandered ambiguously* Jun 1984, *Vanity Fair*
204 *Don't worry, I shall* JM to Goad, 6 Jan 1969, FA
204 *he arrived so late* Michael Nott, *Thom Gunn: A Cool Queer Life*, 2024
205 *Terrible city . . . So long as I* JM to EM, n.d. 1970
205 *I was once stuck, et seq.* Intro to *Persia*, photographs by Roger Wood, 1969
206 *something for my supper . . . a solitary grey heron* Places
206 *Silently, silently trail the pickpockets, et seq. ibid.*
206 *if like me you . . . steamy, mouldy, gourd-like fibrous* ibid.
206 *aesthetic* (Wyoming) *ibid.*
206 *full-blooded aesthetic . . . in Gauguin colours and* ibid.
206 *aesthetic* (Trouville) ATC
207 *guardians of lost identity . . . still seemed at ease* Places
207 *I am a respectable* Conundrum
207 *I did enjoy it . . . I was about the* JM to EM, 2 Nov 1970
207 *If there is one* JM to Monteith, 3 Aug 1970, FA

10 BEING A STAR

209 *shelve* Wolff to Monteith, 14 Jun 1971, FA
209 *I've been travelling en* JM to EM, 9 May n.d.
209 *Stunned . . . ambiguous presence, et seq.* JM to EM, 22 Jan 1971
209 *the happiest of my* Conundrum
210 *Thanks to the jet* Places
210 *a fading genre. Now, et seq. ibid.*
210 *All went off harmlessly* JM to Goad, n.d., FA
211 *Dear Gareth and Chris* JM to Gareth and Chris Morris, 4 Dec 1971, courtesy Trish Morris
211 *Would that be a* Paul Morris to SW
211 *She was very flirtatious* Belinda Mitchell-Innes to SW
212 *I've just finished and* Henry Anglesey to JM, n.d. Sep 1971, FC
212 *It reminds me of* JM to Anglesey, 6 Feb 1995, Plas Newydd Archive
212 *My very dear gurl . . . love and kisses, dearest* various, FC
212 *She and Elizabeth were* Alex Uxbridge to SW
212 *problem of sexual determinacy, et seq.* 10 Mar 1972, *Times*
213 *We are all very* Monteith to JM, 28 Mar 1972, FC
213 *If he has an* Goad, office memo, 11 Apr 1974, FA

375

SOURCE NOTES TO PAGES 214–23

214 *a practical way of* Alistair Horne to JM, 13 Oct 1965, FC
214 *He did not seem* Conundrum
214 *had this lovely Stella* JM to EM, n.d.
214 *non-architecture* JM to EM, 13 Jul 1972
214 *dressed for the corniche* Conundrum
215 *It's over and I'm* JM to EM, n.d.
215 *My chief sensation now* JM to EM, 11 Jul 1972
215 *the clips came out* JM to EM, 12 Jul 1972
215 *Not impressed. You must, et seq.* JM to EM, 13 Jul 1972
216 *I don't feel I've . . . the change came far* JM to EM, 15 Jul 1972
216 *Slight complication this morning* ibid.
216 *Just a line to . . . the chief sensation so* JM to Monteith, 11 Jul 1972, FA
216 *I'm most fearsomely and, et seq.* Monteith to JM, 14 Jul 1972, FA
217 *I would have gone* Conundrum
217 *Torrential congratulations* Monteith to JM, 30 Oct 1972, FA
217 *We got £37,500 for* JM to Monteith, 26 Nov 1972, FA
218 *my first as a* Conundrum
218 *My brothers were sent* SM, 10 Dec 2022, *Sunday Times*
218 *It's very important that* Monteith, 19 Jun 1972, FA
219 *J is away and* EM to Monteith, 11 Jul 1972, FA
219 *They are by necessity* JM to Monteith, 6 Oct 1872, FA
219 *I must confess that* du Sautoy to JM, 11 Sep 1973, FA
219 *Thank goodness she's agreed* Monteith, 21 Sep 1973, FA
220 *It is a perturbing* Conundrum
220 *Dear James/Jan – We love* Rosaleen and Austin J. Tobin to JM, 26 Jul 1972, FC
220 *I want to go* JM to Monteith, n.d. 1972, FA
220 *I thought Jan Morris* Conundrum
220 *This is the first . . . Much love from mummy* Enid Morris to JM, n.d., FC
221 *I began work on* notebook, FC
221 *It was a matter* Jorgensen, *A Personal Autobiography*
221 *I am deep in* JM to Monteith, 24 Jan 1973, FA
221 *It did not make* 4 Jun 2008, *Independent*
222 *feeling of unfluctuating control, et seq.* Conundrum
222 *I'm getting better fast* JM to Monteith, n.d., FA
222 *to assist in the* Sissons to Monteith, 4 Apr 1973, FA
222 *James of Everest is* 31 May 1973, *Daily Mirror*
223 *more explicit about her . . . extreme self-absorption at the* Goad, 22 Jun 1973, FA
223 *commercial* Matthew Evans, 19 Jun 1973, FA
223 *a natural for Pseuds* ibid.
223 *disappointed* Monteith to MM [*sic*], 12 Oct 1973, FA
223 *obsessively . . . it's probably better* Goad, 22 Jun 1973, FA
223 *A long morning* Monteith to Wolff, 26 Sep 1973, FA
223 *It was now a* 'Conundrum: Synopsis for a New Draft', JM to Faber, n.d., FA

223 *I think I failed* Paris Review, No. 143, Summer 1997
223 *perhaps I'm not a* Gareth R. Jones, *The Welsh Agenda*, No. 68, Spring 2022
223 *This proposed book is* 'Conundrum: Synopsis', FA
224 *I certainly did not, et seq.* Conundrum
225 *I would strongly suggest* du Sautoy to JM, 18 Sep 1973, FA
225 *one was either wholly male . . . or wholly female* Georgina Somerset, *Over the Sex Border*, 1963
226 *the archetypal HK colonial* JM to Monteith, 24 Nov 1973, FA
226 *When the story first* Cowell, *Roberta Cowell's Story by Herself*
226 *Mum thought it was* Eleo Gordon to SW
226 *each had loves of* Conundrum
227 *a sort of non-affair, et seq.* JM to EM, 16 Feb 1974, FC
227 *the central saga of . . . a chronicle of squalor* HC
227 *her unteachable gift of* H. V. Morton, cited in Peter Devenish to JM, 14 Jul 2005, FC
227 *kept up their strength, et seq.* HC
228 *How many professional historians* Godfrey Hodgson, 11 Nov 1973, *Sunday Times*
228 *insular British indifference to* Paul Scott, 6 Nov 1973, *Times*
229 *We are in the* Monteith to Wolff, 20 Dec 1973, FA
229 *The trouble is that* JM to Monteith, 3 Nov 1972, FA
229 *Whatever they do to . . . I don't think I'm . . . but as you will* JM to Monteith, 13 Nov 1972, FA
229 *I loathe the jacket, et seq.* JM to Monteith, 1 Jan 1974, FA
230 *Can't Faber ever get . . . it's enough to make* JM to Monteith, 1 Mar 1974, FA
230 *If I am having . . . fairly muddy* JM, *Travels*, 1976
230 *Bath isn't really good* Paul Morris to SW
230 *planners' naïveté, developers' greed* Charles J. Robertson, *Bath*, 1975
230 *If it turns out* JM to Monteith, n.d., FA
231 *The only thing to* theme tune, *Whatever Happened to the Likely Lads?*, BBC sitcom, 1973–4
231 *It will be a* JM to John Bodley, 12 Mar 1974, FA
231 *She is clearly very . . . She is alarmed at* Monteith, internal memo, 25 Jan 1974, FA
231 *I long to get* Russell Harty, 19 Oct 1973, ITV
231 *a very large sum* Monteith, internal memo, 25 Jan 1974, FA
232 *Jan Morris is still, et seq.* Talk-In To Day, 10 May 1974, BBC1
232 *Those of us who* Leo Abse, 26 May 1965, House of Commons
233 *probably the most unnerving* A Day to Remember, 12 Aug 2017, BBC2
233 *She was dreading it* MM, unpublished memoir, private collection
233 *The publication of your* Huw Wheldon to JM, n.d. May 1974, FC
233 *to thank you for, et seq.* JM to Katharine Whitehorn, n.d., GA (Katharine Whitehorn Papers)
234 *I see them as* Conundrum
234 *no single rational explanation* The Dick Cavett Show, 16 May 1974, ABC
234 *Jan Morris is perfectly, et seq.* Nora Ephron, 6 Jun 1974, *RS*

SOURCE NOTES TO PAGES 234–46

234 *THE BOOK EVERYONE IS, et seq.* Germaine Greer, 25 Apr 1974, *Evening Standard*
235 *essentially Jan is an, et seq.* V. S. Pritchett, 26 Apr 1974, *New Statesman*
235 *As a communication of, et seq.* Bernard Levin, 28 Apr 1974, *Observer*
235 *perhaps the finest descriptive, et seq.* Rebecca West, 14 Apr 1974, *NYT*
235 *most women do become* Victoria Glendinning, *Rebecca West*, 1987
235 *a man's idea of, et seq.* West, 14 Apr 1974, *NYT*
235 *(fn) the he was a* Paul Levy, 12 Nov 1989, *NYT*
236 *The Sheer Fun of* 28 Apr 1974, *Sunday Times*
236 *No matter what tortures* Stanley Reynolds, 14 May 1974, *Guardian*
236 *Please, Miss Morris, can, et seq.* FC
237 *When I was ready* n.d., NLW
237 *idyllic marriage . . . creeping Harold-and-Vitaism* Ephron, 6 Jun 1974, *RS*
237 *Your own experience is* Nigel Nicolson to JM, 3 Oct 1973, FC
238 *In her bigoted review* EM, 29 Apr 1974, *Evening Standard*
238 *It wasn't Jan who* Kate Murray-Brown to SW
238 *I was three or* Conundrum
239 *the usual ret-conned narrative* 17 Dec 2022, gendercriticalwoman.blog
239 *Half a lifetime of* Conundrum, 2002 edn
239 *It was like being* PoaTL
239 *One of the problems* Fallowell & Ashley, *April Ashley's Odyssey*
239 *I felt emboldened to, et seq.* 14 Apr 1974, *NYT*
240 *Everest of vanity* Michael Holroyd, *Bernard Shaw*, one-vol edn, 1997
241 *entailed falling deliciously in* JM to Monteith, n.d. Oct 1974, FA
241 *I have seldom been* JM to EM, 28 Jan n.d.
241 *and the least of . . . I think you must* JM to EM, 30 Jan n.d.
241 *All too often, the, et seq.* 24 Nov 1961, *TLS*
241 *I think we're home* JM to Bodley, 2 Jun 1974, FA
242 *Transsexualism is a passionate* Conundrum

11 MON DIEU

243 *For parallel cross-purposes, misunderstandings* HC
243 *He's not allowed to* JM to Monteith, 12 May 1974, FA
243 *Miss Jan Morris needs* 9 Feb 1979, NLW
244 *I always admired the* PoaTL
244 *Lloyd George, the typical Welshman* AWHiW
244 *I found my reportage* AWW
244 *What matter empires fall* n.d., NLW
245 *a larger sales potential* office memo, 4 Nov 1975, FA
245 *I wonder if I* office memo, 28 Oct 1975, FA
245 *Peter is right, I* ibid.
245 *the most thrilling phenomenon* JM, *Destinations*, Oxford, 1980
245 *I took her over* Jann Wenner to SW
246 *instantly* PoaTL
246 *America was a dream* Wenner to SW

378

246 *a journalistic genius* PoaTL
246 *the mystic sheen of* FTT
246 *tempering the* Rolling Stone *Destinations*
246 *The Scum Also Rises* 10 Oct 1974, RS
247 *Against all my better, et seq.* 21 Nov 1974, RS
247 *She didn't need editing* Wenner to SW
247 *LA Turnoff: Driving through, et seq.* 1 Jul 1976, RS
248 *I am – we are* John Gregory Dunne to JM, 19 Jun 1976, FC
248 *Between Tom and you* Wenner to JM, 28 Mar 1977, FC
249 *Late Classic of the . . . Let the Bicentennialists have* 1 Jan 1976, RS
249 *A <u>marvellous</u> day up* JM to Arthur Crook, 25 Nov 1969, NUKA
249 *that you have been* Crook to JM, 22 Dec 1971, NUKA
249 *I am tentatively calling* JM to Monteith, n.d. Jan 1974, FA
249 *on the last of my* JM to Monteith, n.d. Jan 1975, FA
250 *I am giving myself* JM to Bodley, 20 Feb 1975, FA
250 *Whatever you wish us* JM to EM, n.d.
250 *he wandered as a . . . If it is not Travels*
250 *one of the most* 1 May 1976, *Economist*
250 *another of my perennial* JM to du Sautoy, n.d. Jul 1976, FA
251 *Jan sets great store* Monteith and Bodley, office memo, 5 Apr n.d., FA
251 *All being well, work* JM to Monteith, 2 Oct 1976, FA
251 *often despaired . . . and only* EM to Monteith, 3 Dec 1976, FA
252 *What nice people you* JM to Hugo Brunner, n.d. Jul 1977, OUPA
252 *become girlie* Robert McCrum to SW
252 *ROLLING STONE INTERESTED VIENNA* 26 Oct 1977, FC
253 *CONFIRM VIENNA NOW EXPENSES* n.d., NLW
253 *Good-by to Britain, Good-by, et seq.* Mar 1977, *Horizon*
253 *during one of Britain's, et seq.* 20 Apr 1978, RS
254 *vast sums of Arabian* 19 Oct 1978, RS
254 *She may want more* Evans, 7 Dec 1977, FA
254 *a pair of old* McCrum to SW
254 *idea of heaven . . . bowling* Woman of Action, 24 Jun 1978, BBC Radio 3
254 *Mon dieu* n.d., FA
254 *BEST YEAR OF MY LIFE* JM to Monteith, n.d. Jan 1979, FA, and NLW
254 *about to explode, et seq.* 19 Oct 1978, RS
255 *A Good Erection Every* Jonathan Raban to JM, n.d., FC
255 *I'm so frightened of, et seq.* Jonathan Raban, *Arabia Through the Looking Glass*, 1979
256 *I could sense a, et seq.* 19 Oct 1978, RS
256 *festering in the shadows, et seq.* 8 Feb 1979, RS
256 *across the world the, et seq.* FTT
257 *affectionate* 8 Sep 1968, NYT
258 *boats full of dead men* FTT
258 *Gradually it occurred to* ibid.

258 *It was* Heaven's Command Jacob Rees-Mogg, *The Victorians*, 2019
258 *Now I wonder at* James Wood, *London Review of Books*, 4 Jul 2019
259 *So all appears to* Monteith to Goad, 2 Jun 1978, FA
259 *a disaster* 3 Nov 1978, FA
259 *further weakens the links* Monteith to JM, 20 Nov 1978, FA
260 *And gradually there overcame* 1 Jan 1976, RS
260 *like Dunkirk, a failure* FTT
261 *been much criticised. My* ibid., 1998 edn
261 *degree of exoticism . . . Surgery in far-off* Stuart Lorimer, in *Trans Britain*
261 *showed the way forward* Burns, in *ibid.*
261 *It's not bad all* *Julia's Story*, BBC2
261 *I spent the next* Grant, *George and Julia*, 1980
261 *I wanted the films* ibid.

12 THE MATTER OF WALES

262 *yelling into the wind, et seq.* JM, *The Venetian Empire*, 1980
262 *a mighty menagerie of* JM, *A Venetian Bestiary*, 1982
263 *bored of India* Monteith to Faber board, 6 Oct 1980, FA
263 *something deeper: the development* JM to Monteith, 11 Nov 1974, FA
264 *I confess to a* *The Letters of Bruce Chatwin*, ed. Elizabeth Chatwin & Nicholas Shakespeare, 2010
264 *Jan Morris, in his/her* ibid.
264 *As a person he* Jan 1997, *Literary Review*
264 *Everyone else was talking, et seq.* Paul Theroux to SW
265 *The maleness that still . . . a queer thrill when* Theroux, *The Kingdom by the Sea*, 1983
265 *She did influence me* Theroux to SW
265 *I thought I was* JM to Robin Denniston, 14 Jul 1981, OUPA
265 *I hope I'm not* JM to OUP, 4 Mar 1992, OUPA
266 *a reminder of the* AWHiW
266 *if you dye your* Outriders
267 *It is her fatness* JM, *Journeys*, Oxford, 1984
267 *the unbelievably ugly high* 50 Yrs
267 *Have we met? . . . Dad* Paul Morris to SW
268 *exchanging mutually self-congratulatory seditious* JM, *The Princeship of Wales*, Llandysul, Dyfed, 1995
268 *Nobody need employ me* Planet, 1987
268 *I believe that political* AWHiW
268 *in a soupy, pre-Fascist* Nicholas Shakespeare, *Bruce Chatwin*, 1999
269 *emotional approach to history* 8 Sep 1968, *NYT*
269 *a dreadful phenomenon redeemed* MacKenzie, *Cultural History of the British Empire*
269 *I was much moved* PoaTL
269 *about ten years ago* Desert Island Discs, 1 Apr 1983
270 *an insatiable dream, a, et seq.* JM & Paul Wakefield, *Wales: The First Place*, 1982
270 *aggressively romantic view of, et seq.* Simon Jenkins, *The Celts*, 2022

271 *No! I get lonely* Desert Island Discs, 1 Apr 1983
271 *the dottiest ambitions of* South African Winter
271 *looking at the country* TMoW
271 *the lonely magic rowans, et seq.* ibid.
271 (fn) *I once met that* AWW
272 *riddled with minor mistakes, et seq.* Torey Hayden, 28 Apr 1985, *NYT*
272 *very boring* JM to Rubinstein, n.d. May 1984, OUPA
272 *there is more beautiful* Journeys
273 *There are virtually no* 24 Nov 1983, *RS*
273 *Yum yum! I'm eating* n.d., FC
273 *Beijing was too big* Paris Review, No. 143, Summer 1997
273 *Beijing and Shanghai were* Journeys
273 Rolling Stone *didn't matter* Joe Hagan, *Sticky Fingers*, New York, 2017

13 WHAT'S BECOME OF WARING

274 *After half a lifetime* PoaTL
274 *I seldom knew what, et seq.* Epilogue to *Hav*, 2006 (combined edn of *Last Letters* and *Hav of the Myrmidons*)
274 *like one of those* Last Letters
275 *like Waring* ibid.
275 *determined to turn up, et seq.* McCrum to SW
275 *I am an aficionado* JM, *Locations*, 1992
276 *observing that nobody in, et seq.* ATC
276 *It was at Rome* Edward Gibbon, *The History of the Decline and Fall of the Roman Empire*, 1776
276 *illustrate the shifting responses, et seq.* ATC
276 *the Dwyfor of China* JM to EM, n.d.
277 *There hasn't been a* TM to SW
278 *I hope Trefan Bach* Elspeth Huxley to EM, 1 Aug 1980, FC
278 *Dearest Joan, what a* EM to Joan Murray-Brown, n.d., FC
278 *When I did the* AWHiW
279 *Exasperated by the self-control, et seq.* O Canada!
279 *simpler world* 1 Jul 1976, *RS*
279 *It's like old times* JM to Monteith, n.d. Jan 1986, FA
280 *We Made It Mom, et seq.* Manhattan '45
280 *If this is art* Charles Darwent, *Surrealists in New York*, 2023
280 *The skyline was not, et seq.* Manhattan '45
281 *distorted through the pink* Richard Dorment, May 1987, *Literary Review*
282 *Sick of the Tourist* 9 Dec 1987, *Independent*
282 *Save Wales for the* 7 Jul 1988, *Independent*
282 *the English . . . had always viewed the* 50 Yrs
283 *I finally acquired my* Geoffrey Moorhouse to JM, 28 Apr 1992, FC
283 *Somebody speaking on behalf* Matthew Evans to JM, 16 Sep 1981, FA
283 *Hong Kong seems to* American *Vogue*, May 1985

284 *These were the early, et seq.* JM, *Hong Kong: Xianggang*, 1988
284 *I read your excellent* Chris Patten to JM, n.d. 1993, FC
284 *repeatedly nominated the best hotel* *Hong Kong: Xianggang*
284 *debased* PoaTL
284 *Far better to regard* ibid.
285 *I truly don't think* *Desert Island Discs*, 1 Apr 1983
285 *Blood love is the* PoaTL
285 *enjoys shocking her reader* Paul Levy, 12 Nov 1989, *NYT*
286 *So the year ended* EM, diary, 31 Dec 1989
286 *Not that Burgess* Roger Lewis, *Anthony Burgess*, 2002
287 *We barely edited Jan, et seq.* Robert Winder to SW
287 *The doges would have* 23 Mar 2018, *FT*
287 *She loved giving everyone, et seq.* Robert Winder to SW
287 *The most pungently individualistic* JM & Paul Wakefield, *Ireland: Your Only Place*, 1990

14 ON THE BRINK

288 *becoming much like all* *Ireland: Your Only Place*
288 *no more than a* JM, *Sydney*, 1992
288 *It was a full* ibid.
288 *virile postures* FTT
289 *I thought a little* *Sydney*
289 *Most of the world's* ibid.
289 *flavourless advertorial style . . . a* Julian Evans, 14 May 1992, *Guardian*
290 *Dear Jan, What fun!* Harry Evans to JM, n.d. 1981, FC
290 *I'm working up to* JM to Robert Winder, 23 Oct 1992, courtesy Robert Winder
290 *better than* The Hashemites Freya Stark to JM, 18 Oct 1960, FC
290 *more than just women . . . human being* 24 Nov 1961, *TLS*
290 *I am glad to* Stark to JM, 16 Jan 1975, FC
291 *petty failings and trivial* 30 Jan 1993, *Independent*
291 *There is a way* John Carey, *William Golding*, 2009
292 *apparently the only Faber* ibid.
292 *Sometimes we bumped into, et seq.* Arthur Roberts to SW
293 *to tears* Chatwin & Shakespeare, *Letters of Bruce Chatwin*
293 *his cloth cap tilted* 7 Jan 1995, *Independent*
293 *She was enormous fun* William Kerr to SW
293 *I enjoyed almost every* AWW
293 *a debased addiction* PoaTL
294 *Get me out of* Roger Lewis to SW
294 *weakness for grand style* *Fisher's Face*
294 *a jeu d'amour* ibid.
294 *with the ships of* ibid.
295 *kissing his forehead with* ibid.
295 *moments of self-indulgence* *Journal of Military History*, Vol. 60, No. 3, Jul 1996
295 *One by one, the half-dead states . . . Like one of those* 29 Dec 1990, *Times*

296 *It represents an old* 27 Apr 1997, *Sunday Times*
296 *frequently plastered over by* 6 Mar 1993, *Times*
296 *it was one of . . . I am myself a* 50 Yrs
296 *unreliable or even unscholarly* JM to UCNW, 6 Jul 1989, NLW
296 *fifteenth greatest British writer* 5 Jan 2008, *Times*
297 *Wales is essentially a* JM, *A Machynlleth Triad*, 1994
297 *real embarrassment* TM to SW
297 *the awful gorges through* AWW
298 *changed everything* TMoW
298 *a portent of a . . . the dream of a, et seq.* Wales: Epic Views of a Small Country (revised TMoW), 1998
298 *Congratulations on what you* Iwan to SW
298 *I long ago came* 17 Feb 1972, *Times*
298 *this first faint hope* Wales: Epic Views
299 *the dross of Anglo-American* TMoW
299 *an enormous book about* JM to Robert Winder, 26 Apr 1994, courtesy Robert Winder

15 JESTER IN CAMELOT

300 *It was like treading* 50 Yrs
300 *I am now in* Escaping from Liberty, 27 Dec 1996, BBC Wales
301 *waiting for us with* 50 Yrs
301 *The case concerned heroin-trafficking* ibid.
301 (fn) *She was a lousy* SM, 10 Dec 2022, *Sunday Times*
302 *By the 1980s the* 50 Yrs
302 *my mind full of, et seq.* ibid.
303 *I used to be* ibid.
303 *If my book seems* HC, 1998 edn
303 *Mine is an aesthetic* FTT, 1998 edn
303 *greatly depresses and debilitates* JM to Winder, 14 Jan 1998, courtesy Robert Winder
303 *hated . . . distasteful . . . a rag* MM to SW
304 *Sir, At San Francisco* 1 Sep 1997, *Times*
304 *I was the person* 4 Jun 2008, *Independent*
305 SEX CHANGE WRITER'S CBE JM to Trish Morris, 15 Jun 1999, courtesy Trish Morris
305 *Well earned ole gal!* Anglesey to JM, n.d. 1999, FC
305 *I hope you like* JM to Julian Loose, 2 Jun 2001, courtesy Julian Loose
305 *Lincoln was essentially a* JM, *Lincoln*, 1999
305 *In this book, it's* 31 Jan 2000, *Publishers Weekly*
306 *the best book ever* 4 Mar 2000, *Globe and Mail*
306 *Elizabeth was there, but* Nicholas Turner to SW
306 *cold, wet and miserable* FC
306 *How wittily generous of* Ricks to JM, n.d., FC
306 *to thank you for* n.d., NLW

307 *I have not dined* AWHiW
307 *and I made the* Catharine Morris to SW
307 *On this as on* JM to EM, 14 Feb 2000
307 *inner shrine of Welshness, et seq.* JM, *Our First Leader*, Llandysul, 2000
307 *For no amount of* 12 Jan 2001, *TLS*
308 *between every line Trieste* Trieste
308 *Trieste is also a, et seq. 50 Yrs*
309 *What a nightmare hiatus* Trieste
309 *Which way are we* ibid.
309 *There is wonderful writing* Stan Barstow to JM, 16 Aug 2006, FC
309 *Did some of them* Trieste
310 *not a literary sort* JM to Julian Loose, 23 May 2001, courtesy Julian Loose
310 *Nothing on earth would* 'By the Book', 4 Dec 2014, *NYT*
310 *Your last? Ha Ha!* Anglesey to JM, n.d., FC
310 *That was all straight* Joey Casey to SW
310 *The Manhattan skyline shimmered* Manhattan '45
310 *If race is a* Trieste
311 *after a year of* 29 Sep 2001, *Cambria Magazine*
311 *Historically, Trieste has been, et seq.* Trieste
312 *I can't pretend I'm* Desert Island Discs, 21 Jun 2002
312 *entered the vocabulary . . . found themselves caught in* Trieste

16 ANCIENT MARINER

313 *comes straight from the* Intro, Sybille Bedford, *Pleasures and Landscapes*, New York, 2003
313 *a bit Range Rovery* AWW
313 *the irony, the self-amusement* Intro to 2003 edn, Rose Macaulay, *The Towers of Trebizond*, New York, 1956
314 *Why must you always* Last Letters
314 *everyone's patriot* Trieste
314 *consciously modelled* AWW
314 *have sometimes beaten me* 'By the Book', 4 Dec 2014, *NYT*
314 *where will and destiny* JM, in *The Pleasure of Reading*, ed. Antonia Fraser, 1992
315 *All my books are, et seq.* Desert Island Discs, 21 Jun 2002
315 *I am a hybrid* Robert McCrum interviews Jan Morris, 2016, available on YouTube
315 *essence . . . of all I* AWHiW
316 *a whiff of the* Penelope Lively, 20 Apr 2002, *Independent*
316 *sit down, take a* AWHIW
316 *Fifty-odd years after, et seq.* Rahul Jacob to SW
317 *rim to rim* Destinations: *A Collection of* FT *Travel Writing*, 2006
318 *For years and years* 31 Dec 2002, *Times*
318 *culturalism . . . nationalism that has* Sep 2003, *Literary Review*
318 *I'm very depressed* ibid.
318 *only the second time . . . a sort of permanent* JM to Julian Loose, 17 Apr 2007, courtesy Julian Loose

SOURCE NOTES TO PAGES 318–26

318 *Nothing is what it* Allegorizings
318 *We were primed for* MM to SW
319 *With Everest 50 coming* Al Alvarez to JM and EM, 10 Mar 2003, FC
319 *one of the most* CE, 2003 edn
319 *So, too, was hers* Al Alvarez, 24 May 2003, *Guardian*
319 *Now I have to* JM, 29 May 2003 (speech at Royal Gala 'Endeavour on Everest')
319 *the crisis in the* 9 Aug 2003, *Daily Post*
320 *He is much more* Sep 2003, *Literary Review*
320 *a born hybrid* ibid.
320 *coy whimsy* 24 Nov 1961, *TLS*
320 *I liked young Americans* Sep 2003, *Literary Review*
321 *It's not even a* Simon Jenkins to SW
321 *The first British mainstream* Burns, in *Trans Britain*
321 *fundamental attitudes . . . have not, et seq. Conundrum*, 2002 edn
321 *It is very much* Burns, in *Trans Britain*
321 *an early hint that, et seq.* Jane Fae, in *Trans Britain*
322 *100 Key Books of* 12 Oct 1996, *Times*
322 *Nobody who reads her* publicity material, FA
322 *For better or worse* Preface to Evelyn Kaye, *Adventures in Japan*, Colorado, 2000
322 *During my own travelling* Foreword, *Off the Beaten Track*, ed. Dea Birkett, 2004
323 *New Guinea was not* Preface to Kaye, *Adventures in Japan*
323 *This is certainly not* Lynne Jones, 25 May 2004, House of Commons
323 *The government had finally* Lynne Jones, in *Trans Britain*
324 *No. I've had too* Bill Norman to SW
324 *people try to define Desert Island Discs*, 21 Jun 2002
324 *We saw her and* Valerie Kleeman to SW
324 *I admire her very* Patrick Leigh Fermor to Rudi Fischer, 10 Nov 1986, *Dashing for the Post*, ed. Adam Sisman, 2016
324 *beyond cavil the greatest* 24 Oct 1986, *Times*
324 *Mr Fermor is perhaps* ibid.
324 *I wish you could* Leigh Fermor to JM, 2 Jun 2004, FC
325 *imperishable picture of life* 50 Yrs
325 *so fresh and hopeful* Intro, Patrick Leigh Fermor, *A Time of Gifts*, 2005 edn, New York
325 *not only remembering himself* ibid.
325 *The past is a* Trieste
325 *Facing up to Rheumatism* Allegorizings
325 *cosmetic face transformation* note, n.d., FA
325 *We've been together for* EM to JM, 18 Mar 2007
325 *To my very special* EM to JM, 2 Oct 2007
326 *the look of an* IMME
326 *and when passing customers* Allegorizings
326 *It was thought to* 4 Feb 2010, unsent, EM, FC
326 *I don't think much* JM to MM, 2 May 2006, FC

326 *Finding himself in his* PoaTL
326 *multiculturalism was blurring old* publicity note for *Hav* combined edition, 2006, FC
327 *the 2006 Hav is* 2 Jun 2006, *TLS*
327 *Probably Morris, certainly her, et seq.* Ursula K. Le Guin, 2 Jun 2006, *Guardian*
328 *I seem to spend* An Eloquent Sufficiency, ed. Susan Wyndham, Sydney, 1998
328 *I'm not really a* Sandy Nairne to SW
329 *a cheery old cracker* Jonathan Keates, Nov 1997, *Literary Review*
329 *evokes the swagger and* Tom Holland, Dec 2005, *Good Book Guide*
329 *a dreadful phenomenon* MacKenzie, *Cultural History of the British Empire*
329 (fn) *Among the most meaningful* Tom Holland to SW
330 *The British Empire was, et seq.* 29 Aug 1997, *Daily Mail*
330 *Is this the arse-end* www.listener.co.nz, 23 Mar 2012
330 *has succeeded better than, et seq.* Feb 2003, *Literary Review*
331 *Whenever I have felt* courtesy Trish Morris
331 *They had a bond* Catharine Morris to SW
331 *He was born with . . . He was a truly* courtesy Trish Morris
332 *No, alas, we're not* JM to Gareth Morris, 26 Apr 2001, courtesy Trish Morris
332 *Imagine, if Elizabeth died* Paul Morris to SW
332 *which I'm hoping to* JM to MM, 30 Jun 2007, FC
332 *If only Jan had* SM to SW
332 *Glorious . . . divine, however abject* JM to MM, 30 Dec 2007, FC
332 *I prefer to consider* 14 Jan 2008, *Times*
332 *Do you want to, et seq.* W. W. Norton & Company archive
333 *During the Napoleonic Wars* 'An Outsider on Everest', Sir Edmund Hillary Memorial Lecture, 27 May 2010, courtesy The Himalayan Trust
333 *I thought I'd make* Colin Thubron to SW
334 *We were introduced, but* Paul Clements, *Jan Morris*, 2022
334 *insufferably fey and self-indulgent* 25 Mar 2010, *Guardian*
335 *pioneering a new kind, et seq.* Foreword, Robert Byron, *Europe in the Looking Glass*, 2012 edn
335 *stretched dead on a slab* Laurie Lee, *A Moment of War*, 1991
335 *For myself, I doubt* Intro, Lee, *A Moment of War*, 2014 edn
335 *true in the sweep* Travels
336 *Oh my love, my* Four-Letter Word, ed. Joshua Knelman & Rosalind Porter, Toronto, 2008
336 *Must go, don't know* Leigh Fermor, *A Time of Gifts*
336 *the last of a* 12 Jun 2011, *Observer*
336 *One of the great* Intro, Leigh Fermor, *A Time of Gifts*
336 *The fizz was gone* Joey Casey to SW
336 *anything to stop Jan* FC

17 BOTH

337 *Jan was always the* Valerie Kleeman to SW
337 *after all I've put* ibid.

337 Both Alan and Jan ibid.
338 brilliantly ... the endless spectacle, et seq. TA
338 irrevocably mingled in my IMME
338 Everything in Venice is Bookclub, 5 Jun 2008
339 Though I came from PoaTL
339 played Tosca when crossing ibid.
339 Routine is the one 'Loneliness', W. H. Auden, *Epistle to a Godson*, 1972
340 Praying that you win Mike Parker to SW
340 such a great ambassador Leanne Wood to JM, 20 Feb 2015, FC
340 she materialises from what Sarah Lyell, 25 Apr 2019, *NYT*
340 a born hybrid Sep 2003, *Literary Review*
340 I haven't gone from 30 Aug 2018, *Times*
340 Of course I had 23 Mar 2018, *FT*
341 I think more and 30 Aug 2018, *Times*
341 She became more and Trish Morris to SW
341 She has been determined 30 Jan 1993, *Independent*
341 She was one of, et seq. Derek Johns to SW
341 I'll buy you some Angus Cargill to SW
341 because they won't let JM to Hetherington, 10 May 1956, GA
342 I never felt there, et seq. Rahul Jacob to SW
342 Jan is a precious *Taith i Jan Morris / A Journey for Jan Morris*, Plas Glyn y Weddw, Llanbedrog, 2016
342 so-called villains from recorded event, Plas Glyn y Weddw, 15 Oct 2016
342 a flower opening ... wondered, et seq. Michael Palin to SW
342 that very handsome young Charlotte Sacher (Oxford Films) to SW
342 It gets higher every 'Michael Palin meets Jan Morris', BBC *Artsnight*, 4 Oct 2016
343 She was warm and, et seq. Michael Palin to SW
343 I eagerly turned to IMME
343 It's very kind of TA
343 I have entered a IMME
343 that subtle demon of ibid.
343 I, the mere partner TA
344 I'd have been a, et seq. *The Verb*, 18 May 2018, BBC Radio 3
345 A pretty equivocal sort, et seq. *The British Empire: An Equivocation*, 27 Jun 2018, BBC Radio 4
345 Having for the moment IMME
345 Thank you ibid.
345 What is it with, et seq. ibid.
345 We all talk to ibid.
346 Not feeling terribly bright ibid.
346 squalor and disillusion ... Every, et seq. ibid.
347 and thank you most n.d., NLW
347 I have had to, et seq. FC

347 *my emotional needs have* ibid.
347 *extremely conservative older colleague* ibid.
347 *to bring back happy* ibid.
348 *I have always rather, et seq.* TA
349 *Sometimes down by the* Conundrum, 2002 edn

AFTERWORD
351 *I want to be* e.g. 13 Nov 2000, *CBS News Sunday Morning*
351 *reassuringly common* Allegorizings
351 *woodland grotto* TM to SW
352 *INSTITUTION CAUGHT UP IN* 16 Feb 2024, *Times*
352 *both now* 30 Aug 2018, *Times*
352 Conundrum *belongs near the* Stephanie Burt, 19 Jan 2021, *Paris Review*
353 *closed-minded sophistry . . . almost sanctifying, et seq.* CN Lester, Intro to *Conundrum*, Folio 2024 edn
353 *with but not of* Peter Fleming, 28 Mar 1958, *Spectator*
353 *If they did not* Conundrum
353 *She comes across as, et seq.* Sathnam Sanghera, *Jan Morris: Writing a Life*, 13 Nov 2021, BBC Radio 4
354 *Wherever I go, you* Paul Theroux to JM, 2 Oct 1995, FC

ACKNOWLEDGEMENTS

When Mark Morris, Jan's literary executor, asked me to write this biography, we had never met: he had only read some of my books, which is not (quite) the same thing. He did not ask for text approval and cooperated over the long haul with insight, intelligence, humour and good grace. No biographer could ask for more. My deepest thanks go to him. His brother Twm Morys facilitated access to their parents' home over the course of several years, helped in other ways and talked to me at length. Their sister Suki Morys generously gave me her time. Mark's partner Janice Tole and Twm's partner Gwyneth Glyn were endlessly forbearing in the wings, and I suspect I owe them more than I know. Thank you. In the wider family, warm thanks to Trish Morris, Catharine Morris, Mary Morris, Thomas Morris and Paul Morris.

I am grateful to everyone who agreed to be interviewed. They include, in England: Joey Casey; Kate Fetherston-Godley; Alexander Fyjis-Walker; Eleo Gordon; Sir Simon Jenkins; Derek Johns; Andrew Kerr; William Kerr; Valerie Kleeman; Julian Loose (who went to great and awful lengths to retrieve emails); Alberto Manguel; Robert McCrum; Belinda Mitchell-Innes; Sandy Nairne; the late Rev. Bill Norman; Jo Shaw; Elizabeth Skeet and the late Ian Skeet; Arturo di Stefano; Paul Theroux; Alex Uxbridge, Marquess of Anglesey; Paul Wakefield; Robert Winder. *Yng Nghymru*: Dafydd Iwan; Anne Loveland; Morfydd Roberts and the late Rev. Arthur Roberts. In Canada: John Fraser. In the US: Bob Weil; Jan Wenner. In India: Rahul Jacob. Thank you all.

For insightful readings of drafts, thanks to Peter Graham, Catherine Moorehead and Andy Rattue.

I was fortunate to have Victoria Glendinning as a mentor, and I owe her a debt of gratitude. Others I wish to thank include John Arnott and Philippa Arnott; Nicolas Barker; James Barr; Richard Beswick; Robert

ACKNOWLEDGEMENTS

Binyon; Katherine Bucknell; the Hon. Nell Butler; Alan Cameron; David Campbell; Peter Carew; Sam Carter and Leslie Mitchell; Richard Cohen, who had the idea I should take Morris on in the first place; Bill Colegrave; Johanna David and the late Robin David for hospitality in Monmouth; Michael Delgado; Miranda France; Lesley Gerry; Tim Gibbs; Belinda Harley; Matthew Hart; Adrian Harvey; Lucy Hughes-Hallett; Tom Holland; Bruce Hunter; Pico Iyer; Jonno Keates for Venice talk; Susan Kerner; Mary Killen; Petra Lewis; Roger Lewis; Sheila Markham; Patrick McAfee for wisdom on *Trieste*; Dr Helen Miller for guidance on medical matters; Mike Parker; the late Jonathan Raban; Jasper Rees; Sir Christopher Ricks; Catherine Riley at the Royal Society of Literature; Ann Rittenberg; Andrew Roberts, Lord Roberts of Belgravia; Stephen Robson at the Charles Rolls Heritage Trust; Barnaby Rogerson; Ruth Scurr; Nick and John Shakespeare; Linda Shaughnessy; Michael Sheridan for Hong Kong talk; Norena Shopland; Posy Simmons; Sir Peter Stothard; Tom Sutherland; Tom Swick; Colin Thubron; Richard Turner; Stephen Venables for help with (not on) Everest; Jane Walker; Simon Walker; John Walsh; Simon Winchester; Philip Womack; James Woodall.

In the archives: thanks to staff at the National Library of Wales; Janette Martin and the team at the John Rylands Research Institute and Library, University of Manchester; staff at the Eisenhower Centre, home of the Faber Archive, and Toby Faber for showing me how to penetrate the Faber system there; the *Guardian* Archive in London, where Philippa Mole went beyond the call of duty; Nicholas Mays at the News UK Archive at Rainham, Essex; Andrew Riley and Jess Saunders at the archive of Churchill College, Cambridge; Frank Bowles in the Cambridge University Library Archives and Modern Manuscripts Department; Dr Martin Maw at Oxford University Press; Judith Curthoys at Christ Church Archive; Dr Emily Jennings at Magdalen College Archive; Lesley Eastabrook at Lancing College Archive; Natalya Rattan and Zoe Mack at the Fisher Library, University of Toronto; staff at the Wellcome Foundation Library, the British Library and the

ACKNOWLEDGEMENTS

Beinecke Rare Book and Manuscript Library at Yale; National Trust staff at Plas Newydd. And as always, for every book, the incomparable staff at the indispensable London Library.

Thanks to editors Laura Hassan at Faber in London and Noah Eaker at HarperCollins in New York. At Faber, thanks also to Mary Cannam, Angus Cargill, Sara Cheraghlou, Alex Eccles, Ella Griffiths, Leigh Haddix, Mo Hafeez, Hayley Newns, Anne Owen and Robbie Porter; and to Silvia Crompton, Ian Bahrami and Melanie Gee.

I wish to set down my gratitude to Lewis Marks KC for legal counsel and advice. Also Philip Kolvin KC for guidance and support on contractual matters. These two were my rocks; without them there would not be a book.

Thanks to my agents Lisa Baker at Aitken Alexander in London and Kathy Robbins at the Robbins Agency in New York, and to Caroline Dawnay at United Agents, representatives of the Morris estate. For permission to quote: thanks to Curtis Brown Ltd (W. H. Auden), David Higham Associates (Louis MacNeice), Smokestack Books (John Berger); the University of Manchester Library (*Guardian* archive); the estate of Patrick Leigh Fermor and the News UK Archive.

All mistakes are mine.

PICTURE CREDITS

Every reasonable effort has been made to trace copyright holders. Any copyright holder who has not been correctly acknowledged is requested to contact the publisher.

Page 1 Enid at the piano; James and Chris: Family collection
  Walter, Gareth and James: Courtesy Trish Morris
  1 Herbert Road © Sara Wheeler
Page 2 With telescope; at eleven: Family collection
  With Chris in Piccadilly; Chris in the organ loft: Courtesy Paul Morris
Page 3 Morris and Busk in Venice: photographer unknown; military ID card; Palestine: Family collection
Page 4 Wedding; scrapbook images: Family collection
  Heathrow: TopFoto
Page 5 Reading proofs: Family collection
  On Everest: Alfred Gregory, Royal Geographical Society via Getty Images
  With Sherpas: Courtesy *The Times* / News Licensing
Page 6 Shaking hands with Hillary: George Lowe, Royal Geographical Society via Getty Images
  With Hillary in DC; Pye ad: Family collection
Page 7 Morrises on the lawn: Courtesy *The Times* / News Licensing
  With Rolls in the Alps: Courtesy Elizabeth Skeet
  Morris and Henry: Family collection
Page 8 Morrises in Venice: Courtesy *The Times* / News Licensing
  Morris and sons; Suki and dogs: Family collection
  Plas Trefan © Sara Wheeler

PICTURE CREDITS

Page 9   1970: Faber Archive; 1971: Faber Archive © Frances Charteris
On *Dick Cavett Show*: ABC Photo Archives via Getty Images

Page 10 Charles Monteith: Faber Archive
Enid's letter: Family collection
Newsstand poster: Courtesy *The Times* / News Licensing
Morris with bookshelves: Faber Archive © Bruno de Hamel

Page 11 Sketch © Don Bachardy. All rights reserved
With tower of *Pax Britannica*: Courtesy *Bath and West Evening Chronicle*

Page 12 Notebook © Sara Wheeler
Binoculars: Peter Kevin Solness, Fairfax Media Archives via Getty Images
Morris and Twm © Richard Whitehead / courtesy National Portrait Gallery, London

Page 13 Twm, Elizabeth and Mark: Courtesy Mark Morris
With HRH Queen Elizabeth II: Family collection

Page 14 Trefan Morys, exterior and interior © Sara Wheeler
With Jacky Fisher © Matt Thomas

Page 15 Arturo di Stefano portrait © National Portrait Gallery, London
Elizabeth; family group: Courtesy Mark Morris

Page 16 © Antonio Olmos

INDEX

Abbreviations: EM Elizabeth Morris; JM James/Jan Morris. All works are by JM unless otherwise indicated.

Abse, Leo, 232, 236
Academy Club, London, 286
Afghanistan, 140–1
Algeria, 123, 131, 132, 214
All Souls College, Oxford, 102, 119, 166, 167, 179, 204
Allegorizings, 7, 351; JM prepares ground, 318; JM's promotional film, 332–3
Alvarez, Al, 99–100, 101, 319
Amis, Kingsley: *Girl, 20*, 151, 211, 254
Amman, 107, 116, 135
Among the Cities, 276
Anglesey, Henry, 7th Marquess of, 211–12, 264, 305, 310, 340
Anglo-Iranian Oil Company, 64, 73
Anson, Peter, 56
'anthrax' attack on JM, 311
Appleton, Berkshire, 64, 68, 76, 83
Arab News Agency (ANA), 57–8, 60–1, 64, 107
Armstrong-Jones, Tony, Lord Snowdon, 231
Asanuma, Inejiro, 143
Ashley, April, 182–3, 184, 231, 239
Attlee, Clement, 43, 59
Auden, W. H., 3, 22, 26, 59–60, 111, 201, 225, 339
Austen, Jane, 206, 314
Australia, 47, 150, 151, 176, 191, 228, 252, 288–9; newspaper serialisations of *Conundrum*, 231
The Australian (newspaper): review of *Sydney*, 289

Bach, Julian, 165, 233, 291
Bach Agency, 176, 252–3
Bachardy, Don, 247–8
Baldwin, Stanley, 16, 21, 348
Balkan Wars, 297

Ballard, J. G., 327
Bangkok, 140, 167
Barstow, Stan: *A Kind of Loving*, 153, 309; sends JM fan letter about *Trieste*, 309
Bath, 17, 25, 32, 214, 230; *Bath* (Robertson), 230; JM's flat, 217, 222, 230, 251
Battleship Yamato: Of War, Beauty and Irony, 344
Baynes, Pauline, 151
Beaumont, Chevalier d'Éon de, 137–8, 167
Beaumont Society, 138, 181–2
Bedford, Sybille: *Pleasures and Landscapes*, 313
Bell, Gertrude, 241
Benjamin, Henry, 160–1, 180, 183, 214; *The Transsexual Phenomenon*, 161
Berger, John, 77–8; *G.*, 78
Berlin, Irving, 33, 315
Berlin Wall, 295
Bevin, Ernie, 42, 59
Biggar, Nigel, 329
bin Taimur, Sultan Said, 109, 110–11, 113
Bird, Isabella, 323
Birkett, Dea: *Off the Beaten Track: Three Centuries of Women Travellers* (ed.), 323
Black, Eugene R., 152, 197
Blair, Tony, 305
Bletchley Park, 84, 111
Bodley, John, 231, 233, 241, 250, 251, 257
Bosnia-Herzegovina, 297
Bourdillon, Tom, 90, 91, 96
Bourne, Betty, 54, 55, 100
Bourne, George and Bessie, 55
Boustead, Hugh, 113, 187–8
Brain, Dennis, 25, 32, 86
Breitmeyer, Charles, 95, 214
Breitmeyer, Peter, 95, 186, 267
Brenan, Gerald, 163, 165; *South from Granada*, 163
Brennan, Maeve: *The Long-Winded Lady*, 338
Briggs, Chris and Jo, 174
The British Empire: An Equivocation (BBC radio), 345

INDEX

British Empire and imperialism: British weakening and withdrawal, 48, 50, 59, 122, 129, 147, 153, 176, 258; Empire Day celebrations, 20–1; and the 'imperial aesthetic', 47; 'informal Empire' in Middle East, 110, 113; JM's piece for *Daily Mail*, 330; JM's vocabulary when describing, 129, 256–7; and multiculturalism in Britain, 193; museum of, 330; Niall Ferguson on, 330–1; public attitudes (2014 YouGov poll), 330; scholarship on, 190–1, 191n; and schoolroom maps, 21; *see also* Mandatory Palestine; *Pax Britannica* trilogy

Browning, Robert, 71, 275

Bunin, Ivan, 308

Burgess, Guy, 71, 125, 142, 275, 286

Burns, Christine, *Trans Britain: Our Journey from the Shadows* (ed.), 261, 321

Burou, Georges, 182, 183, 214–15, 216

Busk, Martin, 75, 120

Byron, Robert, 140; *Europe in the Looking Glass: Reflections of a Motor Drive from Grimsby to Athens*, 335

Cairo: Black Saturday, 75; EM in, 63, 105–6, 113–14, 118; as 'half-way city', 143; JM in, 58–60, 61–2, 63–4, 72, 73–4, 75–6, 105–7, 118, 132, 149, 254–6; *Saphir* (houseboat), 63, 72, 105–6, 107, 113–14, 116, 118, 149, 255

Callaghan, Jim, 252, 259

Cambridge Five spy ring, 61, 70, 71, 125, 126, 142, 275

Campaign for Nuclear Disarmament (CND), 274

Canada: JM in, 140, 176, 201; Mark Morris in, 276, 279, 334

Capote, Truman: *In Cold Blood*, 199

Carew, Peter (né Breitmeyer), 95, 186, 267

Caribbean, 130, 142, 147, 186, 217

Carpaccio, 38, 139, 339; *Ciao, Carpaccio! An Infatuation*, 339

Casey, William, 67, 74

cats, 2, 106, 118, 171, 187, 317, 318, 325, 326, 328, 329, 347

Cavett, Dick, 233–4

Ceylon: EM's childhood in, 54–5; JM visits, 175

Charles, Prince of Wales, 267, 268, 277, 315

Chatwin, Bruce, 263–4, 268, 293, 322, 328

Cheever, John, 280–1

Chekhov, Anton, 314

China, 346n, 347; JM in, 272–3

Christ Church, Oxford: JM as chorister, 20, 22–5, 27; JM as undergraduate, 66–7, 68, 69, 71; links with intelligence services, 65; Mark Morris at, 211; other alumni, 26, 73, 111, 120, 156; *son et lumière* fundraising event, 201

Churchill, Randolph, 131, 132

Churchill, Winston: concerns about Middle East, 76; concerns about Russian army, 41; death, 132; JM's opinions of, 257; in *Pax Britannica*, 257; RAF Symphony Orchestra plays for, 32; returns as prime minister, 72; rumours of imminent death in Monte Carlo, 131–2; actual death, 132; speeches, 27, 35, 42

Ciao, Carpaccio! An Infatuation, 339

Cities, 167, 168

class differences, widening in Britain, 156–7

class snobbery (JM), 26, 83, 84, 98, 126, 145, 146, 150–1, 157, 168

Clausen, George, 11, 12

Clausen, Katharine 'Kitty', 11, 12

Clevedon: JM's parents' and childhood homes in, 13–15, 17, 19, 21, 25, 351; JM's parents' burial plot, 267; national celebrations in, 20–1, 35; Picture House, 14, 22, 27; wartime bombings, 32

The Climax of an Empire see under Pax Britannica trilogy

coal crisis, 43, 53

Coast to Coast/As I Saw the USA, 102, 103, 105, 108, 116–17, 121, 158, 193

Coca-Cola, 99, 104

'Coca-Colonization', 59, 109

Cold War: beginnings, 41–2, 48–9; end of, 282, 295

Commonwealth Fund Fellowships, 81–2, 96, 98, 121

Commonwealth Trans-Antarctic Expedition, 121

Conrad, Joseph, 206

Conundrum: content and style, 214, 223–6, 238–9, 240, 242; Faber advances, 221, 222; fiftieth-anniversary edition, 353; jacket blurb, 225, 230; JM's dissatisfactions with, 223–4, 229, 230; letters to newspapers in

INDEX

response to, 239–40; Mark's and Suki's responses to, 225; new introduction to 2002 edition, 321, 323; newspaper serialisations, 231, 236; publication and publicity, 231–4; readers' personal letters of gratitude to JM, 236–7, 347; reviews, 232, 234–6, 237, 238, 246, 322, 352; significance and legacy, 238, 240, 261, 321–2, 347, 351, 352–3; writing and redrafting, 221, 222–4

Corbett, Arthur, 182, 183

Corbett v. *Corbett* court case, 183, 219

Coronation Everest, 97, 101–2, 108, 113, 131, 319

Covid-19 pandemic, 348

Coward, Noël, 34

Cowell, Roberta 'Betty', 114, 226; *Roberta Cowell's Story by Herself*, 114

Crawshay-Williams, Robert and Elizabeth, 173, 318

Criccieth, 169, 175, 220, 244, 267, 269, 282, 292, 305, 308, 321, 331, 334, 340, 343

Crook, Arthur, 249, 264

Cymdeithas yr Gymraeg (Welsh Language Society), 203

Cyprus, 122, 123, 124, 147

Czechoslovakia/Czech Republic, 140, 295

dahabiyeh (houseboat), Cairo, 4, 63, 72, 105–6, 107, 113–14, 116, 118, 149, 255

Daily Mail: JM's piece on British Empire, 330; see also Izzard, Ralph

Daily Mirror, 222

Day, Robin, 232–3

Deakin, Ralph, 69–70, 72, 76, 77, 78, 80

Depression, 16–17

Desert Island Discs (radio), 19, 271, 314–15

Destinations, 259–60, 265

Diana, Princess of Wales: in *Allegorizings*, 351; death, 303–4; wedding, 267, 315

Dickens, Charles, 314

Dickson, Mora: *Baghdad and Beyond*, 241

Disney, Walt, 100

donkeys, 172, 187, 218

Doughty, Charles, 49–50, 65–6; *Travels in Arabia Deserta*, 49, 50

du Sautoy, Peter, 196, 202, 225, 245, 250–1

Dunne, John Gregory and Joan Didion, 248

The Economist (magazine), 250

ECSC (European Coal and Steel Community), 67–8

Eden, Anthony, 41, 42, 72, 122, 124

Edward VII, King (funeral), 9

Egypt: Anglo-Egyptian treaty negotiations, 72–3; Britain's changing relationship with, 58–9, 72–3, 106; First Arab–Israeli War, 58, 62; JM in (writing for *Manchester Guardian*), 124; JM in (writing for *Rolling Stone*), 254–6; JM in (writing for *The Times*), 72–7, 105–7, 118; JM travels through en route to military posting in Mandatory Palestine, 44–5; JM's posting with Arab News Agency, 58, 59–62, 63–4; Naguib–Nasser coup, 106; Suez Crisis, 118, 121–5; *see also* Cairo

Ehrlichman, John, 246–7

Eisenhower, Dwight, 98, 100, 124, 246

Eisenhower, Mamie, 99

Eisteddfod, 296, 319–20

Elbe, Lili, 351

Eliot, T. S.: on Charles Monteith, 119; as director at Faber & Faber, 102; *Notes Towards the Definition of Culture*, 57

Elizabeth II, Queen: attends celebration of fortieth and fiftieth anniversaries of Everest ascent, 290, 304, 319; attends premiere of *The Conquest of Everest*, 96; awards CBE to JM, 304; awards Coronation Medal to Everest expedition members, 95, 304; coronation, 76, 93, 94, 105; hosts National Book Day event attended by JM, 304; not informed of JM's transition, 304; receives news of Everest ascent, 93, 95

Encounter (magazine), 77, 139–40, 156, 178, 189, 284

Ephron, Nora, 234, 235, 237, 238

Equality Act (2010), 340, 352

Ethiopia, 143, 153, 188

Eton College, 9, 111, 168, 185, 186, 196, 210, 258, 267; Etonians, 35, 143, 258

European Economic Community: Britain joins, 221; France vetoes Britain's application, 156, 200

European Union: Single European Act (1985), 282

Evans, Charles, 90

Evans, Harry, 231, 290

Evans, Matthew, 220, 223, 254, 283, 292

Evening Standard (newspaper), 234, 238, 301

397

INDEX

Everest expedition: *The Ascent of Everest* (Hunt, book), 97; codes for dispatches to *The Times*, 82, 83, 87, 91, 92, 96, 108; *The Conquest of Everest* (Stobart, film), 96–7, 99; *Coronation Everest* (JM, book), 97, 101–2, 108, 113, 131, 319; Coronation Medal awarded to members, 95; discussions about correspondent for *The Times*, 80–1, 82, 83; Evans and Bourdillon's South Summit ascent, 90; fiftieth-anniversary Royal Gala Celebration, 319; Hillary and Tenzing's South Summit ascent, 90–1; JM as expedition member, 4–5, 82–95, 96, 97; JM climbs to Camp IV, 88–9, 90–1, 97; JM exaggerates height of own ascent, 342; JM recreates in family garden, 159; JM's dispatches, 84, 85, 87, 89, 91, 92, 93, 102; JM's socks later used as Christmas stockings, 173; porters, 83, 131; reunions, 164, 173–4, 222, 290, 319, 337; rival press interest in, 82, 84, 86, 90; Sherpas *see* Sherpas; *The Times* breaks story of successful ascent, 93; *The Times* refuses (then grants) JM permission to publish book on, 97, 101–2, 113; *The Times* sponsorship and story rights, 80; training, 83; other members *see* Bourdillon, Tom; Evans, Charles; Gregory, Alf; Hillary, Edmund; Hunt, John; Lowe, George; Noyce, Wilf; Pugh, Griff; Roberts, J. O. M. 'Jimmy'; Stobart, Tom; Tenzing Norgay; Ward, Mike; Westmacott, Mike; Wylie, Charles

Faber & Faber: 'bank' of, 196, 222, 259; contracts and advances for JM's books, 102, 105, 113, 197, 210, 221, 222, 254; deals with JM's transition and name change, 210–11, 218–20; delays publishing *The Great Port*, 202–3; financial difficulties, 252; JM's impatience with, 202–3, 251; printers' strikes, 229; rights for *The World Bank*, 152; seventy-fifth anniversary celebration, 321; turns down books by JM, 259, 263, 275; *see also* Bodley, John; du Sautoy, Peter; Evans, Matthew; Goad, Rosemary; McCrum, Robert; Monteith, Charles
Faisal II, King of Iraq, 132
Fallowell, Duncan, 239

Fanny, Aunt, 11, 13, 15, 26
Farewell the Trumpets see under Pax Britannica trilogy
Farouk, King of Egypt, 58, 59, 106
Ferguson, Niall: *Empire: How Britain Made the Modern World*, 330–1
Fifty Years of Europe: An Album, 301–3; republished as *Europe: An Intimate Journey*, 329
Fiji, 206, 207
Financial Times: JM's diary column, 345; JM's travel pieces, 317; review of *Oxford*, 179; review of *Pax Britannica*, 194; *see also* Jacob, Rahul; Shanks, Michael
First Arab–Israeli War, 58, 62
First World War, 11–12, 13, 22, 25, 42, 77–8, 172
Fisher, Admiral Lord John 'Jacky', 1, 294–5
Fisher's Face, 294–5
flasher, in Athens, 302
Fleming, Ian: *Casino Royale*, 111; *Thrilling Cities*, 167–8
Fleming, Peter, 111–12, 121, 131, 353; *Brazilian Adventure*, 111; *To Peking*, 111
Florence, 39
Forster, E. M., 194–5; *A Passage to India*, 194, 195
Forward, Mr and Mrs, 145, 171, 203
France: 'aesthetic' of the Second Empire, 206; JM in, 37, 176, 201; JM and family in French Alps, 119–21, 125; Paris, 132, 267, 280; and Suez Crisis, 122, 123–4, 125; vetoes Britain's application to EEC, 156, 200
Franco, General, 162, 166, 254

Gallipoli, 257–8
Gandhi, Indira, 249, 250
Gandhi, Mahatma, 17, 250, 257
Gaulle, Charles de, 156, 200
gender-critical feminism, 238, 239
gender dysphoria, 160, 239, 352; *see also under* gender identity and transitioning (JM)
gender fluidity, 226, 352
gender identity and transitioning (JM): attracting curiosity, 204, 207, 209, 220, 294; conviction of inhabiting the wrong body, 114, 115, 239; Faber's official in-house announcement, 210–11; feelings of femininity, 52, 62, 115; feminising

398

hormones and side effects, 138, 140, 149–50, 157, 163, 184, 202; gender as 'arbitrary sham', 308; gender surgery, 214–16, 217, 222, 224; as 'half a freak show, half a miracle', 204; Harley Street practitioners, 146, 160; having no regrets over transition, 241–2; Henry Benjamin's role, 160–1; hiding physical changes during transitioning, 141, 158, 185, 186; lack of peer support, 181–2; learning about other trans people, 114–16; long-term medication and side effects, 294, 296; medical bills, 140, 151, 196, 217; as much more than problems with own homosexuality, 146; name change and writing names, 218–20; needing to 'transition or die', 138, 140, 146, 224; neighbours' response to gender transitioning, 278; non-binary 'both' identity, 340–1; others finding her attractive, 186–7, 226–7; others' literary slights about, 341–2; pre-transition 'existential terror', 161; presenting as a woman in Oxford, 181, 184–5; press interest, 204, 211, 213, 222; *Private Eye* piece on, 186; refusing to engage with ongoing transgender debates, 2, 238, 242, 323–4, 353; rejecting 'trans woman' identity, 322; self-consciousness during 'chimera' stage, 201, 204; 'smart progressive' people's responses to reassignment, 264; spiritual nature of transitioning, 223, 224; as stereotypical 'feminine type', 222, 238; support from friends, 146, 184, 185–6, 220, 249, 290–1; support from mother, 220–1; tells family members, 185, 211; tells/forgets to tell literary colleagues, 204, 205; transition memoir *see Conundrum*; travels in America as a woman, 209; as two unresolved parts of whole, 137, 223; yearning remaining unresolved after transition, 242, 311–12
Gender Identity Clinic, Charing Cross Hospital, 180, 184
gender reassignment surgery *see* transition surgery
Gender Recognition Act (2004), 323, 340
George Polk Award for Outstanding Foreign Reporting, 147
George V, King: Silver Jubilee and death, 21
George VI, King: coronation, 26; death, 75

Gibbon, Edward: *Decline and Fall of the Roman Empire*, 51, 194
Gillie, Darsie, 132
Giorgione: *La Tempesta* (painting), 39
Glyn, Gwyneth, 342
Glyndŵr, Owain, 245, 259, 271, 320–1
Glyndŵr Award for Outstanding Contribution to the Arts in Wales, 296
Goad, Rosemary, 130–1, 134, 151, 158, 204, 210, 213, 223
Golding, William, 291; *Lord of the Flies*, 103
Goodwin, Dick, 245
The Goon Show (radio), 125
Gorbachev, Mikhail, 282
Gordon, Bill, 226
Gorsedd Beirdd Ynys Prydain (Society of the Bards of the Island of Britain), 296
Gourmet (magazine), 323
Grant, Julia, 258–9, 261
The Great Port: A Passage Through New York, 197, 198, 202–3, 279
Greece, 148, 222, 262, 302, 324–5, 333–4
Greene, Graham, 69, 108n, 111
Greer, Germaine, 232, 234, 238
Gregory, Alf, 91
Grigg, John, 207
Grimond, Jo, 154, 155, 156
Guardian (originally *Manchester Guardian*): 'Herbivore' characterisation of readers, 208; JM approaches again after resignation, 164; JM 'hates' due to 'distasteful' identity politics, 303; JM resigns from, 147; JM taken on, 121; JM's dispatches and pieces, 122–5, 128, 132, 134, 137–8, 140, 142, 143, 147, 148, 149, 150, 157, 164, 175, 288; JM's employee/freelance status, 139; name change, 133; reviews of JM's works, 289, 327–8; *see also* Hetherington, Alastair
Guevara, Che, 142, 198, 342–3; on T-shirt, 271n
Gunn, Thom, 119, 204–5

Haley, Sir William, 78, 105
Halliwell, Kenneth, 119, 204
Handford, Basil 'John', 28, 30
Harcourt, Brace & World: JM's impatience with, 251; JM's titles with, 162, 165, 168, 202, 251; *London* (Pritchett), 162; *see also* Wolff, Helen

INDEX

Harmsworth, Nancy, 129, 130
Hart-Davis, Duff: *Peter Fleming: A Biography*, 111–12
The Hashemite Kings, 132, 134, 135, 164, 219–20
Hav (*Last Letters from Hav* and *Hav of the Myrmidons*), 326–8, 334; *see also Last Letters from Hav*
Hayden, Torey, 272
headstone for JM/EM, 285–6, 294, 318–19, 351
Heaney, Seamus, 205, 328
Heath, Edward, 207, 229, 251, 252
Heaven's Command see under Pax Britannica trilogy
Heinemann Award, 144, 195
Heren, Louis, 70, 74
Hetherington, Alastair, 121, 122, 124, 126, 139, 147, 154, 155, 164, 174–5, 200
Hillary, Edmund, 90–1, 95, 100, 121, 222, 332, 333, 341–2
hiraeth (homesickness), 19, 298, 306, 311
Hirschfeld, Magnus, 115, 160n
hitchhikers, 271n
Hofer, Evelyn, 162, 165–6
Holden, David, 118, 186, 239
Holiday (literary periodical), 189
Holland, Tom, 329, 329n
Hollingworth, Clare, 62
Holmes, Sir Ronald, 226
Hong Kong, 133, 226, 283, 293, 300–1, 342
Hong Kong: Xianggang, 283–4, 316; revisions, 293
Hooper, Tom: *The Danish Girl* (film), 351
Horizon (arts and history quarterly), 253
Horne, Alistair, 213–14
Huddersfield, 153, 156, 172, 189, 329
Hunt, John, 1, 80, 83, 84, 85, 88, 89, 90, 91, 94, 100, 290; *The Ascent of Everest*, 97; *see also* Everest expedition
Hussein, King of Jordan, 107, 116, 132
Hutchinson, Arthur, 82, 83, 84, 86, 94, 95
Hutchinson, June, 83
Huxley, Elspeth, 218, 277–8

In My Mind's Eye, 345–7
Independent (newspaper), 287, 294
India: British withdrawal, 48, 51, 59, 153, 176, 256; economic growth, 346n; Henry Morris in, 227; JM in en route to Nepal, 83; JM in for *Guardian*, 175; JM in for *Venture*, 206; JM in to research *The World Bank*, 153; JM in to research *Pax Britannica* and for *Rolling Stone*, 249–50; JM writes poem in Darjeeling visitors' book, 7–8; JM's lack of emotional involvement with, 176; JM's *Rolling Stone* essay, 316; *A Passage to India* (Forster), 194, 195; in *Pax Britannica*, 191, 192, 227, 249–50, 256, 258, 260; *Raj Quartet* (Scott), 176
indigenous nations, in *Pax Britannica*, 227–8, 243
inflation, in 1970s Britain, 251, 252
intelligence and spies: Cambridge Five spy ring, 61, 70, 71, 125, 126, 142, 275; and Christ Church, 65; MI5 (Security Service), 44, 49; MI6 (Secret Intelligence Service), 44, 49, 58, 75, 111, 120; SIME (Security Intelligence Middle East), 48–9, 61, 107; and *Sunday Times*, 107; and *The Times*, 69, 111, 118
intersex people, 161
Iraq, 107, 129, 132, 134, 288
Iraq Petroleum Company, 109, 112
Ireland, in *Pax Britannica*, 193
Ireland: Your Only Place (photography by Wakefield, with text by JM), 287, 288
Isherwood, Christopher, 60, 247–8
Israel: declaration of independence, 58; First Arab–Israeli War, 58, 62; Jerusalem, 44, 45, 46, 49, 108, 116, 148; JM and EM holiday in, 108; JM in, 116, 122, 123, 148; Suez Crisis, 118, 121–5; *see also* Mandatory Palestine
Istanbul, 256, 260
Italy: Florence, 39; Milan, 39; post-war conditions and politics, 37–9, 40; Trieste, 41–3, 311, 312, 317, 354; Venice, 38–9, 40–1, 57, 74, 133–5, 136, 287, 289–90, 317, 324, 334, 338, 339; *see also Trieste and the Meaning of Nowhere*; *Venice/The World of Venice*
Iwan, Dafydd, 3, 203, 298, 342
Izzard, Molly: *Freya Stark: A Biography*, 291
Izzard, Ralph, 75, 84, 86, 102, 108, 291

Jacob, Rahul, 316, 317, 342
Japan, 132–3, 143
Jenkins, Canon Claude, 23–4
Jenkins, John, 243
Jenkins, Sir Simon, 270, 318, 320–1

INDEX

Jerusalem, 44, 45, 46, 49, 108, 116, 148
Jewish refugees: in Europe, 44, 49; in Mandatory Palestine, 44, 46, 49; Walter (staying with JM's family in Clevedon), 26, 36
Johns, Derek, 291, 305, 341; *Ariel: A Literary Life of Jan Morris*, 341
Jones, Betty, 218, 251, 286, 332
Jones, J. E., 269
Jones, W. S. (Wil Sam), 203
Jordan, 107, 116, 132
Jorgensen, Christine, 115, 160n, 161, 183, 221; *Christine Jorgensen: A Personal Autobiography*, 221

Kennedy, John F., 147, 167, 245
Kenya, 147, 188, 207
Kerr, Andrew, 145
Kerr, Isabel, 120, 127, 136, 145, 173, 305
Kerr, Johnnie, 120, 127, 136, 145–6, 173, 305
Kerr, William, 136, 293
Khrushschev, Nikita, 143
kindness, virtues of, 5, 203, 318, 332, 342, 346, 347
Kinglake, Alexander: *Eothen*, 65, 66–7, 106
Kipling, Rudyard, 22; *Kim*, 329
Kirwan, Laurence 'Larry', 80, 81
kitchen-sink works, 153, 309
Kleeman, Valerie, 324, 337–8
Kuwait, 109, 127, 288

Lancing College, 27, 29–31, 65, 224
Larkin, Philip, 119; *The Whitsun Weddings*, 151
Last Letters from Hav, 274–5, 308; *see also Hav*
Laurie, Lieutenant-Colonel David, 43
Lawley, Sue, 314–15
Lawrence, T. E., 135, 194: *Seven Pillars of Wisdom*, 65, 66
Le Guin, Ursula K., 327–8
Lee, Laurie: *A Moment of War*, 335
Leigh Fermor, Patrick, 324–5, 336; *A Time of Gifts*, 325, 326; *Between the Woods and the Water*, 324
Leipzig Konservatorium, 10–11
Levin, Bernard, 209, 235
Lewis, Roger, 286
Liberal Party, 154–5, 157
Life (magazine), 140, 143, 144, 148, 189, 271
Lincoln: A Foreigner's Quest, 305–6

Literary Review (magazine), 281
Lively, Penelope, 316
Llanbedrog arts centre, day in honour of JM, 342
Lloyd George, David, 1, 170–1, 244
Lloyd, Selwyn, 116
Los Angeles, 247–8, 278, 279, 288
Lowe, George, 91, 337

Macaulay, Rose: *Towers of Trebizond*, 313
A Machynlleth Triad, 296–7
Maclean, Donald, 61, 71, 125, 275
Macmillan, Harold, 122–3, 124, 126, 143, 147, 156
MacNeice, Louis: *Autumn Sequel* (poem), 97; script for *The Conquest of Everest* (film), 96
Malta, 201, 301–2
Manchester Guardian see the *Guardian*
Mandatory Palestine, 43–51, 58; *see also* Israel
Mandela, Nelson, 128
Manhattan '45, 279–81, 310
The Market of Seleukia/Islam Inflamed, 121, 128–9, 152, 164, 275
marriage rights, for trans people, 183, 219, 323
Marshall Plan, 48, 59
Marten, Eliza, 9–10
The Matter of Wales: content, perspective and style, 271–2; discussions with Faber, 244, 245, 251; initial conception as biography of Owain Glyndŵr, 245, 259, 271; OUP contract, 252, 265; reviews, 272; updated and republished (as *Wales: Epic Views of a Small Country*), 298, 303
McCarthy, Joe, 98, 103
McCrum, Robert, 275
McCullough, David: *Truman*, 287
McDonald, Iverach, 81, 93, 97, 105, 117–18
McLeod Innes, Neil, 112
McMillan, Ian, 344
Meibion Glyndŵr (Sons of Glendower), 269, 271
MI5 (Security Service), 44, 49
MI6 (Secret Intelligence Service), 44, 49, 58, 75, 111, 120
Milan, 39
miners' strike, 281
Mitchell, Annie, 10
Mitchell, Joseph, 199
Mitchell, Maria, 10

INDEX

Mitchell-Innes, Belinda, 211, 232
Mitford, Nancy, 144, 146
Monmouth, 9, 10, 11, 12–13
Monte Carlo, 131–2, 133
Monteith, Charles: appearance, 119; attends Auden's funeral, 225; attends *son et lumière* at Christ Church, 201; character, 119, 292; death, 291; Faber career, 102, 259, 279, 283; fellow of All Souls College, Oxford, 102, 119; godparent to Tom (Twm) Morris, 158; learns of Casablanca, 204; as 'Liz Monteith' in *Between Us Girls* (Orton), 119; Matthew Evans' opinion of, 254; relationship with Rosemary Goad, 131; sexuality, 254, 292
  WORKS WITH JM: believes JM has 'lost her edge', 252; *Coast to Coast*, 102, 105, 108; *Conundrum*, 221, 223; *Coronation Everest*, 113; discussions about Afghan book, 140; first meeting, 119; *The Hashemite Kings*, 134; hopes JM will not sever links completely, 259; JM asks if he will accompany her to *Spectator* party, 220; JM informs him that Collins has offered more than Faber, 158; *Manhattan '45*, 279; as 'midwife', 292; *Oxford*, 179; *Pax Britannica* trilogy, 197, 213, 216; signing off letters 'with love', 216; *The Spectacle of Empire*, 263; stays loyal to JM, 245; *Sultan in Oman*, 121; *Venice*, 145, 229; *The World Bank*, 164
  WORKS WITH OTHER AUTHORS: John Osborne, 119; Philip Larkin, 119, 151; Samuel Beckett, 113; Seamus Heaney, 205; Ted Hughes, 204; Thom Gunn, 119, 204–5; William Golding, 103, 291
Moorhouse, Geoffrey, 268, 283
Moraes, Dom, 148, 227
Morgan, Rhodri, 311
Morison, Stanley, 67, 249
Morocco, 214–17
Morris, Catharine, 307, 331
Morris, Christopher: on Gareth's and Enid's music-making, 15; on JM's flirtatiousness, 211
  LIFE: birth, 14; Gareth's funeral, 332; children (Paul and Sallie), 146, 230; closeness to father, 15; death, 338; death of wife, 303; education, 20; fails to recognise JM as Jan, 267; marriages, 74; military service, 32, 35; mother's eightieth birthday, 188; musical career, 146; officially learns of JM's transition, 211; organ loft apprentice at Hereford Cathedral, 28; visits EM and baby Mark, 74; visits JM and EM in Venice, 136; visits JM and EM in Waterperry, 146
Morris, Elizabeth (née Tuckniss)
  CHARACTERISTICS: ability to compromise, 68, 142, 277; beauty, 54, 113; dress, 53; 'heroic', 158; 'incredible strength and courage', 238; loyalty to British government, 122; making the best of things, 74, 99; public loyalty to JM, 238; tension between strength and victimhood, 3, 354
  DIARY ENTRIES: America, 99; Europe, 317–18; Oxford, 336
  FRIENDSHIPS: Al Alvarez, 99–100; Betty Jones, 218, 251, 286, 332; Charles Breitmeyer, 95; Chris and Jo Briggs, 174; Clough Williams-Ellis, 172; Elspeth Huxley, 218, 277; Enid Morris, 64, 74; Gerald Norman, 108; Hugh Boustead, 187–8; Ian and Elizabeth Skeet, 107, 136, 173; Joan Murray-Brown, 278; Johnnie and Isabel Kerr, 120, 127, 136, 145–6, 173; Kate Murray-Brown, 238; Martin Busk, 75; Morfydd and Arthur Roberts, 292, 333; Nancy Harmsworth, 129; Reg and Audrey Mutter, 64, 73, 74; Robert and Elizabeth Crawshay-Williams, 173; Rosemary Goad, 130, 134, 151, 158
  HOMES: Appleton cottage, 64, 68, 76, 83; Hammersmith flat, 71, 76; house in Ickham, Kent, 129–30; houseboat in Cairo, 63, 72, 105–6, 107, 113–14, 116, 118; Nottingham Place boarding house, 53–4, 56; rectory in Wiltshire, 141; Taplow house, 81, 90, 95; Trefan Bach, 217, 218; Trefan Hall (Plas Trefan) *see* Trefan Hall; Trefan Morys *see* Trefan Morys; Waterperry rectory, 141–2, 145, 146, 170
  INTERESTS: cats, 187, 317, 318; gardening, 172, 187, 266; horse riding, 107; natural world, 275
  LIFE: attends Faber launch of *Conundrum*, 232; attends premiere of *The Conquest of Everest*, 96; birth and death of Virginia Mary, 142, 225; birth of other children, 74, 89–90, 158, 168; brief engagement to Peter Anson, 56; celebrates JM's CBE, 305; childhood and family, 54–5, 175, 202; civil partnership with JM, 333; cognitive decline and dementia, 3, 334–5, 343; concerns about adult children, 277, 286, 336; death, 351; depression, 217; financial independence, 218; gynaecological

402

INDEX

procedure and hysterectomy, 187, 209, 217; hospitalisations, 337, 348; increasing frailty, 334; marries JM, 62–3; pregnancies, 71, 72, 81, 83, 142, 147; works at architect's firm, 54, 56; in the Wrens, 55–6

RELATIONSHIP WITH JM: beginnings, 53–4, 56; civil partnership, 333; divorce (as legal necessity), 219, 221; EM defends JM in letter to *Standard*, 238; EM goes along with move to Trefan Morys, 277; EM is frequently left on her own, 67, 72, 74, 75, 76, 81–3, 148, 187; EM is kept in dark about JM's Muscat and Oman journey, 109; EM preferring JM to be away, 325; EM provides feedback on *Conundrum* draft, 222; EM provides JM with emotional stability, 137; EM uses male pronouns for JM after transition, 219; EM's 'fathomless' understanding, 63, 68, 142, 181, 286; engagement and wedding, 62–3; JM as 'guard dog'/'gatekeeper', 218, 334; JM buys EM Dior Trapeze dress, 130; JM commissions joint headstone, 285–6, 294, 318–19; JM continues acting as male stereotype post-transition, 221–2; JM describes as 'ecstatically happily married', 225; JM falls in love, 56–7; JM's double suicide plan, 318–19; JM's enduring love, 148, 187; JM's frustrations with domesticity, 68; JM's paean to EM, 336; letters and cards (EM to JM), 74, 75, 76, 95, 325–6; letters and postcards (JM to EM), 4–5, 56, 57, 72, 73, 74, 75, 83, 84, 85–7, 88, 89, 90, 94, 111, 138, 148, 149, 150, 175, 186–7, 207, 209, 214, 215–16, 227, 241, 250, 273, 286, 307; missed anniversaries, 76, 148; sex as 'subsidiary', 224; staying together after transition, 217–18; telegrams (EM to JM), 62; telegrams (JM to EM), 62, 150, 187; their children's conflicting accounts of, 334; travel together as two women, 209

TRAVEL: America, 99, 100, 102, 147, 209; Cairo, 63, 105–6, 113–14, 118; Caribbean, 217; French Alps, 119–21; Greece, 222; Israel, 108; Monte Carlo, 133; New Zealand, 332; Persia, 201; Portmeirion, 142; Slovenia, 317–18; Spain, 162–3; Switzerland, 332, 335; Trieste, 317; Venice, 133–4, 136, 317, 324

Morris, Enid (née Payne)
CHARACTERISTICS: compulsion to reach out, 16; dauntlessness, 14; love of reading, 15; supporting JM's transitioning, 220–1; unconventional, 14

HOMES: Clevedon, 13–15, 17, 19, 21, 25, 351; with Gareth in London, 64; Saxlingham Hall nursing home, 188, 220; Walberswick, 130

LIFE: birth, 10; childhood, 10; death and funeral, 267; eightieth birthday, 188; failing eyesight, 146; learns of JM's transitioning, 220–1; marriage to Walter, 9, 13, 26; meets EM, 56; sends care parcels to Geraint, 11; stroke, 188; visits JM and EM at Trefan Hall, 173; visits JM and EM in Waterperry, 146; wartime losses, 26–7

MUSIC: composing, 16, 25; education, 10–11; listening, 15–16, 53, 130; opinions on piano-playing, 16; organist, 9, 11, 14, 16, 27, 146; pianist on pleasure steamers, 14; pulling out all the stops, 16; teaching, 14, 15

Morris, Gareth: on Charles Rolls and Enid Payne, 11
CHARACTERISTICS: 'gift for happiness', 331; self-deprecation, 17; trouser braces, 35

LIFE: birth, 14; as boat boy in church, 16; book collecting and nocturnal reading, 33–4; book on flute technique, 332; celebrates JM's CBE, 305; childhood excursions with Christopher, 17–18; closeness with JM, 331–2; at coronation of Elizabeth II, 105; daughter (Catharine), 307, 331; death and funeral, 331, 332; education, 20, 25; exchanges faxes with JM, 282; JM writes to from Hong Kong, 283; mother lives with in London, 64; mother's eightieth birthday, 188; musical career, 43, 104–5, 331–2; musical education, 15, 25, 32; officially learns of JM's transition, 211; pays JM's mess bills, 43; in RAF Symphony Orchestra, 32; visits EM and baby Mark, 74

Morris, Henry: on JM's absence as parent, 334
LIFE: birth, 89–90, 131; Edmund Hillary as godfather, 95; education in Venice, 134; in Goa, 227; learns of JM's transitioning, 227; page at Gillian 'Puff' Harmsworth's wedding, 129; prep school education, 146; sickness on journey to New York, 99

Morris, James Charles, 9, 12–13

Morris, Jan
ARCHIVE: at National Library of Wales, 3, 318; sources in *Times* archive, 3; sources in Trefan Morys, 4–5, 318
CHARACTERISTICS: absence and cruelty as parent, 5, 218, 244, 266–7, 300–1, 301n, 334; addiction to writing, 5, 334, 344, 345;

403

INDEX

as 'aesthetic monarchist', 319; ambition, 6, 62, 81, 82, 87; 'anti-received-wisdom stance', 287; appearance in childhood, 18; attractiveness, 18, 38; aversion to physical touch, 307; aversion to thin/fat people, 267; book tour persona, 309–10; charm, 69; class snobbery, 26, 83, 84, 98, 126, 145, 146, 150–1, 157, 168; conservatism and right-wing views, 124, 267; contradictions, 2, 5; correcting others' publications, 286–7; 'crushing remarks', 31; diplomacy, 69; dislike of dinner parties and functions, 307, 310; dress choices post-transitioning, 2, 220, 245, 246, 255; egocentrism, 6, 68, 81, 82, 127, 223, 234, 235, 244, 341; emotional tone-deafness, 267; exaggerating age to army and EM, 32, 56; exaggerating work experience on application forms, 58; exceeding income and poor financial management, 151, 176–7, 196; facial features, 18, 38; flirtatiousness, 1, 2, 211, 246, 309; hair, 18, 38, 158, 220; hostility towards Prince Charles, 267–8, 315–16; 'hybrid'/ambiguous aspect, 315; Jaeger suits, 158, 220; liberalism and left-wing views, 143, 154–6, 157; 'military aura', 71; as 'outsider', 49, 51–2, 62, 312; personal mythology, 6, 19, 225, 275, 319, 341; playfulness, 317; selective politeness, 310; sensitivity, 69; shrewdness, 74, 325; spirituality without religious dogma, 24; superficial sociability, 271; taking writers under her wing, 286; time management, 62; voice and speech, 255–6, 265, 345; Welsh nationalism *see under* Welsh nationalism; wit, 31, 293, 321

FAMILY: brothers *see* Morris, Christopher; Morris, Gareth; children *see* Morris, Henry; Morris, Mark; Morris, Suki (born Susan); Morris, Twm (born Tom); Morris, Virginia Mary; father's ancestry and family, 9, 12–13; mother's ancestry and family, 9–10, 11–12, 13, 14, 15, 26; nieces and nephews *see* Morris, Catharine; Morris, Paul; Morris, Sallie; parents *see* Morris, Enid (née Payne); Morris, Walter

FRIENDSHIPS: Al Alvarez, 99–100, 319; Alan Whicker, 74, 324, 337–8; Alistair Horne, 213–14; Arthur Crook, 249; Bill Gordon, 226; Bill Norman *see* Norman, Bill; Charles Breitmeyer, 95; Chris and Jo Briggs, 174; Clough Williams-Ellis, 169, 172–3, 203; Cyril Quilliam, 72–3; Geoffrey Moorhouse, 268, 283; Henry and Shirley Paget, 211–12, 305, 310, 340; Ian and Elizabeth Skeet, 107, 125, 136, 173, 305; Johnnie and Isabel Kerr, 120, 127, 136, 145–6, 173, 305; Mike Parker, 340; Morfydd and Arthur Roberts, 292–3, 333; Nancy Harmsworth, 129, 130; Patrick Leigh Fermor, 324–5, 336; Paul Theroux, 264–5, 268, 269, 354; Reg and Audrey Mutter, 64; Robert and Elizabeth Crawshay-Williams, 173, 318; Robert Winder, 287, 303; Simon Jenkins, 270, 318, 320–1; Valerie Kleeman, 324, 337–8

GENDER IDENTITY AND TRANSITIONING *see* gender identity and transitioning (JM)

HOMES: Appleton cottage, 64, 65, 66, 68; Bath flat, 217, 222, 230, 251; Hammersmith flat, 71, 76; house in Ickham, Kent, 129–30; houseboat in Cairo, 63, 72, 105–6, 107, 113–14, 116, 118; Nottingham Place boarding house, 53; Oxford terraced house, 181, 184, 201; rectory in Wiltshire, 139, 141; Taplow house, 81, 95; Trefan Bach, 217, 218; Trefan Hall (Plas Trefan) *see* Trefan Hall; Trefan Morys *see* Trefan Morys; Waterperry rectory, 141–2, 145, 146, 170, 174

INTERESTS: art, 39, 339; cars, 1, 120, 145, 170, 211, 254, 283, 303, 343; cats, 2, 18, 106, 171, 254, 326, 328, 329, 347; place names, 20; second-hand bookshops, 33; ships, 18–19, 20, 103, 145, 294, 344; sketching, 163, 264–5, 282–3; technology, 282–3, 344; telescopes and binoculars, 18–19, 25, 146, 163, 176, 177, 330; urbanism, 275–6

LETTERS TO/FROM READERS, 158–9, 236–7, 306–7, 347

LIFE: begins to withdraw, 343; birth, 14; birth and death of Virginia Mary, 142, 225; birth of other children, 74, 89–90, 131, 168; brain bleeds and fainting, 326, 334, 339; childhood and adolescence, 14–15, 17–31, 351; chorister at Christ Church Cathedral Choir School, 20, 22–5, 27; civil partnership with EM, 333; 'cosmetic face transformation', 325; death and funeral of Gareth, 331, 332; death of Henry Anglesey, 340; as Druid, 296, 319–20; enlistment and military training, 32–4, 35; falls over in street, 326; feelings of mortality, 318; financial difficulties, 96, 150, 161–2, 196, 209, 222, 250–1, 259; godparent to Peter Breitmeyer, 95, 186, 267; high blood pressure, 303; hospitalisation and death,

348–9, 351; is pursued by 'nymphomaniac', 148; joins/leaves Liberal Party, 154–5, 157; joins Plaid Cymru, 157; Lancing College, 27, 29–31, 224; language learning, 53, 57, 162, 244; legacy planning, 318; locks herself and EM in courtesy car, 343–4; marries EM, 62–3; military intelligence work, 45–7; military postings, 36–51; opposes holiday camp development, 201; Oxford entrance examinations, 57, 62, 64; portrait by Arturo di Stefano, 328–9; public speaking, 2, 319, 320–1, 325, 333–4; receives 'anthrax' through post, 311; rhinoplasty, 249; shareholder in local pub, 341; shingles, 332; social media use, 343; travel routines, 339; undergraduate study at Christ Church, 66–7, 68, 69, 71

PRIZES AND AWARDS: Arthur C. Clarke Award for science fiction (shortlisted, *Hav*), 327; Booker Prize (shortlisted, *Last Letters from Hav*), 275; Café Royal Prize (winner, *Coast to Coast*), 117; CBE, 304–5; David Cohen Prize (shortlisted), 328; George Polk Award for Outstanding Foreign Reporting (winner), 147; Glyndŵr Award for Outstanding Contribution to the Arts in Wales (winner), 296; Golden PEN Award for a Lifetime's Distinguished Service to Literature (winner), 328; Heinemann Award (winner, *Venice*), 144; honorary doctorate from University College of North Wales, 296; honorary fellowship at RIBA, 296; John Llewellyn Rhys Prize (runner-up, *Coast to Coast*), 117; Medal of the Honourable Society of Cymmrodorion, 342; Thomas Cook Travel Book Award for Outstanding Contribution to Travel Writing (winner), 328; US Book of the Month Club midsummer choice (*The World Bank*), 164

RADIO: *The British Empire: An Equivocation*, 345; *Desert Island Discs* (twice), 19, 271, 314–15; talks for *At Home and Abroad*, 133; *The Verb*, 344; *Woman of Action*, 254

READING AND LITERARY INFLUENCES: Anthony Powell, 274–5; Anton Chekhov, 314; *Baghdad Sketches* (Stark), 109; Charles Dickens, 314; *Decline and Fall of the Roman Empire* (Gibbon), 51, 194; *Eothen* (Kinglake), 65, 66–7; in final years, 338; first book bought, 25; intimacy achieved through reading, 15; Jane Austen, 206, 314; John Ruskin, 338–9; Joseph Conrad, 206; library at Trefan Morys, 266, 277, 338; library on *dahabiyeh* (houseboat), 106; *The Long-Winded Lady* (Brennan), 338; *Love Story* (Segal), 216; Marcel Proust, 314; Martin Amis, 313; memoirs by trans people, 114, 115–16; *Notes Towards the Definition of Culture* (Eliot), 57; *A Passage to India* (Forster), 194–5; *In Patagonia* (Chatwin), 264; precocious book-collecting, 33–4; published diaries, 345; R. S. Thomas, 174; *Roberta Cowell's Story by Herself* (Cowell), 114; Russian classics, 25, 314; *Seven Pillars of Wisdom* (Lawrence), 65, 66; *Story of Everest* (Murray), 88, 222; *Travels in Arabia Deserta* (Doughty), 49, 50; Twm reads to JM in hospital, 348; *The Welsh Fairy Book* (Thomas), 25, 348

RELATIONSHIP WITH ELIZABETH *see under* Morris, Elizabeth

SEXUALITY: ability to orgasm after transition, 224; attempts to snog Nicholas Turner, 306; 'enjoys' stranger putting hand up skirt, 241; flirtations and 'non-affairs' as woman, 226–7, 241; 'incest' comment in *Pleasures of a Tangled Life*, 285; is attracted to Kim Philby, 126; male assignations in young adulthood, 53, 224; prudishness, 196; relationship with Otto Thwaites, 47–8; schoolboy sexual encounters, 29–30, 52, 224; uncertainties about sexuality, 52

TELEVISION: *Dick Cavett Show* interview, 233–4; documentary about Wales, 263; documentary on Ickham, Kent, 129–30; documentary on Oxford, 159; documentary on turning ninety (with Michael Palin), 342–3; films on cities that influenced her, 300; *Late Show* special about travel writing, 263–4; news piece on *Lincoln*, 306; *Panorama* documentaries, 133, 134; *Talk-In To Day* interview (Robin Day and panel), 232–3; other interviews, 221

TRAVEL *see* Everest expedition; *specific countries/cities*

WRITING: BIOGRAPHY *see Fisher's Face*; *Lincoln: A Foreigner's Quest*

WRITING: BOOK REVIEWS: *Baghdad and Beyond* (Dickson), 241; *Between the Woods and the Water* (Leigh Fermor), 324; contract with *The Independent*, 287; *Empire: How Britain Made the Modern World* (Ferguson), 330–1; *Freya Stark: A Biography* (Izzard), 291; *Peter*

INDEX

Fleming: A Biography (Hart-Davis), 111–12; travel book by Carrington, 141; volume by Kapuściński, 7

WRITING: CHARACTERISTICS: anthropomorphising, 167; bogus self-satire, 248; clarity, 31, 70, 101; cliché, 284; conveying uncertainty, 50–1; direct speech, 7, 31, 117, 175, 224–5, 240, 302; doggerel and limericks, 136, 346; efficiency, 70; exaggerated femininity, 252, 281; exaggeration, 248; finding novelty in the commonplace, 65; generous but waspish reviewer, 287, 325; gift for narrative, 129, 135, 190; honing own style during undergraduate days, 66, 77; humour, 31, 101, 127, 131, 248; immediacy, 31, 284; impressionism, 136, 162, 244; as 'intellectual hopscotch', 250; lacking awareness of wider social and economic context, 154, 156–7, 316–17; 'letting go', 137; 'magpie-style' embedding of detail, 139, 178, 190, 257; 'more truthful than factual', 136–7, 199, 339; New Journalism, 199, 248; 'over-insistent manliness', 157, 158; purple prose, 136, 144, 178, 201–2, 206, 223, 234, 235, 272, 309; shifting interpretations of places and events, 38–9; slights to stockbrokers, 177; 'swank', 147; teasing stories out of single fact or image, 77, 139, 256; throwaway parenthetical remarks, 144; truth 'in the sweep', 250, 335; vocabulary and favoured words, 116–17, 129, 135, 193, 206–7, 256–7, 312; whimsy, 320, 351

WRITING: COLLECTED ESSAYS see *Allegorizings*; *Among the Cities*; *Cities*; *Destinations*; *Places*; *Travels*

WRITING: DURING CHILDHOOD/ADOLESCENCE: *Lancing College Magazine*, 30–1; play and story adaptation for *Bubble and Squeak* pupils' show, 30; Somerset gazetteer, 25; *Travels with a Telescope*, 19

WRITING: JOURNALISM: American *Vogue*, 272, 283; with Arab News Agency (ANA), 57–8, 60–1, 64; *Architectural Review*, 189; *Cherwell* (Oxford University student newspaper), 67; *Daily Mail*, 330; *The Economist*, 77; *Encounter*, 77, 139–40, 189, 284; *Evening Standard*, 301; fame after Everest story, 94–5, 96, 98; *Financial Times*, 317, 345; *Gourmet*, 323; the *Guardian see under* Guardian; *Harper's*, 77; *Holiday*, 189; *Horizon*, 253; *Life*, 140, 143, 144, 189, 271; *The Lighter Lancer*, 46; *London Calling*, 77; *The Nation*, 77; *New Statesman*, 77; *New York Times*, 188–9, 190; *O'r Pedwar Gwynt*, 345; *Planet*, 268; *Rolling Stone*, 245–50, 252–4, 254, 256, 273, 316; *Saturday Evening Post*, 146, 149, 150; *Saturday Night*, 279; *Spectator*, 67; *Texas Monthly*, 272; *The Times see under The Times*; *Times Literary Supplement* (TLS), 77; *Vanity Fair*, 204; *Venture*, 175, 189, 206; *Vogue*, 77; *Welcome Aboard* (BOAC magazine), 189; *Western Daily Press*, 31, 33

WRITING: LETTERS TO NEWSPAPERS: *Cambria* magazine (open letter criticising Rhodri Morgan), 311; inherited compulsion to reach out, 16; *The Times* (on expense of royal wedding), 267; *The Times* (on Liberal Party), 154–5; *The Times* (on Olympic hair test), 212–13; *The Times* (on Princess Diana), 303–4; *The Times* (on the future of Jerusalem), 46; *The Times* (unpublished), 347

WRITING: MEMOIRS/AUTOBIOGRAPHIES/DIARIES see *A Writer's House in Wales*; *Allegorizings*; *Conundrum*; *Fifty Years of Europe: An Album*; *In My Mind's Eye*; *Pleasures of a Tangled Life*; *Thinking Again*; *Trieste and the Meaning of Nowhere*

WRITING: NOVELS see *Hav*; *Last Letters from Hav*; *Our First Leader: A Welsh Fable*

WRITING: OTHER: *Ciao, Carpaccio! An Infatuation*, 339; edits new edition of *Stones of Venice* (Ruskin), 339; edits *The Oxford Book of Oxford*, 252; essay for *Bath* (Robertson), 230; essay for book accompanying *Turner and Venice* Tate show, 290; foreword to *Around the World in 80 Days* (US edition) (Palin), 342; foreword to *Europe in the Looking Glass* (Byron), 335; introduction to *A Moment of War* (Lee), 335; introduction to *A Time of Gifts* (Leigh Fermor), 325; introduction to Harry's Bar cookbook, 290; introduction to *Persia* (Wood), 205–6; introduction to *Pleasures and Landscapes* (Bedford), 313; introduction to *Thrilling Cities* (Fleming), 167–8; introduction to *Towers of Trebizond* (Macaulay), 313; lists, 175; obituary of Clough Williams-Ellis (*The Times*), 173; *The Oxford Entertainment* (stage piece), 189; poem for *Four-Letter Word* anthology, 335–6; preface to *Off the Beaten Track: Three Centuries of Women Travellers* (Birkett),

323; publicity brochure for Portmeirion, 169; *son et lumière* script, 201; text for *Ireland: Your Only Place* (photography by Wakefield), 287, 288; text for *Wales: The First Place* (photography by Wakefield), 263, 269–70, 277, 287; tribute to Edmund Hillary (*The Times*), 332; tribute to Leigh Fermor (*Observer*), 336; *The Upstairs Donkey* (children's book), 151; *see also The Outriders: A Liberal View of Britain*

WRITING: PROCESS: laptop writing on the road, 283; notebooks purchased in Criccieth, 175, 308; 'slapdash' approach to research, 135–6, 192, 284, 305; target-setting, 108, 108n, 113

WRITING: THEATRE REVIEWS: for *Lancing College Magazine*, 30–1; of *This Is the Army*, 33; for *Western Daily Press*, 33

WRITING: TRAVEL AND HISTORY *see A Machynlleth Triad*; *A Venetian Bestiary*; *Battleship Yamato: Of War, Beauty and Irony*; *Coast to Coast/ As I Saw the USA*; *Coronation Everest*; *Hong Kong: Xianggang*; *Manhattan '45*; *Oxford*; *Pax Britannica* trilogy; *South African Winter*; *Sultan in Oman*; *The Great Port: A Passage Through New York*; *The Hashemite Kings*; *The Market of Seleukia/Islam Inflamed*; *The Matter of Wales*; *The Spectacle of Empire: Style, Effect and the Pax Britannica*; *The Venetian Empire*; *The World Bank/The Road to Huddersfield: A Journey to Five Continents*; *Trieste and the Meaning of Nowhere*; *Venice/ The World of Venice*

WRITING: UNFINISHED/UNPUBLISHED WORKS: anthology (*Comparisons*), 151; biography of Lord Mountbatten, 261; book about Cascade Mountains, 209; book about England, 136; book about First Afghan War, 140–1; book about Jerusalem, 151; book about San Francisco, 151; book about the Nile, 136, 139; book on Eton College, 209; book on Ivan Bunin, 308; book on Port of London, 209; children's book about Venice, 136

Morris, Mark: on being uninformed about family news, 334; believes JM was planning double suicide, 318; on change to family after JM's transition, 216; on co-dependency of JM and EM's marriage, 217; on *Conundrum*, 225; on JM acting as gatekeeper for EM, 334; on JM compared to other prep school fathers, 168–9, 185; on JM maintaining control, 348; on JM's addiction to writing, 334; on JM's class sensibilities, 126; on JM's dress choices, 220; on JM's emotional involvement with places, 176; on JM's 'feudal' entertaining at Trefan Hall, 173; on JM's lack of interest in transgender community, 323–4; on JM's lack of parenting, 244; on JM's literary and personal struggles, 157; on JM's loss of interest in politics, 196; on JM's 'mythical' status in Wales, 270; on JM's narcissism, 244; on JM's prudishness, 196; on JM's rhinoplasty, 249; on JM's self-mythologising, 225; on JM's silence about father, 26; on JM's unresolved yearning after transition, 242, 311; on JM's wish to control own death and legacy, 318–19; on nannies in Cairo and Venice, 134; on 'nomadic' family life, 141; on sale of Trefan Hall, 217; on seeing Franco's motorcade in Spain, 162

LIFE: academic career in Canada, 276, 334; birth, 74; at Christ Church, 211; dates Belinda Mitchell-Innes, 211, 232; at Durrell School Summer Symposium, 333–4; education in Venice, 134; at Eton College, 168, 185; first marriage, 244, 276; is lost at Cairo airport, 118; Isabel Kerr, Bill Norman and Martin Busk as godparents, 120; learns of JM's transitioning, 185; Marsh Court boarding school, 158; page at Gillian 'Puff' Harmsworth's wedding, 129; PhD in creative writing, 276; prep school education, 146, 168; second marriage, 277; sickness on journey to New York, 99

MUSIC AND WRITING: *Domesday Revisited: A Traveller's Guide*, 276–7; musicality, 171; 'Songs of Hav' (song cycle), 334

RELATIONSHIP WITH JM: accompanies JM to studios for *Talk-In To Day* interview, 233; estrangement, 276–7, 279, 334; postcards from JM, 158; provides feedback on *Conundrum* draft, 222; receives JM's Jaeger suits, 220; requests authorised biography of JM, 2–3; response to JM's 'incest' comment in *Pleasures of a Tangled Life*, 285; works on third edition of *Oxford*, 179

Morris, Paul, 146, 230

Morris, Ruth, 146

Morris, Sallie, 146, 267

Morris, Suki (born Susan): believes JM was planning double suicide, 318; on Christmas at Trefan Hall, 173; on EM and JM's

INDEX

relationship, 325; on JM as 'lousy parent', 301n; JM's cruelty towards, 5, 218, 266–7, 300–1, 301n, 334; on JM's lack of interest in rural environment, 275; on JM's sole interest in literature, 266; as reincarnation of Virginia Mary (JM's belief), 171; response to *Conundrum*, 225; response to *In My Mind's Eye*, 347
    LIFE: birth, 168; education, 218; learns of JM's transitioning, 185; as schoolteacher, 334

Morris, Twm (born Tom): on bats at Trefan Morys, 316; on Chris Briggs' glass eye, 174; on Geraint Perry, 278; on JM and EM's relationship, 334; on JM's inability to be authentically Welsh, 320
    LIFE: birth, 158; Charles Monteith as godparent, 158; death of JM, 349, 351; at Llanbedrog arts centre's day in honour of JM, 342; music, 277, 351; shareholder in local pub, 341; sings at Blue Plaque ceremony for JM's childhood home, 351; at Trefan coach house, 334; Welsh nationalism, 277, 320; Welsh translations, 277, 296, 307; wins National Eisteddfod bard's chair, 319–20
    RELATIONSHIP WITH JM: close relationship and collaboration, 277, 296–7, 304, 307, 339, 343, 348–9; joint birthday party with JM (thirty-fifth and seventieth), 300; reads to JM in hospital, 348

Morris, Virginia Mary, 142, 171, 225, 351
Morris, Walter, 9, 12, 13, 15, 17, 19, 20, 21–2, 25; death, 25–6, 225
Moscow, 125, 142, 147, 276
Mountbatten, Lord, 260, 261
Mudiad Amddiffyn Cymru (Movement for the Defence of Wales), 243
Murray, W. H.: *Story of Everest*, 88, 222
Murray-Brown, Jeremy, 133, 134, 238, 278
Murray-Brown, Joan, 278
Murray-Brown, Kate, 238
Muscat and Oman, 109–11, 112, 125
Musk, Elon, 344
Mutter, Audrey, 64, 73, 74
Mutter, Reg, 64, 74

Nasser, Gamal Abdel, 106, 118, 121, 124
National Front, 268
National Library of Wales: Morris Collection, 3, 318

New Journalism, 199; 'gonzo', 248
New Labour, 305
New Scientist (magazine), 322
New Statesman (magazine), 77, 178–9
New York, 197–9, 272, 279, 300, 310, 332–3; *see also* *Manhattan '45*; *The Great Port: A Passage Through New York*
New York Review of Books (magazine), 201
New York Times: David Holden's piece on friendship with JM, 239; JM's piece on ascent of Everest, 94; JM's piece on writing *Pax Britannica*, 188–9, 190; letters in response to *Conundrum*, 239–40; names *The Conquest of Everest* one of the best films of year, 96; piece on JM aged ninety-two, 340; piece on 9/11 terrorist attacks, 310; reviews of JM's works, 129, 235, 272
New Yorker (magazine), 199
New Zealand, 150, 209, 332
Nicolson, Nigel, 237–8
Nicolson, Sir Harold, 237
Nigeria, 143, 147
9/11 terrorist attacks, 310
Norman, Bill, 35, 40–1, 42, 45, 51, 120, 324
Norman, Gerald, 82, 84, 95, 96, 101, 108, 112–13, 116, 118
Northern Ireland *see* Troubles
nostalgia: as changeable, 330; as escapism in 1970s Britain, 230–1; JM writes on theme of, 7, 43, 201–2, 311, 327, 330, 354; and Joseph Mitchell, 199; and nationalism, 302; and Stan Barstow, 309
Noyce, Wilf, 108

Observer: JM's tribute to Patrick Leigh Fermor, 336; stance on Suez crisis, 122
oil: American interests in Middle East, 109; Anglo-Iranian Oil Company, 64, 73; and British status in sheikdoms, 110; concession for *The Times*, 112–13; impact on 'romance of old Arabia', 127; Iraq Petroleum Company, 109, 112; oil crisis and three-day week in Britain, 229; and Suez Canal, 107
Oldaker, Reverend Wilfrid, 23, 25
O'r Pedwar Gwynt (literary journal), 345
Orton, John/Joe, 119; *Between Us Girls*, 119
Our First Leader: A Welsh Fable, 307–8
The Outriders: A Liberal View of Britain, 155–6, 266

INDEX

Oxford: JM and EM spend Christmases at, 332, 336; JM presents as a woman in, 181, 184–5; JM's television documentary, 159; JM's terraced house, 181, 184, 201
Oxford, 159, 162, 166–7, 177–9, 196, 252
The Oxford Book of Oxford (JM editor), 252
The Oxford Entertainment (stage piece), 189
Oxford University: All Souls College, 102, 119, 166; Christ Church *see* Christ Church, Oxford; University College, 166–7
Oxford University Press (OUP), 242, 259–60, 265, 276, 342

Paget, Henry (7th Marquess of Anglesey), 211–12, 305, 310, 340
Paget, Shirley, 212
Pakistan, 149, 153, 158, 204, 236
Palestine *see* Mandatory Palestine
Palin, Michael, 144; *Around the World in 80 Days*, 342; documentary on JM, 342–3
Pantheon Books, 108, 152, 164, 165
Paris, 41, 82, 132, 236, 267, 280
Paris Review, 352
Parker, Mike, 340
Pasha, Glubb, 116, 135
Patten, Chris, 284
Pax Britannica trilogy: as 'centrepiece' of JM's life, 6; content, perspective and style, 21, 139, 190–4, 195, 207, 227–8, 243, 244, 256–8, 260, 288, 303, 353; decision to create a trilogy, 197; early discussions and working titles, 140, 147–8, 168, 213; Faber advances, 197; 'James' as author, 219; JM threatens to make second volume an anthology, 209, 213; material for *Heaven's Command*, 205; notebooks and planning, 175; people in, 35, 177, 189, 257; reception and reviews, 190–1, 194, 201–2, 228, 329; as required reading at Eton College, 258; revisions, 261, 303; sales, 202; seeds of, 140, 188–9; translations, 347; writing, 165, 188, 189, 213; Vol. 1 (*Heaven's Command*) (written second), 205, 213, 216, 217, 221, 227–8, 229, 243; Vol. 2 (*The Climax of an Empire*) (written first), 188–94, 195, 201–2; Vol. 3 (*Farewell the Trumpets*), 241, 249–50, 252, 256–8, 260, 288
Payne, Charles, 9, 10, 11, 12
Payne, Edith (née McKenna), 11, 13, 14
Payne, Geraint, 10, 11–12

Payne, Iris, 11, 13
Pen-y-Gwryd, Snowdonia, 83, 164, 173–4, 222, 290, 337
penectomy surgery, 115, 180
Perowne, Stewart, 108–9, 116, 291
Perry, Geraint and John, 278
Persia, 201, 205–6; *Persia* (JM's introduction/essay for), 205–6
Philby, Kim, 70, 126
Places, 210, 219, 259
Plaid Cymru, 157, 203, 245, 268, 296, 340
Planet (magazine), 268
Plas Newydd, Anglesey, 212
Plas Trefan, Gwynedd *see* Trefan Hall
Pleasures of a Tangled Life, 284–5, 326
Pocock, Tom, 113–14
Pope Pius X, 133–4
Pope-Hennessy, James, 194
Port of New York Authority, 197–8
Portmeirion, 142, 169, 172
Potter, Dennis, 104, 153, 180n; *The Glittering Coffin*, 154; review of *Oxford*, 177–8; review of *The Climax of an Empire*, 202; television adaptation of *The Past Is Myself* (Bielenberg), 178n
Powell, Anthony, 274–5; *What's Become of Waring*, 275
Powell, Enoch, 202
Powers, Francis Gary, 142, 147
Prague, 59, 137–8, 201, 295
The Presence of Spain, 162, 163, 165–6, 196; translated editions, 196; updated and republished (as *Spain*), 166, 254
Pritchett, V. S. ('VSP'), 100n, 234–5; *London*, 162
Private Eye (magazine), 186, 223, 254, 292, 339
Proust, Marcel, 314; *In Search of Lost Time*, 314
Pugh, Griff, 90
Punch (magazine), 156

Quilliam, Cyril, 72–3

Raban, Jonathan, 255–6, 268
Randell, John, 180–1, 182, 217
Raymond, Janet: *The Transsexual Empire*, 238
Real Life Test/Real Life Experience (RLT/RLE), 181
Rees-Mogg, Jacob, 258
rhinoplasty, 249

INDEX

Ricks, Christopher, 178, 179, 306
Ridsdale, William, 93
Roberts, Arthur, 292–3, 333
Roberts, J. O. M. 'Jimmy', 84, 85, 90
Roberts, Morfydd, 292, 333
Robertson, Charles J.: *Bath*, 230
Rockefeller, David and Peggy, 198
Rolling Stone (magazine), 234, 245–50, 252–4, 254, 256, 273, 316; books arm publishes *Destinations*, 259–60
Rolls, Charles, 10, 11
Rolls-Royce cars (JM), 120–1, 170, 254
Royal Geographical Society (RGS), 80, 81, 97, 290, 333
Royal Society of Literature, 2
Rubinstein, Hilary, 258–9, 272, 291
Rusbridger, Alan, 124
Ruskin, John: *Stones of Venice*, 339
Russell, Bertrand, 173
Russia: under Gorbachev, 282; JM in, 125, 140, 142, 147, 276

Sackville-West, Vita, 95, 237
Sadat, Anwar, 254, 256
Sampson, Anthony: *Anatomy of Britain*, 156, 201; review of *The Climax of an Empire*, 201–2
San Francisco, 245–6, 288
Sandburg, Carl: 'Chicago', 98
Sanghera, Sathnam, 353
Saphir (houseboat, Cairo), 63, 72, 105–6, 107, 113–14, 116, 118, 149, 255
Saturday Evening Post (newspaper), 146, 149, 150
Saturday Night (magazine), 279
School of Oriental and African Studies, London, 53, 57
science fiction, 327–8
Scott, Paul, 176, 228; *Raj Quartet*, 176, 192
Second World War: air raids, 27, 32, 35; concentration camps, 36; Eichmann trial, 148; German invasions, 27; Jewish refugee stays with JM's family, 26, 36; JM undertakes compulsory junior military training, 30; lead-up and preparations, 26; loss of life, 31; musical entertainment for troops, 32, 33, 34–5; VE Day, 35
Secret Intelligence Service (SIS) (MI6), 44, 49, 58, 75, 111, 120

Security Intelligence Middle East (SIME), 48–9, 61, 107
Security Service (MI5), 44, 49
Segal, Erich: *Love Story*, 216
Selassie, Haile, 17
Self-Help Association for Transsexuals (SHAFT), 182
Sexual Offences Act (1967), 232
Shanks, Michael: *The Stagnant Society*, 154, 155, 156
Sharpe, Tom, 30
Sherpas, 83, 85, 86, 87, 90, 93, 96; *see also* Sonam; Tenzing Norgay
ships: JM lectures on, 325; JM's interest in, 18–19, 20, 103, 145, 294, 344
Shipton, Eric, 80–1, 102
Sissons, Michael, 196, 197, 205, 222
Skeet, Elizabeth, 136, 173, 305
Skeet, Ian, 107, 125, 136, 173, 305
Slade-Baker, John, 107
Slovenia, 317–18
Somerset, Georgina, 161; *Over the Sex Border*, 161, 225
Sonam (Sherpa), 85, 88, 92, 93
South Africa, 128, 188, 205
South African Winter, 131
South America, 149, 260, 292–3
Spain: EM in, 162–3; JM in, 143, 162–4, 165–6, 200; *A Moment of War* (Lee), 335; *see also* *The Presence of Spain*
The Spectacle of Empire: Style, Effect and the Pax Britannica, 202, 263
The Spectator (magazine): announces JM's forthcoming transition, 213; JM attends social gatherings, 220; JM defends Alan Whicker, 337; JM writes for, 67; review of *Coronation Everest*, 131; review of *The Climax of an Empire*, 202
Stark, Freya, 144, 241, 257, 290–1, 341; *Baghdad Sketches*, 109
Stefano, Arturo di: portrait of JM, 328–9
Stewart, J. I. M., 64–5, 66, 68, 71
Stobart, Tom, 91; *The Conquest of Everest* (film), 96–7, 99
Stuart, C. H., 65
Sudan, 108, 117, 331
Suez Canal Treaty, 107
Suez Crisis, 118, 121–5
Sultan in Oman, 117, 121, 126–7, 129, 164, 263

INDEX

Sunday Telegraph: review of *Pax Britannica*, 194
The Sunday Times: links with intelligence services, 107; *The Oxford Book of Oxford* on bestseller list, 252; reviews of JM's works, 135, 179, 228; serialises *Conundrum*, 231, 236
Switzerland, 201, 301, 332, 335
Sydney, 150, 288–9
Sydney, 288–9

Taylor, A. J. P., 178–9
telephone directories, 101, 134, 149, 153, 214, 246
telescopes and binoculars, 18–19, 25, 146, 163, 176, 177, 330
Tenzing Norgay, 84, 87, 90–1, 92, 95, 96, 206
Texas Monthly (magazine), 272
Thailand, 140, 167
Thatcher, Margaret, 259, 281, 282
Theroux, Paul, 264–5, 268, 269, 354
Thinking Again, 348
This Is the Army (troop show), 33
Thomas, Noyes 'Tommy', 73, 183
Thomas, R. S., 174, 201, 203, 274, 304; 'Song at the Year's Turning', 174
Thomas, W. Jenkyn: *The Welsh Fairy Book*, 25, 348
Thwaites, Henry Otto Daniel, 47–8, 110, 309
Time (magazine), 316
The Times: anonymous reporting in, 68; archive, 3; breaks story of Everest ascent, 93; chooses *Conundrum* as one of the '100 Key Books of Our Time', 322; codes in dispatches from Everest, 82, 83, 87, 91, 92, 96, 108; codes suggested for striking oil in Muscat and Oman, 112–13; covers coronation of Elizabeth II, 94; EM's anniversary message to JM in, 76; Everest expedition sponsorship and story rights, 80; JM as acting foreign news editor, 79, 81, 82; JM assigned as Cairo correspondent, 101, 105; JM assigned as correspondent for Everest expedition, 82–3; JM assigned as special correspondent in Egypt, 72; JM is given pay rises, 74, 113; JM resigns from, 117–18, 341; JM taken on as graduate trainee, 68–9; JM works as diplomatic correspondent, 105; JM works in during university vacations, 67–8; JM works on Foreign desk, 69, 70–1; JM's dispatches and pieces, 68, 70, 73, 74, 75, 76, 84, 85, 87, 89, 91, 92, 93, 98–9, 100, 101, 102, 103, 107, 109, 112, 116, 118, 276, 295, 296; JM's letters, 212–13, 268; JM's obituary of Clough Williams-Ellis, 173; JM's tribute to Edmund Hillary, 332; JM's unpublished letters, 347; links with intelligence services, 69, 111, 118; Muscat and Oman story rights, 109; names JM 'fifteenth greatest British writer since the war', 296; office and culture, 69; oil concession, 112–13; permissions for JM's books, 97, 101–2, 113, 117, 121; review of *Heaven's Command*, 228; sailing cutter during Napoleonic Wars, 333; supports JM during Commonwealth Fund Fellowship, 96; *see also* Deakin, Ralph; Norman, Gerald
Times Literary Supplement (*TLS*), 77, 201, 249, 307–8, 327
Tobin, Austin J., 197–8, 200, 220, 310
trans people: and binary/non-binary identities, 340–1; *A Change of Sex/Julia's Story* (BBC TV documentaries), 261; *The Danish Girl* (film, dir. Hooper), 351; and Equality Act (2010), 340, 352; and gender-critical feminism, 238, 239; and Gender Recognition Act (2004), 323, 340; pathologizing by medical profession, 183–4; press and public interest, 115, 183, 204, 239; sending personal letters of gratitude to JM after *Conundrum*, 236–7; support (and lack of support) for, 138, 181–2; *Trans Britain: Our Journey from the Shadows* (ed. Burns), 261; *The Transsexual Empire* (Raymond), 238; *see also* Ashley, April; Beaumont, Chevalier d'Éon de; Cowell, Roberta 'Betty'; Elbe, Lili; gender identity and transitioning (JM); Grant, Julia; Jorgensen, Christine
trans rights, 183, 219, 323, 340, 351–2
transition surgery: April Ashley, 182, 183; Christine Jorgensen, 115; by Georges Burou, 182, 183, 214–15; JM, 214–16, 217, 222, 224; medical establishment recognition, 180; penectomy, 115, 180; recommended by John Randell, 180, 182; Roberta 'Betty' Cowell, 114; vaginoplasty, 114, 180, 214–15, 224
'transsexualism': first uses of term, 160, 160n; *Sex Change?* (BBC documentary), 161

INDEX

travel writing in general, JM on, 141, 143–4, 210, 241, 313, 328, 335
Travellers Club, 150, 204, 310, 325, 336
Travels, 250, 259
Trefan Bach, Abergavenny, 217, 218, 277, 278
Trefan Hall (Plas Trefan), Gwynedd, 169–72, 173, 174–5, 187, 188, 196, 201, 212, 249; coach house and stables, 170, 217, 251, 334; Dafydd Iwan has rooms in, 203, 342; sale of, 216, 217–18; telex machine, 282
Trefan Morys (converted stable of Trefan Hall), 1, 7, 264–5, 266, 269, 270–1, 277, 278, 283, 286, 294, 300, 325, 326, 335, 338, 344, 351; after JM's death, 351; JM's papers remaining at, 4–5, 318; JM's wish for it to be literary centre, 318; *see also A Writer's House in Wales*
Trevor-Roper, Hugh, 65, 148, 163
Trieste, 41–3, 311, 312, 317, 354
Trieste and the Meaning of Nowhere, 307, 308–10, 311–12, 315, 325
Trott du Solz, Adam von, 177, 178n
Troubles, 193–4, 245, 258, 260; mainland violence, 229, 260, 281
Trucial Oman Levies (paramilitary group), 110
Truman, Harry S., 76, 100–1, 287
Trump, Donald, 348, 352
Tuckniss, Austin Cecil, 54–5, 175, 202
Tuckniss, Margaret (née Bourne), 54–5
Tuckniss, Trevor Richard (Dick), 54, 55
Turkey, 256, 257–8
Turner, Nicholas, 306
Tyerman, Donald, 68–9, 74

Uganda: immigrants from, 228, 258; JM in, 147
United Nations: founding, 41; General Assembly, Manhattan, 143; Special Committee on Palestine (UNSCOP), 49, 50, 51
United States: 'Americanisation' and 'Coca-Colonization', 59, 103–4, 109, 120, 143, 163, 167; Cascade Mountains, 209; food and drink, 99; interests in Middle Eastern oil, 109; JM's Commonwealth Fund Fellowship, 98–104; JM's dispatches to the *Guardian*, 140, 143; JM's dispatches to *The Times*, 98–9, 100, 101, 103; JM's other trips to, 140, 143, 147, 176, 188, 201, 209, 272, 279, 288, 300; JM's visit to research *Lincoln*, 305; JM's visit to research *The Great Port*, 197–200; JM's visit to work with *Rolling Stone*, 245–9; Los Angeles, 247–8; Marshall Plan, 48, 59; McCarthyism, 98, 103; New York, 197–9, 272, 279, 300, 310, 332–3; in *Pax Britannica*, 228; police corruption, 103; Port of New York Authority, 197–8; productivity, 104; racism, 103; San Francisco, 245–6, 288; and Suez Crisis, 122–3, 124; technology, 99; Vietnam War, 188, 198, 200; Washington, DC, 246–7; Watergate trial, 246–7; *see also Coast to Coast*; *Manhattan '45*; *The Great Port: A Passage Through New York*
University College, Oxford, 166–7
The Upstairs Donkey (children's book), 151

vaginoplasty, 114, 180, 214–15, 224
Vanity Fair (magazine), 204
A Venetian Bestiary, 262
The Venetian Empire, 210, 222, 262
Venice, 38–9, 40–1, 57, 74, 133–5, 136, 287, 289–90, 317, 324, 334, 338, 339
Venice/The World of Venice: content, structure and style, 136–7, 139; Heinemann Award, 144; JM corresponds with Swedish reader about, 159; publication, 144; reception and reviews, 144, 169; revisions, 137, 229, 262, 289; *Rough Guide* mention, 334; sales, 144, 196, 262; 'truth' of, 338; US publication, 164, 165; writing, 136
Venture (magazine), 175, 189, 206
The Verb (radio), 344
Vienna, 26, 37, 47, 252–3
Vietnam War, 188; anti-war demonstrations, 198, 200
Viking: publish *Last Letters from Hav*, 275; publish *Sydney*, 288
visitors' book, 264–5, 282–3
Vogue (magazine), 77; American *Vogue*, 272, 283
VSP (Victor Pritchett) *see* Pritchett, V. S.

Wakefield, Paul: *Ireland: Your Only Place* (photography, with text by JM) *see Ireland: Your Only Place*; *Wales: The First Place* see *Wales: The First Place*
Wales: Anglo-Welsh intellectual and artistic

set, 173; devolution, 298, 311; Eisteddfod, 296, 319–20; Gorsedd Beirdd Ynys Prydain, 296; JM has 'mythical' status in, 270; JM's family heritage, 9, 10, 12–13, 69, 169, 172, 244, 269–70; JM's homes *see* Trefan Bach; Trefan Hall; Trefan Morys; Monmouth, 9, 10, 11, 12–13; as 'nuclear-free country', 274; Pen-y-Gwryd, Snowdonia, 83, 164, 173–4, 222, 290, 337; Plas Newydd, Anglesey, 212; Portmeirion, 142, 169, 172; unemployment, 268–9; *see also The Matter of Wales*; Welsh language; Welsh nationalism

Wales: The First Place (photography by Wakefield, with text by JM), 263, 269–70, 277, 287

Walker, David, 73

Walter (Jewish refugee), 26, 36

Ward, Mike, 88, 96

Washington, DC, 246–7

Watergate trial, 246–7

Waterperry, Oxfordshire, 141–2, 145–6, 170, 174

Waugh, Evelyn, 53, 179

Weil, Bob, 332–3

Welcome Aboard (BOAC magazine), 189

Welsh community in Patagonia, 292–3

Welsh language, 244, 268, 298, 339, 345; Twm Morris's translations, 277, 296, 307

Welsh Language Society, 203

Welsh nationalism: devolution, 298, 311; JM as 'great ambassador', 340; JM characterises herself as 'Welsh patriot', 253, 316; JM is awarded Medal of the Honourable Society of Cymmrodorion, 342; JM's interest in Welsh language and cultural nationalism, 244, 268, 298, 316, 318; JM's romantic nationalism, 174, 176, 203, 243, 244, 270, 272, 296; JM's writings and speeches about, 282, 296, 298, 319; Meibion Glyndŵr, 269, 271; Mudiad Amddiffyn Cymru, 243; Plaid Cymru, 157, 203, 268, 296, 340; protest fires, 269, 271; 'seed' of JM's nationalism planted by J. E. Jones, 269; and Twm Morris, 277, 320

Wenner, Jann, 3, 245, 247

West, Rebecca, 235

Western Daily Press, 31, 33

Westmacott, Mike, 91–2

Weston-super-Mare, 14

Wheeler, Lyle R., 100

Wheldon, Huw, 233

Whicker, Alan, 40, 74, 317, 324, 337–8; *Whicker's World* (TV series), 337

Whitehorn, Katharine, 208, 233

Williams-Ellis, Amabel (née Strachey), 172

Williams-Ellis, Clough, 169, 172–3, 203, 230

Williams-Ellis, Susan, 231

Wilson, Harold, 146, 189, 200, 207, 231, 252, 374

Winder, Robert, 287, 290, 294, 303

Wolfe, Tom, 199, 248

Wolff, Helen, 164–5, 201, 202, 209, 219, 223, 244, 251

Wolff, Kurt, 164, 165

Wood, James, 258

Wood, Leanne, 340

Wood, Roger: *Persia*, 205–6

World Bank, 152–3, 154

The World Bank/The Road to Huddersfield: A Journey to Five Continents, 152–4, 164, 198, 317

Worsthorne, Sir Peregrine, 69, 70–1, 78

A Writer's House in Wales, 315–16

- Jan Morris — The Venetian Empire
- Jan Morris — Destinations
- The Oxford Book of Oxford
- Jan Morris — Travels
- Jan Morris — Farewell the Trumpets
- Jan Morris — Pax Britannica
- Jan Morris — Heaven's Command
- Jan Morris — Places